T. Ryan Jackson

New Creation in Paul's Letters

A Study of the Historical and Social Setting
of a Pauline Concept

WIPF & STOCK · Eugene, Oregon

Wipf and Stock Publishers
199 W 8th Ave, Suite 3
Eugene, OR 97401

New Creation in Paul's Letters
A Study of the Historical and Social Setting of
a Pauline Concept
By Jackson, T. Ryan
Copyright©2010 Mohr Siebeck
ISBN 13: 978-1-5326-0532-1
Publication date 8/19/2016
Previously published by Mohr Siebeck, 2010

This licensed edition published by special permission
of Mohr Siebeck GmbH & Co. KG

In Memory of

Professor Graham N. Stanton

*No epitaph could increase the honor he deserves
for how he lived his life.*

Preface

This monograph is a slightly revised version of a Ph.D. thesis submitted to the Faculty of Divinity of Cambridge University on the 5th of June 2008. I would like to express my thanks to Prof Dr Jörg Frey for accepting this thesis into such a fine series, and to Dr Henning Ziebritzki and his editorial staff for their professionalism and courtesy in bringing it to publication. I would also like to thank my examiners, Drs Simon Gathercole and Edward Adams. Their helpful suggestions made this work sharper than it would have been.

The 12th century philosopher Bernard of Chartres is reputed to have originated the phrase later picked up by John of Salisbury and Isaac Newton, "We are like dwarfs on the shoulders of giants." The production of this thesis has proven to me that I am, indeed, supported by a number of giants without whom this study would not have been possible. Professor Graham N. Stanton's gentle guidance was much more gracious than I deserved. His scholarship and, more importantly, his character have been an inspiration to me. He was a wonderful supervisor, mentor, and friend. He will be greatly missed.

The thrill of studying in Cambridge was greatly enhanced by the staff and readers of Tyndale House library. The Tyndale community embodies the statement, "The fear of the Lord is the beginning of wisdom..." (Prov 9:10). Many of my colleagues there have been a band of brothers to me.

The staff and church family of Holy Trinity Church, Cambridge were a source of constant encouragement, and it was a great joy to be a part of them if only for a short season.

I am also immensely thankful to Rev Dr John Hedgepeth and the church family of Northwood Temple Church, USA for allowing this goal of mine to be an extension of their ministry. Their prayers and support have been sure foundations for me. Their kindness and sacrificial giving are overwhelming. I am also grateful for the generous grants awarded me by the Faculty of Divinity of the University of Cambridge, St. Edmund's College, and the Panacea Society.

My family have been incredibly patient with me during this process, and I owe them thanks for their constant love and support.

The most wonderful thing I received in Cambridge was my baby girl, Liliann Sarah. She is the apple of her daddy's eye.

My greatest debt of gratitude is owed to my wife, Emily. She has been God's gift to me. This book is a product of her loving encouragement. She has truly been a helper suitable for me, and this husband rises to call her blessed. I dedicate this work to her. Emily, *"Chaque jour...." Soli Deo Gloria!*

T. Ryan Jackson
Raleigh, NC
5 August 2009

Table of Contents

Preface VII
Table of Contents IX
Abbreviations XIII

Chapter 1. Introduction 3

A. Brief History of Research 3
B. Early Christian Understandings of New Creation 7
C. Limitations 9
D. Overview 10

Part I
Historical and Social Contexts of New Creation

Chapter 2. New Creation in the Old Testament 17

A. The Former Things/New Things 19
B. Cosmic Judgment/Cosmic Renewal 22
   The Problem of Idolatry 22
   Cosmological Consequences of Sin 23
   Use of the City in Isaiah 24
C. The Nature of the New Creation in Isaiah 65:17 27
D. CONCLUSION 31

Chapter 3. New Creation in Early Jewish Literature 33

A. The Plight of Second Temple Judaism 34
   Historical Context 34
   Apocalypticism and the Response of People under Pressure 35
   New Creation in Jewish Apocalyptic Works 37
B. The Function of New Creation in the Book of Jubilees 38

    Assimilation to Hellenistic Society and the Loss of Jewish
    Identity in Jubilees 40
    Reclaiming Identity through the Redefinition of Time and
    Space 44
    New Creation in Jubilees 46
  C. New Creation in the Dead Sea Scrolls 52
  D. CONCLUSIONS 58

Chapter 4. Roman Imperial Ideology and Paul's Concept of New Creation 60

  A. Methodological Considerations 62
  B. The Imperial Transformation of the World 63
  C. The Turn of the Ages and the Eternal Empire 71
  D. Rome and the New World Order 75
  E. CONCLUSIONS 79

Part II
New Creation in Paul's Letters –
An Examination of the *Hauptbriefe*

Chapter 5. Paul's Conception of New Creation in Galatians 6:11-18 83

  A. New Creation in the Concluding Verses of Galatians (6:11-18) 84
  B. Paul's Use of κόσμος in Galatians 90
  C. The New Creation and the New Age 96
  D. Paul's Modification of "Jewish Apocalyptic Eschatology" 100
  E. The Christ Event and Inaugurated Eschatology in Galatians 103
  F. Eschatological Unity and New Creation 106
  G. The New Creation and the Israel of God 111
  H. CONCLUSIONS 113

Chapter 6. Paul's Conception of New Creation in 2 Corinthians 5:11-21 115

  A. Paul's Use of Isaiah in 2 Cor 5 116
    2 Cor 5:1-5 116
    The New Creation 119

The Ministry of Reconciliation..123
2 Cor 6:2 and Its Use of Isa 49:8 125
B. New Creation Epistemology as Apostolic Defence........................128
C. The Christ Event and the New Creation..136
D. CONCLUSIONS...147

Chapter 7. Paul's Conception of New Creation in Romans 8:18-25 150

A. Paul's Use of κτίσις in Romans 151
B. Paul's Use of κόσμος in Rom 3-5 152
C. Eschatological Glory and the Restoration of Creation in Romans 8:18-25...155
D. The Effects of Human Sin on Creation 156
E. Creation and Redemption 161
F. CONCLUSIONS..167

Conclusion

Chapter 8. Conclusion..173

A. Summary..173
B. Implications and Considerations for Further Study........................182

Bibliography 187

Index of Ancient Sources..211
Index of Modern Authors...224
Index of Subjects 229

Abbreviations

SBL abbreviations apply throughout. The following abbreviations are also used in this thesis:

ANS	American Numismatics Society
BDAG	Danker, Frederick W., ed. *A Greek-English Lexicon of the New Testament and Other Early Christian Literature*. Chicago: Chicago University Press, 2000.
BDF	Funk, Robert W., ed. *A Greek Grammar of the New Testament and Other Early Christian Literature*. Chicago: Chicago University Press, 1961.
CIL	*Corpus Inscriptionum Latinarum, 1862–*. Edited by Theodor Mommsen, Otto Hirschfeld and Alfredus Domasyewski, Berolini: George Reinger.
IG	*Inscriptiones Graecae, 1873-1998*. Edited by Guilelmus Dittenberger et al., 14 Vols., Berlin.
JAL	Jewish Apocalyptic Literature
LCL	*Loeb Classical Library*, Harvard University Press, Cambridge, MA.
LS	Liddell, H.G., and R. Scott, eds. *A Greek-English Lexicon with a Revised Supplement*. Oxford: Clarendon, 1996.
OCD	Hornblower, Simon, and Antony Spawforth, eds. *The Oxford Classical Dictionary*. Oxford: Oxford University Press, 1996.
PG	Migne, J.-P. *Patrologiae Cursus Completus (series Graeca)*, Paris: Migne, 1857-1866.
RIC	*The Roman Imperial Coinage, Volume 1: From 31 BC to AD 69*. Edited by C.H.V. Sutherland, Rev. ed., London: Spink & Son, 1984.
RPC	*Roman Provincial Coinage, 1992–*. Edited by Andrew Burnett, Michel Amandry and Pere Pau Ripollès, London: British Museum.
Sherk	Sherk, Robert K., ed. *The Roman Empire: Augustus to Hadrian*. Cambridge: Cambridge University Press, 1988.
Smallwood	Smallwood, E. Mary, ed. *Documents Illustrating the Principates of Gaius, Claudius, and Nero*. Cambridge: Cambridge University Press, 1967.
SNTW	*Studies of the New Testament and its World*
TDNT	*Theological Dictionary of the New Testament*

On the third day the friends of Christ coming at daybreak to the place found the grave empty and the stone rolled away. In varying ways they realized the new wonder; but even they hardly realized that the world had died in the night. What they were looking at was the first day of a new creation, with a new heaven and a new earth; and in a semblance of the gardener God walked again in the garden, in the cool not of the evening but the dawn.

– G. K. Chesterton,
The Everlasting Man

Chapter 1

Introduction

The concept of new creation is a fascinating component of the apostle Paul's theology even though the actual phrase occurs only twice in his writings (Galatians 6:15; 2 Corinthians 5:17). This study is an attempt to interpret how this concept was understood by Paul and how it functions in his letters. Considerable amounts of ink have been spilled on the theme of new creation, but few authors in recent scholarship have undertaken to provide sustained explanations of its significance in the context of Paul's thinking as a whole. The two most noteworthy exceptions in contemporary scholarship are the monographs by Ulrich Mell and Moyer Hubbard.[1] These monographs represent two poles of understanding Paul's thinking with regard to the concept of new creation.

A. Brief History of Research

Both Mell & Hubbard have made positive contributions to the discussion and their work will be addressed where appropriate throughout this thesis. They provide the main dialogue partners with which this study interacts. Mell gives a painstaking overview of the occurrences of the phrase "new creation" in Jewish literature; but this strength is also his weakness. His work fails to do justice to the contexts in which new creation appears in Paul's letters and his approach is limited by the well-worn pitfalls of a strictly *traditionsgeschichtliche* method. Focusing on those Jewish texts which support a cosmological understanding of new creation, Mell ignores texts which might have influenced Paul to think of new creation from an anthropological perspective.[2] As Hubbard aptly criticizes, "this prejudicial selectivity not only affects Mell's conclusions, it was probably the *func-*

---

[1] Mell 1989; Hubbard 2002. See the earlier work of Schneider 1959:257-70; Stuhlmacher 1967:1-35.

[2] The term "anthropological" is used in the classical sense of systematic theology rather than the social scientific way of anthropology. In this thesis, "cosmic" and "cosmological" refer to the way in which Paul's theology has implications for all the created order.

tion of these (predetermined?) conclusions, and further illustrates the *de facto* circularity of [his] approach."[3]

In an attempt to avoid this error, Hubbard begins with an examination of the commonly acknowledged origin of new creation themes in the prophecies of Isaiah and incorporates the anthropologically focused promises of the new heart and new spirit in Jeremiah and Ezekiel.[4] Rather than attempting an exhaustive examination of the usage of the phrase "new creation" in the literature of Second Temple Judaism, Hubbard takes a comparative approach focusing on the presence of the theme in two works from the period: *Jubilees* and *Joseph and Aseneth*. Through a keen application of social theory to Paul's letters, Hubbard helpfully reminds us of the importance of the individual in Paul's soteriology. However, if Mell could be criticized for a pre-determined cosmological slant, Hubbard's work surely falls into the opposite error. He too allows his discussion to be pressed into mutually exclusive distinctions with which Paul may not have been comfortable. In my estimation, Paul's conception of the new creation has both anthropological as well as cosmological dimensions.

Hubbard is not the first to be led astray by the false dichotomy which understands Paul's concept of new creation in *either* anthropological (individual or communal) *or* cosmological terms. A brief perusal of the history of research on this issue makes clear that the discussion of new creation has largely focused on one or the other of these emphases. Such a history has been adequately traced elsewhere, but some repetition would prove instructive for our purposes.[5]

The *anthropological* aspect of Paul's thinking about new creation has received the most emphasis in the long history of interpreting the apostle's thought. Calvin and Luther both focused on the anthropological components of this concept. Calvin, for example, translated the phrase as "new creature" in his commentaries on 2 Corinthians 5:17 and Galatians 6:15. This aspect of Paul's thinking about new creation became predominant throughout the subsequent history of interpretation well into the modern period.

Adolf von Harnack's important study on rebirth and related experiences of renewal took special interest in the Jewish background material and considered this material indispensible for understanding Paul's terse phrase.[6] The ensuing emphasis on the importance of the rabbinic sources for understanding Paul suggested that the apostle's conception of new

---

[3] Hubbard 2002:6-7.

[4] Hubbard does not acknowledge how even the more anthropologically focused promises of Jeremiah and Ezekiel maintain a connection between people and the world in which they live. I address this point briefly in Chapter 2.

[5] See Mell 1989:9-32; Hubbard 2002:2-5.

[6] Von Harnack 1918. Cf. Hubbard 2002:3.

creation must have been focused on a change in the life situation of the individual.[7]

In an attempt to expand the individual anthropological perspective of Paul's new creation language, some scholars understood Paul's language in terms of a new community. Driven by heightened interest in the corporate elements of Paul's thought, Wolfgang Kraus has championed the idea of a communal referent.[8] Though this perspective is not widely accepted, it does have the merit of taking seriously the connection between the community and the cosmos in the highly charged new creation language of Isaiah 65-66.[9]

The *cosmological* aspect of Paul's thinking began to receive greater emphasis after the recognition of the importance of Jewish apocalyptic literature for interpreting Paul. Albert Schweitzer's assertion that this material was influential in the development of Paul's eschatological perspective catalyzed an important debate in Pauline studies that would continue to the present.[10] Rudolf Bultmann attempted to *demythologize* the apocalyptic influence and sought to recover the anthropological emphasis which he felt to be central to the message of Paul. Ernst Käsemann came to the defense of the apocalyptic background material and famously dubbed it, "the mother of Christian theology."[11] Efforts were made to return to the anthropocentric perspective of Bultmann,[12] but the cosmological influence of the apocalyptic literature would prove to be an influential voice in the study of Paul – one that still commands a great deal of attention from scholars.[13]

The distinction between between anthropological and cosmological elements of Paul's thinking has actually muddied the waters and led to a generally unhelpful way of approaching Paul's letters because he would not have divided his thinking so neatly into these categories. I shall argue that both of these are aspects of the eschatological soteriology at play when Paul employs the concept of new creation in his writing.

A similar point has been made in the unpublished doctoral dissertations of J. H. Hoover and A. J. D. Aymer.[14] Hoover's work maintains the con-

---

[7] Cf. Sjöberg 1950; Schwantes 1962.

[8] Kraus 1996:247-52. Hubbard also cites the similar work of Klaiber 1982:97-101.

[9] For a fuller discussion on the theme of new creation in Isaiah, see Chapter 2.

[10] Cf. Schweitzer 1911; Schweitzer 1930. See Matlock 1996 for a critique of the "apocalyptic fervor" in Pauline scholarship.

[11] Both Bultmann's and Käsemann's positions are supported by different emphases within Jewish apocalyptic writings – forensic and cosmological – and this supports the claim of this thesis that Paul's thinking should be limited neither to a strictly anthropological nor to a strictly cosmological perspective. For a summary of that discussion, see De Boer 1989:169-90. Cf. Minear 1979:405.

[12] For example, see Baumgarten 1975.

[13] See, e.g., Beker 1980; Martyn 1997.

[14] Hoover 1979; Aymer 1983.

nection between the inner new creation of mankind and the cosmic change which occurred in the Christ event. Furthermore, his thesis recognizes the importance of including Rom 8 in the discussion of Paul's conception of new creation. However, his work completely excludes the Greco-Roman background material and, in my opinion, does not sufficiently secure the exegetical basis for the connection between the anthropological and cosmological elements of Paul's thought in the light of current research. Aymer's work suffers from similar problems. It is no real surprise that neither Hoover nor Aymer address the importance of Roman imperial ideology for understanding Paul's hearers.[15] Further, although Aymer helpfully discusses analogous themes in Paul's writings, his work suffers from inadequate detailed analysis of the most important new creation texts in Paul's letters: Gal 6:15; 2 Cor 5:17; Rom 8:18-25.

Therefore, this thesis maintains that a balanced approach to the apostle Paul's conception of new creation will reveal that this idea is an expression of his eschatologically infused soteriology which involves the individual, the community and the cosmos and which is inaugurated in the death and resurrection of Christ.[16] Moreover, the phrase serves as an encapsulated expression – a kind of theological shorthand – for this soteriology.[17] Before the discovery of the Dead Sea Scrolls and the ensuing attempts to understand the influence of Jewish apocalyptic writings on Paul, most exegesis focused on the individual perspective of Paul's use of καινὴ κτίσις.[18] However, already in the patristic era there was a breadth in the understanding of this expression which contemporary scholarship would do well to reconsider.[19]

---

[15] This omission is certainly understandable given the relatively recent increase in interest in applying it to Pauline studies. However, this background in particular provides important evidence in the discussion of Paul's new creation texts and its inclusion in this study is an important contribution of this thesis.

[16] For a discussion of the eschatological importance of the concept of newness in the NT, see Harrisville 1955.

[17] Hays uses the phrase "new creation" as his own "shorthand signifier for the dialectical eschatology that runs throughout the NT" without acknowledging how the phrase functions in a similar way in Paul. While the claims of this thesis are far more modest than Hays's, I take the phrase καινὴ κτίσις as a tip of Paul's eschatological iceberg (to borrow G. Stanton's imagery). See Hays 1996:198. Cf. Stanton 2004:49-52.

[18] Cf. Hubbard 2002:2-3.

[19] This contradicts the claim that the fathers invariably held to a strictly anthropological view as argued in Hubbard 2002:2. Riches, too, argues that what the fathers have in common is an individual rather than cosmological understanding of καινὴ κτίσις in Paul in Riches 2007:326-7. See his forthcoming work: Riches 2008.

B. Early Christian Understandings of New Creation

The phrase καινὴ κτίσις does not appear in the extant works of the apostolic fathers. Early Christian literature, however, did use creation language to speak about conversion. The *Epistle of Barnabas* 16:8 indicates how the believer becomes the glorious temple of God, "Having received the forgiveness of sins, and having put our hope in the name [of the Lord], we have become new, created again from the beginning (λαβόντες τὴν ἄφεσιν τῶν ἁμαρτιῶν καὶ ἐλπίσαντες ἐπὶ τὸ ὄνομα ἐγενόμεθα καινοί πάλιν ἐξ ἀρχῆς κτιζόμενοι)."[20] When the phrase καινὴ κτίσις appears for the first time in post-NT Christian literature, in Clement of Alexandria, it is also applied to the individual believer.[21] This application has support in a number of early Christian writers.[22]

The conception of new creation in the early church, however, was not limited to an individual conversion experience. One striking example of this occurs when Clement uses the phrase in reference to Jesus, "...What exceptional thing does the new creation (καινὴ κτίσις), the Son of God, reveal and teach?"[23] The use of καινὴ κτίσις in reference to Christ indicates that there is something more than conversion at play in the early church's understanding of this phrase. The application of this idea to Jesus is not unique to Clement of Alexandria. Gregory of Nyssa, for example, calls Christ the "firstborn of the new creation." He understood Christ to be the agent of the original creation which had grown old (παλαιόω) and had become unrecognizable (ἀφανίζω).[24] The new creation was necessitated because the first creation had been made "unavailing (ἀχρειόω) by our disobedience."[25] In this way, we find in the writings of Gregory of Nyssa a strong link between the state of humanity and the created order. Christ brought about a new creation in which he took the lead by being the firstborn of "all the creation of men."[26] Christ accomplished a two-fold regen-

---

[20] This translation is my own.
[21] Cf. Exhortation 11.114; Miscellanies 3.8.62.
[22] Hubbard cites: Tertullian, On Modesty 6; Against Marcion 4.1.6; 4.11.9; 5.4.3; 5.12.6; Jerome, To Oceanus; Augustine, On the Baptism of Infants 1.44; Reply to Faustus 11.1; 19.10; Grace and Free Will 20; Sermons 26.12; 212.1. Cf. Ambrosiaster, Second Epistle of Paul to the Corinthians 5.17; Epistle of Paul to the Galatians 6.15, "Nova creatura est regeneratio nostra...."
[23] Who is the Rich Man that Shall Be Saved? 12.1. The translation is mine.
[24] Cf. Heb 8:13.
[25] Against Eunomius 2.4.3.
[26] Against Eunomius 2.2.8.

eration involving baptism and resurrection by which he is seen to become the "firstborn of the new creation."[27]

The early church believed the Christ event to have had effects on all of creation.[28] Its effects were not simply limited to the sphere of the individual experience but in him, "all things are redeemed and the new creation wrought afresh (τὰ πάντα λελύτρωται, καὶ πάλιν τὴν καινὴν εἰργάσατο κτίσιν)."[29] Athanasius goes so far as to say, "in [his] flesh has come to pass the beginning of our new creation (καινῆς κτίσεως)."[30] What he means by this becomes clear elsewhere in an elaboration on 2 Cor 5:17, "But if a new creation has come to pass, someone must be first of this creation; now a man, made of earth only, such as we are become from the transgression, he could not be. For in the first creation, men had become unfaithful, and through them that first creation had been lost (δι' αὐτῶν ἀπώλετο ἡ πρώτη); and there was need of someone else to renew the first creation, and preserve the new which had come to be."[31] Though Athanasius surely understood the individual importance of the new creation, this passage shows how he saw it as part of the renewal of creation as a whole which had been destroyed (ἀπόλλυμι) because of sin.[32]

Chrysostom's commentary on 2 Cor 5:17 gives a fine example of how some fathers could think more broadly of the concept of new creation than simply a reference to the individual's conversion experience. Chrysostom cites the new creation as the ground for Christian virtue "not because we are not our own only, nor because He died for us only, nor because He raised up our firstfruits only, but because we have also come unto another life."[33] This is perceived as a new birth by the Spirit in which a person comes "to another creative act (εἰς ἑτέραν ἦλθε δημιουργίαν)."[34] The broader soteriological emphasis of the phrase is clear in the description of what is to become new in the new creation: note especially his emphasis of *both* soul (internal) *and* body (external), "But behold, both a new soul, (for it was cleansed,) and a new body, and a new worship, and promises new,

---

[27] Gregory has an in-depth discussion of the meaning of πρωτότοκος (Against Eunomius 2.4.3) in which he associates new creation with the resurrection. See Theodoret, The Letters 146. Theodoret speaks of the new creation in the sense of the resurrection. Cf. Irenaeus, Against Heresies 5.36.1.

[28] Cf. Panagopoulos 1990:169.

[29] Athanasius, Four Discourses Against the Arians I.5.16.

[30] Athanasius, Four Discourses Against the Arians II.21.70. This is especially important in the light of my understanding that the new creation actually began in the Christ event.

[31] Athanasius, Four Discourses Against the Arians II.21.65.

[32] Athanasius also spoke of 2 Cor 5:17 in terms of believers coming into a new way of life in Questions about Holy Scripture, PG 28:760, ll. 51-6.

[33] Commentary on the Second Epistle to the Corinthians, PG 61:475, l. 34.

[34] Commentary on the Second Epistle to the Corinthians, PG 61:475.

and covenant, and life, and table, and dress, and all things new absolutely."[35]

His comments on Galatians 6:15 display similar soteriological breadth. Chrysostom explains that Paul uses the idea of new creation to describe the new life of the believer. This new life is intimately related to the past act of baptism (conversion) as well as the future resurrection. Chrysostom explains that Paul calls this a new creation "both on account of what is past, and of what is to come; of what is past, because our soul, which had grown old with the oldness of sin, hath been all at once renewed by baptism, as if it had been created again. Wherefore we require a new and heavenly rule of life. And of things to come, because both the heaven and the earth, and all the creation, shall with our bodies be translated into incorruption."[36]

Theodoret recognizes this breadth in both 2 Cor and Gal in his ability to see that the new creation which applied to the individual at baptism was actually part of a larger soteriological thrust.[37] This is clear in his assertion that "the strict meaning of new creation is the transformation of all things which will occur after the resurrection from the dead."[38]

Several points become clear after an examination of the teaching of the early church on the concept of new creation. First, they applied the concept to individual conversion initiated at baptism. Secondly, they understood the relation of this to a broader soteriology which encompassed all of creation. The association of the resurrection with the new creation indicates how this is the case. Although various writers in the early church could focus on one aspect or another of Paul's new creation, it is clear that many could hold together both an individual as well as a cosmological thrust to this concept. This thesis attempts to argue that Paul is best understood within such a soteriological paradigm.

C. Limitations

It should go without saying that Paul's own letters are the most important evidence in this investigation. Accordingly, the two Pauline usages of the phrase καινὴ κτίσις (Galatians 6:15 and 2 Corinthians 5:17) are obvious candidates for inspection. Further, our understanding of Paul's thinking is

---

[35] Commentary on the Second Epistle to the Corinthians, PG 61:475f.

[36] Commentary on the Epistle to the Galatians, PG 61:636, l. 17. The translation is mine. For a further association of the use of new creation language with baptism, see Theodoret, Commentary on the Second Epistle to the Corinthians 317; Basil, Letters 8.

[37] Note his comment on 2 Cor 5:17, "Those who believe in Christ have entered a new life. They must be born again in baptism and renounce their former sins." Cited in Bray 1999:249.

[38] Theodoret, Epistle to the Galatians 6:15 (CPE 1:363-4) cited in Edwards 1999:103.

considerably clearer if we move beyond a simple word study approach to incorporate other passages where the concept is clearly employed even if the terminology itself is not. This necessitates the inclusion of Romans 8 into the discussion if we expect to get a balanced picture of what Paul might have had in mind when he thought about new creation.[39] I focus mainly on the three texts mentioned above because they are the clearest and most obvious expressions of Paul's conception of new creation. The fact that these three passages occur in the *Hauptbriefe* will enable me to avoid lengthy discussions of authenticity and provide a helpful cross-section of Paul's usage in the context of various social settings. The closely related conception of resurrection will be incorporated into the discussions of these texts.

Ideally, the enquiry could be broadened to observe how the new creation relates to Paul's use of the theme of newness in general, as well as a fuller exploration of his views of creation. Among other important analogous themes, the discussion could include Paul's death-life imagery, renewal, newness of life, new covenant, new Spirit, new man and new exodus.[40] A discussion of Jesus traditions (e.g. Matt 19:28) and other NT writings (e.g. Col 1:15; Eph 2:15; 2 Pet 3:10-13, Rev 21:1-2) would also prove helpful. Further study in these areas would offer a promising way forward in our understanding of Paul's thought in comparison with other NT writers. Unfortunately, limitations of space will prohibit adequate discussion of these topics but careful exegetical considerations of the most relevant texts in Galatians, 2 Corinthians and Romans alongside passages which are directly related to them will provide an informative study of Paul's thinking regarding this subject.

D. Overview

This thesis is in two parts. After a brief introduction, Part I addresses both Jewish and Greco-Roman backgrounds to Paul's understanding of new creation. It will be argued that the primary background to understanding Paul's concept of new creation is Isaiah. Though other prophetic themes are important to the apostle (such as passages in Jeremiah and Ezekiel), none is as demonstrably crucial to his understanding of new creation as Isaiah. Isaiah's new creation is a mixture of the cosmological/anthropological soteriology also attested in Paul. The new creation

---

[39] Both Hubbard and Mell exclude significant discussions of Rom 8. It is, however, included in the unpublished doctoral work of J. Hoover. See Hoover 1979.

[40] Hubbard trades heavily on Paul's death-life imagery and gives helpful attention to the Spirit in the course of his discussion.

functions in Isaiah as the ultimate expression of redemption from the corruption caused by sin. It involves a restoration of social structures which were directly related to cosmic order (Chapter 2).

In the apocalyptic writings of the 2nd c. B.C. to the 1st c. A.D., the idea of new creation took on an increasingly cosmological emphasis but it remained connected to the Isaianic application of the concept as a solution to the problem of exile and oppression by foreign powers. This is instantiated in Qumran where the community expected to be a part of YHWH's work of judgment (i.e. destruction) and restoration which they spoke of in terms of new creation. All of this is important background for deciphering Paul's terse statements about the new creation. As many scholars have shown, Paul does appear to be influenced by the apocalyptic traditions of Judaism. But, though Paul's message of the crucified and risen Jesus may be influenced from these traditions, it has its own remarkably different character. What that is and how it is distinct from the Jewish soil from which it grew will become clearer in the course of this study (Chapter 3).

In order to understand the complexities of the Pauline conception of new creation, we will attempt to incorporate evidence from the broader social influences at play. Far from being excess background noise to Paul's message, the imperial ideology of Rome and its conception of new creation help to indicate the missionary thrust of Paul's writing (Chapter 4).[41] Drawing on the rich theological soil of Judaism, Paul articulated his gospel in the context of a world under the ubiquitous influence of the Roman Empire. Though he did not explicitly polemicize against the empire with his writing about a new creation, he was interested in delineating a society with an eschatology and epistemology in stark contrast to that of his contemporaries.

The language of new creation would have resonated with the recipients of Paul's letters. They would have been aware of the imperial ideology which gave cosmic significance to the reality of the empire and sought to bring all of life under its influence. Because of this, Paul's articulation of a new creation would have suggested far more than just an individual conversion. It would have suggested a completely alternative social order. Paul's interaction with the imperial powers of his time is no novelty. The theme of new creation had previously been used by other Jewish writers to speak about God's deliverance for his people. But Paul's application of this theme came about in an innovative and surprisingly different way. Incorporating this element into our enquiry offers an attempt to "sound out"

---

[41] See Wagner 1998:222; Hays 2005:26.

at least one way in which Paul's writing might have been understood by its original recipients.[42]

The second part of the argument moves into a closer examination of the three most important Pauline texts with due consideration to related ideas along the way. First, Gal 6:15 communicates the concept of new creation in the form of an appeal for a new social structure which is not built on the same principles or religious distinctions as that of the agitators who are distorting his gospel. These were the fundamental building blocks of the old age which had been destroyed on the cross. Paul encourages his readers to build their lives with new materials provided in the new creation – faith working through love (5:6). Paul's belief that the world had been crucified to him (6:14) should not be limited to the apostle's own religious experience but should be connected with the eschatological concept of the ages which permeates his thought. This represents a modification of Jewish apocalyptic eschatology (Chapter 5).

The language of 2 Cor 5:17 takes up a greater interest in the individual as the phrase ὥστε εἴ τις ἐν Χριστῷ makes clear. This presents a real challenge to an overly apocalyptic view of Paul which precludes Paul's interest in the individual in the attempt to give this language its cosmological force. However, it is a mistake to focus this entirely on the existential. The phrase ἐν Χριστῷ creates a powerful link to the Christ event discussed in vv. 14-15. It is common to understand his resurrection as being the firstfruits of the general resurrection at the eschaton. A logical corollary of this is that the destruction of his physical body on the cross is the beginning of the destruction of the old world. Thus, the reference to the new creation here is the entrance of the believer into the new realm which had dawned in the death and resurrection of Christ (Chapter 6). This eschatological thrust is attested in Paul's repeated use of Isaianic imagery in the immediate context of 2 Cor 5:17.

Chapter 7 argues that in Rom 8 Paul insists that the salvation of the individual is specifically linked to the salvation of creation. Beginning with an analysis of Paul's uses of κτίσις and κόσμος, this chapter seeks to show how the argument in Rom 1-8 moves from creation to new creation. This resonates with OT prophetic traditions which envisage eschatological restoration of people and the world in which they live. The eschatological matrix which has been so influential in our discussions of other Pauline letters is certainly at play in Romans as well, and Paul uses it as a foundation for much of the hope he offers in Rom 8. The parallel between the groaning creation in Rom 8 and the groaning believer longing to put on the resurrection body in 2 Cor 5 provides evidence that salvation for Paul was

---

[42] This represents a different approach to a similar question raised in Hoegen-Rohls 2001:143-53.

not simply an individual experience but involved the resurrection of the body as part of the general renewal of creation envisaged in Jewish traditions. A concluding chapter will summarize these results and suggest possible implications of this study.

Part I

Historical and Social Context

Chapter 2

New Creation in the Old Testament

The clearest, most explicit Old Testament formulation of the theme of new creation occurs in Isaiah.[1] Although the term "new creation" does not occur in the Old Testament, the Isaianic expression "new heavens and new earth" (65:17; 66:22 MT) is a clear instance of the typical Hebrew use of merism and should be understood as a way of expressing this concept.[2] A strong case could be made to show that the idea of new creation is related to a whole constellation of OT themes, such as new covenant and new spirit, which become more prominent in Jeremiah and Ezekiel. It is beyond dispute that these works, too, were important for Paul's thinking.[3] However, for a number of reasons this study will focus on the Isaianic material.

First, it is commonly recognized that Isaianic passages bore particular importance for Paul and we should not be surprised to find that they significantly contributed to his thinking.[4] If the thrust of this thesis is correct – that Paul's concept of new creation maintains both cosmological as well as anthropological elements – the Isaianic portrayal of new creation becomes particularly significant background since it makes a similar connection. Furthermore, all three of the major new creation passages in Paul addressed in this thesis may appear in contexts which reflect specific Isaianic influence.[5] Secondly, the Isaianic material serves as the *Ursprung* for

---

[1] The use of a verb for creation (ברא, יצר, עשׂה) with YHWH as the subject and חָדָשׁ as the object occurs outside of Isaiah only in Jer 31:22 (38:22 LXX) where the language is used in the context of a return from exile (similar to the Isaianic texts). The passage describes a new action of YHWH's deliverance but the difficulty of Jer 31:22 is clear in the discrepancy between the MT and LXX. Where the MT has, "For YHWH has created a new thing in the earth," the LXX reads, "For the Lord has created deliverance for a new planting." The cosmological emphasis should be noted in either text. For an explanation of the difficulties of Jer 31:22, see, e.g., Sawyer 1999:99-111; Keown, Scalise, and Smothers 1995:116-24.

[2] E.g. Gen 1:1

[3] Hubbard's work, in particular, shows how the prophecies of Jeremiah and Ezekiel are important for understanding Paul's conception of new creation. See Hubbard 2002:17-25.

[4] Cf. Hays 2005:25-6.

[5] A thorough examination of these correspondences is beyond the limitations of this thesis. However, Chapter 6 has an in-depth discussion of the Isaianic influence on Paul's thinking in 2 Cor 5.

many streams of tradition which may have influenced Paul. The high concentration of new creation language in Isaiah (particularly in chapters 42, 43, 48, 65 and 66) presents the overwhelming likelihood, "daß seine Prophetie den historischen Entstehungspunkt der theologischen Neuschöpfungsvorstellung markiert."[6]

Any attempt to examine themes within Isaiah must take into account standard divisions of the book recognized by the majority of scholarship (1-39; 40-55; 56-66). These three sections seem to address three distinct historical periods and are characterised by stylistic variations. The disjunction has led critical scholarship to attribute Isaiah to a number of different authors and to deal with the text in a disconnected manner. This perspective has often obscured important insights which can only be gleaned from recognizing the literary unity of the book.[7] More recent scholarship has recognized this oversight and attempted to deal with the unity and composition in a more nuanced manner.[8]

Most important for this study is the recognition that "Jewish and Christian readers of the first century viewed and interpreted the work as a unified whole."[9] As our investigation is ultimately aimed at how the apostle Paul might have understood the theme of new creation in the book of Isaiah, it is sufficient to acknowledge that he had access to these materials and that they present themselves as a "single literary work" by the time Paul would have encountered them.[10]

The theme of new creation in Isaiah reaches its climactic expression in chapters 65-66 (esp. 65:17; 66:22). This universal and cosmic expression of YHWH's redemptive purposes is the natural progression of an idea which has been developed throughout the material. Many commentators view the new creation envisaged in chapters 65-66 as categorically different from the restoration envisaged earlier in the book.[11] It may be true that the later passages represent a development and intensification of the earlier thought; but, given the intense cosmological emphasis of 1-39 and 40-55, it seems clear that this theme has been woven throughout the material from the very beginning. The force of the imagery of 65-66 is impossible to un-

---

[6] Mell 1989:47.

[7] See Childs 1979:329; Rendtorff 1984:319-20.

[8] For a summary of the discussion, see Vermeylen 1989:11-53. See also: Rendtorff 1984:295-320.

[9] Wilk 1998:8. Cf. Strauss 1995:235.

[10] Sweeney 1996:51ff. For a discussion on the redactional unity of Isaiah, see Sweeney 1988:11-25.

[11] The radical description of restoration expressed here has been cited by some scholars as an early development of the apocalyptic style. This may be true; but the writing itself could not be classified as apocalyptic even though it is intensely eschatological. The "proto-apocalyptic" view is most thoroughly expounded in Hanson 1979.

derstand without the framework which has been developed in the earlier parts of the book.

A closer examination of how this theme is developed will shed light on how "new creation" functions within Isaiah as the solution to problems raised in the book. This chapter begins with an examination of the "former/new" contrast which appears in the context of the new creation promise in Isa 65. Though this contrast is employed in various ways throughout the book, it is consistently used to indicate the superlative nature of the promised future action of God on behalf of his people.

God's judgment against sin bore consequences for the natural world and the restoration promised in terms of a new creation at the end of the book is directly related to the cosmological destruction which appears earlier. The themes of cosmic judgment and restoration are developed in Isaiah through the use of the city motif. The intent of this chapter is to show how the Isaianic material maintains a strong connection between humanity and creation. Human sin leads to natural destruction and the promise of new creation restores both God's people as well as the world in which they live. As we shall see in the second half of this thesis, Paul may well have appropriated similar ideas in his understanding of God's eschatological program of salvation.

A. The Former Things/New Things

The most direct reference to a new creation in the Old Testament, Isaiah 65:17, articulates YHWH's promise to create a new heaven and earth between two references to "former (ראשׁנות)" things (65:16c, 17b).[12] The recurrent "former/new" theme within Isaiah is concentrated in Isa 40-66 (42, 43, 48, 65) and can be employed in various ways.[13] The former things may refer to ambiguous historical events, to God's past acts of deliverance and even to Israel's sin.[14] "New things" typically refers to acts of deliverance. What has not been commonly recognized is what the various usages have in common. The Isaianic "former things/new things (חֲדָשׁוֹת/רִאשֹׁנוֹת)" contrast is regularly employed in the context of a challenge or comparison between YHWH and idols. Space does not permit a comprehensive treat-

---

[12] It should not be missed that this term is from the same root as the Hebrew title of the book of Genesis, בְּרֵאשִׁית.

[13] This theme is one of those strands which serve to tie the book of Isaiah together into a literary unity since it occurs in the earliest and latest parts of the material (e.g. Isa 9:1, 65:16-17). Cf. Brueggemann 1998:4; North 1950:111-26.

[14] Cf. Hubbard 2002:15-16.

ment of the contrasts but examination of a few of them will helpfully inform our inquiry into the meaning of the new creation passage in Isa 65:17.

Isaiah 43:18-19 places the חֲדָשׁוֹת/רִאשֹׁנוֹת contrast in the immediate context of a reference to the deliverance of Israel from Egypt during the Exodus (43:17). This passage may very well be the key passage of Isaiah's new exodus theology in which the original Exodus provides the paradigm for speaking about YHWH's new acts of deliverance for his people.[15] The combination of redemption and creation in Isaiah 40-55 is commonly recognized.[16] Just as the original Exodus was spoken of as the creation of God's people, the theme of new exodus in Isaiah announced a new creation of his people – a new act of deliverance so spectacular as to bring about a complete reorientation of Israel's identity. They were being encouraged to forget the Exodus event in the sense that YHWH was not bound to past actions or past paradigms. Rather, as creator God, he could act in new and astonishing ways. The new thing which God would accomplish for his people would be the miraculous deliverance and liberation from Babylon.[17] In the same way that the original Exodus was a victory over a pagan nation and the gods associated with it, the new exodus from Babylon would be a miraculous display of YHWH's power over those forces which opposed his people.[18] This new exodus would supersede the original one in important ways described in the following verses.

The appearance of wild animals honouring God in verse 20a brings to mind the paradisiacal conditions associated with the coming of the Branch from the root of Jesse in Isa 11:6ff (cf. 65:25).[19] Whereas the sinfulness of humanity had brought about a deterioration of stable conditions, the restorative act of redemption proposed by YHWH would bring the hostile elements of nature under control. Blenkinsopp calls the inclusion of these beasts "an Isaian topos associated with ecological degradation and the collapse of urban life (cf. Isa 13:22; 34:13)."[20] YHWH's role as redeemer and creator was thus merged. Sin had affected not only the people of God but

---

[15] For further investigation of the use of Exodus traditions in Isaiah, see, e.g., Kiesow 1979. For a study of the use of new exodus themes from Isaiah in the New Testament, see Watts 1997.

[16] The theme is carefully expounded in Stuhlmueller 1970. See also: Lee 1995. This theme is very important for Paul.

[17] Watts 1997:80.

[18] An analysis of how the plagues on Egypt represent the defeat of the Egyptian pantheon through YHWH's control of nature would repay careful study.

[19] Motyer 1993:337.

[20] Blenkinsopp 2002:228.

also the world in which they lived. The great deliverance envisaged by Isaiah would restore creation as well as its inhabitants.[21]

Isaiah 48 also employs the חֲדָשׁוֹת/רִאשֹׁנוֹת contrast in a way that further illuminates chapter 65. Israel is described in Isa 48 as a people who take oaths "not in truth or righteousness" (48:1). Significantly, the restoration later envisaged in 65:16 indicates a reversal of this practise. YHWH has announced הָרִאשֹׁנוֹת (v. 3) in order to prevent the people from crediting his actions to idols (48:5). In addition to foretelling previous acts from Israel's past, YHWH also promised to tell of new things (חֲדָשׁוֹת) previously unknown (v. 6). The use of the verb בָּרָא in verse 7 highlights the fact that the new things referred to are beyond the ability of the idols and are only able to be performed by the true creator God who "laid the foundation of the earth" and "spread out the heavens" (48:13).

Finally, in Isa 65:17 הָרִאשֹׁנוֹת is used differently from its previous occurrences. Whereas the term had been used in an overwhelmingly positive manner, here the former things are presented in a pejorative light. This is in keeping with the context of 65:7 where the "former deeds" refer to idolatrous practices. YHWH announces judgment upon Israel for a history of rebellion and seeking after foreign gods. Again in verse 16 the troubling history of Israel's recalcitrance is invoked in the phrase הַצָּרוֹת הָרִאשֹׁנוֹת, "the former troubles." The troubles here likely refer to the consequences following from Israel's sinful past. Though YHWH had delivered them from past distresses (63:9), Israel was continually unfaithful to him (63:10). The situation from which the writer cried out for redemption is intimated in 63:18-19, "Your holy people took possession for a little while; but now our adversaries have trampled down your sanctuary. We have long been like those whom you do not rule, like those not called by your name." Sin and rebellion against God lie undeniably at the heart of Israel's problem in Isaiah (cf. 64:6). The internal condition, however, has material ramifications – judgment which often comes in the form of foreign oppression.[22]

---

[21] Clifford 1994:170-1. Notably, in Wis 19:18-22, YHWH's redemptive plans cause a change to the very elements of the world to deliver his people from slavery.

[22] M. Lind argues that this problem is characterised by a violation of God's rule in two ways: in Israel's attempt to participate in the power politics of the ANE and in their own domestic relationships. Chapters 2-5 integrate these internal relationships with international ones and use Jerusalem as the universal exemplar which will ultimately be used to draw in the nations (5:26; cf. 66:18-21). Chapter 6 connects these emphases in the narrative of the prophet's experience "with the cosmic, terrestrial rule of YHWH of hosts, the Holy One...whose realm he and his people had violated." See Lind 1997:317-38.

The writer prays for retribution against the nations by YHWH's cosmologically destructive act of rending the heavens to come and intimidate them (64:1-2).[23] Such cosmic judgment language has been repeated throughout the book and comes to particular expression in chapters 13, 24-27, 34, and 65-66.[24] The prayer for restoration throughout this chapter culminates in 64:9-12 and this prepares us for the promise of restoration of Zion/Jerusalem issued in the next chapter given in terms of a new creation. In the climactic conclusion of the book of Isaiah, God's response is an act of deliverance so complete that it is spoken of in terms of a new creation in 65:17. The radical renewal makes former acts of deliverance pale in comparison and will bring such joy as to erase completely the sorrow which afflicted God's people before its advent.

Focus on the Isaianic use of "former/new" alerts us to the sustained rhetoric of the book against idolatry and the Isaianic use of the cosmic judgment/cosmic renewal in order to deal with this problem. We now turn our attention to an examination of this cosmic motif in order better to show how the new creation, most explicitly communicated in Isa 65:17 and 66:22, functions in the material.

B. Cosmic Judgment/Cosmic Renewal

The Problem of Idolatry

Warnings against the threat of idolatry are woven throughout the entire book of Isaiah. From the very beginning of the book, an indictment is made against the people of God.[25] R. Bergey points out that chapter 1 "provides not only a prologue to the Isaianic prophecies in general but also, by its position, a preface to the block of judgement pronouncements against Jerusalem and Judah in chs. 1-11 (12)."[26] In what Blenkinsopp calls a "great arraignment," chapter one opens with a call to heaven and

---

[23] The phrase, "tear open the heavens (קָרַעְתָּ שָׁמַיִם)" (MT 63:19) is unique in the OT but it does seem to express the common understanding of a theophany in which God would break through what was viewed as a solid barrier between heaven and earth (cf. Ps 18:9; 144:5; Isa 40:22). Cf. Oswalt 1998:620.

[24] The cosmic destruction language prepares the way for the new creation language in chapters 65-66.

[25] The holiness of God stands in sharp contrast to the depravity of humanity both on the level of the individual as well as the nation (Isa 44:20; cf. 6:7; 53:6; 57:1, 15; 59:4). The appellation "Holy One of Israel (קְדוֹשׁ יִשְׂרָאֵל)" is a favourite in Isaiah. It is used 26 times – more than all the other occurrences in the Hebrew Bible combined.

[26] Bergey 2003:36-7. Sehmsdorf recognized a deuteronomistic influence upon Isa 65-66. See Sehmsdorf 1972:517-62.

earth to be witnesses in the case YHWH has against his people (1:2ff).²⁷ The charge in Isaiah 1:2 is that YHWH has "reared children (בָּנִים גִּדַּלְתִּי) and brought them up (רוֹמַמְתִּי), but they have rebelled (פָּשְׁעוּ) against [him]." The rebellion involves turning away from trusting YHWH and engaging in relationships with foreign nations. Whatever the exact historical background of 1:2-4, it is apparent that the rebellion against or turning away from God has in mind the reliance upon other nations which consistently vexed Israel's relationship with YHWH (Isa 2:22; 10:20; 20:5; 30:1-5; 31:1).²⁸

Of course, fraternization with pagan nations was viewed as a dangerous thing in Israel at least partially because it threatened to divert Israel's attentions to other deities besides YHWH (2:6-8).²⁹ The allure of relying upon other nations was not simply political opportunism. In the context of the ancient Near East, the most powerful nation was that nation with the most powerful gods. Israel's reliance upon foreign nations carried an implicit acknowledgment of the power of those nations' gods (Isa 1:29; 2:8, 18, 20). Isaiah 42:17 seems to have this in mind in the midst of praise for deliverance. YHWH promises mighty acts of salvation for his people, but those who trust in idols, that is, those who have turned away from him, will be "turned back (נָסֹגוּ) and utterly put to shame."³⁰

Cosmological Consequences of Sin

The rebellion of which the people of Israel are accused in Isaiah does not go unanswered. The invective of Isaiah 1:4-9 indicates that the conditions the people face are the direct result of their unfaithfulness to YHWH.³¹ Not only do the people suffer personal injury but the land itself has felt the effects of sin, "Your country lies desolate, your cities are burned with fire; in your very presence aliens devour your land; it is desolate, as overthrown by foreigners" (Isa 1:7). After the opening salvo against faithless Israel, Isaiah turns to a series of judgement oracles in chs. 2-4.³² The poem in 2:10-21 gives a thorough description of this judgment using imagery from nature (vv. 13-14).³³ The climax of the poem (vv. 18-9) refers to this judgment as a time when YHWH "rises to terrify (לַעֲרֹץ) the earth (הָאָרֶץ)."

---

²⁷ The concept of sin in Isaiah is frequently portrayed as rebellion against God. Isaiah uses at least four different roots in reference to sin (פשע, סרה, מרה, עוה).

²⁸ The issue of failure to trust God is at the heart of the sin (12:2; 50:10).

²⁹ Hanson 1995:113.

³⁰ Likewise, the Lord "turned himself (יֵהָפֵךְ) to become their enemy" (63:10).

³¹ Oswalt 1986:86-93.

³² Cf. Childs 2001:28-37.

³³ Motyer 1993:67-73.

In the final movement of the preface to the book (5:1-30) bleak judgment is pronounced against the rotten fruit of YHWH's vineyard (5:2-4; cf. 1:8; 3:12-15). The climactic judgment of vv. 25-30 is described as a devastating earthquake. Earthquakes were commonly seen in the ancient world as acts of divine wrath. Isaiah uses this cosmological judgment to show that, "the created world, in all the complexity, splendour and ferocity of its powers, is a controlled tool in the hand of the Creator, serving his righteous purposes."[34] Just as creation was an instrument in his hand, so are the foreign nations whom God will use to judge his people. Their onslaught will be tireless and two images of chaotic primordial creation are invoked to express how helpless Israel will be at their (i.e. God's) mercy: the roaring lion seizing prey and the storm which churns the sea and obscures the land (Isa 5:29-30). The wild beast and the storm evoke images from the time of creation where light and darkness and the chaotic sea were subdued by YHWH and nature dwelt in harmonious cohabitation. The cosmic judgment which has been described above is developed in Isaiah through the use of the city motif.

Use of the City in Isaiah[35]

The importance of the city of Jerusalem and Mount Zion cannot be overestimated for the Jewish people.[36] They were the focal point of God's commitment to Israel as his chosen people.[37] When the status of the city and the locus of the temple are compromised, the veracity of promises from YHWH which necessitated political and religious centrality for Jerusalem and Zion is challenged. R.E. Clements argues that questions about Zion's future in the context of the destruction of the temple and the city of Jerusalem frame the entire collection of prophecies.[38] The city and its holy mountain are used in Isaiah as symbols of hope for the continuing covenant relationship between YHWH and his people (cf. Isa 37:31-2).

The story of this hope in Isaiah begins with the initial account of the rebellion of the city against YHWH. It continues throughout the prophecies with his efforts to restore it to a position of prominence (1:21-26; 40:2; 60:14; 61:4). The role of Zion as apostate city (1:21) and as focal point of

---

[34] Motyer 1993:73.

[35] This theme in conjunction with Isaianic new creation may provide an interesting background to Paul's allegory in Galatians 4:25. Horbury 2003:189-226 argues that Paul "expresses hope for a kingdom of Christ in a renewed, not just a heavenly, Jerusalem" (p. 191). Such a connection would contribute to the argument of this thesis and would be a promising avenue for further research.

[36] Watts 1985:79-80. For a full discussion, see Fritz 1995.

[37] See Van Oorschot 2004:155-79.

[38] Clements's insightful article shows how this theme can help to explain the relationship between chapters 1-30 and 40-66. See Clements 1997:1-17.

world order (2:1-5) is found throughout Isaiah and comes into sharpest focus in chapter 66.[39] It therefore seems likely that W. Beuken is correct in his argument that these chapters relate to one another in ways which bind the material together as a literary unity and could be thought of as bookends for the collection of prophecies in between.[40] He concludes, "The renewal of Zion, population and city, is presented in the...opening of [the book of Isaiah] as the all-embracing object of YHWH's dealings with his people."[41]

Cities are also used in Isaiah in reference to people other than the people of God and embody competing political, social and religious realities.[42] This symbolism is employed to great effect in depicting the conflict between the purposes of God and the prideful human self-reliance which opposes his sovereignty. Different historical cities are used in Isaiah to illustrate godless society.[43] Chapters 13-23 give a highly concentrated focus on these cities which culminates in the judgement and deliverance depicted in 24-27.[44] Strikingly, the judgment against the "city of man" is communicated in cosmic terminology.[45] In this context, the earth itself is defiled by the sinfulness of the people against YHWH (24:5-6). Creation strains under the awful weight of guilt from this rebellion against God (24:20).[46]

The sins of humanity corrupt all of creation and bring God's judgment upon it.[47] He judges not only Israel but all of arrogant humanity which exalt their own purposes above those of the only true God. The judgement of YHWH against the nations (particularly those which have oppressed Israel) is announced in chapter 34 in cosmological terms (cf. Isa 36-37). As a result of his destructive wrath, "all the host of heaven shall rot away, and the skies roll up like a scroll" (Isaiah 34:4). After this has taken place,

---

[39] For R. Gordon, the correspondence between 2:1-4 and 66:18-24 stands out clearly [since chapter 1 is introductory]. "It is as if the encompassing vision of the book is that the Zion beloved of 'Isaiah of Jerusalem' is destined to become the focus of universal pilgrimage." See Gordon 2004:86.

[40] Beuken 1991:204-21. Beuken argues that the latter chapters are not necessarily allusions to the earlier chapters since the correspondence is on the level of single words and not phrases. Rather, he makes the case that the borrowing of terms from throughout chapter one would seem to suggest that the themes addressed are similar in both texts.

[41] Beuken 2004:469.

[42] E.g. Damascus, Samaria, Babylon, Edom, etc.

[43] Most saliently, Babylon in chapter 13. Ulrike Sals argues that "Babylon ist eine *politische* und *theologische* Größe, die immer wieder im Laufe des Jesajabuches behandelt wird [emphasis mine]." See Sals 2004:217.

[44] Cf. Anderson 1994:206.

[45] Isa 24:1, 3; cf. 24:18-23; 34:1-4.

[46] This text will be dealt with further in chapter 7, "Paul's Conception of New Creation in Romans 8:18-25."

[47] Cf. Hos 4:2-3. Brueggemann 1998:188-216.

chaotic nature overruns the strongholds of the pagan societies (vv. 13-15). In stark contrast, destitute creation itself rejoices (35:1-2; cf. 65:18) because it is brought from a condition of inhospitable barrenness to a place of life and peace (vv. 6b-7).[48] The term for rejoicing (גִּילָה) in 35:2 occurs only here and in 65:18 where the rejoicing of the new creation is described. This transformation of desolate nature is the physical component of the restoration which God will accomplish for his people. The "Holy Way" which results from this act creates paradisiacal conditions reminiscent of 11:6-9, 16 (cf. 65:20-5). The new conditions of peace which subdue the hostility of natural predators (e.g. lions; 5:29; 11:6-7; 35:9) pave the way for a return of God's people to the land (35:10; cf. 65:19).

The result is the deliverance of Israel wherein those who had been oppressed by the human powers return to worship the Lord "on the holy mountain in Jerusalem" (27:13; cf. 2:2).[49] The Hebrew text draws a contrast between the pagan city/cities and the powers of foreign domination which it/they represent(s) and the city of Jerusalem in Judah.[50] Thus, there is established a "city of God" which Motyer describes as "a new world order constructed by God on his plan, with himself at the centre and from where he reigns over a universe of righteousness and peace."[51] This is ultimately expressed in Isa 65:25 where the promise of new creation culminates in a rehearsal of the promise from 11:6-9. Creation is set right when YHWH's holy mountain takes its rightful place as the focal point of world order (cf. 66:18, 21, 22-3; Deut 28:1).[52]

After the terrifying predictions of the destruction of the earth in Isaiah 1-39, Isaiah 40-55 offers comfort to those whose actions had compromised their responsibilities in upholding the covenant with YHWH. They would have been liable to the judgments pronounced against those who violated the covenant stipulations. Nonetheless, YHWH was still firmly in control of the flow of the history which had apparently gone so far off course. Despite the fact that sin had brought the threat of utter destruction, YHWH's faithfulness was resilient. He encourages the people: "Lift up your eyes to

---

[48] The Hebrew noun גִּילָה is only used twice in the book of Isaiah and both appearances occur in the context of a renewal of creation (35:2; 65:18).

[49] Doyle's study on the use of metaphors draws out the relational importance of the language. Essentially, the cosmic judgment language reflects divine displeasure with the land (אֶרֶץ) and its inhabitants. The absence of YHWH's presence leads to reversal of creation. The "city of chaos (קִרְיַת־תֹּהוּ)" (Isa 24:10) recalls to mind the chaos which was said to characterise the "earth (אֶרֶץ)" in the original creation (cf. Gen 1:2). See Doyle 2000:214-16.

[50] Van der Kooij 2000:183-98.

[51] Motyer 1993:17.

[52] Oswalt offers a parallel argument that in its final form, Isa 56-66 functions theologically and literarily to draw the themes of the book together. Oswalt 1997:177-91.

the heavens, and look at the earth beneath; for the heavens will vanish like smoke, the earth will wear out like a garment, and those who live on it will die like gnats; but my salvation will be forever, and my deliverance will never be ended" (Isa 51:6; cf. 54:10). These texts help to link the horrific judgment described vividly throughout the book with the ultimate image of redemption in the conclusion of the material.[53] A closer examination of the nature of the new creation in Isa 65:17 will help to show how this is the case.

C. The Nature of the New Creation in Isaiah 65:17[54]

The nature of the new creation in Isaiah 65:17 (cf. 66:22) is contentious. Does this prophecy envisage a creative act wherein the physical universe is either completely recreated or renewed? Or, is this exaggerated language, only a metaphor for the renewal which YHWH plans for human society? According to C. Westermann, Isaiah's use of the new creation does not envisage a destruction of the cosmos and a recreation of its constituent parts but, rather, a renewal of the world.[55] This line of thinking is picked up by later commentators and exemplified in Blenkinsopp's suggestion that "the new heavens and earth are thought of more as the context for social and political transformation and therefore are not themselves the focus of attention, as is the case in apocalyptic writings from the Greco-Roman period."[56] There is evidence which may support this claim.

First, contrary to the extraordinary cosmological focus of the authors of apocalyptic, Isa 65 turns immediately from the new creation in verse 17 toward the city of Jerusalem in verse 18. D. Gowan considers this to be part of the larger theological thrust of the Isaianic material in which the cosmological elements of the text are subordinated to an interest in the wilderness and Zion.[57] Then, the LXX of Isa 65:17 translates the Hebrew verb (ברא) with the future tense of εἰμί: ἔσται γὰρ ὁ οὐρανὸς καινὸς καὶ ἡ γῆ καινή, "for there will be a new heaven and a new earth...." This could represent an attempt of the translators to avoid evoking the creation account of Gen 1:1 where the MT has ברא and the LXX has ποιέω fol-

---

[53] Cf. Houtman 1993:178-81.
[54] Isa 66:22 is also an important reference but it seems to rely on the description from the previous chapter and does not further our understanding of the nature of the new creation drastically. Thus, attention is mainly given to 65:17.
[55] Westermann 1969:408.
[56] Blenkinsopp 2003:286.
[57] Gowan 2000:113.

lowed by a reference to heaven and earth.⁵⁸ The omission in Isa 65:17 would be the result of an editorial effort on the part of the LXX translator to downplay the cosmological significance of the passage (cf. v. 18). Only when the Hebrew text takes a clear object other than the heavens and earth (i.e. Jerusalem) does the LXX give a direct translation of the phrase, "for behold I create (כִּי־הִנְנִי בוֹרֵא)" (repeated in MT of vv. 17a, 18b).⁵⁹

However, there is even stronger support for an alternative point of view. First, though the passage does move from the cosmological newness language of verse 17 to the renewal of Jerusalem and Zion in the following verses, the passage articulates this renewal in cosmologically important imagery. The lifespan threatened during the oppressive "former time" (cf. 65:16-7) would no longer be a source of mourning (vv. 19b-20);⁶⁰ and the hostile predatory relationships in creation would be calmed (65:25). Furthermore, the stability and enjoyment of the land's productivity (Isa 65:21-22) are direct reversals of the curses pronounced as a result of the broken covenant relationship with YHWH. There is a focus on the city (Jerusalem) and mountain (Zion) of God but it is never separated from creation as a whole. Though U. Berges goes too far in his argument that the new creation involves no radical effects to the cosmos but only to social structures, he is correct (in continuity with the earlier work of Kraus) that the city of Jerusalem is used in Isaiah as the epitome of creation.⁶¹ Thus, the extension of the creation terminology to Jerusalem in 65:18 is not simply a reference to post-exilic reconstruction projects designed to restore national morale; but, a microcosm of the newly created world spoken of in verse 17.⁶²

Secondly, even without the verb of creation and the more personal statement of YHWH's activity in creation in the LXX of 65:17, it is clear that the actor is God. The absence of the verb could have other explanations. Parablepsis from הָרִאשֹׁנוֹת of verse 16 to הָרִאשֹׁנוֹת of verse 17 may explain how the LXX translates the Heb. at the end of verse 16 with such an obviously different phrase: וְכִי נִסְתְּרוּ מֵעֵינָי = καὶ οὐκ ἀναβήσεται αὐτῶν ἐπὶ τὴν καρδίαν. The translator's eyes may have passed to the second appearance of this word and then picked up the normal translation

---

⁵⁸ Isa 65:22 seems to condemn this line of thought. Where the MT reads, "as the days of a tree shall be the days of my people" the LXX reads, "for the days of my people shall be as the days of the tree of life." This seems to be an intentional reference to Gen 3:22, 24. O. Steck argues that Isa 65:16b-25 reflects reception of the text of Gen 1-3. See Steck 1997:349-66. Contra Steck, see Blenkinsopp 2003:287.

⁵⁹ The translation is mine.

⁶⁰ This verse does not seem to eradicate the possibility of death as is the case in 25:7-8 (cf. 26:19). However, the language could be metaphorical.

⁶¹ Berges 2002:13. Quoting: Kraus 1990:241. Cf. Brueggemann 1998 :2.

⁶² Dim 2005:106.

C. The Nature of the New Creation in Isaiah 65:17

with the beginning of verse 17. The difference in verbs used at the end of vv. 16 and 17 may be stylistic variation.[63]

However, this would not explain why the language at the beginning of verse 17 is altered. D. Baer argues that this is part of a larger problem with vv. 16-17. In his helpful textual analysis of the LXX of Isa 65-66, he makes the case that the depersonalization of verse 17 (MT = LXX) is "part of a sustained evacuation of God from the vulnerable pathos of this context."[64] It could be that the Hebrew (v. 16) כִּי נִשְׁכְּחוּ הַצָּרוֹת הָרִאשֹׁנוֹת וְכִי נִסְתְּרוּ מֵעֵינָי ("because the former troubles are forgotten and are hidden from my sight") held the concepts of forgetfulness and something's being hidden from God in too close a proximity for the translator's comfort. Not only is the final phrase changed but the penultimate clause has been transposed from the passive form in Hebrew (נִשְׁכְּחוּ) to the "active and unmistakably human ἐπιλήσονται γὰρ τὴν θλῖψιν αὐτῶν."[65] Thus, the exclusion of the first person reference to God in verse 17 is most likely not an attempt to dilute the cosmology of the passage; but, rather a well-known tendency of the translator to "soften anthropomorphic descriptions of God and to avoid affirmations of divine limitations."[66]

Thirdly, it is difficult to excise cosmological reference from the language of Isa 65:17 even though social and political upheaval may be implied.[67] Particularly if Isaiah is viewed as a literary unity, it is not hard to imagine how the recreation of the world could be a fitting conclusion to the cosmic destruction mentioned earlier in the book and discussed above.[68] Further, the combination of the terms אֶרֶץ and שָׁמַיִם is used throughout the OT in reference to the entire created order. This point is strengthened by the clear and unambiguous understanding of this text as cosmological in a majority of the subsequent Jewish and Christian literature which picks up the theme.[69] Whether Paul would have taken this text

---

[63] Cf. Ziegler 1934, pp 51, 173. Seeligman argues that there could be other Greek texts influencing the translation: Seeligmann 2004:222-4.

[64] Baer 2001:142.

[65] Baer 2001:142.

[66] Baer 2001:140. For a discussion of the evidence for this strategy throughout chapters 56-66, see Baer 2001:154-9.

[67] J. Watts' attempts to translate אֶרֶץ consistently as "land" are unconvincing, especially in Isa 65:17 where it appears in connection with שָׁמַיִם. Cf. Watts 1987:349, 53-4.

[68] Though he does not deal extensively with the issue of creation, Sweeney argues convincingly that 65-66 serve as the conclusion for the book as a whole. See Sweeney 1997:454-74.

[69] 2 Peter 3:10-13 presents this theme in remarkable clarity. The day of the Lord would cause cosmic destruction and the hope for new creation was not far removed. Hubbard acknowledges this point but argues that this stream of Jewish tradition was not what influenced Paul's conception of the new creation. See Hubbard 2002:16-7

to intimate a complete destruction and recreation or only a renovation of the present world is not of utmost importance. Both traditions are represented well in later developments of the Isaianic conception of new creation. The essential point is that there is an intimate connection between the world and humanity.

The declaration of the new creation in Isa 65:17 and its subsequent description culminating in 65:25 indicates the importance in the book of Isaiah of maintaining a strong connection between God's people and God's world. The salvation referred to by the promise of a new heaven and earth is not a disregarding of the created order. Quite the contrary, it is the recognition that the fate of humanity and the world are intertwined. The promised deliverance from the judgment of the exile and from the instrumental foreign rulers used by God to exact the penalty for the sin of rebellion was a political victory for the people of God over the nations. But it was far more than a political affair. The deplorable spiritual condition of Israel had an effect on creation itself. The ultimate promise of salvation in Isaiah 65-66 represents not only a reversal of the political and social situation of the people but also a rectification of the internal issues concomitant with a fracturing of the covenant relationship with YHWH.[70]

Isa 66:22 has been given less attention because it mostly assumes the discussion of new creation in chapter 65. However, it offers at least one clue concerning the nature of new creation in Isaiah. This verse speaks of the endurance of God's people in direct relation to the endurance of the promised new heavens and earth. What happens to humanity is directly related to the world in which they live. The text supports the premise that the fates of both are intertwined, "For *as* the new heavens and the new earth, which I will make, shall remain before me, says the LORD; *so* shall your descendants and your name remain."

Other OT books which are also important for Paul's concept of new creation (namely, Jeremiah and Ezekiel) also maintain the connection between the world and its inhabitants.[71] In the well-known new covenant passage of Jer 31:31-38 the endurance of the cosmos is cited as evidence for the endurance of YHWH's faithfulness. The restoration context of this chapter declares a solution to the plight addressed by the prophet which focuses attention on the need for renovation of the heart. That emphasis certainly dominates but does not obfuscate the restoration of the earth's productivity and the geocentricity of Zion so important in the wider Jewish tradition (cf. Jer 31:12-14, 23-4). The characteristics of the new creation

---

[70] Cf. Russell 1996:69-77.
[71] Cf. Hanson 1979:23.

described in Isa 65:17-25 are similar in content to the promises of Jer 31 (cf. 31:4-6, 12-13, 15-6, 27-28).[72]

Ezekiel's restoration message in chapters 34-6 is also delivered in the context of cosmologically important language. As in Isaiah and Jeremiah, the restoration spoken of here involves both an internal as well as a physical, cosmological element. D. Russell expresses this well in his recognition that "the alienation between humanity and the earth is removed due to the implanting of a new heart and new spirit (36:25-30). Thus, the restoration of a proper relationship between God and his people will affect even the created order."[73]

D. CONCLUSION

In the Old Testament, the promise of new creation provided hope that YHWH would bring restoration after the ravishing effects of Israel's own sin. Particularly in Isaiah, that sin ultimately led to judgment spoken of in terms of an actual destruction of the world. The cosmological judgment texts in Isaiah anticipate the ultimate act of redemption – when the cosmos itself is made new. Though the later passages may reflect development or intensification in terms of their cosmological scope, this chapter has attempted to show that cosmological themes are important throughout this collection of prophecies. It is impossible to understand the Isaianic prophecy of new creation without the cosmic disasters which had necessitated it. Furthermore, it would be a serious misreading of the text to take the prophecies of new creation in Isa 65-66 to be an external solution required by an external problem. As we have argued, the state of the world is directly related in Isaiah to human sin.

Contrary to our contemporary scientific view of reality where the material world stands in isolation from the spiritual and moral state of humanity, the world of ancient Israel held an indissoluble link between the spiritual and physical. This means that we cannot speak of what happens to them politically in isolation from their religion. And we cannot view these things in isolation from the creation. The state of the world is directly related to the state of the people. When viewed as a literary unity, the book of Isaiah combines the soteriological emphasis with a cosmological emphasis throughout. The new creation functions as the ultimate expression of redemption from the corruption caused by sin. It involves a restoration of social structures which were directly related to cosmic order. The importance of this concept for Paul's conception of new creation will become

---

[72] Keown, Scalise, and Smothers 1995:122-3.
[73] Russell 1996:69-70.

clearer when we deal directly with his letters. But before we turn our focus to the Pauline epistles, further examination of Jewish and Greco-Roman background will be necessary.

Chapter 3

New Creation in Early Jewish Literature

As the previous chapter suggested, the concept of new creation in the Old Testament, particularly in Isaiah, provided the headwaters for many streams of Jewish tradition. The idea of new creation became an especially important concept in Jewish literature spanning roughly the 3rd century B.C. to the 1st century A.D. and was developed and expanded in a number of ways. It is my intention here neither to suggest any particular lines of development nor to give an exhaustive survey of the use of the concept in our period.[1] The argument focuses on how the idea of new creation functioned within the socio-historical framework of Second Temple Judaism.

As the concept of new creation comes to particular expression in the apocalyptic literature, this material will be examined to support the claim that new creation was employed as a way of dealing with a perceived problem. I do not suggest that a common social setting should be assumed for the entire genre.[2] This body of literature covers such an expanse of time and is comprised of such an eclectic collection of material, it would be imprudent to impose the conception of a single setting upon the entire corpus.[3] However, the modest observation that apocalypses were written out of perceptions of some form of distress is generally recognized and need not obscure the diversity of the material.[4] The use of the concept of new

---

[1] For such an analysis, see Mell 1989. I have already pointed out how Mell's rigid *traditionsgeschichtliche* approach to the material yields an inaccurate picture of Paul's thought. Mell nonetheless provides a tour de force through the use of the phrase "new creation" in early Jewish literature.

[2] It is not assumed that apocalyptic literature was written by a monolithic movement or group. The literature is diverse and was adapted to speak into various contexts. All that is argued here is the commonly accepted concept that apocalyptic writers attempted to provide a means of assuring their readers that the course of history was being directed by God despite all appearances to the contrary. Davies 1989:264-70. See Rowland 1982:194-213.

[3] M. Hengel put it well in describing his reaction to his assignment to write about the social setting of apocalyptic writing. He claimed that this was "so etwas wie eine Gleichung mit zahlreichen Unbekannten. Man sieht die Aufgabe und weiß zugleich, daß sie unlösbar ist, weil wir darüber zu wenig wissen und die einzelnen Größen daher nicht eindeutig zu erfassen sind." Hengel 1989:655.

[4] Collins 1998:38; See Sappington 1994:83-123; Adela Yarbro Collins 1986:1-11; Hubbard 2002:35.

creation in the context of foreign oppression caused by sin is particularly relevant for this thesis.

The argument of this chapter advances in three sections. First, in order to address the question of how the idea of new creation functioned as the solution to a perceived plight, it will be necessary to explore how the plight itself was understood in early Jewish thought. Apocalyptic literature served as a way of dealing with the tensions precipitated by these challenges. The second section of this chapter undertakes a detailed analysis of how the concept of new creation could be used in one form of Jewish Apocalyptic literature – the book of *Jubilees*. *Jubilees* offers a helpful example of how the apocalyptic literature could conceive of the problem faced by the Jewish people in both political and religious terms. The solution it offers to this problem, spoken of in terms of new creation, involves God's action on both cosmological and anthropological levels. This is perfectly consistent with the connection between humanity and creation described in the previous chapter. Such a connection supports the argument of this thesis that Paul's understanding of new creation involved anthropological and cosmological soteriology.

A final section examines the use of the concept of new creation in the Dead Sea Scrolls. The eschatological soteriology represented in the Qumran communities offers helpful comparative material for our inquiry into how Paul understands new creation.

A. The Plight of Second Temple Judaism

Historical Context

M. Hengel's thorough study of Judaism and Hellenism includes an attempt to understand Jewish apocalypticism within its social and cultural setting.[5] He cites considerable evidence to show that apocalyptic literature was Judaism's response to the crisis created by the encroachment of the Hellenistic worldview on Jewish society.[6] Of course, the roots of apocalypticism are much earlier but the genre did become especially prominent from the time of the Maccabean revolt of the 2nd century B.C. From the time of the Babylonian exile in 587 B.C., the nation of Israel was subject to a series of foreign powers. The Persians returned a modicum of autonomy to Jerusalem but essentially made it a province of the Persian Empire. The hopes of a glorious return from the exile were never realized and the seeds of cognitive dissonance created by the apparent failure of the promises of God may

---

[5] Hengel 1973.

[6] Hengel also acknowledges the reciprocal influence of Hellenistic society on Jewish apocalyptic literature. Cf. Nickelsburg 1989:642-4.

be evidenced in the prophecy of Haggai 2:3, "Who is left among you that saw this house in its former glory? How does it look to you now? Is it not in your sight as nothing?"[7]

The subsequent years brought little resolution to that strand of Jewish tradition which awaited a glorious fulfilment of restoration promises. In fact, the relatively benign conditions in which they found themselves would grow far worse before they would be ameliorated. The rise of the Hellenistic Empire in due course brought with it a philosophy of imperialism which was not content with allowing subject peoples to enjoy their own culture and traditions in isolation from Hellenism.[8] When the Seleucid king Antiochus IV issued decrees against the temple cult and the practice of the Mosaic Law, it was the spark that ignited the smouldering embers of discontent among the dominated people of Israel.[9] The resulting Maccabean Revolt succeeded in establishing a measure of independence. It did not succeed in bringing Israel to the heights anticipated by some of the OT restoration promises. Further, the relative success was short-lived as the rise of the Roman Empire would soon draw the nation deeper into the network of an imperial power structure.[10]

Apocalypticism and the Response of People under Pressure

Apocalyptic literature played an important role in influencing the practise of Judaism in the period between the Maccabean Revolt and the destruction of the temple.[11] While this literature was certainly influenced by various sources, the thrust of the material is founded upon an OT conception of salvation history.[12] Therefore, it is possible to appreciate a variety of settings in which apocalyptic writing could have flourished and, at the same time, to recognize that these writings articulated in similar ways the prob-

---

[7] Cf. Ezra 3:12. From this period, two streams of tradition developed which interpret the post-exilic situation in radically divergent ways. The *theocratic stream* views the restoration as having taken place in the return of captives from Babylon at the beginning of Persian hegemony. The *eschatological stream*, apparently intimated by Haggai and Ezra, indicates that the people of Israel remain under the wrath of God and have not yet enjoyed the fulfilment of restoration promises. See Scott 1996:786-8. Cf. Talmon 2001:107-46.

[8] This was not the case in the earlier expansion under Alexander the Great. He prided himself, among other things, with the eclecticism and "multiculturalism" of his empire. It was actually the ruling class of Judea that would later attempt to implement Hellenistic reforms and thereby catalyse the Maccabean Revolt.

[9] Hengel 2001:16-22.

[10] Horsley 1987:3-19.

[11] Hengel 1974:253. For a recent discussion on the nature of apocalyptic literature, see the collection of essays in Grabbe and Haak 2003.

[12] Hengel 1974:251. This observation challenges J.L. Martyn's view that apocalyptic excludes any ties with salvation history in Paul. See Martyn 1997.

lems faced by different communities and the solutions to those problems. Apocalyptic was the "distinctive form taken by imagination in late Second Temple Jewish society ... [and] could serve as the medium through which Jews held fast to their faith under foreign oppression."[13] Apocalyptic literature represents an attempt to confront the reality of the world which seemed to challenge the promises and faithfulness of God with an alternative way of viewing the world and the course of history.

The worldview projected by the apocalyptists was an application of the traditional "symbolic universe" of the OT in the historical situations in which they found themselves.[14] They addressed the apparent problem faced by their audience in a way that was consistent with the biblical revelation of God's redemption and judgment. God's actions were cosmic in scale and provided a basis for maintaining group identity and hope in the face of forces which challenged the social cohesion of the people of God.[15] For example, the concepts of resurrection and dualism were newly expressed in the apocalyptic context.[16] Resurrection offered ultimate vindication of the righteous struggle of God's people to maintain their faithfulness and dualism spoke of that struggle in a way that allowed them to demonize the forces which represented the oppression.

Rightly interpreted, apocalyptic should be rooted to its historical context.[17] It attempted to expose and demystify the oppressive power structures of pagan foreign rule as well as the apostate Jewish leaders who aligned themselves with them.[18] With the story of the Exodus as a historical model, the apocalyptic writers were able to challenge their contemporary situation with the idea that, despite all appearances, God's sovereignty would prevail over the temporal sovereignty of pagan rulers and he would ultimately bring justice when his ordained time had come.[19] As will be made clear later in this chapter, the political oppression in which the people of God found themselves was directly connected to their spiritual condition.[20]

---

[13] Elliott 1994:149ff.
[14] Cf. Horsley 1987:133-5.
[15] Nickelsburg 1989:645.
[16] These were likely based on ideas inchoate in the OT.
[17] Horsley 1987:133-5. Contra Hanson 1979:26ff.
[18] Horsley 1987:140.
[19] The necessity of discerning the times is an important theme in this literature. Elliott 1994:163-4.
[20] This point is intended to balance R. Horsley's over-emphasis on the political nature of these writings. See, e.g., Horsley 1987. We should avoid seeing the ancient communities in the image of 20th century victims of imperialism. Although the congruencies are striking and important, the apocalyptists themselves did not restrict their language to this aspect of their experience to the exclusion of the spiritual/religious points they wished to make.

Within this broad social and historical framework, the apocalyptic use of new creation provides a way of speaking about divine deliverance from the predicament faced by the people of God. How this is the case may be seen from a brief look at the use of new creation in Jewish apocalyptic literature in general followed by a more detailed analysis of an exemplary text: *Jubilees*.

New Creation in Jewish Apocalyptic Works

The idea of God's bringing eschatological renewal was a familiar theme in Jewish apocalyptic works in general and the concept of new creation was understood in various ways throughout the literature.[21] The renewal of the world was portrayed both as an incremental progression (*Jub.* 1:29; *1 En.* 45:4-6) as well as a cataclysmic event (*1 En.* 91:14-16; cf. 1 Pet 3:10, 12).[22] Broadly speaking, the literature may be divided between two approaches to the question of continuity between creation and new creation.[23] Some works envisage a completely new creation (e.g. *1 En.* 72:1; 91:14-16), usually understood to follow a total destruction of the earth, and others foresee a renewal of the present world (e.g. *1 En.* 10:18-22; 45:4-5). These two perspectives may occur in the same book (e.g. *4 Ezra* 6:13-16, 24-25; 7:30-2, 75; *2 Bar.* 32:6; 44:12-15; 57:2) and it is sometimes difficult to determine which of these ideas is predominant.[24]

M.C. de Boer observes a further distinction of apocalyptic literature between a *cosmological* and a *forensic* track.[25] In *cosmological-apocalyptic eschatology*, the world has fallen under the dominion of hostile spiritual powers and the faithful await God's invasion of the present to bring about a new age in which all opposition to his sovereignty is silenced.[26] *Forensic-apocalyptic eschatology* minimizes the evil powers and focuses on human freedom and responsibility to choose obedience to

---

[21] For an overview of the use of new creation in apocalyptic writing, see Mell 1989:113-78. For an analysis of early Jewish views of the corruption and redemption of creation, see Hahne 2006:153-68.

[22] Russell 1964:280-4.

[23] N. Dahl sees at least seven different ways in which the relationship between the first and last things is described. See Dahl 1956:425-8. For a recent study of this issue in Paul, see Schrage 2005:245-59.

[24] This may support the observation that the apocalyptic writers were not as interested in systematic consistency as they were in the use of evocative language and imagery. However, the inconsistencies could also be explained by the composite nature of much of this material. Cf. John J. Collins 1986:345-70. However, note Klijn's attempt to harmonize the discrepancy in Klijn 1970:65-76; cf. Hahne 2006:139.

[25] De Boer 1989:169-90.

[26] Cf. *1 En.* 5, 10, 16, 19, 21.

the Law.[27] Particularly interesting for this thesis is de Boer's observation that both these strands are present within the apostle Paul's writings and this may explain how Paul is able to hold together both *cosmological* and *anthropological* soteriology.[28]

Cosmological-apocalyptic eschatology, which speaks of God's salvific actions in terms of new creation, anticipated that God was going to do something in the future that would extirpate evil from the world and ultimately establish his reign. God's rule would bring restoration and cleansing to the created order on such a scale as to be conceived of in terms of a new creation (*1 En.* 45:4-6).[29] Thus, the new creation may be thought of as a return to the paradisiacal conditions of the original creation either in an earthly or heavenly sense (*T. Levi* 18:10ff.; *1 En.* 61:12; *2 En.* 8:1ff.; *2 Bar.* 4:3; et al.).[30]

Given the diverse nature of this material, a detailed examination of its social setting and the function of new creation within it would not be possible in the confines of this thesis. Analysis of the use of new creation in a sample work, the book of *Jubilees*, will suffice for our argument here.

B. The Function of New Creation in the Book of Jubilees

Current scholarly opinion dates *Jubilees* between 170 and 150 B.C.[31] That is, it is roughly contemporary with the beginning of the Maccabean period which began during the first of the three major Jewish revolts of antiquity. *Jubilees* almost certainly reuses earlier apocalyptic traditions[32] and thereby stands firmly within the stream of apocalyptic interpretations of new creation. There are a number of justifications for focusing on this

---

[27] Cf. *2 Bar.* 54:13-22.

[28] De Boer argues that in both Rom 1-8 and Galatians, Paul's "conversation partners" embrace the *forensic-apocalyptic eschatology* track and that Paul balances that perspective with a *cosmological-apocalyptic eschatology*. See De Boer 1989:182-5.

[29] The new creation would be like the original creation in the sense that the old is an analogy for the new – both are sovereign acts of God accomplished completely by his power and according to his will for his glory (*Jub.* 1:29; *2 Esd* 7:30ff.; *1 En.* 24-5; 91:16; *Tg. Jer.* 23:23). See Dahl 1956:422-443.

[30] Russell 1964:282-4.

[31] VanderKam 1989:v-vi. This date is narrowed by Vanderkam to a date between 160 and 150. This period is widened by Davenport who applies form-redaction criticism to assert that the book was written by several authors in at least three editions. The earliest sections he dates to the end of the third or the beginning of the second century. He believes that the latest sections could have been written as late as 104 B.C. For a fuller discussion of this possibility, see Davenport 1971:10-8. For a fuller discussion of the issues of dating, see VanderKam 1977:207-85.

[32] VanderKam 1978:229-51. Cf. VanderKam 1993:96-125.

book as a case study of how new creation could be utilized in pre-A.D. 70 Jewish literature.[33] First, *Jubilees* is the only extant literature outside the Pauline corpus in which the phrase "new creation" occurs twice.[34]

Secondly, it offers insight into the Jewish response to the encroachment of Hellenization and, more particularly, illumination of the Hasidim who may well have been predecessors to the Pharisees.[35] As Paul considers himself a Pharisee (Phil 3:5; Acts 23:6; 26:5; cf. Acts 5:34; 22:3), his ministry is directed towards Gentiles and he deals with the issue of Jew/Gentile relations, the way *Jubilees* deals with the Jew/Gentile culture clash offers helpful comparative material.

Thirdly, *Jubilees* falls into the category of those works labelled historical apocalypses.[36] The book offers a reinterpretation of history which serves to bring understanding to the present circumstances faced by the readers as well as to offer hope for the uncertain future out of a situation which might have appeared disastrous for those faithful to YHWH.[37] This makes it a helpful comparison with Galatians and 2 Corinthians as these letters are not part of the apocalyptic genre but they do reframe history in terms of the Christ event.

Finally, M. Hubbard's book uses the concept of new creation in *Jubilees* as an example of the type of cosmological influence which he argues is *not* present when Paul uses the term "new creation." On the contrary, it will be argued here that *Jubilees* embodies the dual cosmological/anthropological focus, which the previous chapter of this thesis argued is present in Isaiah. This dual reference is acknowledged by Hubbard, but he focuses on the cosmological nature of the concept in *Jubilees* and fails to address the importance of this dual focus for understanding how Paul used the term "new creation."[38]

---

[33] In his recent work on new creation in Paul's letters, M. Hubbard analyses the function of new creation in *Jubilees* as a representative work of Jewish apocalyptic literature. See Hubbard 2002:26ff. This thesis does not affirm that *Jubilees* serves as a representative of all Jewish apocalyptic literature; and neither, I think, does Hubbard's. However, it does provide an important example of how the concept of new creation could be used in literature with characteristics shared by the larger corpus of apocalyptic writings. For an exemplary objection to classifying this book as apocalyptic, see Lange 1997:25-38.

[34] Of course, the concept could be present where the phrase is not but this should not lead us to neglect those relatively few passages (4 in total: *1 En.* 72:1; *Jub.* 1:29; 4:26; *2 Bar.* 44:12) where the phrase actually appears.

[35] Hubbard 2002:26ff. Cf. Wintermute 1985:46.

[36] Mell 1989:152. The commonly recognized reliance of this text upon Enochic literature roots it firmly within the apocalyptic tradition. Hubbard compiles a substantial bibliography of scholars who take *Jubilees* as an apocalyptic work. See Hubbard 2002:27-8.

[37] Hall 1991:43-44.

[38] Hubbard 2002:52.

Hubbard brings important insights to our understanding of how new creation is used here as well as in the writings of the apostle Paul. However, Hubbard's focus on the question of whether the term "new creation" should be understood anthropologically or cosmologically obfuscates the more important issue of how the author of *Jubilees* preserves Jewish identity during difficult times. Despite Hubbard's valuable insights, his argument that the concept of new creation functions as an *external* solution to an *external* plight does not adequately communicate the message of *Jubilees* and contributes to a misunderstanding of Paul's soteriology as an *internal* plight requiring an *internal* solution. A closer look at the sense of dilemma in the book of *Jubilees* and the way in which new creation functions to solve that dilemma will support this charge.

Assimilation to Hellenistic Society and the Loss of Jewish Identity in Jubilees

At first observation, it may seem strange that the Jewish religion should be oppressed at all by the Seleucid power. The culture was quite pluralistic and Antiochus IV Epiphanes apparently espoused a partial tolerance of foreign religion and politics. An example of this policy may be seen in the fact that Samaria's worship on Mt. Gerizim was allowed to continue, while the Jerusalem temple was defiled and an attempt made to remould the inhabitants of the city in the image of Hellenism.[39] The difference in imperial attitudes between Samaria and Jerusalem reveals an important point about the nature of Judaism at the time. The problem was that the Jewish religion was exclusive and particularistic. This offended the cultural sensibilities of the 2nd century Mediterranean world in much the same way as these ideas transgress the sensibilities of modern pluralism.[40] To add YHWH to the pantheon of Hellenistic gods may not have been a serious problem. But this was not an option for the Jewish faithful of the time. Their position is reflected in Josephus's account of the roots of conflict between Israelites and Midianites.[41] By rejecting the gods of the Seleucids along with the cultic exercise of their religion, these Jews *de facto* rejected the political establishment and the means whereby they could cultivate a suitable relationship with the reigning powers.[42]

A group of Jews who sought reform to counter this problem may well have postulated that the exclusivistic, particularistic elements of their re-

---

[39] Cf. *Ant.* 12:257-264. Of course, the Samaritans brought their religious practices into conformity with Hellenism and even requested of Antiochus that their temple be called the Temple of Jupiter Hellenius.
[40] Cf. 1 Macc 1:41-2; 2 Macc 4:11-17.
[41] *Ant.* 4:129-30; *Ant.* 4:137-8.
[42] Bickerman 1979:82-85. See also: VanderKam 1997b:20-1.

B. The Function of New Creation in the Book of Jubilees

ligion were not original but represented a corruption of their ancestral ideals (cf. 1 Macc 1:11).[43] The author of *Jubilees* is very much concerned with maintaining the purity of Israel's national identity.[44] The struggle for identity may be clearly seen in the way that the author of *Jubilees* addressed the vicissitudes of the contemporary situation by reworking the Genesis traditions of the Old Testament. The author of 1 Macc 1:14 cites first the building of a gymnasium in Jerusalem as the action taken by those who were interested in eradicating Jewish particularity. The offensive Greek practise of exercising in the nude is confronted in *Jubilees*' handling of the account from *Genesis* 3 of the covering of Adam's nakedness in the Garden of Eden.[45] The Hellenists were criticized by the author of *Jubilees* not only for being "uncovered as the Gentiles are uncovered" (*Jub.* 1:31), they also sought to reverse the appearance of their circumcision and outlaw the ritual among other Jews (1 Macc 1:15, 48-50; *Ant.* 12:241). As circumcision was one of the most important identity markers of Judaism, the attempt to hide the marks of circumcision was, in essence, an attempt to erase their identity as Jews.

The abandonment of the religious traditions of Israel and the attempt to merge Jewish society with the Hellenistic world is echoed in the interest *Jubilees* displays in maintaining cultic and racial purity. In chapter 1, the future apostasy of Israel is predicted when they will, "walk after the Gentiles and after their defilement and shame" (1:9). According to our author, mixing with the Gentiles causes Israel to forget God's commandments and corrupt the observances of holy times and the honouring of holy places ordained by God (1:10-11, 14; 6:35-8). The idea of separation from foreigners is stressed throughout the book (cf. 22:16; 25:1, 3, 5, 8-10, 12; 30:7-17). The retelling of history in *Jubilees* devalues the spiritual and political pressures that oppose Israel and creates a backdrop to the hope that God will act for his people to bring resolution to their difficult circumstances.[46]

Central to the worldview of *Jubilees* is fidelity to the Law.[47] The identity of the recipients of the book is being threatened. This can only be reinforced through return to God's commandments.[48] The entire book is set on Mt. Sinai where Moses received the "tablets of the Law and the commandment by the word of the Lord."[49] These commandments draw the

---

[43] For a fuller discussion of this hypothesis, see Bickerman 1979:78-86. This study points out other Hellenistic material which refers to a previous time when there was no such separation between people groups.

[44] Hellerman 2003:421.

[45] Van Ruiten 1996:313-15.

[46] Mell 1989:117-18.

[47] O. Wintermute claims that this is the book's central message. Wintermute 1985:40.

[48] Frey 1997:286-7.

[49] This statement occurs in the book's original title.

lines of identification around the people of God and obedience to them firmly establishes their identity as his chosen ones.⁵⁰

The author of *Jubilees* used the Law to serve as an identity marker for Israel. Three themes from the book illustrate this point. First, *Jubilees* is predicated upon the concept of a chronological system based on a 364 day solar calendar. In its ancient descriptive title, the work is referred to as: "The Account of the Division of Days of the Law and the Testimony for Annual Observance according to their Weeks (of Years) and their Jubilees throughout all the Years of the World." Though the history only incorporates the time through the giving of the Law at Sinai, the pattern established from creation is meant to reveal how God will deal with his people throughout time. Strict observance of this system is required in order to maintain the purity that God intended for the religious festivals which he revealed to his people. Chief among the calendrical observances was honouring the Sabbath. The Law given to Moses at Sinai was only a continuation of the ordinance rooted in creation itself.⁵¹ In fact, the recognition of Sabbath on the earth was a reflection of what even the angels did in heaven (cf. *Jub.* 2:17-19, 30-1; 1 Macc 1:39). Obedience to God's commandments puts the people of Israel back into harmony with the divine order of creation.⁵²

Secondly, the emphasis on circumcision in *Jubilees* was designed to reinforce Jewish identity in a time when this rite was being challenged by the political powers of the day (*Jub.*15:25-6, 28-9; cf. *Ant* 12:254).⁵³ Antiochus "compelled the Jews to dissolve the laws of their country, and to keep their infants uncircumcised..." (*J.W.* 1:34). Josephus credits this kind of imperial behaviour with provoking the Maccabean Revolt.⁵⁴ The assertion that circumcision is an "eternal ordinance" (15:25, 28-29) is supported, as was Sabbath observance, by the fact that the angels, too, had observed the rite even from the day of their creation (16:27). Failure to uphold this divine mandate not only surrendered their identity as Jews on a personal level but also on the national level. One of the consequences of disobedi-

---

⁵⁰ The author of *Jubilees* seeks to support the concept that the Law given at Sinai was in effect long before the tablets were received by Moses. According to B. Ego, "Das Gesetz des Mose wiederholt somit, was bereits in der Ur- und Vätergeschichte initiert wurde." See Ego 1997:207. This position is reflected in Van Ruiten's work on the interpretations of biblical traditions in *Jubilees*. See Van Ruiten 2003:190; Van Ruiten 1996:305-17; Van Ruiten 2000:70. The connection between the law and creation is also evidenced in later rabbinic works.

⁵¹ For a discussion of the significance of the Sabbath in *Jubilees*, see Doering 1997:179-205.

⁵² Ego 1997:216.

⁵³ Hellerman Hellerman 2003:414-15.

⁵⁴ *J.W.* 1:35.

B. The Function of New Creation in the Book of Jubilees

ence was that they would be uprooted from the land.[55] Breaking the covenant relationship with God resulted in exile.[56]

A third emphasis of the book of *Jubilees* that is intricately related with the previous two examples is the interest of the author in securing Israel's identity through separation from Gentiles and purity from the pollution of pagan foreign ideology.[57] This is expressed in the sustained assertion that Israel alone is the people of God and that the Jewish ancestry should be kept in pristine isolation from foreign contamination.[58] In Rebecca's motherly instructions to Jacob regarding marriage, she implores him, "My son, do not take for yourself a wife from the daughters of Canaan...but from my father's house and my father's kin...and the Most High God will bless you, and your children will be a righteous generation and a holy seed" (*Jub.* 25:1-3). Jacob promises to avoid the failure of his brother, Esau, in this regard. Vowing never to take a foreign wife, he is able to say, "I will walk uprightly and will never corrupt my ways" (*Jub.* 25:10).[59] Racial separation between Jews and Gentiles was augmented by geographical divisions coming from the time of Noah (*Jub.* 8:10-11).[60] *Jubilees* has Noah pronounce a curse upon those who do not honour these divisions of land (9:14; cf. 10:27-34). In this way, the foreign occupation of Jerusalem is repudiated and the divine right of the Jews to live in this territory is established.

As these examples show, the law serves an identity-forming role for the people of Israel. If the law helps to define the people of God, violation of the law, or sin, poses a direct challenge to Israel's identity as the elect of God. Although *Jubilees* does not postulate a fully developed doctrine of original sin, it is clear that sin is responsible for shortening the lengthy life spans which are related in the early chapters of Genesis.[61] *Jubilees* does acknowledge individual responsibility with regard to sin but the bulk of the

---

[55] *Jub.* 15:28, 34.

[56] For a thorough discussion of how many Diaspora Jews of the Greco-Roman era perceived themselves in a state of exile, see Scott 1997:173-218.

[57] See Ravid 2002:61-86.

[58] Such exclusivism is pronouncedly different from the universalism encountered in Isaiah where the nations ultimately are taken into Israel. Here, only those physically related to Abraham can take part in the covenant. Note the unusual inclusion of women into the genealogies to stress the significance of racial purity (e.g. 4:7-15, 27-28). Cf. VanderKam 1997b:19. For a fuller discussion of the role of women in *Jubilees*, see Halpern-Amaru 1994:609-26.

[59] The penalty for disobeying this restriction is recorded in the context of the rape of Dinah (*Jub.* 30:4, 7-17).

[60] Hellerman Hellerman 2003:417. What would later be called the "promised land" was given to Noah's favourite son, Shem.

[61] Endres 1987:52-3.

culpability is ascribed to the Gentiles and to Satan.⁶² This nefarious duo works in conjunction to lead the people of Israel away from the observances which define their identity. Evil spirits are responsible for the depravity of the Gentiles (*Jub.* 15:31).

Consequently, the Gentiles are viewed by the author of *Jubilees* as corrupting influences who pollute the worship of Israel with idolatrous practices and bear some responsibility for Israel's sin (*Jub.* 1:9; 22:16). When Israel is led into erroneous behaviour, God ultimately judges them by delivering "them into the hand of the Gentiles for captivity, and for a prey, and for devouring, and [removing] them from the midst of the land, and [scattering] them amongst the Gentiles" (*Jub.* 1:13). The Gentiles become God's instrument of judgment. The nature of the judgment takes the form of exile just as it had done in 586 B.C. at the hand of the Babylonians.⁶³ The foreign oppression/rule over Israel, including being "uprooted from the land" (*Jub.* 15:34), is the physical manifestation of the spiritual bondage/exile in which the people of God find themselves.⁶⁴

Reclaiming Identity through the Redefinition of Time and Space

As part of a comprehensive program to make sense of the history of Israel, the author of *Jubilees* retells the paradigmatic story of the creation of the cosmos in tandem with the story of Israel's election. Whereas the events of history may have brought the faithfulness of God to his people into question, the author represents history as moving forward according to God's plan and subject to his sovereign control. The division of time and history into an orderly structure serves to reveal how God will act in the future based on his actions in the past.⁶⁵

Alongside the chronology, the topography of the book helps to motivate the readers to strengthen their identity as the chosen people of God. The geographical boundary of the land of Canaan further separates the people

---

⁶² Cf. Hubbard 2002:39.

⁶³ There is strong evidence to support the proposition that the Jews of this era viewed themselves as still living in a period of exile which began during the Babylonian period. In fact, many apocalyptic works may not have envisaged a historical return at all. The exile is often viewed as a perpetual condition which may only be fully resolved in the eschaton. See, e.g., *Pss. Sol.* 17. Cf. VanderKam 1997a:109.

⁶⁴ The connection between the Gentiles and Satan in *Jubilees* and the apocalyptic literature as a whole would repay further investigation.

⁶⁵ J. Scott sees in the book of *Jubilees* a tripartite division of history in which the end is a mirror image of the beginning where the decline noted during the era of the Patriarchs is gradually reversed during the area of restoration until the time of the new creation. Apparently, there is no concept of an end to history, but rather a return to the paradisiacal conditions of Eden. For a fuller discussion, see Scott 2005:150-2, 155-6.

B. The Function of New Creation in the Book of Jubilees

from the surrounding nations. The spatial and temporal elements of *Jubilees* serve as integral parts of the readers' collective identity.[66]

The author of *Jubilees* is attempting to make an important point by his retelling of history and using the concept of the Jubilee Year in which servants are freed and land returned to its rightful owners (cf. Lev 25). Just as God delivered the Israelites from Egypt, he will deliver his people from oppressive circumstances. Divinely orchestrated history involves a cycle of Jubilee Years where the nation's identity as God's liberated people is re-established. As his chosen people, they have a right to the redemptive restoration of the Year of Jubilee. The pattern of history set out in *Jubilees* ensures that God's acts of redemption will continue in the future for his people. The concept of new creation in this work is the encapsulation of this idea.

It is significant that the discussion of the Jubilee Year in Lev 25 continually refers to the God who delivered people from Egypt. No one was to be a slave because YHWH had delivered his people from slavery. Both the national identity of having been granted land by God and the individual identity of having been set free from bondage are reinforced. The point is made clear by J. Milgrom's discussion of the passage where he acknowledges the connection between national and individual redemption. YHWH redeems Israel as a nation from foreign hegemony to restore them to the Promised Land. He also redeems them on a more individual level from slavery.[67] This supports the assertion that *Jubilees* envisages both a cosmological and anthropological change regarding the new creation.

Correlative to a redefinition of time, the author of *Jubilees* also redefines holy space in order to deal with Israel's crisis of identity. This is most clearly evinced in the support offered for Israel's right to the land promised them by God. This interest in the land is closely related to the chronological framework of the book. The series of Jubilee Years consisting of a jubilee of jubilees culminates in the Exodus from Egypt and the entrance into Canaan.[68] Time from the creation is measured in terms of weeks of years and overlaid with the paradigm of the jubilee to reinforce the idea that the important identity-supporting act of deliverance in the Exodus from Egypt not only serves as the model for history but also the means by which God acts to provide his chosen people with the Promised Land. Scott astutely argues that this land, with its central sanctuary, is the epicentre of God's plan to realign the earthly pattern with the heavenly

---

[66] Frey 1997:288.
[67] Milgrom 2001:2233-2271. Cf. Scott 2005:14.
[68] Scott 2005:12.

original.⁶⁹ A closer look at significant new creation texts in *Jubilees* will help to clarify how this concept functions in the book.

New Creation in Jubilees

The clearest expression of the new creation motif in *Jubilees* occurs in chapter one. Given the importance of this chapter in introducing themes which recur throughout the material, the significance of the use of the term here should not be underestimated. Similarly to the prophecies of Isaiah, where the new creation is articulated as an expression of the theme of second exodus, the term appears in *Jubilees* in the context of the deuteronomic *Sin → Exile → Restoration* pattern (Hereafter, SER; cf. 1:11, 13, 15).⁷⁰ This pattern is employed within the chronological structure of the book to indicate that the pattern by which God had acted in delivering his people in the past remained a valid indicator of how he would deal with them during the present crisis.

The commonly recognized pattern is at work here to depict redemption by way of a second exodus from the exilic conditions in which the people of God found themselves. This is supported by the fact that the entire book is placed in the context of "the first year of the Exodus" (1:1). The Exodus from Egypt and the conquest of Canaan are intended to be exemplars of God's deliverance and designed to set Israel apart from the nations.⁷¹ Just as the deliverance of the Exodus had an identity forming function in OT literature from Moses' time forward, the author of *Jubilees* uses this salvific act as a mark of the identity of the people of God: "But they are your people and your inheritance, whom you saved by your great might from the hand of the Egyptians" (1:21).

The victory over Egypt was both a spiritual and political victory. The Gentiles are led by evil spirits (15:31). Victory over the spirits implies victory over the political forces which are under their control just as victory over the army of pharaoh was considered victory over the gods of Egypt. After the restoration promised by God, "every angel and spirit will know and acknowledge that they are [his] sons and [he] is their father in uprightness and righteousness" (1:25). God's dealing with Israel was a testimony to the powers over the nations and to the nations, themselves (*Jub.* 1:28; cf. Isa 45:1-3; Ezek 36:23; 37:28). This is important because the nations and the spirits which control them bear responsibility for Israel's violation of YHWH's covenant with them (1:19-20). In establishing the Exodus as the paradigmatic act of God's deliverance, the author intends to hold out hope to those who would have strained under a foreign oppression which

---

⁶⁹ Scott 2005:208.
⁷⁰ See Sanders 1983; Scott 2005:77ff.
⁷¹ VanderKam 2001:96.

the Jews of his day would have understood in terms of the Egyptian oppression in Moses' time or the Babylonian oppression of the 6th century B.C. The hope that God would free them from this type of bondage and once again lead them into possession of the land would have resonated strongly with the population of Judah at the time.

It is in this context that *Jubilees* employs the concept of new creation to articulate an eschatological renewal of the cosmos. The author gives three explanatory clauses concerning the nature of the new creation in 1:29:

> The angel of the presence, who was going along in front of the Israelite camp, took the tablets (which told) of the divisions of the years from the time the law and the testimony were created – for the weeks of their jubilees, year by year in their full number, and their jubilees from [the time of the creation until] the time of the new creation when the heavens, the earth, and all their creatures will be renewed like the powers of the sky and like all the creatures of the earth, until the time when the temple of the Lord will be created in Jerusalem on Mt. Zion. All the luminaries will be renewed for (the purposes of) healing, health, and blessing for all the elect ones of Israel and so that it may remain this way from that time throughout all the days of the earth.[72]

First, it is to be a time "when the heavens, the earth, and all their creatures will be renewed like the powers of the sky and like all the creatures of the earth." This language is reminiscent of Isaiah 65:17 and 66:22 and occurs in a similar second exodus context. The language of cosmic renewal is used by the author to indicate how God will resolve what has gone wrong in the universe. In the context of this chapter and of the book as a whole, this renewal refers to a time when the people of God would be restored to the purity of their land, their worship and their own spirit. The spiritual powers which stand behind the Gentiles and oppress the people of God are ultimately dealt with. At that time, "They will no longer have any satan or any evil person. The land will be pure from that time until eternity" (50:5).

The connection between the cosmic renewal and the restoration of the people of God is made clear in chapter 19. Though the actual term "new creation" is not used there, the language of renewal of the heavenly luminaries is employed.[73] In this passage, it is the seed of Abraham through Jacob which will "serve (the purpose of) laying heaven's foundations, making the earth firm, and renewing all the luminaries which are above the firmament" (19:25). This pure and holy seed is to be the agency through which the cosmic order is set right. Distorting their role as the chosen people of God causes cosmic imbalance described in 1 Macc 1:28 in cosmological terms where, as a result of the defilement of the evil Antiochus, "even the land trembled for its inhabitants." Abraham goes on to pray that the spirit of Mastema would not rule over them. This freedom from the in-

---

[72] This translation is from VanderKam 1989:6-7.

[73] For a discussion of the importance of the luminaries in other ancient texts for determining proper times and seasons, see Iwry 1970:41-7.

fluence of the evil spiritual powers is to be a condition of the ultimate restoration expected during the eschaton. Its arrival is anticipated throughout the book in the absence of sin, Satan and Gentiles (40:9; 46:2; 50:5; cf. 22:22).

Secondly, the new creation is presented in parallel to the time when "the temple of the Lord will be created in Jerusalem on Mt. Zion." Mount Zion is cited in chapter 4 as one of the four sacred places upon the earth which were to be sanctified during the new creation (4:26). It is quite significant that "new creation" is used in context with Mount Zion. Our author is interested in purity of people and purity of worship. It is well known that Antiochus deliberately sought to defile the Jewish ceremonial worship when he "arrogantly entered the sanctuary" (1 Macc 1:21; *Ant.* 13:243). The time of renewal envisaged in the new creation would restore purity to the land.

Interestingly, just after mentioning Mount Zion's sanctification in the new creation *"for the sanctification of the earth,"* the author informs us that "for this reason the earth will be sanctified from all its sins and from its uncleanness into the history of eternity." As the Gentiles were a source of the pollution of Israel, it is no stretch of logic to deduce that the author envisages a Gentile-free future (cf. 22:22).[74] This stands in contrast to the Isaianic proclamation: "In days to come the mountain of the LORD's house shall be established as the highest of the mountains, and shall be raised above the hills; all the nations shall stream to it" (Isa 2:2). The universalistic tendencies in Isaiah are narrowed in *Jubilees*. This is consistent with the idea that the author was attempting to preserve Jewish identity during the oppressive domination of pagan powers.

Finally, the new creation in 1:29 is a time when "all the luminaries will be renewed for (the purposes of) healing, health, and blessing for all the elect ones of Israel." The heavenly lights are important for the author of *Jubilees* because they provide the heavenly pattern which earthly worship is meant to imitate.[75] Two things are significant in this regard. First, the renewal of the heavenly lights refers to the renewal of the cosmic order initiated in creation by which all proper worship should be determined.[76] Restoration of calendrical purity would bring the earthly community further in line with what was going on in heaven.[77] To renew the cosmic order would be to set right the contaminated worship patterns of Israel. Secondly, and perhaps more intriguingly, this renewal brings healing, peace

---

[74] Cf. Hubbard 2002:42-3.

[75] The emphasis on the 364 day solar calendar is also important at Qumran.

[76] A similar world view is attested in Jewish wisdom literature where "human destiny, history and eschatology are all bound up with the structure of the universe." Collins 1977:128.

[77] J. Scott argues this point convincingly in Scott 2005.

and blessing for all the elect of Israel. Even here, in profoundly cosmological language, the author's message is not separated from what God does in the lives of his people. The cosmic/anthropological blessing given to God's people is intended to endure "from that time throughout all the days of the earth."

Although it is clear that *Jubilees* deals with an external problem – Satan and the Gentiles – the solution offered to the plight of the people is not given entirely in external terms, neither is the problem entirely external. Without underplaying the significance of the external problem, we should not pass over the fact that the kind of restoration envisaged by the author is not merely a nationalistic dream for military dominance. It involves circumcision of the heart of Israel so that that they will not continue to turn away from God (1:23). They will be given a new, holy spirit and will be children of God (1:21-25).[78] This anthropological transformation is spoken of in terms of a new creative act in 5:12a, "He made a new and righteous nature for all his creatures so that they would not sin with their whole nature until eternity."

Restoration of the covenant position of Israel is intended to suggest the ultimate eschatological restoration when God would "descend and live with them throughout all the ages of eternity" (1:26). The heavenly tablets being revealed in the book of *Jubilees* confirm this paradigmatic plan of restoration by disclosing their message in the form of "the divisions of the years from the time the law and the testimony were created – for the weeks of their jubilees, year by year in their full number, and their jubilees from [the time of the creation until] the time of the new creation..." (1:29a). This will secure their identity against the challenge of hostile political and spiritual powers which threaten their rightful place as the sons of God.

One final text from *Jubilees* will illustrate the function of the concept of new creation in this book. Chapter 23 does not use the term "new creation" but it offers parallel themes and explanatory comments which are very helpful in unlocking the author's meaning.[79] This chapter is recognized, together with chapter 1, as the most eschatologically charged passage of the book. It offers a prediction of the progressive decline of humanity in connection with the familiar SER pattern already seen in chapter 1. The lengthy lifespan of the earlier patriarchs related in *Genesis* is shortened because of the evil which has corrupted the land. In contrast to the near 1000 year lives of Adam and other early patriarchs, anyone who lives to be 75 years old will be said to have "lived for a long time" (23:12). The land, itself, is contaminated and underproductive because of this evil: "The

---

[78] This prayer from Moses on behalf of Israel echoes the penitential prayer from Ps 51:10: "Create in me a pure heart, O God, and renew a steadfast spirit within me."

[79] Hubbard draws out these parallels. Hubbard 2002:43-8.

earth will indeed be destroyed because of all that they do. There will be no produce from the vine and no oil because what they do (constitutes) complete disobedience..." (23:18). The worship of Israel is also polluted to the point that even the holy of holies is contaminated (23:19-21).[80] God's response is to send a great plague in the form of Gentile oppression (23:22-23).[81]

The result is that people would seek to "return to the right way" (23:26). This brings a reversal to the shortened lifespan (23:27-29) and likely stands in parallel to the new creation of chapter 1. J. Scott argues that this reversal of the shortening of human longevity is a clue to the concern of the author to represent the idea that history has three phases in which the final phase is a mirror image of the first. In this way, the gradual improvement of conditions on the earth is an incremental "repristinization culminating in the new creation itself and the establishment of God's eschatological Temple on Zion."[82] In language reminiscent of Isaiah 65:20, *Jub.* 23:28 predicts, "There will be no old man, nor anyone who has lived out his lifetime, because all of them will be infants and children." Whereas, according to *Jubilees*, septuagenarians would have lived long lives, the Isaianic prophecies indicate that in the new creation those who die at 100 "will be considered a youth." The prophecy continues in Isaiah with promises that the curse of the exile will be overcome. Houses and vineyards will no longer be stolen and occupied by foreigners but the promised peace would be so inclusive that the wolf and lamb would feed together (65:21-25). *Jubilees* carries on in the same line to speak of a time when there was to be no more Satan and when the Gentiles would be driven out from the land. But far from the universalistic tendency of Isaiah,

---

[80] This may echo Antiochus's defilement of the temple by offering a swine on the altar.

[81] The use of the term "plague" is interesting here in the light of the plagues against the Egyptians in the original Exodus. These plagues were intended to display YHWH's control over nature and his victory over the gods of Egypt. The use of this imagery in *Jubilees* 23 resonates with the idea that God's new act of deliverance for his people will occur in the form of a new exodus where the people are set free from the bondage of foreign oppression and sin and are given the Promised Land free from Gentile pollution (23:30).

[82] Scott helpfully points out that, "*Jubilees* helps us to see that what scholars have often held as mutually exclusive alternatives in early Christian chiliasm – fixed period vs. incremental process, present creation vs. eternal state, heavenly intermediate state vs. interim earthly kingdom – all of these supposed strict alternatives can actually be held in creative tension with one another." Scott 2005:156, 233. Rather than the commonly anticipated cataclysmic apocalypse of God's kingdom, the "messianic kingdom" in *Jubilees* "will come...by gradual process in a renewed heaven and earth in which god's people will grow in spiritual awareness as they give themselves to a study of the Law of God." See Russell 1992:50.

Jubilees envisages a peaceful rest for God's people where the nations are judged by God and become recipients of the hardships which they once endured (23:30-31).

Hubbard is correct in this regard to speak of the hope for new creation in *Jubilees* as the articulation of nationalistic aspirations.[83] However, despite the fact that the plight addressed by *Jubilees* is largely understood as an external plight (either caused by Gentiles or Satan), *Jubilees* does not appear to isolate the political dilemma of Israel from the spiritual dilemma. The solution which the new creation offers clearly restores the cosmic order, which intrinsically determines the identity of Israel. This inherently deals with the overwhelming sense of oppression brought about by the corrupting presence of foreign pagan powers. However, the blessings of the new creation are not articulated in isolation from what God does for the community and for the individual.

The concept of the new creation is used in *Jubilees* to reset what has gone wrong with the world. It functions as a kind of theological shorthand for God's eschatological program of restoring his people from the estranged condition brought about by sin and exacerbated by Satan and the Gentiles.[84] It would be a mistake to limit the author to a single category, whether anthropological, communal or cosmological, in attempting to explain what he had in mind with the use of this concept. While we do not find the same emphasis on the cosmological that we find in the Enochic literature, the cosmological emphasis is very much present. There is also emphasis on individual and corporate renewal of Israel. These are inseparably bound together in the book of *Jubilees* and this supports the argument of this thesis that these emphases should not be separated in Paul's thinking.

Jubilees was used in various Jewish social settings in the 1st c. B.C. to the 1st c. A.D. It is notoriously difficult if not impossible to determine what these social settings were but one historical association is promising.[85] *Jubilees* was a very important work for the Qumran communities.[86] The number of *Jubilees* texts among the DSS is second only to a handful of biblical texts.[87] An examination of how new creation was understood in the Qumran communities will supplement our examination of new creation in

---

[83] Hubbard 2002:48.
[84] Cf. Mell 1989:173.
[85] Cf. Knibb 1989:16-17; Hempel 2000:195.
[86] This is not to say that *Jubilees* was a sectarian writing. Much of the Qumran library was comprised of non-sectarian texts. For a comparison of the theologies of *Jubilees* and Qumran, see Noack [Hahne 68].
[87] Hempel 2000:187-96. There are 14-15 copies of *Jubilees* extant among the DSS. Only Psalms (36), Deuteronomy (29), Isaiah (21), Exodus (17) and possibly Genesis (15) are better attested. See VanderKam 2000b:437.

Jubilees and offer helpful comparative material for our inquiry into Paul's conception of new creation.

C. New Creation in the Dead Sea Scrolls

The DSS communities stand out from their contemporaries in the intensity with which they pursued common hopes of the time.[88] While the actual identity[89] of the people who lived within the DSS communities is far from being settled, the documents reveal ideals which bear some resemblance to those of the early Christian communities.[90]

Paramount for our purposes is the community's eschatological worldview which comes to particular expression in the abundant use of the phrase "the end of days."[91] A. Steudel's detailed study of this expression indicates that this final era, believed to precede the ultimate salvation, could entail aspects of the past, present and future.[92] This accords well with further evidence from the DSS which suggests a kind of inaugurated eschatology in which the final time of testing as well as final salvation had already begun to some degree (cf. 4Q394-399; 1QH 11:19-22, 19:10-14).[93] Future expectations are also preserved in texts such as 4Q246 and 1QH XI where the pain of a coming period of distress is described "like a woman giving birth the first time" (1QH XI 1-18). The resolution was expected in the ultimate defeat of God's enemies and the rule of someone called "son of God" (4Q246 I-II).[94] The distress would be the indicator that the time of

---

[88] E.P. Sanders points out four components of a future hope which were common strands throughout Judaism: 1) the tribes of Israel would be re-assembled; 2) the Gentiles would be converted, destroyed or subjugated; 3) Jerusalem would be made glorious with a rebuilt purified temple; 4) the people would be pure and righteous and would offer proper worship. These hopes were anticipated differently within the different traditions of Judaism but the general hope for restoration characterised by these four components achieved near ubiquitous status within the Judaism of the Second Temple period. Sanders 1992:291-4.

[89] Wright posits that the DSS seem to contain conflicting information which contributes to the common assertion that they are the product of more than one community. Cf. Wright 1992:203ff. For further discussion on the identity of the Qumran communities, see VanderKam 1999:487-533.

[90] Martínez 1996:lii-iv. Cf. Fitzmyer 1999:599-621.

[91] Collins 2000:256-61. Cf. Schiffman 1989; VanderKam 2000a:113-34.

[92] Steudel 1993:225-46.

[93] Collins 2000:257-8. The belief that angels lived among the community may also be evidence of a form of inaugurated eschatology. See Collins 1998:174. Cf. Kuhn 1966.

[94] Fitzmyer 2000:46-54. These texts indicate the expectation of the coming "Messianic Woes." For further study of the role of messianism and eschatology in the DSS, see Knibb 1999:379-402.

C. New Creation in the Dead Sea Scrolls

God's judgement was imminent when Gentiles as well as apostate Israel would either be destroyed or brought within the covenant community of which Qumran was the chief representative.

The DSS do not represent a coherent, systematized eschatology but the expectation of eschatological warfare is well-attested (cf. 1QM).[95] The communities considered themselves the "advance guard" of God's plans to wage a final, catastrophic war against unrighteousness. As true Israel, they were to be God's means for reordering the world.[96] Through their community, the embodiment of faithful Israel, God was preparing for a renewal of the depraved world order that would restore the remainder of Israel and possibly even Gentiles to fellowship with him (1QS VIII 1-11; 1QH XIV 25-9). Renewal was viewed as a future expectation of something God would bring about *through* the community and *within* the temporal world. The contrast between the present world and the hope of God's future intervention to change things was an expression of the widespread hope within Judaism for a "new age" which would come about at the end of time.[97]

The exact nature of the end times is unclear.[98] While it is clear that the eschatological war between Sons of Light and Sons of Darkness would bring "a time of salvation for the nation of God and a period of rule for all the men of his lot, and of everlasting destruction for all the lot of Belial,"[99] the salvation is not clearly described in the DSS.[100] However, there is evidence that the earth as well as humanity would be renewed as part of this soteriological program.[101]

The renewal of the earth, which was to occur in the "new age," involves restoration of what had gone wrong in God's creation. The eschatological hymn of 4Q88 IX 10 speaks of heavens which would give dew and an earth which would yield its fruit "in its season." Strikingly, the idea of the heavens giving their dew is connected with the idea that there will be no

---

[95] Harrington 2006:175-83. Cf. Duhaime 2004.

[96] Wright 1992:203-9.

[97] Sanders 1992:298-303. For a discussion of how this last period of time involved past, present and future, see Steudel 1993:225-46.

[98] Schiffman argues that the eschatology of Qumran merged ideas of "restorative" and "utopian" messianism in which restoration could be conceived of either as that "naturalistic process of historical events that will lead to the restoration of what was" or a new age "that will come about through cataclysmic, usually violent events." Schiffman 2001:203-21.

[99] 1QM I 5.

[100] For an extensive argument that final salvation would involve bodily resurrection, see Puech 1993. This is disputed, for example, by Nickelsburg 1972. H. Lichtenberger suggests that the Qumran community believed that the dead would have a part in salvation even if they did not articulate this in terms of bodily resurrection in Lichtenberger 2001:79-91.

[101] Cf. Sjöberg 1955:131-6.

corrupt dealings in its territories. The earth which yields its fruit "in its season" is said to have produce which will not fail and springs which will not deceive. The correlation between physical plenty and moral purity is intended to be an explanation of what the world will be like after YHWH, "comes to judge every cre[at]ure, to obliterate evil-doers from the earth." A stable and productive physical world is associated with moral and social stability free from destruction and deceit. Thus, the new order for which the Qumran community hoped could be spoken of in terms of the renewal of the physical world.[102]

Without offering details about the fate of the physical universe, new creation in the DSS primarily involves the eradication of evil which had brought the faithfulness and integrity of God's promises under question. Those who felt this oppression in whatever form it manifested and who feared YHWH could eat the fruit produced by the restored earth and be satisfied – they could take part in the new order with contentment (v. 11; cf. Isa 11:6-8; Ezek 34:25-7). Again, the focus is on a future goal affected through the community itself – a new age on earth.

Although the term "new creation" does not occur often in the extant documents of Qumran, the community conceptualized renewal of the world in new creation language.[103] Speaking of God's judgment being enacted through the community, the writer of 1QH V writes:

These are those [you] fou[nded before the centuries,] to judge through them...[according to] all your design for all the eternal ages and the eternal task. For you have established them before the centuries, and you have [...] the work of [...] in them, so that they can recount your glory throughout all your dominion; for you have shown them what they had never s[een,...] what was there from of old and creating new things, demolishing ancient things and [erec]ting what would exist for ever.[104]

This passage seems to suggest that God's plan has not been thwarted by whatever contemporary troubles faced the readers. His plan was established "before the centuries." He had already chosen those through whom he would display his glory. What he was doing was both old and new in the sense that it had been in his plan long before it came to pass and that it had not been witnessed before that time (cf. 11Q5 XXVI 9-15). This may provide evidence that God was acting in continuity with his plan from the beginning and that that plan did not include a final stage which simply returned to the original state.[105]

---

[102] Cf. Ringgren 1995:164-6.

[103] Cf. Derrett 1988:597-608. Derrett concludes that the Isaianic new creation which encompassed heaven and earth was a "collective experience of which individuals might be granted, at most, some foretaste" (p. 607). Cf. Mansoor 1961:178.

[104] Excerpts from 1QH V 13-18.

[105] Texts such as 11Q19 XXIX 7-10 indicate that what God is doing in the present is of the same material with what he will do in the future. The community saw great lines of

C. New Creation in the Dead Sea Scrolls

The idea that God was showing things formerly unseen and creating new things also occurs in Isa 48:6-7 (cf. 42:9; 43:19).[106] The passage in Isaiah ends with YHWH's declaration, "My glory I will not give to another" (48:11). 1QH V, similarly, indicates that God's purpose for establishing the community and working in them was so that they would recount his glory throughout his dominion. For both Isaiah and Qumran, his dominion operated through restored Israel governing and illuminating the nations with knowledge of YHWH (cf. Isa 14:2; 42:6; 49:6; 60:3). Thus, the renewal of the world began in and came about through the community.[107]

More explicitly, 1QS IV 23-25 indicates that God has sorted the spirits of truth and injustice which feud within the human heart into equal parts until the "appointed end and the new creation." The context posits that at that time, injustice will be no more and that "all the glory of Adam" shall belong to "those God has chosen for an everlasting covenant" (cf. 1QH IV 15; 4Q88 IX 1-5; Jer 31:31; 2 Cor 3:6-18).[108] The Qumran texts (as well as the rabbis) indicate a belief that Adam lost God's glory at the fall and that it would be restored when the Messiah came at the time of the end.[109] The appointed end and the new creation are parallel ways of speaking of the time of "the visitation" (v. 26) when God would restore fellowship with his people. Israel's experience of exile was like the expulsion of Adam from the garden. They awaited the glorious restoration prophesied in the OT and thought of it as a time of renewed fellowship with their covenant God.[110] This restoration was viewed as an eschatological action of God, spoken of interchangeably as "the time of the end" and "the new creation," which had already begun in the embodiment of their own community.[111] Whatever

---

continuity between what God was increasingly doing among them and what he would consummately do in the time of the end.

[106] J. Hughes does not recognise this connection in her broader discussion of scriptural allusions in the Hodayot. But note her helpful chapter on methodology in Hughes 2006:35-62. Cf. Holm-Nielsen 1960:210-17. Holm-Nielson argues that the idea of new creation in this text should not be limited to the individual but is much more in line with the apocalyptic streams which speak of a new world. However, he makes the essential observation that, "at the same time, this thought is linked to the existence of the community...[which] belongs to and forms part of the new creation, and ... has, on the strength of the revelation, gained insight into what is taking place in reality" (p. 217).

[107] For an argument that the Hodayot understood the community as a new creation (1QH 16:4-27a), see Daise 2000:293-305.

[108] Cf. Derrett 1988:599-600.

[109] Cf. Noffke 2007:618-24.

[110] It is no surprise that the OT refers to this time as a time of a "new covenant" (cf. Jer 31:31). They had a new circumcision – the heart was circumcised – and even thought in terms of new birth (1QS V 5; 1QpHab XI 13). Cf. Derrett 1988:599-600.

[111] Stuhlmacher considered this a kind of inaugurated eschatology within Qumran and cited 1QH III 19-22; XI 10-14 in support. See Stuhlmacher 1967:1-35.

else they thought the new creation was, Qumran viewed the new creation as a reordering of the structures of the world hostile towards God. The new creation primarily referred to the new age which would be brought about through the community – the renewed world as pure as the original creation had been where evil was extirpated and God's rule ultimately established.

Yet as much as the re-ordering was primarily understood in terms of the new age within history affected through the community, two caveats are essential. First, as U. Mell points out, 1QH V 11ff, 1QS IV 25 and 11QT XXIX 9 could be understood as having significance for the physical universe. This is especially true since these texts convey the idea that the new creation would be an eternal one which would not allow for the corruption inherent to the old creation.[112] This possibility becomes clearer in apocalyptic Jewish writings. Mell, however, goes so far with the cosmological explanation of the new creation that he asserts that "die priesterlich orientierte Qumrangemeinde eine individuelle eschatologische Neuschöpfung nicht kennt."[113]

Thus, the second caveat is that individuals who took part in the community should be seen as experiencing the hope of renewal (cf. 1QH XIV). Mell correctly notes that individuals are not directly named "new creation" in the extant writings at Qumran. He also correctly recognizes that 1QH XIX 13-14 refers to daily renewal and that 1QH XI 21 refers to the entrance of a person into the community.[114] However, 1QH XIX 13-14 speaks of a renewal "with everything that will exist" and 1QH XI 19-21 points out the hope of one "fashioned from dust" (i.e. a part of humble, evanescent creation) and being purified to become part of an "eternal community."

Although the individual is not called a "new creation," it does seem that the concept of renewal linked the individual to the community and thereby to the renewal that would come about at the end of the old age. This is borne out in 1QS V 1-6 where those who would "freely volunteer to convert from all evil and to keep themselves steadfast in all he commanded in compliance with his will" were encouraged to "circumcise in the Community the foreskin of his tendency and of his stiff neck in order to lay a foundation of truth for Israel, for the Community of the eternal covenant." Here, the community is underlined as the true remnant of God's people. That the individual joins the community "in order to lay a foundation of truth for Israel" stresses the importance of the role of the individual.[115]

---

[112] Mell 1989:93-112.
[113] Mell 1989:110.
[114] Mell 1989:93-112.
[115] The later writings of the rabbis referred to individual converts as "new creations" (*Gen. Rab.* 39:4).

This text seems to hold together both the corporate conception of the community as the locus of God's activity and the importance of the individual's participation in it. There seems to be a progression from a focus on what God did in the community (with individual participation in that action) to God's intention for the world as a whole.[116] The Qumran documents suggest that this community anticipated the future action of God who had chosen their community to carry out his plans and they spoke of this future hope in new creation terms.

One final observation can be made about the nature of the renewal. The renewed world would be a place where all opposition to God's rule through his people would be eradicated. The DSS sectarian communities were living metaphors of exile. Not only did their wilderness existence underscore their separation from the religious establishment of Jerusalem, it became increasingly evident that the communities viewed Rome as their primary enemy.[117] This is clear in the generally accepted view that the Kittim were eventually identified with Rome (cf. 1QpHab VI 3-5; *J.W.* 6:316).[118] Although earlier references to the Kittim suggest that the foreign oppressors were God's means of judgment against "the last priests of Jerusalem" (1QpHab IX 4), the War Rule makes them the earthly manifestation of a satanic army which represents the ultimate foes of God's people (cf. 4Q285).[119] Spiritual and physical, cosmic and earthly realities are kept in close relation in the presentation of the final eschatological battle in the DSS.[120] Strikingly, the aftermath of the great eschatological battle is described in 4Q285 *Frag.* 1 where blessings are pronounced upon the natural order,[121]

... [Blessing, dew and] rain, ea[r]ly and lat[e] rains in their season, and to give [you fruit, the harvests of wheat,] [of wine and of o]il in plenty. And for [you] the land [will yie]ld delicious fruits. And you shall eat (them)] [and be replete. In yo]ur [land] there will be no miscarriage nor [will one be sick; drought and blight] will not be seen in [its] harves[ts; there will be n]o disease at all [or stumbling blocks in your congregation, and wild animals will vanish] from the land. There will be no pesti[lence in yo]ur [land.] For God is wi[th you and his holy angels are in the midst of your Community.]

---

[116] Ringgren sees the dualism of the two spirits (1QS IV 23-26) as an essential part of the creation until the time of God's new creation. He rightly understands these two spirits to represent not only a struggle within the human heart but also a "world-wide battle between two principles, which finally will end in a terrible war between the children of light and darkness." Ringgren 1995:72, 76.

[117] Lim 2000:469-71. Cf. Esler 2005:9-33; Hengel 2000:46-56.

[118] Cf. Vermes 2005:20-25.

[119] Vermes 1998:56.

[120] 1QM XIX 2-8; 1QM XVIII 1-3. Cited in Vermes 1998:85. Cf. 1QM I 1-17; XV 12-16; XVI 11-16.

[121] The text quotes from Isa 10:34 in *Frag.* 5 and may reflect influence of the Isaianic new creation of Isa 65-66.

D. CONCLUSIONS

Our study of the early Jewish literature has provided helpful comparative material for our study of Paul's "new creation." Three observations about this material are of particular importance for our purposes. First, it has been shown that the concept of the new creation invariably was a future expectation in the extant Jewish literature. Although some of the works could be represented as having a form of inaugurated eschatology, the eschatology they embody is not entirely consistent with Paul's conception of the inaugurated eschaton. It is true that some of the writings found at Qumran indicate a belief that God was already beginning the creation of the new age in their community. This helps to explain their intense asceticism. They wanted to restore the purity of the original creation through perfect observance of the Law. However, the centre of gravity of God's action to bring about the new creation was yet to be reached. What God was doing in them was only *preparatory action* awaiting future consummation.

The apocalyptic writers, too, had their eyes firmly fixed on the horizon of history in eager anticipation of the dawning of a new day. In this company, the OT prophets knew God to be active among them but seemed convinced that his greatest work was yet to come. Paul, on the other hand, had an eschatology that was altogether different. As will be shown in the remainder of this work, the centre of gravity for Paul's eschatology lay indisputably in the past event of Christ's life culminating in his death and resurrection.[122] Though Paul certainly maintained future expectation, the primary event in God's plan had already occurred. On the basis of this event, everything to follow was made possible.

The second observation is related to the first. Especially in the Qumran literature, but also in the apocalyptic writers and OT prophets, there is the idea that God had a chosen people through whom he was working to bring about his ultimate purposes for the world. Paul maintained the concept of a people of God but that conception was radically transformed. Rather than moving from God's action within the community to God's purposes for the world as a whole, as seems to be the case in the writings surveyed here, Paul moves from what God did on a universal scale – in Christ – which brings about his community which, in turn, continues his work in the cosmos.[123] In both the early Jewish literature as well as in Paul there is a strong connection between the cosmological, communal and anthropological emphases.

Finally, *Jubilees* provides evidence of some very interesting strands of thought within this period of Judaism which will be useful for comparing

---

[122] Cf. Beker 1980.
[123] Cf. Hafemann 1997:172-89.

with the apostle Paul. The emphasis in *Jubilees* on the identity of the people of God is particularly relevant to Paul's letter to the Galatians. The agitators of Galatia asserted that one's Christian identity cannot be separated from one's identity as a descendent of Abraham. Like the author of *Jubilees*, they were concerned to honour circumcision and obey proper calendrical observances (Gal 4:10) in order to establish their identity in connection with the Law. It may be that the opponents of Paul saw in his inclusion of the uncircumcised Gentiles in the "Israel of God" (Gal 6:16) the same type of compromise with Hellenistic society which so threatened the identity and covenant position of Israel during the time of the Maccabean Revolt. This makes perfect sense in the light of the parallel between the way that *Jubilees* sees the Gentiles and the way they are probably presented by the agitators in Galatians: "Gentile sinners" (*Jub.* 23:24; Gal 2:15).

Furthermore, the new creation motif in *Jubilees* deals with the identity struggle caused by the foreign oppression which is directed by the evil spirits. Similarly, Galatians may confront the evil social sphere (Gal 1:4) and its understanding of identity with Paul's conception of the new creation. For Paul, however, the struggle is not about Jew vs. non-Jew. Where he comes into agreement with *Jubilees* is that the new creation is God's way of righting what has gone wrong with the world. Though Paul did not write a specifically anti-imperial polemic, he would have recognized that the powers of imperial Rome advocated a social structure in which the identity of God's people was challenged.[124] Paul used the concept of the new creation to create his own social sphere in contradistinction to that of Rome and his interlocutors in Galatia and Corinth. Before we turn our attention to a closer analysis of Paul's letters, a broader understanding of the cultural environment into which he wrote will be facilitated by a look at how the ubiquitous ideology of the Roman Empire spoke of its transforming influence in eschatological and cosmological terms.

---

[124] Howard-Brook and Gwyther 1999:77-85.

Chapter 4

Roman Imperial Ideology and Paul's Concept of New Creation

As the previous chapters have argued, Jewish eschatology provides the raw materials from which Paul's concept of new creation is constructed. Yet the recipients of Paul's letters were not all Jews and they were influenced widely by sources other than Jewish traditions. One influence which has recently been gaining attention in New Testament studies is that of the Roman Empire.[1] Even though Paul may have taken up or modified the Jewish traditions to which he was indebted, he communicated his ideas in a society whose worldview was heavily influenced by imperial Rome.[2] This chapter explores the ways in which the ideology of the empire was communicated in strongly cosmological and eschatological (even soteriological) categories.[3]

The first Roman emperor, Augustus, set out on such an all-encompassing program of reform that it was communicated in terms of a transformation of the world.[4] The worldview portrayed by Augustus became the prototype upon which later emperors patterned their own thinking. The rulers contemporary with Paul's writing (i.e. Claudius, Nero) may have embodied character strikingly different from Augustus, but they did little to alter the essence of the vision Augustus had articulated. It is fair to say that Caligula and Nero, in particular, intensified the imperial rhetoric to the point of distorting its original sounding. Yet even they operated within the power structures secured by the ideology which Augustus set in

---

[1] Note, in particular, the recent issue of *JSNT* 27 (2005) devoted to the study of the Roman Empire as background for study of the NT. For an overview of the issue and bibliographic information on the theme, see Horrell 2005:251-5. Cf. Georgi 1991; Elliott 1994; Horsley 1997; Carter 2001; Oakes 2001a.

[2] Rather than suggesting a simple cause-effect relationship between the ideology of Rome and Paul's writing, I am arguing along similar lines as A.Y. Collins; she has shown that the cultural experiences, undoubtedly influenced by the imperial ideology, of the Pauline communities could well have influenced how his message was understood. Cf. Collins 1999:234-57.

[3] For a discussion of eschatological traditions in the first century, see Downing 1995:99-109.

[4] Cf. Brunt 1990:433-7.

motion.⁵ This is especially true for Claudius who was well-known for his interest in aligning himself with the Augustan prototype.

At the same time that Paul was employing his concept of new creation, which this thesis will argue is an expression of his eschatological soteriology, imperial Roman propaganda was broadcasting an ideology throughout the empire that articulated its own form of eschatology.⁶ As part of a program to create a new society, the empire developed a new system of visual communication through which its ideology could be communicated *en masse*.⁷ Philo provides us with the perspective of an Alexandrian Jew roughly contemporary with the apostle Paul upon the way this ideology had permeated the world:

> The whole habitable world voted him [i.e. Augustus] no less than celestial honours. These are so well attested by temples, gateways, vestibules, porticoes, that every city which contains magnificent works new and old is surpassed in these by the beauty and magnitude of those appropriated to Caesar and particularly in our own Alexandria.⁸

As a Jewish citizen of Rome who had travelled throughout the empire, Paul would have been keenly aware of the impact of Roman society and its ideology on the peoples it subjugated. This ideology serviced a vision of the world, time, space and history which could be spoken of as eschatological. At just the right moment of history, Augustus had come into the world, become its saviour and benefactor, inaugurated a new age of peace and prosperity and established a new world order.⁹ The similarities between this eschatological/soteriological vision and Paul's are striking and deserve closer examination. An examination of these parallels could inform how Paul's auditors understood his conception of the new creation. Three important aspects of the imperial ideology will be examined. First, it was communicated in cosmological terms. Secondly, it was predicated upon a turn of ages. Finally, it sought to articulate the establishment of a new world order.¹⁰

---

⁵ Nero blatantly claimed to "rule according to the principles of Augustus" (Suetonius, *Nero* 10.1). By Roman ideology, I mean "Roman discourse which sustains certain power relations." Oakes 2005:301-22 (302); cf. Thompson 1990.

⁶ This is not altogether dissimilar to how John used the imagery of the imperial cult to articulate his own vision of what God was doing in the world – even though John did this far more blatantly than Paul. See Friesen 2005:351-73.

⁷ Zanker 1988.

⁸ *On the Embassy to Gaius XXII.150*

⁹ Cf. Harrison 1999:79-91.

¹⁰ As these areas are intricately interrelated, some overlapping in the discussion is unavoidable.

A. Methodological Considerations

We can be certain that both Paul and his readers had abundant exposure to the imperial ideology. The evidence for its influence in every part of the empire is plentiful and strong. In the course of this chapter we shall see that it was certainly present in Rome and very much alive and well in the colony of Corinth and the province of Galatia (both north and south). Though this ideology was complex and could vary from location to location both in its propagation as well as its reception, there is sufficient evidence to conclude that the recipients of Paul's letters would have been inundated with the ideology of the empire.

The most immediate problem raised by this inquiry is, of course, the question of whether Paul had the Roman imperial ideology in mind at all as he employed the concept of new creation in his writings. It is a fair question to ask how many points of reference Paul could have intended in any given assertion. What place would a statement about imperial ideology have found in the middle of a defence of Paul's apostolic authority (2 Cor) or a polemic against agitators who contradicted his teaching (Gal)? Does Paul encrypt an anti-imperial message in his writings even if a subversive motivation is not immediately obvious?[11] If Paul's letter to the Galatians, for example, embodies an imperial critique, we might ask the question, "What has Caesar to do with circumcision?" More to the point, "What has Paul's understanding of new creation to do with Roman ideology?" There do appear to be significant parallels between the imperial ideology and Paul's understanding of new creation. But would an examination of these parallels be one more excrescence of the well-known problem of "parallelomania"?[12] The lack of any exact verbal parallels between Paul's καινὴ κτίσις and Roman ideology makes the case even more difficult.[13]

Before proceeding, we would do well to keep in mind a few caveats. First, we should be aware of the possibility of unconscious correlations. Similar language does not necessarily imply borrowing, influence or engagement at any level at all. It could be that there were standard ways of speaking about certain subjects that are used in both imperial ideology as well as in Paul's writing.[14] Secondly, conscious correspondences could be

---

[11] Indeed, in some cases, Paul's writing could even be construed as taking a positive stance toward the Roman authorities (e.g. Rom 13:1-7). But note that even this text which encourages civic obedience relativizes the absolute claims of Roman authority by acknowledging that those authorities are "instituted by God" (v. 1). Cf. Wright 2002b.

[12] Cf. Sandmel 1962.

[13] The case is far easier to make in Paul's letters which contain more direct verbal parallels with the imperial ideology (e.g. 1 Thessalonians and Philippians). Cf. Harrison 2002:71-96; Oakes 2001a.

[14] For an example of this approach, see Zeller 1988:141-76.

incidental engagements which have little or no bearing on the point Paul is actually making. Here, Paul could simply employ common expressions to communicate his message. Thirdly, we should beware of over-interpreting the historical background to the point that it actually obfuscates the text itself. The importance of external parallels should be tempered with evidence that both Paul and his readers at least could have been exposed to the purported references. Fourthly, each correspondence should be examined on its own merits. Accepting the presence of external parallels does not require affirming every possible connection. Fifthly, we must keep in mind that Paul is not addressing the Roman authorities; he is addressing the Jesus-believing communities of Galatia, Corinth and Rome. Although we have evidence of the kinds of things the authorities were saying, the Romans are, at best, third party to Paul's correspondence with local Jesus-believing communities.

Unless specific evidence can be garnered which connects Paul's writing to imperial ideology, we should avoid seeing Paul's letters as an anti-imperial polemic. Even where the evidence suggests strong connections, these claims must be tempered with the evidence offered in the letters themselves as to why and to whom they were written.[15] What I am suggesting is not that Paul engaged in an attempt to bring about the collapse of the imperial power structure. We would expect to find significantly stronger and more direct confrontation with the authorities if that were the case.[16] This is not, however, to say that he was not concerned with the "cultural situation" heavily influenced by Rome. The gospel he preached called for a radically different understanding of world transformation from that envisaged in the imperial ideology.[17] The important point for our purposes is that the evidence which we shall set out below gives an indication of how Paul's understanding of new creation could have been heard in the communities to which he wrote. With these caveats in mind, it is possible to address what could be legitimate confrontations with pagan culture within Paul's writing in a way that could significantly nuance our understanding of Paul.

B. The Imperial Transformation of the World

The first aspect of the imperial ideology which may offer insight into Paul's conception of new creation is the idea that it was presented in cos-

---

[15] This issue will be taken up more thoroughly in the second half of this thesis.
[16] In line with Jewish traditions before him, Paul could well have understood pagan nations to be instruments of God's purposes.
[17] Cf. Crossan and Reed 2004.

mological terms. In the ancient world, there was an inextricable link between the cosmos and the state.[18] What happened in one was reflected in the other.[19] This partially explains why signs such as comets and earthquakes were so important for the ancients.[20] The connection between the physical and political order meant that what happened in the cosmos was directly related to the state (and vice versa). During the time of Augustus, the earth itself was thought to respond to the peace Rome offered the world. The victory of Augustus over factions and civil unrest brought order from chaos. The earth itself was said to have responded favourably.[21] In Virgil's *4th Eclogue*, commonly described as "messianic," the poet describes the hopes and expectations of the Augustan age.[22] In similar fashion to Isaiah's depiction of the new heavens and new earth, his work shows how the peace offered by the empire affected not only the state but the natural world as well.[23] In deference to a ruler who would usher Rome into an age of paradise, Virgil writes,

But for thee, child, shall the earth untilled pour forth...her first pretty gifts.... Uncalled, the goats shall bring home their udders swollen with milk, and the herds shall fear not huge lions; unasked, thy cradle shall pour forth flowers for thy delight. The serpent, too, shall perish, and the false poison-plant shall perish.... The earth shall not feel the harrow, nor the vine the pruning-hook; the sturdy ploughman, too, shall now loose his oxen from the yoke.... Behold the world bowing with its massive dome – earth and expanse of sea and heaven's depth! Behold, how all things exult in the age that is at hand![24]

In the *Aeneid,* the connection between the state and the cosmos is portrayed in a different way. There, Rome expands to fill the entire world. Whereas Lucretius had described the world as a city, Virgil presented the city of Rome as the world itself.[25] In *Aeneid I.278-9* Jupiter declares, "For these I set neither bounds nor periods of empire; dominion without end

---

[18] This was especially true in the East as far back as Hesiod. For a fuller discussion of cosmos/state parallels, see Kahn 1960.

[19] Plato's *Republic* had expounded a conjunction between the physical and political order of the universe. The idea was picked up, for example, by Cicero and Virgil. Cf. Hardie 1986:71-6.

[20] See Ramsey and Licht 1997.

[21] Jones 1977:47. Cf. Paterculus II,89.

[22] For a discussion of how the emperor could be seen as a "messianic" figure, see Wistrand 1987. Wistrand sees a connection between the ideas of *imperium, auspicium, felicitas* and *triumphus*. He argues that the religious idea of *felicitas* became attached to the emperor and that it was strongly promulgated in the imperial cult.

[23] See the helpful comparison between Virgil's view of creation in *Georgics* and that of John in the book of Revelation in McDonough 2000:227-44.

[24] Virgil, *Eclogue* IV.18-25, 40-41, 50-52. Translation by H. R. Fairclough in LCL (1934 ed.).

[25] Hardie 1986:190. See Hardie's discussion of how Virgil's thought was related to Lucretius.

have I bestowed." For Virgil, the expansion of the empire mirrored the universal order of the cosmos. His *Aeneid* served as a creation story of the empire in which "the themes of cosmology and Roman power are inextricably intertwined."[26] Although Virgil does not use the expression "new creation," it is clear that he understood the establishment of Rome in universal terms on par with the establishment of the cosmos itself.[27] In Greek literature, κτίσις is used as a virtual "technical term for the activity of city-establishing" and offers a particularly illuminating connection with Paul's "new creation."[28] Two examples will suffice to support this claim.

First, in Plutarch's account of the life of Romulus, Rome's first king, the term κτίσις is used explicitly in reference to the founding of Rome, "Now it is agreed that the city was founded (ἡ κτίσις . . . γένοιτο) on the twenty-first of April, and this day the Romans celebrate with a festival, calling it the birthday of their country."[29] The foundation of the city was to have been attended with cosmic events and the time of its foundation could be discerned from its history since "a city's fortune, as well as that of a man, has a decisive time (κύριον . . . χρόνον), which may be known by the position of the stars at its very origin."[30] Though Plutarch notes suspicions of the "fictitious and fabulous" quality of such accounts, he explains that "the Roman state would not have attained to its present power, had it not been of a divine origin, and one which was attended by great marvels."[31]

Secondly, Josephus's *Antiquities of the Jews 18:373* actually uses the phrase καινὴ κτίσις (in the plural) in a way perfectly congruent with the typical pagan usage of κτίσις in reference to the founding of a city.[32] Josephus relates how the Jews left Babylon and formed new settlements (καιναὶ κτίσεις).

---

[26] Hardie 1986:200.

[27] For a fuller discussion of the political context of Virgil's writing, see the collection of essays in Stahl 1998.

[28] Adams 2000:77. Grimal points out that the establishment of cities in the empire reproduced the image of the mother city in the East and West. Cities were strongholds of "a cultural, religious, social, and political system which formed the very structure of Roman civilization." See Grimal 1983:4-6.

[29] Plutarch, *Romulus* 12.1. The verb κτίζω is used in 12.2, "...Romulus founded (ἐκτιζεν) the city..." (cf. 13:1).

[30] *Romulus* 12.6; cf. 12.2-6. The principle was thought to apply in either direction, i.e. to foretell the end from the nature of the beginning or to divine the beginning from the subsequent events.

[31] Plutarch, *Romulus* 8.7; cf. 12.6.

[32] This is the only occurrence of this usage of the term κτίσις with the adjective καινή in the extant literature. The term καινὴ κτίσις (*nova creatura/creatio*) does not occur at all in the first centuries B.C. to the first centuries A.D. outside Jewish or Christian sources.

Heard in this light, Paul's expression καινὴ κτίσις could take on important associations not typically recognized in Pauline studies. If the Roman colonies in Corinth and Galatia served as outposts on the imperial frontier, the use of καινὴ κτίσις could very well have suggested the establishment of a new social order very different from that propagated by the imperial ideology. This point will become clearer in the next chapter when we turn our attention more fully to the letters of Paul.

Rome's colonies advanced its ideology in the provinces and throughout the known world. This ideology expressed a form of soteriology which was cosmological in nature, and this is portrayed in vivid detail in the imperially sanctioned architecture.

Perhaps the most poignant example of this may be found in the artwork of the *Ara Pacis* (Altar of Augustan Peace) in Rome where civil relations are interwoven with the natural order. The goddess Pax[33] is shown surrounded by symbols of fertility and plenty: children, cattle, and bountiful crops. In interesting juxtaposition, the goddess Roma sits "enthroned on a mound of armour."[34] The images, taken together, underline the concept of Roman peace procured through conquest. The adjacent walls depict Augustus with his family as well as representatives from the senate, the military and the cults. At the centre of it all is the figure of Augustus, himself, the author of this new era of peace. Through this finely crafted image, Augustus was changing the idea of what it meant to be a citizen of the empire. Based on ancient traditions, he developed a new order of participation in society which he controlled and which centred upon his person as much as it did the city of Rome.[35]

At the bottom of the altar and surrounding its exquisite reliefs, the altar is covered with vines, acanthus, flowers and swans. There were even new species of plant life to signify the advent of paradise in which the world had been remade.[36] The symmetry of the nature scenes in precise mirror image reflects the Roman proclivity for order and the rule of law.[37] The use of such imagery is universally found in Roman art and reflects the abundance of the new age of stability in the harmony of nature.[38] The ensuing peace would afford such bounty as to provide happiness for everyone. That this imagery had begun to affect changes at all levels of society

---

[33] Other options include Tellus or a personification of Rome.

[34] Zanker 1988:175.

[35] The emperor stood as representative and source of all things and one's complete sphere of existence could be spoken of as "in him." Suetonius, *Augustus* 98.2; Seneca, *To Polybius, On Consolation* 7.4; cf. Acts 17:28. The emperor's personality represented the corporate personality of the empire. See Brent 1999:66.

[36] Jewett 2004:29.

[37] Zanker 1988:181.

[38] Castriota 1995:139.

is apparent from the words of Aristides, "Thus the existing conditions are naturally satisfying and useful for both the poor and the rich, and there is no other way of living. Thus a single harmony of state order has developed which embraces all."[39] Alongside Augustus's ustrinum, mausoleum and horologium-solarium, the *Ara Pacis* was part of an important complex in the Campus Martius which serves as a "cosmological centre" designed to reorganize time, space and cosmos around the person of Augustus.[40] "The complex...serves as an eschatological 'museum' of Augustus's life and accomplishments."[41] Appearance of the *Ara Pacis* on coins minted in Lugdunum from A.D. 64-67 indicates that Augustus's successors perpetuated the ideology of the *Pax Romana* that had been so important for the first Roman emperor.[42]

Though Virgil was used as a textbook in education throughout the empire, not everyone would have had the privilege of an education.[43] Further, the *Ara Pacis* is a magnificent symbol of imperial ideology but it was located in Rome, roughly 1200 miles away from Galatia and 800 miles from Corinth. This leaves the case for the cosmological emphasis of Roman ideology vulnerable to the claim that it was not accessible to the provinces where Paul's communities were located. Furthermore, it should also be noted that much of the imperial ideology we have observed is based on the message that the emperors themselves or the Roman elite would have embraced. Put simply, how and to what degree was the imperial ideology received in the provinces of the empire?

It should not surprise us that the most well-preserved witness to the ideology of the period is that which was endorsed by the power structure of the time. What may surprise us, however, is the degree to which the propaganda was successful. This is not to say that everyone accepted the new imperial ideology with equal amounts of enthusiasm.[44] Several voices of dissension must be heard. Tacitus recapitulates Calgacus, a chieftain of Briton, who has no delusions about the *Pax Romana*:

Harriers of the world, now that earth fails their all-devastating hands, they probe even the sea: if their enemy have wealth, they have greed; if he be poor, they are ambitious; East nor West has glutted them; alone of mankind they behold with the same passion of con-

---

[39] *Eulogy of Rome* 66 as translated in Wengst 1987:50.
[40] Rehak 2006:143-5.
[41] Rehak 2006:146.
[42] Kreitzer argues that "the association of the person of the Emperor Nero with the Pax Romana seems intended by the deliberate issue of these coins." Kreitzer 1996:121.
[43] In an interesting irony of history, fragments of Virgil's texts have been found at the Jewish stronghold of Masada. Probably belonging to one of the Roman soldiers who besieged the fortress, the text begs comparison with the competing claims of the Jewish and Roman communities.
[44] Zanker 1988

cupiscence waste alike and want. To plunder, butcher, steal, these things they misname empire: they make a desolation and they call it peace.[45]

When Gaius dressed as Jupiter and made proclamations from a high platform, his performance provoked laughter from an onlooker. Charged by the emperor to pass verdict on his appearance, the man responded that he was, "a big humbug."[46] Seneca's *Apocolocyntosis* ("Pumpkinification") famously satirized the "apotheosis" of Claudius.

In Talmudic tradition Rabbi Simon contests Roman benevolence and expresses the sense of oppression from those outside the circles of power, "All what they made they made to themselves, they built marketplaces to set harlots in them; baths to rejuvenate themselves, bridges to levy tolls for them."[47] Yet despite grievances, wide-scale and rapid proliferation of the imperial cult throughout the empire indicates, at least, an awareness of the contemporary structure of power and the desire to participate in it.[48] The positive changes wrought by the Roman government were often noted, even in the provinces.[49]

Roman literature and architecture both provide examples of ways in which imperial ideology could be expressed. It was through the imperial cult, however, that the ideology of *Romanitas* was communicated most blatantly.[50] Of course, the imperial cult was no monolithic entity. In the West, the cult was instituted and advanced by Augustus and his successors. In the East, the cult followed in the wake of the Hellenistic ruler cults and was more readily embraced and advanced by the provincials themselves.[51] But the situation was even more complex. In fact, the cult "takes on different character from area to area; the pattern of development is uneven and the nature of the worship offered tends to vary from province to province."[52] Furthermore, the cult developed and evolved under each of the Julio-Claudian emperors.[53] The important point for this argument is that its presence is evidence of the influence of the imperial ideology.

---

[45] Tacitus, *Agricola* 30. Shotter, however, stresses the positive contributions of the empire and argues that the majority of provincials would not have agreed with the sentiment Tacitus attributes to Calgacus. Shotter 2005:89.
[46] Dio Cassius 59.26.9.
[47] *b. Šabb. 33b*, quoted in Wengst 1987:28.
[48] Griffin 1991:24.
[49] Cf. Branigan 1991; Stockton 1980:5-17.
[50] Brent 1999:67.
[51] Fishwick 1993:92-3.
[52] Fishwick 1993:93.
[53] Rowe 2005:281. For comparative purposes, see the evidence for the presence of the cult in the Roman colony of Aphrodisias in Reynolds 1996:41-50.

B. The Imperial Transformation of the World

In the Roman colony of Corinth, the cult was established ca. 54 A.D.[54] Its influence in Corinth is widely accepted and the civic cults in the forum have been closely related to the Roman state.[55] In conjunction with the status of Corinth as a colony of Rome, we can be reasonably certain that "ceremonies and sacrifices pertaining to the emperor and to state cults were performed at the same time and in the same way as in Rome."[56] Furthermore, the temple designated as Temple E was situated in a dominant location in the forum. It has been variously identified as the Temple of Octavia, Gens Iulia or the Corinthian Capitoleum.[57] Whichever of these is correct, it was clearly associated with "Roman imperial religious traditions."[58] The symbolism is even stronger if the altar in the centre of the forum (which aligns with Temple E) bore resemblance to the *Ara Pacis* in Rome. If that were the case, this altar may be taken as a place of imperial sacrifice.[59] This would place the imperial cult quite literally at the centre of all public life in the city of Corinth.[60]

In Galatia, evidence suggests the imperial cult was in operation as early as 25 B.C.[61] In addition to literary works which indicate a general acceptance of the divinity of the emperor, the imperial temples discovered in Pisidian Antioch as well as in Ankyra would have been striking testimony of the new religio-political system propagated by Rome.[62] Inscribed around the base with the *Res Gestae* (an autobiographical account of Augustus's greatest accomplishments) in Greek and decorated with the same types of nature scenes found on the *Ara Pacis* in Rome, these temples attest to the pervasive influence of the cult. The inscriptions help to transmit the image of the city of Rome including that ordering of society which places the emperor at the centre of everything.[63] Even if people were not entirely aware of the significance of the inscriptions, the impressive architecture of the cults along with the imperial statues and symbols which filled public spaces provide considerable evidence to suggest that "the ideology of the imperial cult was an influential component in the public cul-

---

[54] See Walbank's helpful article: Walbank 1996a:201-213.
[55] Lanci 1997:102-4.
[56] Bookidis 2005:157. Cf. Gradel 2002:15-18.
[57] See Photopoulos 2003:135-9.
[58] Lanci 1997:103-4.
[59] Lanci 1997:103. Cf. Scranton 1951; Walbank 1996b.
[60] Cf. Engels 1990:92-116.
[61] Gill 1997:402. For a recent and thorough study on the development of the imperial cult in Asia Minor, see Witulski 2007.
[62] Cassius Dio records that the provincial centre of the cult in Ankyra was used as an example for other provinces to emulate in other parts of the empire. Cf. Mitchell 1993:102.
[63] Griffin 1991:46.

ture of the empire."⁶⁴ These cults took their cues from the mother city and sought to replicate the ideology and image of the empire embraced in the capital.⁶⁵

Apparently following on the heels of the traditional Hellenistic ruler cults of the East, practice of the imperial cult found its way into the private culture as well. Imperial images in private shrines and on household items indicate, to some degree, the saturation of the world view Rome was articulating.⁶⁶ Whatever the individual's attitude towards the imperial cult, it is clear that the populace of the first century Roman Empire would have been thoroughly inundated with its ideology.⁶⁷

The imperial cult helped to redefine the world in terms focused upon the city of Rome and the personality of the emperor. This underscored the centrality of the emperor in the new society. He was placed alongside the Olympian branch of the Pantheon in order to identify him with the mythological foundation of the world; and he was credited with establishing a new world order.⁶⁸ This cosmogonic emphasis is expressed in the famous Priene inscription (9 B.C.),

> ...Whether the birthday of the most divine Caesar is more pleasant or more advantageous, the day which we might justly set on par with *the beginning of everything,* in practical terms at least, in that he *restored order* when everything was disintegrating into *chaos* and gave a *new look to the whole world,* a world which would have met destruction with the utmost pleasure if Caesar had not been born as a common blessing to

---

⁶⁴ Meggitt 2002:149.

⁶⁵ It was through the imperial cult that the provincials participated in the Roman power structures. It would be a mistake to think that it was solely the military might of Rome which kept provinces like Galatia in check. The sacrificial system of Rome gives great insight into the nature of Roman religion. Through the imperial cult, the relationships between politics, economic oppression and religion were closely linked. That this form of euergetism was presented as benevolence in the new imperial imagery made it an excellent vehicle for the social adhesive which held together the new community created by the emperor. A poorly preserved decree from Coan quoted by S. Price bears this out: "Since Emperor Caesar, son of god, god Sebastos has by his benefactions to all men outdone even the Olympian gods...." An enormous bureaucracy to rule the vast empire was unnecessary if the citizens accepted the idea that they could advance their own status through acts of devotion to Rome and to the emperor. It made perfect sense that the benefactions which Augustus gave to the world should be recognized and reciprocated even if at a very different level. The system modified the "stick and the carrot" form of rewards and punishment to increase the size of the carrot and underplay, though not diminish, the role of the stick. See Price 1984:55; Ando 2000:4-8; Gordon 1997:126, 30, 37.

⁶⁶ Meggitt 2002:151.
⁶⁷ Cf. Oakes 2001b:174.
⁶⁸ Friesen 2001:123.

all. For that reason one might justly take this to be the *beginning of life and living,* the end of regret at one's birth....[69]

The *Decree of the League of Asia Minor* reveals the eschatological significance of the claims being made by the imperial regime. In essence, it expressed the view that the Roman Empire served as the pinnacle of human history. Augustus ushered in a new age of peace and prosperity which was envisaged as a return to the paradisiacal conditions at the foundation of the world – a renewal of creation.[70] It is impossible to know whether Paul ever saw such an inscription. However, Paul did not articulate his eschatological matrix in a vacuum. To whatever degree Paul's auditors embraced the imperial ideology, the evidence cited here suggests that his proclamation of a new creation was not the first time they had heard such claims.

C. The Turn of the Ages and the Eternal Empire

A second aspect of imperial ideology which may provide insight into Paul's eschatology is the fact that it was predicated upon a turn of the ages. Unlike the linear Jewish conception of a history comprised of two ages, Roman history was considered to be cyclical[71] and was believed to consist of ten ages (*saecula*).[72] Each of these ages was associated with a metal characteristic of the age (silver, iron, etc.) and a patron deity.[73] The tenth and final age was to be represented by Sol (Roman god of the sun) and characterised as an age of gold.[74] Virgil's *4th Eclogue* asserts that this last age of history had come during the time of Augustus:

---

[69] *Decree of the League of Asia,* in Ehrenberg and Jones 1976:82-3. Translated in Braund 1985:57-58. Cf. Laffi 1967:5-98.

[70] Cf. Virgil, *Aeneid VI.788-94.* "Hither now turn thy two eyes: behold this people, thine own Romans. Here is Caesar, and all Iūlus' seed, destined to pass beneath the sky's mighty vault. This, this is he, whom thou so oft hearest promised to thee, Augustus Caesar, son of a god, who shall again set up the Golden Age amid the fields where Saturn once reigned...."

[71] The Etruscan traditions had bequeathed Rome with the idea that history was cyclical and that the cycles lasted roughly the length of the longest life in a generation. Once all the former generation had passed away, a new age (*saeculum*) was said to begin.

[72] The Augustan view of the *saecula* was a conglomeration of the contemporary Roman view and the Etruscan view. The view presented here is that offered in the imperial propaganda. See the thorough discussion in Hall III 1986:2564-2589. The idea of cyclical history was first attributed to Pythagoras (born ca. 582 B.C.). See Kee 1985:135.

[73] Jewish apocalyptic literature also spoke of ages of human history in terms of characteristic metals. Cf. Daniel 2:32-33.

[74] The "golden age" was an idealized era of history in which humanity lived in a state of paradisiacal bliss. It was usually associated with Saturnus or Cronus and is marked by

Now is come the last age of the song of Cumae; the great line of the centuries begins anew. Now the Virgin returns, the reign of Saturn returns; now a new generation descends from heaven on high. Only do thou, pure Lucina, smile on the birth of the child, under whom the iron brood shall first cease, and a golden race spring up throughout the world! Thine own Apollo now is king![75]

The god Justice was thought to have left the earth at the end of the first age (also an age of gold) but was to return at the final age. The reference to the reign of Apollo (Greek god of the Sun), Augustus's patron god, makes it clear that Virgil was asserting that this final and greatest age of history had arrived.[76]

In 17 B.C. Augustus made the most blatant possible proclamation of the commencement of the new age by reinstituting the *Ludi Saeculares* (Secular Games). These games were to be celebrated approximately every hundred years to commemorate the passing of history into a new age and to celebrate the foundation of the Republic. The important tradition was long overdue as it had last been celebrated in 146 B.C. The games came on the tide of public hopes for the return to a utopian time of happiness.[77] Augustus used the massive celebration to announce that he had ushered in the anticipated golden age.[78] With the expectation of a comet in 17 B.C., there could hardly be a better time to proclaim that this new age had begun.[79]

---

a time of prosperity and happiness. Hopes for a return to the idyllic time were ripening during the years prior to the rise of Augustus. This gave impetus to the poets of the Augustan age who heralded that he had ushered in the expected age. This concept became a vital part of the new imperial ideology which Augustus used to communicate his rule to the empire. For a fuller treatment of the development of this idea, see Kubusch 1986. The developments of the idea may be discerned within the writings of Virgil who was most enamoured with the concept. See Ryberg 1958.

[75] *Eclogue* IV.4-10.

[76] Virgil's attitude towards the empire is debated among classicists. The issue is to what degree Virgil actually believed the propaganda he was perpetuating. Whether he embraced the imperial image or participated in its promulgation with an attitude of scepticism is difficult to know. For our purposes, however, what Virgil truly believed is not as important as the way his writing was applied to the imperial worldview. The public image of the empire was one created by Roman authority and was presented in terms amenable to their agenda. If the message was derided, it would have made Paul's own message more attractive. If it was embraced, Paul's message would have been seen as a direct challenge to what was coming out of Rome.

[77] This is referred to by Virgil as the Golden or Saturnian age. See *Aeneid* VI.756-789; XI.243.

[78] Taylor and Price 1996:1378.

[79] For a full discussion of the comet and its significance, see Ramsey and Licht 1997, as cited above. For a fuller discussion of how astronomical events were interpreted within Roman society, see Cramer 1954.

C. The Turn of the Ages and the Eternal Empire 73

The games made a salient statement about imperial eschatology. The hopes of humanity had been realized in Augustus.[80] The peace and security which he had brought with his rise to power, though costly for those outside Rome's favour, permeated society and was believed to affect the natural world. Horace's *Carmen Saeculare*, a poem written specifically for this occasion, expresses a universal harmony of nature which results from the new regime, "May Mother Earth, who is fertile in crops and livestock, present Ceres with a crown of corn; may Jove's wholesome showers and breezes nourish all that she brings forth."[81] It petitions the gods for the virtue, peace and glory which were synonymous with the era (ll. 45-8). Sung by an antiphonal choir of children, the hymn exalted the eternity of Roman greatness expressed in the fecundity of the new age.

The eschatological thrust of this propaganda left little place for development or advancement beyond the Augustan ideal. An interesting excerpt from Ovid's *Fasti* concerning the peace brought to the world by Augustus indicates the desire that such conditions would last forever, "...ask the gods, who heed pious prayers, that that house, the champion of peace, may live with her [Rome] forever."[82] Even after Augustus's death, the hope for continuation of the age he had inaugurated is evidenced in an inscription found in Umbria from 32 A.D., "To perpetual Augustan safety and the public liberty of the Roman people...To the providence of Tiberius Caesar Augustus, born for the eternal endurance of the Roman name...."[83] The idea was that Augustus had inaugurated the greatest age of peace the world had ever known. He had established himself at the apex of the world's power structure and in so doing created an entirely new society that was to be as eternal as the immortal cosmos.[84]

It is very interesting that Claudius celebrated these games again only 65 years later in A.D. 47. He recalculated the date of the games to coincide with the 800 year anniversary of the founding of Rome.[85] Of course, this recalculation was not exactly consistent with the Augustan propaganda. This attests to the fact that the imperial ideology was not developed according to a rigidly consistent system. What is important is that Claudius employed the Augustan ideology and placed himself firmly within the Augustan tradition.[86] Repealing much of the work of Gaius, Claudius's reign

---

[80] Cf. Georgi 1997:33-46.

[81] Horace, *Carmen Saeculare* 29-32.

[82] *Fasti* 1.721-22 as translated in Braund 1985:31.

[83] Translated in Braund 1985:99.

[84] There is a long and important history of the association of the ruler with eternity. See Instinsky 1942.

[85] Bowman, Champlin, and Lintott 1996:239.

[86] Claudius's predecessor, Gaius was notorious for his cruel and capricious rule. Something of the contempt felt towards him may be evidenced in Dio's remarks about

was a welcome relief from Gaius's brutal instability and coins were minted announcing the return of the Augustan peace and liberty.[87] His particular interest in the province of Galatia may be seen from the numerous cities founded or re-founded there which bear his name.[88]

Thus, just a few years prior to Paul's writing Galatians, the emperor of Rome celebrated another new age which had dawned. Though the Secular Games occurred only in Rome, public festivities and celebrations in the provinces would have communicated similar ideologies.[89]

The idea that the coming of Augustus was the fulfilment of humanity's expectations is evidenced in an inscription from Halicarnassus in Asia Minor,

> ...Since the eternal and immortal nature of everything has bestowed upon mankind the greatest good (τὸ [μέ|γ]ιστον ἀγαθὸν) with extraordinary benefactions by bringing Caesar Augustus in our blessed time the father of his own country (πατέρα μὲν τῆς [ἑαυ]τοῦ πα|τ[ρ]ίδος), divine Rome (θεᾶς 'Ρώμης), and ancestral Zeus, saviour (σωτῆρα) of the common race of men, whose providence has not only fulfilled but actually exceeded the prayers of all. For land and sea (γῆ καὶ θάλαττα) are at peace (εἰρηνεύο[υ|σ]ι) and the cities flourish with good order (πόλεις δὲ ἀνθοῦσιν εὐνομία[ι]), concord and prosperity – it is the prime crop of all good, as mankind, filled with high hopes for the future and high spirits for the present (ἐλπίδων μὲν χρηστῶν πρὸς τὸ μέλλον, εὐθυμίας | δ]ὲ εἰς τ[ὸ] παρὸν), with festivals, dedications, sacrifices and hymns...their...[about 25 lines missing]....[90]

The eschatological hope of Rome, however, had to be reinvented when new emperors took the throne. When Claudius died and Nero rose to power in A.D. 54, his accession was proclaimed in Egypt in similar terms to the ways Augustus had been heralded as the one who would fulfil the hopes of the world,

> The Caesar owed to his ancestors, god manifest, has gone to them, while the imperator expected and hoped for by the world has been proclaimed. On account of this we should

---

his assassination, "Thus Gaius...learned by actual experience that he was not a god" (59.30.1). Yet even *he* sought, at least initially, to be seen in line with the standards of his predecessors. Cf. Dio Cassius 59.3.7-8.

[87] Especially in comparison with the excesses of Gaius who demanded worship in Rome itself, Claudius was particularly conservative in his rule. Cf. Nock 1966:496-9; Charlesworth 1966:669.

[88] Hardin 2008:64-5 lists: Claudiconium, Claudioderbe, Ninica Claudiopolis, Claudiolaodiceia, Claudioseleuceia and Claudiocaesareia Mistea.

[89] It is clear that the provincial cults intentionally modelled themselves after Rome. The elaborate festivities given to perpetuate the Roman ideology by the cults of Galatia during the time of Tiberius is evidenced in the list of priests and their benefactions cited in Mitchell 1993:108.

[90] As translated in Braund 1985:59.

all wear garlands and sacrifice oxen to show thanks to the gods. Year 1 of Nero Claudius Caesar Augustus Germanicus, 21st of the month New Augustus.[91]

The ideology created during the time of Augustus was employed by successive emperors.[92] Under the *new* "new age" brought by Nero, the hopes of humanity were to be met in the continuation of Roman peace and prosperity. During the period various emperors were said to have brought Rome into a golden age and were spoken of as father of the country, saviour of humanity and guarantor of peace, concord and prosperity, Paul wrote about the "peace ... from God our Father and the Lord Jesus Christ, who gave himself for our sins to set us free from the present evil age, according to the will of our God and Father" (Gal 1:3b-4). This important convergence will be discussed further in the next chapter.

I do not wish to argue that Paul wrote his letter with the lines of poetry and the inscriptions quoted above in mind. However, it seems reasonable to postulate at least that Paul's auditors could have been struck by the challenge which his new age presented to ideology of the purportedly eternal city of Rome. Into an atmosphere where the empire was supposed to offer a new era of history upon which no improvement could be imagined, Paul preached about a new age, inaugurated by the cross and resurrection of Christ that was spoken of in terms of a new creation. For Paul, something far greater than Roman citizenship is on offer (cf. Phil 3:20). Those who embrace his message become the sons of God (Gal 4:4-7).[93]

D. Rome and the New World Order

The imperial ideology of Rome was essentially directed towards establishing a new way of perceiving the world. As the above arguments show, this new order was thought to affect the cosmos and to be the result of a new age of human history. On a practical level, the new order was expressed through the transformation of space and time to reflect the ideology of the age. When Augustus came to power, he immediately began a building project of massive proportions. His renovations of the city of Rome were so extensive, Suetonius records, "he could justly boast that he had found it

---

[91] Braund 1985:94 (No. 235).

[92] This was achieved to varying levels of success. Suetonius records that Nero "declared that he would rule according to the principles of Augustus, and he let slip no opportunity for acts of generosity and mercy, or even for displaying his affability" (*Nero 10.1*).

[93] Imperial coinage and inscriptions heralded the emperor as son of the divine (DIVI F = *divi filius*). See, for example: *ANS* 1941.131.1150; 1944.100.4821; 1967.153.219. The resonance this would have created for early believers in Jesus as Son of God, as well as the adoption of believers into the family of God, deserves further study.

built of brick and left it in marble."[94] One reason behind the building was to provide Rome with an architectural splendour commensurate with her status as commander of the world.[95] It is commonly acknowledged by architects and anthropologists alike that the ordering of space is both influenced by and influences social formation. This order combines "morality, social relations, space, time and the cosmos."[96] Winston Churchill has said that we design our buildings and then our buildings design us.[97] In this way, the architecture of Augustan Rome was meant to reflect the all-encompassing ideal of his regime.[98]

By constructing the new architectural projects with sturdy materials and designing a new bureaucracy to maintain the public works, Augustus clearly intended to communicate that his work was directed beyond his own time.[99] In his treatise on the practice of ancient architecture, Vitruvius wrote that Augustus had "such a regard to public and private buildings, that they will correspond to the grandeur of our history, and will be a memorial to future ages."[100] The refurbishment of the city was far more than an aesthetic improvement upon the visage of the empire. It represented something much greater. In addition to providing gravity to the proclamation of the dawning new age, the construction actually embodied the ideology of the age in the physical world. This transformation of space was used to publicize the ideology of the new order and, in a very real sense, structured the reality of the empire.

The transformation of space was not limited to Rome. S. Price offers a persuasive case that the imperial ideology would have been included in every aspect of civil life not only in Rome but in the East as well.[101] Through the mechanism of the imperial cult, the images of imperial power would have been positioned in the most prominent places within the cities of the empire, East and West.[102] The Forum of Augustus in Rome would have done this in unparalleled grandeur and it was the pattern emulated by the cities which wanted to participate in the power mechanisms of the imperial regime.[103] In the cities of Ancyra, Pessinus and Antioch where prominent provincial cult temples were located, there is sound evidence to

---

[94] Suetonius, *Augustus*, 28.3.
[95] Cf. Vitruvius, *On Architecture* 1.2
[96] Pearson and Richards 1994:10.
[97] Churchill made the remark during a 1943 speech to the House of Commons, "We shape our buildings, and afterwards our buildings shape us." See Churchill 2006:358.
[98] Richardson 2002:23.
[99] Favro 1996:247-8.
[100] Vitruvius, *On Architecture* 1.3 as translated in Chisholm and Ferguson 1981:454.
[101] Cf. Price 1984.
[102] See the most recent instalment of Fishwick's massive work on the imperial cult emphasizes the place of the cult in the provincial centres of the West in Fishwick 2004.
[103] Cf. Hendrix 1991:14-17.

D. Rome and the New World Order

support the fact that these temples were not isolated structures. Rather, they were "linked topographically and functionally with other structures in the centre of the new Augustan cities."[104] In Antioch, the temple was positioned in such a way as to be visible upon approaching the city from miles away.[105] By including imperial images, art, architecture and inscriptions in prominent places in the cities, the ideology of the new world order was given tangible expression.

It would be a mistake to imply that the influence of imperial ideology was confined to the imperial cult. Though many examples could be cited, one quite obvious way that the ideology served to transform the space of the empire that would have been important for Paul was in its system of roads. Rome was renowned for its contribution to travelling and commerce in the ancient world. Though many of the roads were built for military purposes, they opened new trade routes and helped to expand the land and the economy of the empire. There were very few areas of the empire without some system of roads. Travellers along these roads would have been reminded at every mile of who it was that provided such benefits.[106] One such milestone, found in the province of Galatia, declares the status of Augusts as Son of God, "Imperator Caesar Son of God Pontifex Maximus, ... made the Via Sebaste under the care of his legate Cornuto Aquila...."[107] To make the imagery even more explicit, Augustus had a golden milestone placed near the Roman Forum.[108] This, along with the thousands of milestones throughout the empire, served as an indicator that the world was a wheel of which Rome was the hub. All roads truly did lead to Rome. In the new world order which was being constructed there could be no doubt, the emperor and Rome were at its centre.[109]

If the transformation of space could be said to be an important part of the new world order, so could the transformation of time. The *Solarium Augusti*, the Roman Empire's largest sundial, stood at thirty meters high and covered a significant area of public space, probably in proximity to the *Ara Pacis*, with markings to display dates and times. The Egyptian obelisk which served as the gnomon is believed to have been positioned in such a way that on September 23, the birthday of Augustus, it would cast its shadow directly towards the altar.[110] The symbolism of this monument is striking. Crowned with a sphere to portray supremacy over the *orbis ter-*

---

[104] Mitchell 1993:104.
[105] Mitchell 1993:105.
[106] Galinsky 1996:384.
[107] *CIL* 3.6974. Cited in Crossan and Reed 2004:201. Cf. French 1981.
[108] Zanker 1988:143.
[109] Renovation of the roads of Galatia was part of Claudius's building program. This attests to the perpetuation of this aspect of the ideology in his reign.
[110] Zanker 1988:143.

rarum, the gnomon was spoil from Roman conquest in Egypt.[111] That the Roman military might had pointed the way to Roman peace was a principal component of the ideology of the time. That Augustus was its author was of utmost importance. The machine symbolizes a "restoration of cosmic order, paralleling Augustus's political 'restoration' of the Republic."[112]

Just one year after the *Solarium* was dedicated (10 B.C.), Augustus's coming into the world was called the "beginning of everything" (ca. 9 B.C.) in Asia Minor because he had brought this peace into the chaotic and disintegrating Republic.[113] It is interesting to note that the League of Asia which set out (ca. 29 B.C.) to find the greatest honour for Augustus because of this beneficence offered an enticing reward to whoever could devise the greatest honour for the world's "saviour." From the famous Priene inscriptions of 9 B.C., we know that the proconsul, Paullus Fabius Maximus, was awarded the prize for suggesting that time should begin from [Augustus's] birthday,

> [He] has devised to honour Augustus something hitherto unknown to the Greeks: to begin time from his birthday. For that reason, with good fortune and safety, the Greeks of Asia have decided that the New Year in all the cities should begin on 23rd September, the birthday of Augustus....[114]

A new calendar was developed which included Julius (July) and Augustus (August) into the ordering of time.[115] The realignment of the calendar served to redefine the meaning of time. Fears of the collapsing order were so acute, it was believed that the cosmos would have been destroyed had Augustus not been born to bring it into a new phase of existence. In this way, Augustus was shown to have brought a caesura in which time stopped and an altogether new age of history had begun.[116]

This is especially important for Paul in the light of the term used to describe this new world order in the Priene inscription,

> ...Caesar who by his epiphany (ἐπιφανεὶς) exceeded the hopes of those who prophesied good tidings (εὐαγγέλια), not only outdoing benefactors of the past, but also allowing no hope of greater benefactions in the future; and since the birthday of the god first brought to the world the good tidings (εὐαγγελίων) residing in him...

---

[111] Hardie 1986:368.

[112] Rehak 2006:95.

[113] *Letter of Paullus Fabius Maximus* in Braund 1985:57.

[114] *Decree of the League of Asia* in Ehrenberg and Jones 1976:82-3. Translated in Braund 1985:57-58. Cf. Laffi 1967:5-98.

[115] Roetzel 2002:74.

[116] Cancik 2000:99. This caesura and subsequent new era would have been quite similar to the way Christians would later count history from the birth of Christ thus splitting time into two ages.

Whereas the term εὐαγγέλια occurs in the plural in the inscription, Paul uses the term only in the singular. As this term in its various forms plays a more prominent role in Galatians than any of Paul's other writing, G. Stanton points out that its concentration in the opening of Paul's letter would have reminded the Galatians of Paul's insistence that the singular gospel of Jesus Christ stood in direct contradiction to the "gospels" of the Roman emperors.[117] It is highly significant for the argument of this thesis that the imperial ideology employed the term εὐαγγέλια in the context of an eschatological shift and a new world order. The fact that these ideas functioned together in the Greco-Roman world should alert our attention when they appear together in Paul's letters. How these ideas converge for Paul is the subject of the next chapter.

E. CONCLUSIONS

This chapter has sought to explore some of the ways in which new creation language could have been heard in a world under the ubiquitous influence of Roman imperial ideology. Though the actual expression "new creation" does not appear in extant Roman literature or inscriptions, the concept is heavily employed in the eschatological ideology of Roman imperial propaganda.

The peace procured by the empire was said to have renewed creation. Crops were more fertile, livestock more productive and fears of destruction of the world by the dissolution of the state were laid to rest. This was articulated in terms of a change of ages in which a new and golden age was inaugurated. The new age was to be a time of utopian ideal. It was to be the climactic age of history when no greater time could be imagined. The embodiment of the new age was in the establishment of the Roman world order. This world order offered by Rome was constructed around the personality of the emperor and the city of Rome. The society it engendered was to be eternal and the emperor was heralded as a saviour, the Lord of the whole cosmos, guarantor of peace, concord and prosperity.[118] Space and time were reordered to express this ideology.

As the Roman ideology was proclaimed throughout the empire, East and West, it is not altogether unlikely that Paul's proclamation of the new creation could have alerted the sensibilities of those familiar with the imperial message.

---

[117] Stanton 2004:35-46.

[118] Note Harrison's stimulating article which examines the way in which the benefactions of Augustus paralleled the overflowing grace of God in Christ: Harrison 1999:79-91.

Though Paul's primary objective in his letters is not to deal with imperial ideology, it could be that he intends his message to be seen in the sharp relief of that ideology. If that is the case, the concept of new creation in Paul's writing could be seen from a fresh perspective which may promise insight into Paul's thinking. Due consideration of this background material takes more seriously the missionary nature of Paul's letters to the churches of Galatia, Corinth and Rome and stands perfectly in line with Jewish interaction with pagan empires as the previous chapters have sought to show.[119] We now turn our attention to an examination of Paul's understanding of new creation in each of these communities.

---

[119] For a fuller discussion of how Paul's critique of empire stands in line with his Jewish roots, see Wright 2005:59-79.

Part II

New Creation in Paul's Letters – An Examination of the *Hauptbriefe*

Chapter 5

Paul's Conception of New Creation in Galatians 6:11-18

This chapter attempts to show how Paul used the concept of new creation to deal with a crisis of potential apostasy in the churches of Galatia.[1] From the very first verse, we get the sense of a visceral response to the issue there. He begins by establishing the divine origin of his apostolic calling with the emphatic negation of human influence, "Paul an apostle – not from men and not through man but through Jesus Christ and God the Father...."[2] Paul dispenses with the usual niceties of his more cordial openings and, in the place of the expected thanksgiving or words of encouragement, we find an accusation, "I am astonished that you are so quickly deserting him who called you in the grace of Christ and are turning to a different Gospel" (1:6). The pitch of his polemic is not diminished in the course of his argument (cf. 1:6; 2:11; 3:1; 4:11, 19-20; 5:7, 12) and this letter can only be understood properly when this is taken into account.[3]

A careful exegesis of Gal 6:15 and its immediate context will support the overall argument of this thesis that Paul's concept of new creation is an expression of his eschatologically infused soteriology which involves the individual, the community and the cosmos and which is inaugurated in the death and resurrection of Christ. In order to make this case, this chapter proposes that Paul's καινὴ κτίσις should be understood as an expression of the new age. Paul's thinking is marked, in this regard, by his adaptation of Jewish apocalyptic eschatology to his understanding of the Christ event. The importance of this event for Paul's conception of new creation will be shown in the course of this argument.

---

[1] For a recent discussion, see Wilson 2004:550-71 and the fuller treatment in Wilson 2007.
[2] The translation is mine. Rowland argues that the revelation of Christ to Paul "enabled him to act on his eschatological convictions" in Rowland 2003:155-8.
[3] Cf. Betz 1979:14-25. See, e.g., Gaventa 1986:309-26. Gaventa acknowledges that "Paul's comments...also have an apologetic purpose, [even if] that interpretation by no means exhausts the purpose and function of the text" (p. 315). Sumney 2005:18 warns against the polemical reading advocated by Betz. While the entirety of this letter may not be best understood from a strictly rhetorical viewpoint, the polemical characteristics of Galatians may nevertheless provide a helpful starting point for our inquiry.

A. New Creation in the Concluding Verses of Galatians (6:11-18)

A number of scholars have recognized the importance of Gal 6:11-18 as a conclusion for the letter as a whole.[4] The conclusion is emphasized by the phrase ἴδετε πηλίκοις ὑμῖν γράμμασιν ἔγραψα. In addition to providing a safeguard against possible forgeries, a move from the stylized and uniform letters of the amanuensis to the "large letters" of Paul's own hand is, in effect, first century bold print.[5] Lightfoot observes that Paul's "handwriting may reflect the energy and determination of his soul."[6] H.D. Betz's rhetorical approach to the book underscored the nature of the section as *conclusio* and argued that it should "be employed as the hermeneutical key to the intentions of the apostle."[7] This challenge was taken further in the work of J. Weima who has argued convincingly that a series of four contrasts made in the closing "allow us to cut through the confusing (at times) rhetoric of Galatians and to see clearly what Paul believed to be the central issue at stake in the Galatian controversy: the cross of Christ."[8] Exploring the contrasts noted by Weima in the letter closing will prove helpful for our purposes.

The first contrast which Paul highlights in this passage is that between the agitators who "want to make a good showing in the flesh"[9] and who are compelling the Galatians to be circumcised in order to "boast in [the Galatians'] flesh (6:12, 13)," and versus Paul who boasts only in the cross. Two points should be made here. First, the use of flesh (σάρξ) in these verses is not identical even though there is considerable overlap. In verse 13, there is a commonly acknowledged reference to the foreskin.[10] While this allusion certainly operates in verse 12, the use of "flesh" there further indicates that their actions are a performance for people and not for God (cf. 1:16).[11] Though "flesh" may signify "whatever is external,"[12] it is not intended here simply to set up an external/internal contraposition. This explanation would not fit the text since the agitators boast in the flesh and

---

[4] Meyer 1884:337; Lightfoot 1896:220; Matera 1988:79-91; Longenecker 1990:286-7, 301.
[5] Cf. Betz 1979:314. For a strong critique of this approach, see Kern 1998.
[6] Lightfoot 1896:220.
[7] Betz 1979:313.
[8] Weima 1993:106. Cf. Weima 1994; Schnider and Stenger 1987:145-51.
[9] Cf. *The Tebtunis Papyri* 1:19 (B.C. 114). Cited in Moulton and Milligan 1930:264. For further discussion of the meaning of εὐπροσωπῆσαι ἐν σαρκί, see Winter 2002:60-8; Hardin 2008:85-115.
[10] Martyn 1997c:561. Martyn sees the two uses as virtually synonymous.
[11] BDAG, pp. 914-16.
[12] Longenecker 1990:291.

Paul boasts in the cross. Paul's boast in the cross is not a reference to his own experience (though it certainly entailed an experience) but to what God had done in Christ (cf. 1 Cor 1:18-25). Furthermore, this occurrence of the term may resonate with the flesh/Spirit antithesis which operates throughout the letter (3:3; 4:29; 5:16-17, 19, 22; 6:8).[13]

Paul's use of "flesh" in vv. 12-13 may indicate a chiastic structure in these verses. However, as Ciampa's comments indicate, there is some ambiguity as to whether the emphasis should lie on the outer or inner units. The ambiguity is mitigated if, rather than the ABC-C′B′A′ pattern, we arrange the units in simple parallelism: ABC-A′B′C′:

	Gal 6:12		Gal 6:13
A	Ὅσοι θέλουσιν εὐπροσωπῆσαι ἐν σαρκί	A'	οὐδὲ γὰρ οἱ περιτεμνόμενοι αὐτοὶ νόμον φυλάσσουσιν
B	οὗτοι ἀναγκάζουσιν ὑμᾶς περιτέμνεσθαι,	B'	ἀλλὰ θέλουσιν ὑμᾶς περιτέμνεσθαι,
C	μόνον ἵνα τῷ σταυρῷ τοῦ Χριστοῦ μὴ διώκωνται.	C'	ἵνα ἐν τῇ ὑμετέρᾳ σαρκὶ καυχήσωνται.

This arrangement incorporates these verses much better into the context of the letter and suggests some illuminating connections which have been overlooked in scholarship.[14] If Winter is correct that εὐπροσωπῆσαι (6:12a) should be understood in a legal context, this indicates the agitators' concern with vindication before the current political powers rather than vindication before God. They are actually concerned with securing a good

---

[13] There is a higher concentration of the term σάρξ in Galatians than in any of Paul's other letters. In this context we see that the term may be used somewhat innocuously referring simply to humanity or bodily existence (1:16). However, even that for Paul is tinged with the idea of weakness or inferiority (2:20; 4:13, 14). Several times in Galatians it is likely used in reference to the foreskin which had become such an issue in these churches (3:3; 6:13). The term also takes on a more sinister connotation. It is contrasted with the promise (4:23) and the Spirit (4:29) and even takes an active role in hostile antagonism against the Spirit (5:16-17). The flesh is thus used in reference to "the personal propensity towards sinfulness" which manifests the "meta-personal, meta-cultural power of Sin" (5:13, 19; cf. Rom 3:9; 5:21; 7:8, 11, 17, 20). Cf. Longenecker 1998:38-41.

The Flesh-Spirit contrast in Galatians is one indicator that Paul is operating within an eschatological paradigm which has been influenced by Jewish apocalyptic literature. In this way, σάρξ is "associated with 'the world' and 'the present age' which stand in contrast to the new creation." Barclay 1988:205.

[14] See Ciampa 1998:371.

(legal) status[15] with the authorities but not with honouring the essence of God's Law (6:13a).[16] They compel/desire the Galatians to be circumcised (6:12b, 6:13b) in order to avoid persecution for the cross (6:12c). Boasting in the Galatians' circumcision (i.e. not the cross, 6:13c) should be seen in relationship to 6:12c since both phrases consist of a ἵνα clause with a subjunctive verb, which explains the purpose of the agitators' actions. In contrast to Paul who boasts in the cross and even embraces persecution for its sake (cf. 6:17; 2:20, see below), the agitators' attempts to avoid such identification with Christ's sufferings (and, consequently, those who follow them) leave them reliant upon the flesh and severed from Christ (3:1-5; 5:4).[17]

Next, Paul's boast in the cross is a shocking reappraisal of that instrument of torture which would have struck fear and revulsion into the hearts of Jew and Gentile alike.[18] Meyer memorably refers to Paul's boasting in the cross as an "apostolic oxymoron."[19] This emphasis highlights the motivating force of Paul's ministry (cf. 1:10; 6:14) in contrast to the self-serving motivation of the agitators (cf. 4:17) and underscores the crucial role of the cross in this letter as a whole. If the cross had been at the centre of the agitators' message, they would have been the objects of persecution just as Paul had been.[20]

The second contrast presents the agitators' desire to avoid persecution for the cross (6:12) against Paul's cruciform lifestyle (cf. 2:20) demonstrated by the marks of Jesus on his body (6:17).[21] Hardin cites the major

---

[15] Cf. Winter 2002:75.

[16] Cf. Rom 2:26-29. Dunn 1993:338-9; Bruce 1982:269-70. J. Barclay argues that the intense polemic of this statement obscures the facts and that this is Paul's attempt to discredit the agitators. This "paradoxically confirms our impression from the rest of the letter that the agitators expected the Galatians to observe the law in conjunction with their circumcision." See Barclay 1988:65.

[17] Cf. Mell 1989:293-8.

[18] Crucifixion was taboo in Roman society. Cf. Cicero, *Pro Rabirio* 16, cited in Bruce 1982:271. Cf. Hengel 1977.

Hubbard rightly emphasizes the inner change experienced by the individual in his explanation of Paul's new creation language. However, his overly strict anthropocentric interpretation misses the way in which Paul employs the crucifixion of Christ. Paul's language of boasting in the cross is so powerful precisely because of the public and "external" image it would have evoked in the first century (cf. Gal 3:1; 1 Cor 1:18, 23).

[19] Meyer 1884:346.

[20] Mell 1989:323.

[21] The majority of commentators understand τὰ στίγματα τοῦ ᾽Ιησοῦ as scars from injuries sustained at the hands of Paul's persecutors. Paul was clearly no stranger to suffering for the sake of the message he preached, see 1 Cor 4:9-13; 2 Cor 1:5; 6:4-5; 11:23-29; Phil 1:29; 3:10; 1 Thess 3:4; 2 Tim 1:12; 2:3, 9 (cf. Acts 14:19-20; 16:19-24). For a helpful summary of scholarship on this issue, see Tolmie 2005:227-32.

options for who might have done the persecuting: "Jewish syncretists, Gentile proselytes concerned with either *Heilsgeschichte* or local Jewish persecution, Jewish-Christian Gnostics, Judaen Jesus-believers attempting to quell reprisals from the Zealot cause, or even local *non*-Jesus-believing proselytes at work in the Galatian churches."[22] Essentially following Winter, Hardin proposes that the agitators were a local group of Jewish Jesus-believers who sought to avoid possible repercussions to their status with the Roman authorities if the Pauline communities were not considered a *religio licita* by virtue of being a Jewish group.[23] This historical reconstruction offers a plausible explanation for the social setting of the Galatian controversy but it should not obscure the central aim of this passage.[24] Paul is making the case to the believers of Galatia that the agitators' message of circumcision compromises the gospel (cf. 1:6-9) thereby calling into question the efficacy of the centrepiece of its message: the cross (5:11).

Thirdly, in contrast to the opponents who compel circumcision (6:12-13), Paul relativizes its importance altogether (6:15). This underscores the soteriological divide between Paul and the agitators. Barclay has argued for the probability that the agitators expected the Galatian converts to obey the law and not just undergo circumcision.[25] In contrast, Paul has completely disqualified "nomistic observance as a necessary feature of salvation in Christ" (cf. 2:16, 21; 3:11-14; 5:2, 6, 11).[26] The eradication of circumcision as the most fundamental identity marker of the people of God reverberates with the eschatologically infused soteriology which has been at play throughout this letter and which is particularly emphasized in its opening and closing sections.[27] It testifies to the presence of a new era in God's dealings with humanity (3:28-9). The old era for Paul was characterised by "religious pairs of opposites" reflecting an ancient view that the universe was constructed upon the principle of cosmic polarity (e.g. Sir

---

Tolmie passes over the meaning of καινὴ κτίσις except for the perspicacious observation in a footnote that this phrase could be understood as "ecclesiological, soteriocosmological or soterio-anthropological...depending on the way in which one uses the 'evidence' from the rest of the letter" (Tolmie 2005:223). Cf. Du Toit 1994:403-12.

[22] Hardin 2008:90.
[23] Hardin 2008:113-15. Note the recent study on the relationship between Jews and the imperial cult in McLaren 2005:257-78.
[24] See Davies's discussion of Paul's historical and political context in Davies 1999:698-702.
[25] Barclay 1988:60-72. Cf. Longenecker 1998:30-33. Martyn suggests that they may have been selective in their obedience and may have offered a similar flexibility to those in Galatia who would take up circumcision. But this goes beyond the evidence of the text. Martyn 1997c:563.
[26] Longenecker 1998:146.
[27] This idea will be worked out in further detail later in this chapter.

33:15).²⁸ These antinomies met their end in the cross of Christ and their eradication amounted to the dissolution of the world. Thus, Paul's use of the language of new creation in this context announces his soteriological plan predicated upon the cross.

Finally, the structure of this passage underscores the most important contrast for our purposes: the "world" (6:14) versus the "new creation" (6:15).²⁹ Verse 14 begins with ἐμοὶ δέ marking an immediate contrast between Paul and the agitators who boast in the Galatians' circumcision (6:13).³⁰ As previously noted, Paul's boast is in the cross. In itself this is a striking claim, but his writing is even more salient in the next phrase, δι' οὗ ἐμοὶ κόσμος ἐσταύρωται κἀγὼ κόσμῳ.³¹ Here Paul repeats the idea of participation in the death of Christ which had surfaced earlier in the letter (2:20; 5:24).³²

Exactly what is meant by the crucifixion of the world in this context has been the subject of much debate. The most recent attempt to explain this striking expression was undertaken by Moyer Hubbard. Hubbard argues that the repeated personal pronouns serve to confirm the anthropological emphasis of 6:14. For him, "the 'world' which ended for Paul was the only 'world' he had ever known: his 'former way of life in Judaism' (1:13)."³³ Hubbard's view mitigates the difficulty of this verse because it does not require any kind of cosmic event, but merely an internal existential change. However, if Hubbard's social-scientific study helps to restore some of the poignancy of the idea of the κόσμος in reference to the individual, it also fails to give Paul's cosmic and eschatological emphases due consideration.³⁴

---

²⁸ Martyn 1997a:115-19.
²⁹ Weima 1993:94; Mußner 1974:414. Note the interesting (if not always convincing) structural observations in Ciampa 1998:372.
³⁰ Note the emphasis on personal pronouns in this verse: ἐμοί...ἐμοί...κἀγώ. These pronouns primarily serve the purposes of setting Paul apart from the agitators and indicating what effect the cosmic plan of redemption had upon Paul's own life. The world had been crucified and this involved rescue from "the present evil age" (1:4) and the enslaving elements of the cosmos, including the law (4:3, 9) but this is only experienced by those who unite with Christ (cf. 5:6; 6:15). Cf. Brinsmead 1982:65-6.
³¹ The δι' οὗ could refer to the cross ("through which") or to Christ ("through whom"). It is better to take this as a reference to the cross since a reference to Christ might have been more naturally rendered as ἐν/σὺν ᾧ. Cf. Lightfoot 1896:223.
³² Cf. Tannehill 1967:62-5.
³³ Hubbard 2002:218. Hubbard acknowledges that κόσμος as both soterio-cosmology and soterio-anthropology "can claim support elsewhere in Paul's letters" and that they "[represent] a different aspect of Paul's soteriology, broadly understood." Hubbard 2002:216.
³⁴ Cf. Dunn 1993:341.

A. New Creation in the Concluding Verses of Galatians (6:11-18)

There are two factors which directly contribute to Hubbard's misunderstanding of the meaning of κόσμος in Galatians. First, Hubbard is correct to begin with the immediate context in his attempt to ascertain Paul's meaning here. He rightly understands circumcision to be an important part of the κόσμος to which Paul refers. But Hubbard takes this too far in his hypothesis that κόσμος is "defined" in the preceding and subsequent context by circumcision. Paul is not simply saying that he is crucified to circumcision and circumcision is crucified to him. Nor should this phrase be limited simply to Paul's previous Judaizing lifestyle. That κόσμος is not limited to Paul's personal experience is intimated by his relativization of *both* circumcision *and* uncircumcision in 6:15.

Secondly, there is a significant problem with Hubbard's attempt to divide Paul's thinking into mutually exclusive anthropological and cosmological categories. The attempt to explain "the world" in Gal 6:14 as Paul's inner experience does not do justice to the very real effects of the cross of Christ on the cosmos. Furthermore, such an individual focus would represent a unique usage of κόσμος in the Pauline corpus. As Minear astutely argues in his criticism of Bultmann, the separation between history and nature erroneously reflects a modern cosmology in which an interpreter is compelled to choose between either an "objectivistic cosmology or an existentialist anthropology."[35] It would press this point too far to insist that Paul had in mind the crucifixion of the physical world in Gal 6:14 but that does not mean that Paul did not have an objective event in mind.

Enslavement under the law, which Paul portrayed as tantamount to enslavement to the στοιχεῖα τοῦ κόσμου (3:23-4:3), was not merely an existential crisis. It was an expression of the power of the present evil age from which believers had been rescued (1:4). The crucifixion of the world represents for Paul the victory won by the cross of Christ over those hostile forces. Of course, this does not preclude an existential referent.[36] The use of the personal pronouns in 6:14 serves to distinguish Paul from the agitators (and those Galatians who fell under their sway). This implies that there was a reality which applied to him which had not been embraced by them. Understanding how Paul can address both the individual and the cosmos requires modifying our contemporary cosmology/ontology which can allow for this without a "demythologizing" appeal to experience.[37]

---

[35] Minear 1979:405. In Bultmann's response to Minear, he argues that Paul (in addition to Jesus and John) does not envisage a cosmic catastrophe which brings change to the world. Rather, "the liberation from the world [consists in] ... the fact that 'this' world, which has gained its character through men who have succumbed to evil, is finished for the one who by faith in the word spoken by God in Jesus Christ has become a new creature and has found freedom." The quotation is from Kegley 1966:268.

[36] Minear 1979:406-7.

[37] On this issue, see the excellent study by Stuhlmacher 1967:1-35.

B. Paul's Use of κόσμος in Galatians

The meaning of κόσμος in 6:14 may be illuminated by its only other occurrence in the letter to the Galatians (4:3). In one of the theological peaks (4:1-7) of the letter, 4:3 introduces one of Paul's most perplexing phrases: τὰ στοιχεῖα τοῦ κόσμου. The variety of ways this phrase has been interpreted evinces the lack of consensus on how it should be understood. It is taken variously as: "elementary religious teachings," "elements of religious distinction," "physical elements of the universe," "astral powers," "demonic powers" and "elemental spirits."[38] De Boer has recently expanded the conclusions reached by Blinzer, Schweizer and Rusam, who argued convincingly that τὰ στοιχεῖα τοῦ κόσμου would most likely have been understood in the sense of actual physical elements of the universe (cf. Wisdom 13:1-2).[39] De Boer makes the case that Paul employs this phrase as a metonym for the "religious beliefs and practices associated in Galatia with the four elements (earth, air, fire and water) of the physical universe."[40]

This view is not incompatible with the earlier argument of C. Arnold that Paul had in mind the spiritual powers which ruled over the old aeon.[41] The relegation of both Jewish and Gentile religious observance in the time before the Christ event is not a simple recognition that they both participated in calendrical observances (De Boer) but that both were manipulated and exploited by malicious spiritual powers (cf. 1 Cor 8:5; 10:20-21; 2 Cor 4:4; Epistle to Diognetus 8:2).[42] In line with the temporal dualism of the ages of Jewish apocalyptic writings, Paul saw these powers as ruling over an age of evil from which the cross of Christ had procured deliverance (Gal 1:4; cf. 1 Cor 2:8).

Martyn proposes that Paul transforms the common understanding of τὰ στοιχεῖα τοῦ κόσμου to speak of "the ancient equation of the world's

---

[38] Cf. Adams 2000:228-9.

[39] De Boer 2007:207; cf. Blinzer 1963:429-43; Schweizer 1988:455-68; Rusam 1992:119-25.

[40] De Boer 2007:223. He also argues for the less compelling idea that Paul only drew a connection between Jewish observance of the Law and Gentile devotion to the elements on the basis of their mutual concern with calendrical observances. Interestingly, Josephus gives an example of how a Jewish writer could apply the common conception of a four-element universe to the temple as microcosm of the entire world (*Antiquities of the Jews* 3:183). See the most recent discussion of the elements in Woyke 2008:221-34.

[41] Arnold 1996:55-76. See the similar position taken in Forbes 2001:81-3.

[42] Adams 2000:230-1; Delling 1971:670-87. This does not necessarily exclude the notion that the calendrical observances referred to by Paul in Gal 4:10 may reflect observance of the Roman imperial cult practices. This has been argued in Witulski 2000:152-68 and is taken up by Hardin 2008:116-47. Earthly powers were typically associated with spiritual powers in the ancient world.

elements with archaic pairs of opposites to interpret the *religious* impact of Christ's advent."[43] Despite the intriguing and creative insight this may bring, it strains the text beyond reasonable limits. It is not at all clear that the Galatians would have concluded from the pairs of opposites mentioned in the baptismal confession of 3:28 that this understanding was at play. Furthermore, this interpretation does not adequately deal with Paul's understanding of the elements' relationship to the "beings (τοῖς φύσει)" of 4:8.[44] Yet Martyn does acknowledge the idea that however we understand the expression τὰ στοιχεῖα τοῦ κόσμου, it is best viewed in some relation to the physical elements of the cosmos.[45]

Even if this point may be granted, Paul can obviously use terms differently in various contexts.[46] What evidence is there to suggest that Paul's use of κόσμος in 6:14 would have reminded the Galatians of its occurrence in 4:3? The objection could be raised at this point that Paul's understanding of his own crucifixion to the world as having occurred in the past (Gal 6:14) in conjunction with the present reality of the new creation (Gal 6:15) necessitates a non-cosmological understanding of these terms. This is especially true given the evidence that Paul understood the renewal/recreation of the physical world to be a future reality (cf. 1 Cor 15:23-28, 51-5; Rom 8:18-25). However, Paul understands the Christ event to have brought an eschatological revolution which he articulates in terms reminiscent of Jewish apocalyptic eschatology. In this context the term "world" may be understood similarly to Paul's conception of the ages (cf. 1:4).

One text which makes this clear occurs in his later writing to the Corinthians. In 1 Cor 7:31 Paul sees this age "tottering on its last legs and passing away."[47] The ethical stance which he takes toward the issue of marriage in this passage is founded on his conviction that "the form (σχῆμα) of this world (κόσμου) is passing away (παράγει)."[48] Paul's inaugurated eschatology is clearly at work in his use of the present tense of παράγω. The Christ event has brought the present world under judgment so that "time has been shortened/compressed (ὁ καιρὸς συνεσταλμένος ἐστίν)"

---

[43] Martyn 1997b:139.

[44] Martyn 1997c:410-11. Martyn acknowledges the reality of spiritual beings but focuses in his explanation of 4:8 on the idea that "Idols, however, are mere things, not beings in their own right...." This may be true but it fails to note how Paul understood demonic powers to lie behind the idols (cf. 1 Cor 8:5; 10:20-21). He does, however, acknowledge that the starting point for understanding this phrase is the material world.

[45] Martyn 1997c:128.

[46] The term κόσμος elsewhere in Paul provides a good example of this principle.

[47] Garland 2003:65.

[48] Fee 1987:338.

(1 Cor 7:29).⁴⁹ Paul allows for participation in the normal affairs of life but urges participation ὡς μή (7:29-31) because of the uncertainty of life and the evanescence of the present order.⁵⁰ As Adams cogently argued,

> There is no contextual warrant for assuming that the cosmological overtones of the traditional apocalyptic motif which Paul is taking over here are either being eliminated or played down...The apocalyptic event of the cross and resurrection has, in principle, set in motion the process that will lead to final cosmic destruction.⁵¹

In essence, there has been a temporal shift in the ages catalysed by the Christ event (1 Cor 10:11; Gal 3:19-4:7). It is precisely in this event that the anticipated cosmic renewal has begun. Although the "form of the world" remains intact in some sense, there is a real sense in which the death of Christ marks the beginning of the destruction of the old cosmos and his resurrection – the actual renewal of his physical body – marks the inauguration of the expected renewal of creation which was to occur at the end of time.⁵² In this way, the apostle Paul can be said to espouse a "Christological eschatology" and this is perfectly in line with what Betz refers to as "Christological soteriology" in his comments on 1:4.⁵³

The first evidence we can garner to support the claim that Paul's use of the term κόσμος in 6:14 may have resonated with the cosmological associations of 4:3 is in the way that the verb στοιχέω is used in this letter.⁵⁴ Paul uses στοιχέω twice in Galatians to great rhetorical effect (5:25; 6:16).⁵⁵ In 5:16 Paul gives the admonition to walk by the Spirit and not to gratify the desires of the flesh. The verb used for "walk" in this verse,

---

⁴⁹ Garland 2003:328. Note the use of καιρός (1 Cor 7:29) rather than χρόνος (7:39). See Thiselton's excellent discussion on the language of "Eschatological Imminence" in Thiselton 2000:580-3.

⁵⁰ Here "world" is not the constant universe of stoicism but should be understood in the "dramatic world-view characteristic of late Jewish eschatology." Schweitzer quoted in Thiselton 2000:586.

⁵¹ Adams 2000:135, 130-6.

⁵² This gives a fuller explanation to Adams' argument that, "For Paul, the cross has not brought about the expected cosmic transformation or re-creation, but it has in some way started the ball rolling toward that end." Adams 2000:227. Cf. Longenecker 1998:45.

⁵³ Hamilton 1957:38. Betz articulates this specifically in contrast to anthropologically or cosmologically focused soteriology. See Betz 1979:37. Note the Christocentric position argued in Gaventa 1991:147-59. Cf. Lambrecht 1994:299-306.

⁵⁴ Στοιχέω is used twice outside Galatians (Rom 4:12; Phil 3:16).

⁵⁵ If the following interpretation is correct, the appearance of συστοιχέω in 4:25 could be extremely significant. As Bruce 1982:220 argues, "If [Hagar] corresponds to the present Jerusalem...it is not so much the literal city that is meant as the whole legal system of Judaism, which had its world-centre in Jerusalem." Martyn explains this correspondence in terms of the Pythagorean understanding of the world's arrangement in polar opposites (Martyn 1997c:438-9).

περιπατέω, is used 17 times in Paul in each case essentially meaning "to behave." At the end of the passage of ethical exhortations in vv. 24-5, Paul asserts that those who have crucified the flesh and live by the Spirit should also "walk" by the Spirit (NAS, RSV, ESV). However, the verb often translated "walk" in this context is not περιπατέω but στοιχέω.

This verb change could be a simple stylistic variation, yet a synonymous understanding of these terms would be unique to the NT as στοιχέω was understood in the Greek world as "to be in agreement with."[56] It was even used in the military sense "to belong to a series" or "to be in rank."[57] This background gives important nuance to the meaning of the term as it is used here in the context of the cosmic battle between flesh and Spirit. Paul is exhorting the readers to be in agreement with the Spirit, to file in the ranks of the eschatological war against the flesh. Although care must be taken not to assume that words with similar roots necessarily share a semantic field, the term στοιχέω may very well have reminded the Galatians of the enslavement to the στοιχεῖα to which Paul referred in 4:4, 9.[58] The crucifixion of the former world (along with its enslaving forces) made its building blocks obsolete for the new creation. Paul exhorts his readers to build with better materials – the Spirit and not the flesh. Thus, it seems to miss the force of Paul's language simply to translate this verb as "walk." In effect, Paul was saying, "You have been enslaved to the elements of the cosmos. Those elements are no longer valid for constructing your lives. Instead, build your lives according to the blueprints of the Spirit – with the elements of the new creation. Order your existence with these things and you will experience freedom."[59]

The verb is used again in 6:16 where Paul pronounces a benediction to "those who follow this rule (ὅσοι τῷ κανόνι τούτῳ στοιχήσουσιν)." The conditional blessing of the benediction stands in stark contrast to the curse at the beginning of the letter (1:9).[60] As the term κανών means literally "a straight standard of measurement," the use of στοιχέω in the sense of ordering something according to a particular standard would have had particular resonance. In this case the standard is stated in v. 15 – new crea-

---

[56] Delling 1971:668.

[57] Delling 1971:666-69.

[58] This is especially possible given G. Stanton's discussion of Galatians as an oral text in which the "sound map" should be given consideration. Cf. Stanton 1996:99-116.

[59] Thanks to G. K. Beale for prompting my thinking along these lines. See the significant study on the theme of freedom as new creation in Vollenweider 1989. Though, somewhat disappointingly, the title suggests more discussion of the Pauline καινὴ κτίσις than the book contains.

[60] See the helpful discussion in Weima 1995:194-7.

tion.⁶¹ Those who live in synchronous harmony with this rule are called the Israel of God.⁶² This usage of στοιχέω in association with καινὴ κτίσις, and in immediate proximity to the reference to κόσμος in 6:14, may have triggered the Galatians' memory of Paul's earlier discussion of the στοιχεῖα τοῦ κόσμου and may provide evidence that he would have expected them to take his cosmic language at face value.

Further evidence to support this may be found in Paul's identification of the Law in Gal 4 with the enslaving elements of the cosmos (4:3, 5) and his limitation of its influence. He makes clear that the enslaving power of the elements, and by extension the law, has passed. The change is said to occur in the "fullness of time (τὸ πλήρωμα τοῦ χρόνου)" when "God sent forth his son."⁶³ In 6:14 it is the cross of Christ which brings about the demise of the old cosmos. This leads negatively to the end of the religious distinctions inherent to the law (6:15a) and positively to the new creation (6:15b). Thus in both chapters 4 and 6 we have an "old world," of which the Law was an integral part, which meets its end through the Christ event.

Unlike some strands of Jewish tradition prevalent in Paul's day in which the law was eternal and intrinsic to the creation and sustaining of the cosmos (Prov 8:22-30; *1 En.* 99:2; *2 Bar.* 59:2; *Pss. Sol.* 10:4; *Jub.* 6:14; 13:26; 15:25; Philo, *Planting* 1:8; Matt 5:18), Paul placed a temporal restriction upon its efficacy.⁶⁴ Thus, Paul's teaching about the Law would jeopardize the stability of the created order and "result in nothing else than [its] complete collapse."⁶⁵ The reference to καινὴ κτίσις in this context

---

⁶¹ See the section, *"New Creation Epistemology as Apostolic Defense,"* in the next chapter. Note the recent discussion of Paul's epistemology with an emphasis on Galatians in Scott 2006.

⁶² See the section below on *"Israel of God."*

⁶³ For a discussion of links between this sending formula and Rom 8:3-4 in the context of broader discussion about how Paul applied Jewish thinking about "exalted transcendent figures" to Christ, see Chester 1991:78, 72-3.

⁶⁴ For an excellent discussion on the "Perpetuity of the Law," see Moore 1927:263-80. In a tantalizing discussion of the perpetuity of the Law as compared with the limitations on the natural order where the Law's longevity is said even to outlast the material world (cf. Isa 51:6), Moore points out that the meaning of eternity cannot be pressed beyond the "present order." He acknowledges the anticipation of cosmic catastrophe which would make way for a new world which the Jews referred to as "the age to come" in distinction from "this age" (cf. Isa 24-27; 65:13ff). Moore 1927:270-1.

⁶⁵ Longenecker 1998:118-19. Note Philo's emphasis on the eternity of the world (e.g. *Eternity* 1:109). For support of the idea that the Law is eternal and provides the foundation of the world, see Philo's *Planting* 1:8; *Moses* 2:48, 51. Philo also held that "the law corresponds to the world and the world to the law" (*Creation* 1:3).

suggests that Paul may have been aware of this tradition. Paul's challenge to the law's potency would therefore necessitate an entirely new world.[66]

As Longenecker points out, Paul would not have feared the dissolution of the world because he saw Christ "as the embodiment of wisdom (e.g. 1 Cor 1:24; Col 1:15-20) and found in him all the attributes of wisdom previously associated with Torah."[67] Indeed, Paul holds the crucified Christ as the wisdom of God (1 Cor 1:24) who not only created and sustains the world (1 Cor 8:6; Col 1:16-17) but whose work brings reconciliation and redemption to all things (Col 2:20; Rom 8:19ff.). For Paul, "Christologie ist...die Krisis der Theologie."[68] He understood the new creation to have begun in Christ's death and resurrection.

Understanding the intricate connection between the law and the cosmos is part of a broader correspondence between chapters 4 and 6.[69] In both passages, Paul makes note of the previous connection which believers had with the κόσμος (4:3; 6:14), and in both passages this connection was severed (4:5, 7, 9; 6:14). The Jew/Gentile distinction is part of the old κόσμος (4:3-4; 6:15a); so, to receive circumcision was to return to the κόσμος from which they had been rescued (1:4). These corresponding components make a significant case that κόσμος is used similarly in both passages. When seen in this light, the contrast between κόσμος and καινὴ κτίσις represents an "apocalyptic framework" of "spatio-temporal dualism" which functions as "[a tool] for constructing in Galatia a Christian social world separate from the Jewish community."[70]

---

[66] It would be intriguing in this context to explore how the Law was considered foundational for the world and how the new covenant would imply a change in the created order. Cf. Philo, *Creation* 1:3, 143; *Gen. Rab.* 1:1.2.B, "...the Torah speaks, 'I was the work-plan of the Holy One, blessed be he.' In the accepted practice of the world, when a mortal king builds a palace, he does not build it out of his own head, but he follows a work-plan. And [the one who supplies] the work-plan does not build out of his own head, but he has design and diagrams, so as to know how to situate the rooms and the doorways. Thus the Holy One, blessed be he, consulted the Torah when he created the world. So the Torah stated, 'By means of "the beginning" [that is to say, the Torah] did God create...' (Gen 1:1). And the word for 'beginning' refers only to the Torah, as Scripture says, 'The Lord made me as the beginning of his way' (Prov 8:22)."

[67] Longenecker 1998:119.

[68] Mell 1989:293.

[69] Adams 2000:229. Adams employs points out how 6:14-15 can enlighten our understanding of 4:3, 9. I am using the earlier statement to interpret the latter which seems to me to be what the original hearers are more likely to have done.

[70] Adams 2000:231-2. Adams's research makes clear that σάρξ rather than κόσμος is the prevailing negative term in Galatians as opposed to Corinthians where κόσμος plays a much more significant role. His explanation for this is that Paul's letter to the Corinthians was an attempt to distinguish believers from the surrounding (Greco-Roman) society. Σάρξ, Adams argues, is obviously more appropriate in the light of the Galatian controversy regarding circumcision and the group-boundary between Christians and Jews. If

One further observation from the dominant culture in which Paul operated may help us understand how the term κόσμος might have been heard in the Galatian congregations. Despite various understandings of the κόσμος in Greek/Hellenistic culture, there were some standard ideas which the use of the term κόσμος brought to mind.[71] Particularly interesting for our purposes is the way in which the κόσμος was viewed as a unified whole: the sum of all existence. Humans serve not only as constituent parts, but to embody the superlative characteristics of the cosmos; the individual is considered to be a microcosm of the cosmos itself.[72] This microcosm-macrocosm relationship is not restricted to the individual. It also applies to human society in relation to the cosmos.[73] Therefore, if the Greco-Roman world could envisage such a connection between the individual and the cosmos and if, as argued above (see my chapters on New Creation in Jewish Sources), such a connection was also possible within Judaism, the broad soteriology advocated in this thesis which involved both the person and the world should be considered as a serious alternative to those approaches which emphasize one of these entities at the expense of the other.

C. The New Creation and the New Age

In P.T. O'Brien's work on Paul's introductory thanksgivings, he has made the compelling case that the concerns of the letters may often be discerned from their opening remarks.[74] Paul's letter to the Galatians is, however, not included in this study because the usual thanksgivings are absent. This fact makes the opening statements of this correspondence all the more impor-

---

this is true, it would weaken my case, at least in Galatia, that the Roman imperial ideology is at play. However there may be a way to avoid this, especially if we understand imperial ideology at play elsewhere under the surface of the letter.

[71] I am relying here on E. Adams' careful study. He lists five of these perceptions. See Adams 2000:64-9.

[72] Plato, *Timaeus* 30d; 44d-45b; Cicero, *On the Nature of the Gods* 2:11-14. Cited in Adams 2000:66. Cf. Ego 1989.

[73] This issue is taken up in my chapter on "The State and the World" in reference to Roman Imperial influence. Note especially the sociological study of Adams 2000:71 which shows that, "By encoding the microcosmic-macrocosmic link between society and the cosmic order, ... κόσμος (= world/universe) served not only to justify and endorse the existing social and political order, but to do so in a comprehensive and powerful way." Cf. Philo, *Joseph* 1:29; *Moses* 2:37; *Rewards* 1:23. Aune intimates this as well in Aune 1993:30-1.

[74] O'Brien 1977:2-3.

C. The New Creation and the New Age

tant for understanding it.[75] Two quite significant pieces of information from the opening (1:1-4) play an important role in this letter.

First is the highly unusual reference to the resurrection in the very first verse (cf. Rom 1:4) which secures the importance of this aspect of the Christ event in the letter as a whole.[76] Given the eschatological associations which this idea would have evoked, we have good reason to suspect that the remainder of this letter will be articulated in an eschatological matrix.[77] While the only explicit reference to the resurrection occurs here, it operates in connection with the crucifixion throughout the argument. The connection is clearest in two locations: 2:19-20 and 6:14-15.[78] Both of these texts speak of a co-crucifixion with Christ and both suggest a resulting new life. Since both of these passages are constructed upon the principle of identification with Christ and both portray his crucifixion followed by life, it is perfectly sensible to take this as an intimation of the resurrection.[79] This adumbrates Paul's later comments on the believer's identification with Christ's resurrection in Rom 6:4-11 (cf. Eph 2:6; Col 2:12; 3:1),[80] identification which becomes especially important if resurrection was understood as part of YHWH's renewal of creation (e.g. Isa 65-66; Ps 103:30 LXX).[81]

Secondly, if both the beginning and the ending of the letter connect organically to its body, we may reasonably posit a relationship between the introduction and conclusion. Like complementary bookends, these two

---

[75] Note Hubbard's recognition that the contrasts which mark the closing of the letter are important for understanding the way Paul distinguishes himself from the agitators in the beginning of the letter (Hubbard 2002:192). Nevertheless, he somewhat surprisingly argues that the reference to the "present evil age" is too far removed from the context to influence the interpretation of 6:15.

[76] Note the reference to the "promise of life that is in Christ Jesus" in 1 Tim 1:1. This is interesting given the eschatological thrust of this letter and especially the attempt by the writer to refute the erroneous teaching that the resurrection had already taken place (2:18).

[77] Note the way in which the resurrection is specifically associated with the age to come in *Adam and Eve* 51:2.

[78] These two passages are discussed in detail below in the section, *"The Christ Event and Inaugurated Eschatology in Galatians."*

[79] Silva 2001:177-80.

[80] It is acknowledged that Rom 6 sees the completion of this identification in the future (note the future tenses of vv. 5, 8 – ἐσόμεθα, συζήσομεν). However, Paul sees this as having already begun in the life of the believer at present (Rom 6:4). This verse focuses on the ethical quality of the life of the believer based on the power of the resurrection but it does not simply refer to ethical improvement. Through the believer's identification with Christ, Paul views the believers already in some way as participants in the power of his resurrection existence. See Eckstein 1997:8-23.

[81] See my chapter on New Creation in Romans. Cf. Wright 2003, 219-25; Chester 2001:77.

parts of the letter hold together the message which Paul communicates between. Several pieces of evidence support this observation. First, both the introduction and conclusion are concerned with a defence of Paul's apostolic authority. Paul goes out of his way in the letter's opening to establish the divine, rather than human origin of his office. His apostleship is "not from men and not through man but through Jesus Christ and God the Father..." (1:1).[82] Similarly, the conclusion takes pains to place Paul's life in sharp contrast to that of the agitators (6:14, 17). Secondly, as mentioned above, the use of the "resurrection formula"[83] can be associated with the new creation since the resurrection was viewed in contemporary Judaism as a characteristic part of the renewal of the world.[84] Finally, the redemptive accomplishment of the Christ event was seen to rescue (ἐξαιρέω)[85] the Galatians from "this present evil age" (1:4).[86] Paul's use of the term αἰών resonates with the eschatological construct of Paul's thought. The term may be used interchangeably with κόσμος (cf. 1 Cor 1:20; 2:6, 8; 3:18-19).[87] The Christ event serves as the bridge from the present age to the new age.[88]

Whether or not Gal 1:4 actually signals the beginning of a new age is disputed. Betz (cf. Kwon, Hubbard, et al.) argues that Paul merely speaks of the end of one age and not the beginning of another. In first century Judaism, however, there was a fundamental conception of history in terms of a division of ages (*4 Ezra* 7:12-13, 113; 8:1; *2 Bar.* 44:11-14; cf. 1QpHab 5:7) and the influence of this tradition on Paul has been commonly recognized among Pauline scholars.[89] To be sure, this interpretational paradigm could become something of a procrustean bed. The charge of approaching Paul with overly enthusiastic apocalyptic fervour could be levelled against some current interpretations of his writing.[90] This, however, should not be allowed to obscure the fact that apocalyptic literature could have influ-

---

[82] We should avoid attempting to mirror-read the charges against Paul brought by the agitators at this point but it is nonetheless clear that Paul is making a significant point of the divine origin of his commission.

[83] Betz 1979:39.

[84] See Schwantes 1962.

[85] For a discussion of Paul's use of this term in conjunction with αἰών, see Silva 1994a:110, 119-20, 141-3, 167-8. Note the works which examine the use of Exodus themes in this letter: Kirschläger 1986:332-9; Keesmaat 1997:300-33; Wilson 2004:550-71; Morales 2007:1-16, 108-83.

[86] Cf. *L.A.E.* 29:3, "this age"; *2 En.* 66:6, "this age of ills"; Bovon 1978:91-107.

[87] Schlier 1962:33. This becomes especially poignant in the light of the contrast between the κόσμος and the καινὴ κτίσις in 6:14-15.

[88] Schlier 1962:34.

[89] Most notably in J.L. Martyn. See Martyn 1997c:97-105. For a helpful discussion on the use of the term, see Sasse 1964:197-209. Cf. Dunn 1993:36.

[90] This tendency is artfully critiqued in Matlock 1996.

enced Paul. Long before such "apocalyptic fervour" became fashionable, Burton observed,

> There is no doubt that Paul held the current Jewish doctrine of the two ages, and though he never definitely places the coming of the Lord in judgment on the wicked and salvation for believers at the boundary line between the two ages, his language is most naturally understood as implying this....[91]

In contrast to the eschatology of the Jewish traditions which influenced him, Paul shifts the eschatological focus from strictly future to a view which incorporated the past so that the Christ event becomes God's decisive incursion into the world.[92] Of course, the rescue provided by Christ is not a rescue from corporeal existence but it is intimately connected with the resurrection life of the future based ultimately on a positive valuing of creation and its Creator. Believers "share the risen life of Christ (cf. 2:19f.), who has already entered the resurrection age."[93] The Spirit both empowers the life of faith which anticipates the fullness of future salvation and enables believers to live this victorious life in the present (5:16-26).[94] The presence of the Spirit is itself an indicator that the anticipated last days had arrived (Gal 3:2-5, 14; 4:6; 5:5, 16-18, 22, 25; cf. Isa 44:3; Joel 2:28; Acts 2:17).[95] In this regard, it is difficult to improve on the words of Gordon Fee:

> Absolutely presuppositional to the Pauline understanding is the Spirit as the main eschatological reality, the certain evidence that the future has begun and the guarantee of its consummation. Although this note is sounded less here than elsewhere, it is so foundational for Paul that it can scarcely stay silenced. Hence in 5:5, besides everything else, the Spirit supersedes Torah precisely because his presence guarantees our hope that Christ's righteousness has afforded. But even more so, as in 2 Corinthians 3, Paul understands the Spirit himself as the fulfilment of God's promise, in this case, including the promise made to Abraham that included his blessing of the Gentiles (3:13-14).[96]

---

[91] Burton 1921:14; cf. pp. 426-31.
[92] Martyn 1997c:97-105.
[93] Bruce 1982:76. On the Spirit's role in new creation, see Yates 2007.
[94] Hamilton 1957:17-40.
[95] Cf. Philip 2005. The recent work of Morales argues that the eschatological life given by the Spirit is the fulfillment of YHWH's restoration promises to Israel through the prophets. See Morales 2007:233-8.
[96] Fee 1994:470; cf. pp. 390-5, 417-19, 803-26. Kwon strongly objects in Kwon 2004:107-15. However, Kwon has misunderstood Paul's conception of the Abrahamic promise. The point Paul is making has to do with the blessing YHWH promises *upon the nations* through Abraham by means of the seed (Gal 5:8, 16-18). This is crucial to understanding Paul's message of the gospel (cf. 5:8). The inclusion of Gentiles, without the need for circumcision, is an eschatological sign that the promise is being fulfilled.

The most explicit statement of identification for the new age in Galatians occurs in 6:15 where Paul speaks of the new creation.[97] As argued above, the links between the opening and closing of this letter suggest that these statements are not isolated assertions separated by the length of the argument. The curse pronounced upon those who disagree with Paul at the beginning (1:6-9), and the conditional blessing upon those who fall into line with Paul's understanding of the gospel in the end (6:16), support the idea that the opening and closing of the letter are closely linked.[98] Furthermore, the already noted contrast between the κόσμος in 6:14 and the καινὴ κτίσις in 6:15 makes the association of the καινὴ κτίσις with the new age more likely.[99]

D. Paul's Modification of "Jewish Apocalyptic Eschatology"

It should be no surprise that the concept of new creation held great eschatological import for Paul as it had been quite significant for Jewish writers who employed it to speak of the zenith of God's actions in the future. The extent to which Jewish apocalyptic eschatology has influenced Paul's thought has been the subject of much debate within Pauline scholarship since Albert Schweitzer's initial emphasis on its importance in the early 20th century.[100] In the ensuing debate, R. Bultmann and E. Käsemann represent opposite poles of understanding. Bultmann focused on Paul's interest in the actualization of the message of faith in the experience of the individual and sought to "demythologize" the cosmological apocalyptic traditions. Käsemann, on the other hand, argued against such an anthropocentric interpretation of Paul's theology. He accused Bultmann of an over-realized eschatology and sought to preserve the aspect of God's future working as it was recorded in the Pauline corpus. He argued that Jewish

---

[97] Hubbard 2002:216 argues that Gal 1:4 is too far away in the context to influence our understanding of 6:15 in this way. But this fails to take into consideration the importance of the letter opening and closing and the relation between them.

[98] Betz 1975:378-9.

[99] An impressive array of texts and scholars support this association. See *Jub.* 1:29; 4:26; *1 En.* 72:1. Cf. Isa 65:17; 66:22; Rev 21:1; 2 Pet 3:13; *1 En* 91:16-17; *4 Ezra* 7:75; *2 Bar.* 32:6; 44:11-12. Cf. Kwon 2004:172. Kwon rejects the proposition that καινὴ κτίσις is a reference to the new age on the grounds that the phrase functions ethically in Galatians. He interprets καινὴ κτίσις as a way of speaking about the rule (κανών) to which the believers should aspire. See my criticism of this position below.

[100] De Boer 1989:169-90.

D. Paul's Modification of "Jewish Apocalyptic Eschatology"

apocalyptic eschatology should be thought of as more cosmologically than anthropologically oriented.[101]

J. Beker took up the mantle carried by Käsemann by developing further the centrality of apocalyptic eschatology for Paul's thinking though he saw Galatians as an exception to the general rule since it did not indicate an imminent expectation of the parousia.[102] J. L. Martyn, however, applied this interpretive paradigm to Galatians to great effect. In his commentary on Galatians, Martyn argues that Paul's theological matrix is one of apocalyptic eschatology. He achieves valuable insight but his use of the term "apocalyptic" presents difficulty. This term has been used in contemporary scholarship in various and sometimes contradictory ways which has left us far from a consensus on its meaning. Martyn seems to use the term to refer to the revelatory nature of God's action in and through Christ. However, the use of the terms "apocalyptic" and "apocalypse" to describe Paul's gospel obfuscates the distinction between Paul's writing and the actual literary genre of Jewish apocalyptic writings. Although Paul's writings bear theological resemblance to and reflect parallels with the ideas found in the genre of Jewish apocalyptic, they are not technically in this genre and should rather be seen as documents which embody what Paul perceived to be the nature of the end-times. Thus, it is more accurate to speak of Paul's writings as eschatological.[103] In fact, it is through Paul's eschatology that his writings are thrown into sharp contrast with the Jewish apocalyptic works.[104]

The contrast can be seen quite clearly in Paul's understanding of the new creation.[105] It has been suggested that an essential difference between Paul and apocalyptic literature is that apocalyptic literature sees the major problems of humanity as being external – generally the oppression of foreign powers.[106] The cosmic language of new creation would then serve as a way of offering a solution to this perceived plight. In contrast, Paul considered the more pressing problem to be human sin, an internal dilemma requiring an internal solution – the complete renovation of the person.[107] However, as we have seen in our exploration of the Jewish apocalyptic lit-

---

[101] Ibid. Interestingly, M. de Boer astutely shows that both Bultmann's and Käsemann's positions are supported by different emphases within Jewish apocalyptic writings: forensic and cosmological.

[102] Beker 1980.

[103] Cf. Stanton 2000:264-70.

[104] The term "eschatological" is used here to indicate the sense that "God has acted, continues to act, and will ultimately act decisively, establishing a world set right that will, in the end, include all things without remainder." See Longenecker 1998:22ff.

[105] Whether the phrase was used in this manner in pre-Pauline Christian traditions is beyond the scope of this thesis. See Weima 1993:101-2.

[106] Hubbard 2002:52-3.

[107] Hubbard 2002:153-60.

erature, these works also can focus on the problem of human sin and have both an internal as well as an external emphasis.[108] Likewise, Paul's concern is not simply with the individual but with the external powers under which people are held hostage.[109]

The real distinction between Paul and the apocalyptic writings occurs in an area where there is clearly similarity – the division of time into two successive ages. The present age, a world hostile in its manifold rebellion against God, will be overtaken by the new age of the Spirit when God will overcome all opposition to his rule (cf. *4 Ezra* 4:26; 7:50). Whereas this intervention of God is viewed as a future event in the apocalyptic literature, Paul interpreted the Christ event as the pivotal crux of history which brought the old age to a close and initiated the subsequent and final age of God's reign.

In this manner, Paul modified the Jewish thinking in which he had been steeped. He placed the time of God's most radical invasion of the world in the past in the events of the life, death and resurrection of Christ.[110] Paul inverts the future oriented hope of God's actions described with new creation language in Jewish writings into an eschatological system where the epicenter of God's cosmic earthquake was located in the past; and, at the same time, he maintained an expectation for the consummation of that action in the future.[111] There was a form of this eschatological tension in some Jewish writings from our period (see my chapter on "Early Jewish Literature") but the focus lay in the future whereas Paul's writing included two foci: the future as well as the past.[112] This is placed in sharp relief in

---

[108] Thanks to Jonathan Moo for helpful discussions on this point. See his forthcoming work which recognizes this phenomenon in *4 Ezra*.

[109] These can be spiritual and even take physical form as in the "elements of the world" or in the political ideologies which make conflicting claims of sovereignty with the rule of God in the world.

[110] Furnish 1984:333-4.

[111] Kwon prefers to speak about an organic relationship in eschatological perspectives rather than an eschatological tension. However, a tension does arise when we attempt to explain how Paul can seem to suggest so much has been accomplished for the believer in one instance and in another suggest so much is left to come. The tension is not with God but with how to explain the presence of evil even after the cross. In the end, Kwon's preference for an organic relationship between the present and future may just be a way of sneaking in the old understanding of inaugurated eschatology under cover of different terminology.

[112] See the excellent work of Minear 1962:23-37 on apocalyptic cosmology. Interestingly, the book of Revelation is the exception which proves the rule. This is the only actual apocalyptic writing which has a similar eschatological tension and this is precisely because it is predicated on the Christ event.

Galatians where Paul's bifocal eschatology is in operation throughout the argument.[113]

E. The Christ Event and Inaugurated Eschatology in Galatians

Despite a paucity of explicit references to the future (5:5; 6:8) or to the resurrection (1:1), the eschatology of Galatians maintains the bifocal character just noted. This eschatology is predicated on the accomplishment of Christ in his death and resurrection. The crucial placement of eschatological themes within the letter provides the framework upon which Paul builds his theological construction. The terrain of the discussion in this letter rises to at least three major points of emphasis which form a series of peaks in the letter (2:19-21; 4:4-6; 6:14-16).[114] Depending upon one's approach to Galatians as a whole, any of these peaks could be taken to represent the epistle's theological centre; however, taken together, they form an important range of theological ideas reaching its summit in the final passage which encapsulates the theological force of the letter as a whole. It is the concept of καινὴ κτίσις which forms the highest point of this eschatological landscape.

The first of these peaks (2:19-21) is especially important given that it contains a parallel concept with 6:14. It serves as the conclusion to a very difficult passage full of exegetical conundrums but our purposes will be served by focusing on the intensely eschatological nature of the passage.[115] In a striking assertion, Paul indicates that he has died to the law through the law itself. This death occurs through co-crucifixion with Christ, an important identification, but there is another element of identification with Christ which is intimated but left unspoken, that of resurrection. Paul is said both to be dead to the law and alive to God. The life which follows

---

[113] For a study of the eschatological associations of the concept of newness in the NT, see Harrisville 1955:69-79.

[114] To this list could be added Paul's autobiographical statements in Gal 1:15-17. These verses maintain Paul's apologetic thrust in support of his apostolic authority. They embody some of the anthropological elements of Paul's soteriology. They also indicate that Paul places himself in line with prophetic tradition. See Sandnes 1991:69; Ciampa 1998:295-6. However, Paul's individual experience is only important insofar as it is "moulded by the 'master pattern' of the crucifixion and new creation." See Barclay 2002:153. Cf. Horrell 2002:166-8.

I have chosen to focus on these three passages because of their generally recognized importance in the flow of the letter and because of the insight they offer into the eschatological pitch of Galatians as a whole.

[115] Silva 1994b:149ff.

death here is a new kind of life which is lived by faith. That this life follows death (crucifixion) by way of identification with Christ, and in reference to the Christ event, is an unmistakable indication that the resurrection is in mind, since Christ's resurrection followed on the heels of his crucifixion and was believed by Paul to provide the basis for a resurrection hope for believers (cf. 1 Cor 15:3-4, 12-28).

While Paul clearly shifts his focus to the cross in Galatians, it must not be overlooked that the invasion of God into the old age did not end with the cross.[116] Rather, God's ultimate battle of the ages was marked by a victory so great it defeated the most potent enemy of all – death itself. It was admittedly a victory only partly realized (since death is still in operation until the final resurrection), but in some way the effects of the ultimate end-time resurrection promised to believers are viewed as already operative (1:1, 4; cf. Rom 6:4, 11).

The second theological peak (4:4-6) is important for understanding the eschatological outlook of the letter. Leaving aside the question of the provenance of vv. 4-5,[117] essential to this thesis is the eschatological context in which Paul places the "sending" of Christ,[118] which is to occur "when the fullness of time had come."[119] Betz notes that this phrase "belongs to the Jewish and Christian eschatological language which Paul shared."[120] These verses form part of a larger section replete with eschatological emphases. In Paul's explanation of the function of the law (3:19), he underscores the transitory nature of the law's effectiveness.[121] It was given for a period, "until the offspring should come to whom the promise had been made." Paul had already argued that the offspring referenced here is Christ. His coming marks the end of the era of redemptive history determined by the law and the beginning of that determined by Christ.[122] The new period is characterised by faith rather than law: "...before faith came...until the faith which was about to be revealed," "now that faith has come..." (3:23, 25).[123] As Paul has held up the exemplary faith of Abra-

---

[116] Cf. Martyn 1997c:97ff.

[117] For fuller discussion, see Longenecker 1990:166-70.

[118] See the important work on this idea in Schweizer 1966:199-210.

[119] The occurrence of this phrase in the papyri indicates that it may refer to the temporal fulfillment of contractual terms (P Tebt II. 374; P Oxy XIV. 1641; P Lond 1168). Cf. Moulton and Milligan 1930:520. Contra: Martyn 1997c:389.

[120] Betz 1979:206. Betz cites: Eph 1:10; Mark 1:15; 16:14; John 7:8; Heb 1:2; 1QS 4:18f; 1QM 15:15; 1QpHab 7:13.

[121] Cf. Smith 2006:197-214; Gordon 1989:150-4.

[122] Silva 2001:177-80.

[123] The translations are mine. For an excellent study of Paul's understanding of faith, see the unpublished doctoral work of Taylor 2004. Taylor argues against recent attempts to downplay the importance faith as an individual response to the gospel. For him, Paul's understanding of faith is Christocentric and eschatological in nature.

E. The Christ Event and Inaugurated Eschatology in Galatians

ham earlier in this chapter, it is clear that he did not believe faith to have been absent before the coming of Christ (3:6-8), but this faith looked forward to the faith to be revealed in Christ. Paul intimates this in the assertion that what Abraham believed was actually the gospel (3:8). The coming of faith, then, is the primary means thorough which the eschatological blessings are to be received (3:2, 5, 26, 28).[124] It is Paul's way of marking the passing of one era and the beginning of a new era. This new era is signalled in 4:4, "But when the fullness of time had come, God sent his Son...."[125]

Paul communicates this same idea in the final theological peak of his letter: 6:14-15. The use of the verb σταυρόω in 6:14 conveys the centrality of the Christ event for what happened to Paul and to the world. Paul's identification with Christ had meant severing all ties to the old world to the extent that he was completely removed from its sphere of influence. But the old world died, too, when Christ's body, a representative part of that old world, died on the cross. If the new creation (v. 15) is set in opposition to the old world which was destroyed in Christ's crucifixion, it follows that Christ's resurrection was an incipient part of the new creation. It is not just in the cross that the new creation has come about but in the Christ event as a whole. Thus, it is clear that this is no passing reference to the resurrection in the beginning of the letter and no pious rhetoric about the new creation at the end. The Christ event marked the eschatological turn of the ages for Paul and he writes his letter to the Galatians sandwiched between two intricately related references to this theme. This point becomes even stronger when we consider that the letter closing itself apparently serves as an interpretive key to the epistle.[126]

The fact that there is no direct reference to the resurrection in Gal 6 can probably be explained by the idea that this was not one of the planks of Paul's message contested by the agitators.[127] The cross, on the other hand, was in danger of being made redundant because of their teaching that observance of the law was the means for obtaining justification (2:21). Paul focuses on the cross as the eschatological warfare of God in which he invaded the present age and defeated it along with the spiritual powers associated with it (the enslaving voice of the law included) in order to inaugurate an altogether new age. Yet it was not a war fought simply on ethereal cosmic planes. It was warfare in which believers were called to participate in terms of being crucified with Christ (2:19-20; 6:14). This sort of battle imagery is especially suitable since this was given in the context of a de-

---

[124] Taylor 2004 :103.
[125] Cf. *2 Bar.* 30:1 (note the new creation reference in 32:1-7); Mark 1:15; Luke 1:20.
[126] See Weima 1993:90-107.
[127] Martyn 1997c:98-9.

fence of Paul's gospel against the agitators, the struggle with whom was exhibitive of the overlapping of the ages when the old age was defeated but still active.

Paul had spoken of being dead *to the law* in 2:19. In 6:14 he testifies to having been crucified *to the world*. This unexpected connection relates the κόσμος to the νόμος and confirms J. L. Martyn's assertion that the Law is one of the principles which governs the old world, the regency of which has been terminated by God's invasion into it in the Christ event.[128] The period during which the Law was intended to function as παιδαγωγός (3:24-5) had been brought to an end (4:1-5). This is made more palpable in the claim that not only has he died to the world but that the world has died to him. Christ's death had not only destroyed the old order but created a totally new one which came about in the death throes of the old. Paul appeals to this new world in his assertion that the old distinctions no longer matter (6:15), yet, he knew himself to be living in a time of vigorous struggle when some (i.e. the agitators) still operated according to the old distinctions. Though the old world had been defeated, pockets of resistance dotted the terrain of the period best described as the overlapping ages.

F. Eschatological Unity and New Creation

Besides the obvious association with 2 Cor 5:17, two other texts in the Pauline literature are generally recognized to bear close resemblance to Gal 6:15 and are frequently used as aids in the interpretation of Paul's laconic expression, καινὴ κτίσις: Gal 5:6 and 1 Cor 7:19. The similarities between 5:6 and 6:15 were noticed very early as is evidenced by the scribal attempt to assimilate the latter verse to the former by inserting the phrase εν γαρ Χριστω Ιησου ουτε and replacing εστιν with ισχυει. Both verses consist of a devaluation of circumcision *and* uncircumcision followed by the assertion of what Paul feels transcends this previously critical distinction.

Gal 5:6 – ἐν γὰρ Χριστῷ Ἰησοῦ **οὔτε περιτομή** τι ἰσχύει **οὔτε ἀκροβυστία ἀλλὰ** πίστις δι' ἀγάπης ἐνεργουμένη.

Gal 6:15 – **οὔτε γὰρ περιτομή** τί ἐστιν **οὔτε ἀκροβυστία ἀλλὰ** καινὴ κτίσις.

The clear relationship between these texts begs the question of how πίστις δι' ἀγάπης ἐνεργουμένη relates to καινὴ κτίσις.

Galatians 5:6 confirms that Paul's understanding of new creation is certainly applied to humanity, especially in the community of believers. Given his subsequent emphasis on loving one's neighbour as a means of

---

[128] Martyn 1997d:111-123.

F. Eschatological Unity and New Creation

fulfilling the law, it is likely that the love of 5:6 refers to love among those "in Christ,"[129] but the previous statement gives us a clue as to how this fits in with Paul's broader soteriology. In Paul's exposition of freedom in Christ, verses 5 and 6 serve as independent explanatory clauses for verse 4 which states that seeking justification through the law is futile. Paul declares this is true because it is only through the Spirit and by faith that "we eagerly wait for the hope of righteousness" (v. 5). Verse 6 explains this in different terms, and we can understand that statement better if we understand Paul's point in verse 5. The point is not an internal/external juxtaposition (as important as that may be in the broader scope of Paul's thinking). The point at stake is the contrast between works of the law and the gracious work of the Spirit received by faith.

The eagerly awaited hope of righteousness (ἐλπίδα δικαιοσύνης ἀπεκδεχόμεθα) should be seen in the light of Paul's other uses of this anticipatory language. The verb ἀπεκδέχομαι is used exclusively in eschatologically charged contexts in Paul. Bearers of heavenly citizenship, the Philippians "eagerly await" the parousia (Phi 3:20). In close connection with a similar term (ἀποκαραδοκία), Rom 8:19 indicates that "the *eager expectation* (ἀποκαραδοκία) of creation *eagerly awaits* (ἀπεκδέχεται) the revelation of the sons of God."[130] How this passage plays into our understanding of new creation will be discussed in the next chapter. For the time being, it will suffice to point out the eschatological thrust of the language (cf. 1Cor 1:7).

In the context, being ἐν Χριστῷ Ἰησοῦ (5:6) stands over against being "estranged (κατηργήθητε) from Christ" (5:4).[131] The determinative feature securing one's relationship to Christ is not circumcision but faith. The object of the faith mentioned in 5:6 is Christ Jesus.[132] The identification with Christ language has been important throughout (e.g. 2:20) and not surprisingly appears once more in Gal 6:14.

Given the way that the "coming of faith" has been used to speak of a new stage of God's salvific overtures (Gal 3:23-6), it is fairly straightforward to suggest that the new creation which stands in similar position to the working of faith in 5:6 should be seen in a similar eschatological context.[133] The change in scope of the language from 5:6 to 6:15 illustrates well the soteriological breadth of Paul's understanding of the Christ event.

---

[129] Note the following warning against biting, devouring and consuming one another in 5:15 versus the compassionate and unifying interactions of those who walk in the Spirit in 6:2.

[130] The translation is mine. Cf. Rom 8:23, 25.

[131] BDAG, p. 526.

[132] For a helpful discussion of the πίστις Χριστοῦ debate, see Taylor 2004:77-85.

[133] The sonship motif is very important in this regard and will be discussed in the chapter on Romans.

Paul is not writing a cosmology here. Philosophical speculation about the nature or structure of the universe would not have served his pastoral concerns. However, in his understanding, what had happened in the death and resurrection of Jesus had affected the cosmos, particularly when viewed from the temporal perspective of Paul's writings which may have been influenced by the temporal understanding of Jewish apocalyptic literature. Paul's use of the phrases "new creation" and "faith expressing itself through love"[134] represents this chronological change and shows how appropriate is Martyn's observation that sees Galatians as an answer to the question: "What time is it?" Yet this observation does not exhaust the process of interpretation.

Another text which helps to enlighten our perception of 6:15 is 1 Cor 7:19. The phrase corresponding to καινὴ κτίσις is τήρησις ἐντολῶν θεοῦ.

1 Cor 7:19 – ἡ περιτομὴ οὐδέν ἐστιν καὶ ἡ ἀκροβυστία οὐδέν ἐστιν, ἀλλὰ τήρησις ἐντολῶν θεοῦ.

Gal 6:15 – οὔτε γὰρ περιτομή τί ἐστιν οὔτε ἀκροβυστία ἀλλὰ καινὴ κτίσις.

The apparent contradiction between announcing the unimportance of circumcision while at the same time advocating keeping God's commandments has contributed to the opinion held by some scholars that Paul is inconsistent and hopelessly incoherent in his teaching on the law.[135] But the fact that Paul can make such an apparently contradictory statement in a vital attempt to communicate to the Christian community at Corinth is an indication that this approach may not be the most judicious – even if it rightly underscores the difficulty of decoding this enigma. The literature on Paul's understanding of the law is immense and cannot be dealt with adequately within the confines of this thesis.[136] However, a final decision on this exegetical puzzle is not necessary for our purposes.[137]

In the context of 1 Cor 7 the focus of Paul's argument is on compelling his readers/hearers to remain as they are (7:17, 24).[138] The status of cir-

---

[134] The translation is mine. I take ἐνεργουμένη to be present middle as opposed to passive. Mußner 1974:353-4 argues convincingly for this. Cf. BDAG, p. 335.

[135] E.g. Räisänen 1987.

[136] For some important examples, see Dunn 1996; Thielman 1994; Hübner 1984; Sanders 1983.

[137] For further discussion, see Tomson 1996:251-70; Thielman 1994:80-144. In all probability, the reformational concern with justification by faith as opposed to works has led to an association of commandments with works of the law which has been unhelpful in attempts to explain 1 Cor 7:19. See Fee 1987:313.

[138] This broader principle is clear from the following discussion on slavery based on the idea that, "whoever was called in the Lord as a slave is a freed person belonging to

F. Eschatological Unity and New Creation

cumcision/uncircumcision, slave/free and marriage/ singleness are all addressed under the aegis of this principle. Very important for our purposes is the fact that this principle is in part based upon Paul's eschatological perspective.[139] Moving from the discussion of circumcision/uncircumcision to his views on marriage, Paul gives the eschatological ground for his argument in vv. 29-31 (see the above discussion on this passage), and this corresponds to the generally acknowledged eschatological matrix in which this letter is articulated (cf. 1 Cor 1:7-8, 20; 2:6-8; 3:18; 10:11; 15:47-9).[140] This new eschatological reality provides the basis for the ethic which Paul advocates and stands in direct connection to the way Paul applies the new creation ethically in Gal 6:15.

One further text should be considered in this discussion: Gal 3:28. Although this verse is not a syntactic or verbal parallel to Gal 6:15, it bears significant conceptual correspondence. The περιτομή and ἀκροβυστία of Gal 6:15 surely refer to the rite of circumcision but this is obviously the distinguishing mark between Ἰουδαῖος and Ἕλλην (3:28; cf. Gal 2:7-9; Rom 10:12).[141] The connection with 6:15 is strengthened when we see that the three contrasting groups of 3:28 are reflected in 1 Cor 7. The correspondence is not precise and should not be pressed too far, but the similar progression in these two passages can be clearly seen in the following table.

Gal 3:28	1 Cor 7
Jew/Greek	Circumcised/Uncircumcised (7:17-20)
Slave/Free	Slave/Free (7:21-24)
Male/Female	Married/Single (7:25-28)
One in Christ?	Divided Interests/ Undivided Devotion? (7:32-35)

---

the Lord, just as whoever was free when called is a slave of Christ" (7:22). For an investigation of how the scriptures of Israel informed the ethics of Paul, see Rosner 1994.

[139] Winter's suggestion that the ἀνάγκη of 1 Cor 7:26 refers to specific social tensions caused by the grain shortages of ca. A.D. 45-47 does not mitigate the eschatological importance of this passage. It only serves to indicate that Paul's eschatology could envisage, in line with his Jewish contemporaries, changes in the eschaton to affect the natural order. See Winter 1989:86-106.

[140] Adams 2000:105-7. Cf. Hays 2005:1-24.

[141] Contra Hubbard 2002:218-9.

Paul's focus on these three categories poses an interesting question, perhaps having to do with those daily Jewish prayers in which God would be thanked for not creating them as a Gentile, a bondman or a woman.[142] In essence, the very core of the identity of the people of God is redefined, not in terms of one's connection to Abraham but in terms of one's relationship to Christ. Bruce recognizes the similarities between Gal 3:28 and 1 Cor 7, but he does not draw out the implication of this connection.[143] Both of these passages are written in an intensely eschatological context. As argued above, the principle "remain as you are" of 1 Cor 7 is constructed around a view of reality heavily influenced by Paul's eschatology.

His argument is based on a detachment from the importance of human affairs because the "form of this world is passing away" (1 Cor 7:31). In similar fashion, the eschatological nature of Paul's thinking is woven into his letter to the Galatians and is a crucial part of his argument in the context of Gal 3:28. In fact, this verse appears in one of the most unmistakably eschatological passages in the letter.[144] These texts stand in parallel to Gal 6:15, providing evidence that Paul's eschatology was at play in that verse as well.[145] Paul's soteriology was a function of the eschatologically determinative Christ event. This event certainly involved the individual but it also occasioned a change in the very nature of time and space.[146] It made possible a restoration of creation which began in the individual. However, the "event" which set this change in motion was the Christ event.

Unlike the other parallels, Gal 3:28 is not predicated upon a strong adversative.[147] Rather, the γάρ provides further explanation for the eradica-

---

[142] Bruce traces this back to R. Judah b. Elai (t. Ber. 7:18) or R. Me'ir (b. Men. 43b) c. A.D. 150. Bruce 1982:187. This would not preclude the possibility that Gal 3:28 reflects an early baptismal formula. Cf. Betz 1979:181-201.

[143] Bruce 1982:188. A possible further similarity could be noted between the unity of Gal 3:28b and the divided interests of 1 Cor 7:34-5. It is already apparent that these passages are not exactly parallel but they follow conceptually similar lines. Whereas the focus is on unity in Christ in Gal 3, 1 Cor 7 focuses more on how a married person is unable to give sole attention to pleasing the Lord in the same way as the unmarried.

[144] Merklein argues that this text can provide an important perspective on the connection between creation and redemption. Note his discussion of "neither male nor female" with regard to a connection between protology and eschatology. Merklein 1997:236-45.

[145] Hubbard argues strongly against seeing Gal 3:28 as a parallel text to 6:15 on the grounds that the former text speaks of "*baptism → reclothing → oneness*" whereas the latter speaks of "*death → life → newness.*" However, both texts simply apply different imagery to the identification with Christ motif and should not be seen in such an arbitrarily disconnected manner. Hubbard's failure to see this point can probably be put down to his interest in arguing against the ecclesiological understanding of new creation in 6:15. See Hubbard 2002:223.

[146] Mell 1989:317. Cf. Minear 1962:25-8.

[147] Gal 5:6; 1 Cor 7:19

tion of the contrasting identities.[148] The ground for Paul's perceived change in these fundamental identity groups is that his hearers are supposed to be "one in Christ Jesus."[149] Identification with Christ and consequent freedom from the demands of Torah lie at the heart of the soteriological engine of this letter. It is of utmost importance that this soteriology be articulated in connection with the Christ event – an event which naturally embodies eschatological reality.[150] All those who take on the new identity offered in Christ are part of the soteriological equalization characteristic of the new creation.[151]

G. The New Creation and the Israel of God

As argued above, Paul's use of στοιχέω in Gal 6:16 is significant in the context of his reference to καινὴ κτίσις in the preceding verse. It contributes to the way that Paul has used κόσμος and κτίσις in this letter to construct a new social reality for the Galatian churches.[152] The new social reality which Paul envisages is called "the Israel of God." The identity of this group has been vigorously disputed.[153] Interpretation of this verse hinges upon whether the καί should be understood conjunctively or epexegetically.

---

[148] Cousar 1990:145 calls this an "equalization of creation." This may be supported by the variation in structure of the final parallel of 3:28. Whereas the Jew/Gentile and Slave/Free contrasts are set apart with the standard οὐκ...οὐδέ, the final contrast Male/Female is expressed with οὐκ...καί. This probably reverberates with the influence of Gen 1:27 and supports the idea that the eschatological unity which Paul has in mind affects the order of creation itself. The implications of this for how we interpret Gal 6:15 cannot be ignored.

[149] We should note especially how Paul's "Christological-soteriology" speaks both of believers' being in Christ as well as Christ being formed in them (4:19). Cf. Fee 2007:212.

[150] Paul's use of "in Christ" language supports this notion. This is particularly important for 2 Cor 5:17 and will be discussed in the next chapter.

[151] Mell 1989:310-15.

[152] Adams' work is particularly helpful here. However, he emphasizes that Paul uses these terms "as tools for constructing in Galatia a Christian social world *separate* from the Jewish community" (emphasis his). See Adams 2000:232. I would nuance this by saying that, in fact, Paul does not just want to delineate Christians from Jews (even if this is a major thrust of the letter) because the new creation is inclusive of both Jew and Gentile. He is interested in establishing communities built not with the enslaving elements of the age prior to the Christ event but with the elements of the new creation – the Spirit and not the flesh. See Duff 1989:285-9.

[153] For further discussion, see Horrell 2000:321-44. Cf. Dahl 1950:161-70. Note the recent objection of Das 2007:242-3. Cf. Das 2003:44-6.

A conjunctive καί would suggest that Paul refers to two groups in Gal 6:16 – those who "follow this rule" (i.e. the Gentiles) and the "Israel of God" (i.e. faithful Jews).[154] An epexegetical καί would imply only one group and, given the eschatological unity presented in the preceding verse, this option is more likely. Several clues support this decision. First, the very context of Paul's letter has been to disparage the distinctions inherent in the old world – especially those between Jew and Gentile.[155] It would make little sense to maintain these distinctions at the close of a fiery polemic against them.[156] Then, the distinction between a faithful and unfaithful Israel is not foreign to Paul (Rom 9:6) and, since Paul has argued in this letter that Gentiles are spiritual descendants of Abraham, it follows that they could be included in the term "Israel." It is no great stretch to see this term in reference to the eschatological people of God as a whole, whether Jew or Gentile, who have died to the old world and become part of the new creation through union with Christ. This conclusion is further supported by the occurrence of τὴν ἐκκλησίαν τοῦ θεοῦ in 1:13, which may anticipate the similar syntax of the reference to the Ἰσραὴλ τοῦ θεοῦ in 6:17.

The question remains as to how this verse is related to the previous one. The demonstrative pronoun of 6:16a clearly refers back to 6:15. The rule/standard (κανών) to which Paul refers is the new creation. The word κανών is used only four times in Paul, and only here with the meaning "rule/standard."[157] Philo could use the term as a virtual synonym for νόμος.[158] Given the way new creation stands in contrast to the legal distinction of circumcision, it likely has a similar function in its usage here (cf. 6:2), thereby rehearsing the contrast between the law and the new creation and serving as one further appeal to the Galatians to avoid becoming "under law."

Paul's proclamation of blessing upon the Israel of God sustains the eschatological pitch of this letter.[159] This is consistent with the idea at-

---

[154] See, e.g., Betz 1979:319-20.

[155] Longenecker 1990:298-9.

[156] This need not imply that Paul completely repudiated Jewish identity any more than he rejected male and female roles. For further discussion, see Das 2003:44-6.

[157] It occurs in 2 Cor 10:13, 15-6 where it is used in reference to geographical spheres of influence. Note the roughly contemporary text of 4 Maccabees 7:21 and its reference to those who prevail over torture through philosophising by "the whole rule (κανόνα) of philosophy." These are said to control "the passions of the flesh (τῶν τῆς σαρκὸς παθῶν)" (v. 18) on the grounds that despite their impending doom, they "live to God (ζῶσιν τῷ θεῷ)" (v. 19; cf. 16:25). Paul uses a similar expression where he announces his death to the law in crucifixion with Christ and corresponding life to God (Gal 2:19; cf. Rom 6:10-11, Luke 20:38).

[158] *Posterity* 1:28; *Giants* 1:49. Cf. Beyer 1965:596.

[159] Bruce 1982:275.

tested within Jewish traditions contemporary with Paul that the end times would involve the inclusion of Gentiles in God's soteriological program. As argued in Chapter 2, this was a striking feature of the new creation passage in Isa 65-66. The degree to which Isaianic language actually influenced Paul's writing about the new creation is difficult to ascertain,[160] but the broad Isaianic soteriology, which connects the redemption of God's people with the redemption of creation, is very likely to have influenced Paul's understanding of the concept.[161] The association of καινὴ κτίσις with Ἰσραὴλ τοῦ θεοῦ suggests that this is the case and the point will be made even stronger in Paul's letter to the Romans.

H. CONCLUSIONS

This chapter has attempted to examine the way in which the phrase καινὴ κτίσις is used in Paul's letter to the Galatians. It began with a consideration of Gal 6:15 in the immediate context of the letter closing (vv. 11-18) and argued for the importance of this theme in the letter as a whole on the basis of the function of the closing as a recapitulation of the major themes which Paul addressed. Through a carefully crafted series of contrasts, the apostle sets the agitators in a very negative light and reveals how different is the message he preaches from theirs. Each of these contrasts draws the Galatians' attention to the central thrust of Paul's message – the cross of Christ. Most significantly for our purposes, the crucifixion of Christ results for Paul in the crucifixion of the κόσμος followed by καινὴ κτίσις. Based on Paul's use of κόσμος in this letter, it is argued that the Galatians would have understood the term in a cosmological sense and would not have restricted it to the private experience of the individual. This is perfectly resonant with ancient cosmologies which viewed the individual as a microcosm of the universe. The fates of the individual and the world were intricately connected. This suggests that the expression καινὴ κτίσις should be understood in a cosmological context.

Paul constructs his broad soteriological vision through an eschatological matrix based on the death and resurrection of Jesus. Through an innovative modification of Jewish apocalyptic eschatology, Paul views Christ's death and resurrection to have brought an end to the old age and to have inaugu-

---

[160] Greg Beale argues forcefully that the unusual combination of peace and mercy in Gal 6:16 in the context of "new creation" likely reflects the influence of Isa 54:10 and the general new creation themes present in Isa 30-66. Beale 1999:204-23. Cf. Beale 2005:1-38.

[161] This becomes even clearer if those arguments are correct which recognize the presence of the Isaianic new exodus themes in Paul. In particular, see Davies 1997:442-63; Keesmaat 1997:300-33; Oropeza 2002:87-112; Wilder 2001.

rated the new age which is expressed in this letter as καινὴ κτίσις. In the light of several important parallels which underscore the intensely eschatological thrust of Paul's thinking as well as the unity accomplished by the Christ event, Paul's soteriology is seen as a function of that event which should not be spoken of in isolation as cosmological, anthropological or ecclesiological. Rather, a Christological focus holds together these mutually *inclusive* emphases which Paul would not have imagined as *exclusive* categories.

Unlike the Roman imperial ideology, Paul could not refer to the age in which he lived as "golden" (cf. Gal 1:4). He entertained no illusions about the state of his world (cf. 1 Cor 2:6-8); but he did offer a solution – God's eschatological invasion of the world in Jesus (Gal 4:4-5).[162] The crucifixion and resurrection of Christ marked the defeat of the old age and the beginning of the new. For Paul, the cross of Christ had changed time itself. There could be no return of the old age and no further improvement on the age which had been inaugurated in Christ. The glory of Paul's new age in which even the most divisive factions of humanity (Jew and Gentile) could be reconciled is expressed in the term καινὴ κτίσις.

Thus, Paul uses new creation language to communicate the all-encompassing effects of the Christ event. This new reality provides the standard (6:16) by which the Galatians should live their lives. The next chapter will argue how this amounts to a new epistemology which calls for a whole new means of evaluation by the cross.

---

[162] Cf. Plutarch's "decisive time" in *Romulus* 12:2-6.

Chapter 6

Paul's Conception of New Creation in 2 Corinthians 5:11-21

This thesis has been advancing the proposition that the Pauline use of the phrase "new creation" is a kind of theological shorthand which encapsulates his eschatological soteriology. This chapter asks how Paul used the concept of new creation in 2 Corinthians 5:17.[1] This second occurrence of the phrase καινὴ κτίσις in the Pauline corpus occurs in the context of an apostolic defence.[2] Paul's strategy is to articulate an epistemology which radically challenged what would have been standard fare for the people of Corinth.[3] As a Roman colony, Corinth would have been exposed to the epistemology on offer from the imperial ideology of Rome.[4] This epistemology was all-encompassing and was predicated on the Roman transformation of the world. Paul's epistemological transformation is based upon the all-encompassing death and resurrection of Christ. Paul's association of the new creation with the Christ event is an indispensable key to his thought.

Crucial to understanding how Paul articulates his vision of new creation in 2 Cor 5:17 is the recognition that this verse resounds with Isaianic imagery. While this is routinely acknowledged by interpreters, the importance of the connection is not always taken into account. I am neither arguing that Isaiah is the only background to 2 Corinthians 5 nor that it should always be considered the most important source material for Paul. Examination of links with other background literature (Jewish and Greco-Roman) is essential for a proper understanding of the apostle's thought. But I do

---

[1] The issue of the unity of this letter is problematic but it need not impinge upon our discussion here since the majority of scholars at least recognise the essential integrity of chapters 1-9. For further discussion, see Thrall 1994:13-47.

[2] Space prohibits this argument from addressing in any detail the longstanding debate concerning the identity of Paul's opponents in Corinth. See the recent work in Porter 2005:1-6.

[3] It is not at all unusual for the Jews to articulate their beliefs against others in this way. See the fuller discussion of this concept above in Chapter 3.

[4] See the discussion of this above in Chapter 4, "Roman Imperial Ideology and Paul's Conception of New Creation."

want to show how it was the Isaianic prophecies, in particular, which provided an important framework for Paul's thinking about new creation.[5]

I propose, therefore, to examine the context of 2 Cor 5:17 for Isaianic influence. Though ideas from other texts influence the argument in this section, the Isaianic influence is strongest. The cumulative weight of evidence of Isaianic influence in this section contributes to the assertion that Paul had this portion of Israel's scripture in mind when he formulated his thinking about new creation in this passage.[6] Paul understands the new creation as the eschatological fulfilment of the soteriological program of Isaiah. After a closer look at the Isaianic influence upon Paul's thinking in this passage, this chapter will examine how Paul employs new creation epistemology in defence of his apostleship and how his understanding of it is inextricably linked to the Christ event.

A. Paul's Use of Isaiah in 2 Cor 5

2 Cor 5:1-5

The first intimation of an Isaianic connection comes in the opening verses of chapter 5. Immediately following Paul's explication in 4:16-18 that the path to glory leads through suffering, the apostle moves to deal with the issue of the ultimate suffering – that of the possibility of his own physical death. He expresses confidence even in this most dire of circumstances based on the promise of the ultimate redemption to a state of being with the Lord, of which he already enjoys the guarantee (ἀρραβών, 5:5) of the Spirit. In anticipation of that redemption he "groans" and longs for what is mortal to be "swallowed up by life" (5:2, 4). This language represents possible Isaianic influence in this text. An examination of two interesting parallels to 2 Cor 5 (1 Cor 15 and Rom 8) supports this assertion. The connection with Romans 8 will be taken up more fully in the next chapter, but it would be prudent here to take a closer look at the relationship between 1 Cor 15:50-7 and 2 Cor 5:1-5.

The relationship between 2 Cor 5:1-5 and 1 Cor 15:50-57 is a matter of scholarly dispute.[7] However, the thinking in both these passages revolves

---

[5] See my discussion of new creation in Isaiah in Chapter 2. Note Sandnes's argument that Isaiah plays a "tradition-shaping role upon the prophets in general" in Sandnes 1991:42.

[6] For a general methodology for assessing what constitutes Isaianic influence, see Hays 1989.

[7] For a discussion on the issue of continuity between the present creation and the new creation which deals with the apparent discrepancies between 1 Cor 15 and 2 Cor 5, see Schrage 2005:245-59. Schrage explains this in terms of a dialectic tension which Paul

around what Paul views as an eschatological fulfilment of an Isaianic prophecy. Isaiah 25:8 is quoted in 1 Cor 15:54 and alluded to in 2 Cor 5:4.[8] Yet the fact that this same scripture surfaces in both texts alongside other similar imagery (e.g. clothing/putting on) and similar themes (e.g. the post-mortem state of the believer) should not be ignored. The themes, however, appear in the context of different discussions and this may help to account for the discrepancies sometimes noted between these two passages. In 1 Cor 15 Paul is answering objections to the possibility of resurrection. In 2 Cor 5 he uses the idea of resurrection as part of an apostolic defence. Again, in both passages, the resurrection is seen as the fulfilment of Isaianic prophecy.

The ὅταν...τότε construction of 1 Cor 15:54 makes clear that Paul views the resurrection of believers as the fulfilment of Isa. 25:8.[9] He explicitly acknowledges that his message of the death, burial and resurrection of Christ was κατὰ τὰς γραφάς (v. 3).[10] 1 Cor 15:54 makes specific Paul's general appeal to scripture earlier in this chapter.[11] As Isaiah 25:8 was seen in ancient Judaism as a prediction of YHWH's end-time solution to the problem of death, Paul's appeal to it, especially in conjunction with Hosea 13:14 (1 Cor 15:55), should be seen as proof that he viewed the resurrection of believers as eschatological fulfilment of these promises.[12] Earlier in this chapter, Paul has told us that the eschatological fulfilment has already begun in the resurrection of Christ who is the ἀπαρχή of those who belong to him (v. 23).[13] So, Paul did envisage a future resurrection but the end-time resurrection had already begun in the resurrection of Christ.

---

maintains by means of a "processual eschatology." For an explanation of how Paul's thinking may be consistent between these two passages, see Gillman 1988:439-54; Woodbridge 2003:241-58.

[8] For a brief discussion of differences between quotation, allusion and echo, see Moyise 2000:18-19.

[9] Stanley effectively argues on the basis of agreements between Paul and the later Jewish versions that "Paul has most likely followed a pre-existing Greek text at this point." Stanley 1992:210-11. Also, a number of other Isaianic allusions in 1 Cor 15 cumulatively indicate the likelihood of Isaianic influence on Paul. See Oropeza 2002:87-112.

[10] For fuller discussion, see Dodd 1952.

[11] Note the quote of Gen 2:7 in 1 Cor 15:45.

[12] Wilk 2005:146-7. Interestingly, both Isa 25:8 and Hos 13:14 represent an uncommon personification of death. This may help to explain why these texts presented themselves to Paul at this juncture. The personification of death is an important piece of evidence which reveals that Paul's ideas here are fully resonant with the cosmological track of Jewish apocalyptic eschatology which sees death as a "quasi-angelic power that stands opposed to God." See De Boer 1988:90-1.

[13] The eschatological fulfilment of this promise in Isa was to be signalled with the blast of "the great trumpet" (Isa 27:13). Cf. 1 Cor 15:52; 1 Thess 4:16; Rev 11:15; *4 Ezra* 6:23; 6:13, 20

To be sure, Paul's discussion of the resurrection in 2 Cor 5 has a different perspective to that in 1 Cor 15 and is used in a different way.[14] Yet far from representing a revolution in Paul's thought from a Jewish understanding of resurrection (1 Cor 15)[15] to a Platonic one (2 Cor 5)[16], Paul's fundamental understanding of the resurrection of Christ and the subsequent resurrection of believers as the fulfilment of Isa 25:8 remains intact (cf. 5:5).[17] The emphasis here is not a move away from the resurrection expected at the parousia but rather an acknowledgment that the power of the resurrection is already at work in his life. It is this transforming and life-giving power which sustains him despite affliction, perplexity, persecution and the threat of death itself (1:8-9; 4:7-14)[18]

On one level, the flow of Paul's argument in this section of 2 Corinthians is puzzling. Why does Paul engage in a discussion of post-mortem existence in the midst of a sustained defence of his apostolic authority?[19] The issue is that Paul is facing physical suffering which, in the eyes of his opponents, challenges his authority as an apostle. Far from being a momentary diversion from his larger argument, Paul makes the case that the suffering should be viewed as part of the transient world (4:16-18). His weakness is strength because it is the weakness of Christ. Paul's apostolic identification with Christ's sufferings entails the subsequent identification with Christ's resurrection (5:14-15). This prepares the way for the alternative epistemology which comes to fuller expression in 5:16.

---

[14] Wright argues that the change in perspective is that Paul recognizes the possibility of his own death before the parousia (2003: 370). There is also a shift from future to present emphasis: "In 1 Corinthians the movement is primarily towards the future, straining towards the resurrection and discovering what needs to be done in the present to anticipate it, in 2 Corinthians the movement is primarily towards the present, discovering in the powerful resurrection of Jesus and the promised resurrection for all his people the secret of facing suffering and pain here and now." Wright 2003:300.

[15] Winter makes a helpful distinction between Paul's cultural and theological backgrounds. See Winter 2001:xii. Rosner applies this distinction to a study of the resurrection and how "Paul's teaching is framed in sharp relief by Graeco-Roman contrasting views, sketched in outline from biblical and Jewish sources but given its distinctive hues from the palette of the risen Christ." See Rosner 2004:205. This thesis has been moving towards a similar point regarding Paul's understanding of new creation.

[16] For a recent articulation of the strong discontinuity of these passages, see Boismard 1999. Cf. Glasson 1990:145-55.

[17] Matera 2002:400-5.

[18] This coincides with the eschatological perspective which Lambrecht argued is inherent in Paul's earlier reference to the resurrection in 2 Cor 4:14. He argues against Murphy-O'Connor's view that the resurrection should be understood existentially (not eschatologically) here in reference to the "authentic Christian life on earth." Lambrecht 1994a:335-49.

[19] Martin regards this as a "short digression." Martin 1986:107.

The convergence of similar motifs and language in 1 Cor 15, 2 Cor 5 and, as we shall see in the next chapter, in Rom 8, and the presence of Isaianic influence in each of these texts makes a reasonable case that Isaianic texts play an important role in the construct of Paul's thought.[20] Isaiah 25:8 appears in the context (Isa 24-7) of cosmic judgment designed to punish sin and bring salvation. Restoration is both for the nation and for the individual. In particular, the eschatological banquet of 25:6-8 maintains a connection between the person, the nation and the creation and this connection would have been acknowledged by readers of the Second Temple period.[21] Paul's use of this Isaianic material indicates that his concern with the physical resurrection of Christ and of believers has been influenced by the association of creation and redemption in Isaiah. Thus, Paul's discussion of post-mortem existence in 2 Cor 5:1-5 is far from a rhetorical sidetrack. He speaks of post-mortem existence because he realises that *that* represents the ultimate vindication of his sufferings.

The New Creation

The similarity of language in 2 Cor 5:17 and in Isaiah 43:18 is noted in the margins of NA 27 and recognized by many scholars.[22] However, precisely how this language is used and why the Isaianic background to this verse is important deserves further comment. Although 2 Cor 5:17 is not a direct quotation, its closest verbal and syntactical parallels are found in Isaiah; in particular, in the frequently used Isaianic contrast between the former/old things and new things.[23] As G. Beale has shown, this contrast, connected by ἰδού plus creation vocabulary, is found only in Paul or in early Christian literature alluding to 2 Cor 5:17 or Isa 43:18-9.[24] Lambrecht acknowledges that Paul could have been influenced by the contrast of ἀρχαῖα and

---

[20] It is not assumed that every hearer of Paul's letters would have understood the full impact of Isaianic influence on Paul. But even though some of the Corinthians would have missed its full impact, they could not fail to grasp that he was articulating a message in stark contrast to the contemporary attitudes about the nature of life and death. Paul's use of Scripture to communicate this message would have helped to secure his role in the minds of the Corinthians as a spokesman from God (cf. 2 Cor 5:20). See Stanley 2004:38-61.

[21] For a fuller explanation of how this is the case, see my Chapter 2, "New Creation in Isaiah." Cf. Wright 2003:116-8.

[22] Tertullian believed 2 Cor 5:17 to be a fulfilment of the prophecies of Isaiah (*Against Marcion* V.12).

[23] The parallels in other Jewish literature are not nearly as close as the Isaianic text (1 En. 91:16; 1QH 13:11-12). Beale 1989:553.

[24] Beale 1989:553.

καινά in Isa 43:18-19, but he qualifies this by pointing out that the contrast in the two contexts is different.[25]

Lambrecht makes a valid point but his caveat should not obscure the correspondence between the Pauline and the Isaianic material. Both in Isaiah 43 as well as in 2 Cor 5:17 there is a radical change from the former/old things to something new.[26] Isaiah communicates this by saying that the new will be so wondrous the old will not be remembered (43:18). Paul writes that the old has passed away (παρῆλθεν). Secondly, the prophetic promise marker ἰδού (Isa 43:18; 2 Cor 5:17) and its repetition in 2 Cor 6:2 (where Isa 49:8 is quoted) signals that Paul was aware that he was employing prophetic tradition.[27] Thirdly, both texts contain cosmologically related language.[28] The transformed wilderness and desert in Isa 43:19 are part of an Isaianic motif which considers the effects of human sin on the creation and expresses restoration in terms of a renewal of creation. Cosmological restoration language is present in the earlier portions of Isaiah and it comes to fullest expression in Isa 65-66.

There is strong ground for taking Isa 65:17 as influential background of 2 Cor 5:17. Although the phrase καινὴ κτίσις does not occur in Isa 65:17, the use of the phrase "new heaven and new earth (ὁ οὐρανὸς καινὸς καὶ ἡ γῆ καινή)" clearly conveys the same idea.[29] The phrase καινὴ κτίσις probably came to Paul either through his own reflection on Isa 65 or through contemporary apocalyptic reflection on that text.[30] Thus, cosmological reference should be assumed unless a significant case can be made to exclude it.[31]

---

[25] Lambrecht 1994b:380.

[26] The LXX translates רִאשׁוֹן alternatively as πρῶτος and πρότερος (except in 41:27).

[27] Furnish 1984:315.

[28] Hubbard argues that κτίσις should not be taken as having any cosmological referent. However, every other occurrence of the term in Paul has creation in view. If this term should be construed in strict anthropocentrism here, it would be a unique usage in Paul (with the possible exception of Gal 6:15). Even if the term should be translated "creature" rather than "creation" it still points out the change to the created order insofar as the individual is part of the cosmos.

[29] This is a literal Greek translation of the Hebrew שָׁמַיִם חֲדָשִׁים וָאָרֶץ חֲדָשָׁה. The Hebrew merism "heavens and earth" is a common way of expressing the concept of creation as is the case, for example, in Gen 1:1.

[30] Mell argues strongly that the phrase came to Paul through apocalyptic literature. See Mell 1989:113-257. Hubbard 2002:54-73 has argued that the conversion imagery of *Jospeh and Aseneth* represents a greater influence for Paul. However, the phrase καινὴ κτίσις does not appear in the Jewish literature which Hubbard takes to be most influential for Paul's conception of new creation.

[31] Adams 2000:226-7 makes a similar point. Simply indicating that the term has individual ramifications does not necessarily make this case. The failure of Hubbard's at-

The verbal correspondence of Isa 65:17 with 2 Cor 5:17 is not high. But Isa 65 stands at the end of a sustained series of prophecies and offers the ultimate reversal of the cosmic destruction envisaged earlier in the book (Isa 24-27, 34-35). The promises of restoration are intertwined throughout with cosmological/creation language and it is commonly recognized in Isaiah scholarship that it is impossible to separate the themes of creation and redemption (particularly in Deutero-Isaiah). The promise of the new heavens and the new earth in Isa 65 represents the ultimate image of restoration and brings to a crescendo the promise of deliverance which has been building throughout the material. The old-new contrast supports this conclusion (Isa 43:18; 65:17).[32] Important for our purposes, this crescendo does not introduce a new theme but brings to a climax a motif which has played harmoniously throughout the composition.

A recent attempt to explain Paul's use of Isaianic material may be found in Florian Wilk's argument that Paul's language in 2 Cor 5:17cd reflects the usage of the language of the LXX of Isa 43:18-19 and Isa 48:3-7 fashioned according to the sentence structure of Isa 42:9 (Symmachus).[33] He concludes that the unique connections made in these verses between ἀρχαῖα, ἰδού and καινά make Paul's use of Isaianic tradition virtually in-

---

tempt to do this is related to his misunderstanding of the way in which Paul appropriates Isaianic texts. Hubbard 2002:24 says that Isaiah contains two different "but not unrelated" expressions of the motif of new creation. Deutero-Isaiah is seen to focus more on anthropological soteriology while Trito-Isaiah takes in a cosmological perspective. Thus, Paul's language is said to reflect the Deutero-Isaianic tradition. This supports Hubbard's argument that Paul's new creation is more influenced by the anthropological-soteriology of Second Isaiah rather than the cosmological-soteriology of Trito-Isaiah. The result is that Hubbard wants to see the new covenant and new Spirit themes of Jeremiah and Ezekiel as more important for Paul's thinking. He is right to point out the influence of other prophetic writings on Paul. However, he allows a contemporary understanding of a divided Isaiah to determine his understanding. Paul would not have seen "Trito-Isaiah" in such a different light to "Deutero-Isaiah." See the chapter above on the idea of new creation in the OT.

[32] Although ἀρχαῖος does not occur in Isa 65:17, πρῶτος is used in Isaiah virtually synonymously (e.g. 43:18).

[33] Wilk 1998:276-80. He sees glimmers of Isaiah in 2 Cor 5:16 as well. Most interesting is the Isaianic use of ἀπὸ τοῦ νῦν (48:6) and νῦν (48:7) in the context of YHWH's new (τὰ καινά) acts of deliverance (as opposed to the former things, τὰ πρότερα, 48:3). Isaiah 48:3-7 speaks of the former things (πρότερα) coming to pass, it uses language of knowing (ἔγνωτε) and it uses temporal language (νῦν, ἀπὸ τοῦ νῦν) in the context of YHWH's bringing new things (τὰ καινά) to pass (γίνεται). Surprisingly, Wilk does not satisfactorily address how Isa 65 could also have influenced Paul's thinking about new creation. Perhaps this exclusion is what leads Wilk to conclude that Paul's understanding of new creation has in mind neither a cosmic event nor an individual conversion experience but rather "die Erneuerung der Menschheit, die sich proleptisch an den Mitgliedern der christlichen Gemeinde realisiert" (p. 278).

disputable.³⁴ However, Wilk could be accused of taking the level of dependence upon Isaianic material too far.³⁵ There are certainly affinities between 2 Cor 5:17 and these verses but Wilk's convoluted argument cannot be fully substantiated. Rather than requiring Pauline dependence on each of these verses, this seems to suggest that the prophecies of Isaiah formed a paradigm which influenced Paul's thinking. He has managed to offer a *feasible* explanation of how Paul *could have* stitched together various Isaianic texts. But this kind of analysis does not fully consider the way in which Paul had actual access to the OT material. These ideas were present in Isaiah and they were influential on Paul not simply in the language or syntax he used but in the way he constructed his thought.³⁶

The soteriological themes of Isaiah focus on the nation through an application of the new exodus motif interwoven with creation imagery.³⁷ The final chapters of Isaiah focus increasingly more on the creation; but, at least from Paul's perspective, this should not be taken to mean that national restoration is the concern of Deutero-Isaiah while the soteriological interest of Trito-Isaiah involves the entire cosmos. These theological strands are strongly related in the Isaianic material and should not be separated.³⁸ As Webb has argued, "The new exodus patterns or mirrors God's ultimate act of new creation. It is the final step in the restoration process.... In this respect the new exodus *anticipates* the ultimate re-creation, and in turn the eschatological new creation *finalizes* the process begun in the second exodus."³⁹

This is immediately recognizable in Isa 43 where the promised restoration entails blessings even for the created order, "The wild animals will honour me, the jackals and the ostriches; for I give water in the wilderness, rivers in the desert, to give drink to my chosen people" (Isa 43:20). Furthermore, this restoration is spoken of with creation language in vv. 6-7, "I will say to the north, 'Give them up,' and to the south, 'Do not withhold; bring my sons from far away and my daughters from the end of the earth –

---

³⁴ Wilk 1998:277.

³⁵ For example, he sees the use of ἐπῆλθεν in 48:3 as a possible parallel with παρῆλθεν in 2 Cor 5:17. But despite the corresponding root, these verbs have very different meanings and are used in radically different ways in the two contexts.

³⁶ For a recent survey of the scholarship on Paul's use of Scripture, see Aageson 2006:152-81.

³⁷ Morales explores new creation and new exodus themes in ancient Jewish literature and in Galatians. Note particularly his work on Isaiah in Morales 2007:20-39. Cf. Hickling 1996:367-76.

³⁸ Chapter 2 of this thesis explains how the cosmic restoration envisaged at the end of the Isaianic material (65-66) is necessitated by the destruction of creation earlier in the material (24-27; 34-5).

³⁹ Webb 1993:124-5.

everyone who is called by my name, whom I created (κατεσκεύασα) for my glory, whom I formed (ἔπλασα) and made (ἐποίησα)'" (cf. vv. 15, 21). As argued more fully in Chapter 2, the themes of creation and redemption are intricately interconnected throughout this collection of prophecies.

Paul interprets Isaianic material as prophecy of eschatological salvation which God has accomplished in Christ.[40] The lack of exact verbal correspondence should not blind us to the appropriation of this theme to Paul's argument as a whole. The next step in Paul's argument in 2 Cor 5 confirms that the Isaianic texts helped to form his thinking in this passage.

The Ministry of Reconciliation[41]

The probability that Paul's conception of new creation was thoroughly influenced by the Isaianic material is further strengthened when the relationship between 5:17 and 5:18-21 is taken into account. It is *possible* that Paul could have used Isaianic language for his expression of new creation in 2 Cor 5:17 without regard for its context and that the subsequent discussion of reconciliation is a new and unrelated subject in his argument. However, the presence of reconciliation themes in Isaiah in connection with the language that Paul used to express his understanding of the new creation in v. 17 makes it much more probable that Paul employed ideas already present in the Isaianic material.[42] Though the term καταλλαγή only appears once in Isa (9:4), the concept is compatible with Isaiah's discussion of restoration and, as we shall see, may well have derived from Paul's consideration of the Servant Songs of Isaiah.

First, Isa 43:18-19 calls on Israel to trust YHWH for miraculous restoration from Babylonian exile. The act of deliverance which will accomplish this restoration will exceed the most significant event of his deliverance to that time, the Exodus from Egypt (vv. 16-17). The promised deliverance brings both a physical return to the land as well as a restoration to a relationship with YHWH (43:1, 5-7, 15) and is spoken of in new creation terms (43:1, 15, 19-21). The combination of restoration with new creation is especially common throughout Isaiah 40-55.[43]

---

[40] Wilk 1998:278, 280. He understands καινὴ κτίσις as a universal-anthropological term because of his interpretation of ἐν Χριστῷ from an ecclesiological perspective. Exactly how this should be understood will be left to our discussion in the next section. Here, I simply want to build the case that the Isaianic background was important for Paul throughout chapter 5.

[41] Note the remarkable change in emphasis from 2 Maccabees where God is reconciled to people (1:5; 7:33; 8:29) to Paul where people are reconciled to God (Rom 5:10; 2 Cor 5:18-21). On this point, see the lexical work of: Porter 1994; Porter 1996:693-705.

[42] For a fuller discussion of this, see Beale's important article: Beale 1989:554-59.

[43] Beale cites: Isa 40:28-31; 41:17-20; 42:5-9; 44:21-23, 24-28; 45:1-8, 9-13, 18-20; 49:8-13; 51:1-3, 9-11, 12-16; 54:1-10; 55:6-13. Beale 1989:555.

Secondly, Isa 65:17-25 specifically speaks of the restoration in new creation terminology.[44] In the new heavens and new earth envisaged in this passage, sorrow turns to rejoicing as the longevity and productivity of God's people are established (vv. 20-22). The futility of life threatened by hostile foreign power is overcome and even death is made subject to the sovereignty of YHWH (65:20). The salvation of God's people is not distinguished from the salvation of God's world.[45]

Since the concepts of new creation and restoration are connected in Isaiah, it is highly significant for this argument that Paul enters into a discussion of reconciliation in Christ immediately following new creation language. The τὰ δὲ πάντα ἐκ τοῦ θεοῦ (2 Cor 5:18) makes this connection absolutely clear.[46] Given the connection of these themes in Isaiah, it is perfectly reasonable to suggest that Paul's discussion of reconciliation in the immediate context of new creation is influenced by the Isaianic understanding of new creation as restoration of Israel in its relationship to YHWH.[47]

The question of how Paul came to use the terminology denoting reconciliation is a difficult one and a vortex of scholarly endeavour.[48] It has been suggested that the language of 2 Cor 5:19-21 reflects early Christian

---

[44] For a more detailed discussion of this passage, see my chapter on new creation in Isaiah.

[45] Paul's language of reconciliation of the κόσμος in 2 Cor 5:19 certainly includes a reference to humanity since it is the antecedent of the pronoun αὐτός (αὐτοῖς) in v. 19b where trespasses are not counted "against them." However, the term was fraught with temporal and spatial connotations in the Greco-Roman world and apocalyptic literature. If Paul picks up the Isaianic understanding of the connection between creation and redemption, there is strong likelihood that his use of κόσμος here would have reverberated with these associations, especially in the context of his discussion of καινὴ κτίσις. See my discussion of Gal 6:14 in the preceding chapter. Cf. Theobald 2005:435-41.

[46] Furnish notes that this phrase reflects a doxological formula which came to Paul from Stoic pantheism by way of the Hellenistic synagogue. Even if this is the case, Judaism infused this Hellenistic idea with its understanding of God and his relationship to creation. It is interesting that Paul has chosen language with such cosmological reverberations in the context of his discussion of new creation. This coincides with Paul's missionary interest in communicating his message in terms especially poignant to his audience. It suggests a sustained interest in the cosmological consequences (vv. 16, 17) of the Christ event (vv. 14-5; cf. Col 1:20, 22). See Furnish 1984:316.

This may have important implications with regard to the discussion of Paul's interaction with Roman imperial ideology. See Knohl's fascinating comments on the messiah of Qumran and Roman eschatology in Knohl 2000:96-101.

[47] Beale 1989:556-8.

[48] Harris suggests the term is "exclusively Pauline" in the NT. However, similar terms are attested by two other writers (cf. Matt 5:24; Luke 12:58; Acts 7:26). Nevertheless, its influence is undoubtedly Pauline. Harris 2005:435. For a discussion of how Paul might have come to use the term, see Porter 1994.

tradition and this may well be the case.⁴⁹ O. Hofius argues that Paul's thinking about reconciliation should be understood against the background of Isa 52-53.⁵⁰ He understands Isa 53 as the source of Paul's thinking about reconciliation and atonement; but he holds that Paul develops the idea of representative place-taking, in which the offending party is still included, from the substitutive place-taking of Isaiah.⁵¹ Morna Hooker disagrees with Hofius's attempt to distinguish *exkludierende* from *inkludierende Stellvertretung* (i.e. substitution from representation). She sees the idea of *inclusive place-taking* in the original context of Isaiah.⁵² While steadfast in her original thesis of 1959 that the use of Isa 53 to interpret Christ's ministry did not begin with Jesus himself, Hooker allows in more recent work on the subject that the use of Isa 53 to interpret the mission of Jesus very well may have begun with Paul and just how this is the case will be made more clear in the next section.⁵³

The concepts of new creation and reconciliation are corresponding concepts for Paul and these ideas appear in similar proximity in Isaiah. This suggests that Paul could have had Isaiah in mind in the construction of 2 Cor 5:18-21. The point is that being a part of God's end-time new creation means being reconciled to God.⁵⁴ In the context of Paul's argument, the message is clear. Repudiation of Paul's ministry, who stands as God's ambassador, is the rejection of Christ's offer of reconciliation. To be reconciled to God is to be reconciled to Paul.

2 Cor 6:2 and Its Use of Isa 49:8⁵⁵

Finally, the direct quotation from Isa 49:8 (LXX) in 2 Cor 6:2 contributes to the likelihood that Paul had an Isaianic background in mind in the

---

⁴⁹ Käsemann 1971:49-64. Stuhlmacher 1965:74-9 has argued for a more limited influence of tradition (v. 19 rather than vv. 19-21). Porter 1994:129-30 insists, against Käsemann and Martin, that the language of vv. 18-21 is not pre-Pauline. Cf. Furnish 1984:334.

⁵⁰ Furnish 1984:334; Hofius 1980:196.

⁵¹ Hofius 1993:414-37.

⁵² Hooker 1998:98.

⁵³ Hooker 1998:103. See Hooker 1959:116-23. She specifically discusses the connection of Rom 4:25 with Isa 53 (vv. 5, 11f.). Through the idea of "interchange in Christ" (cf. 2 Cor 5:21), Hooker shows how the explanation of why Christ's death and resurrection are efficacious is spelled out in chapters 5:12-21, 6:3-14 and 8:1. See her fuller thoughts on the importance of Rom 4:25 in Hooker 2002:323-41.

⁵⁴ Beale 1989:559.

⁵⁵ Paul does not quote Isa 49:8b: καὶ ἔδωκά σε εἰς διαθήκην ἐθνῶν τοῦ καταστῆσαι τὴν γῆν καὶ κληρονομῆσαι κληρονομίαν ἐρήμου. This important reference indicates that the LXX maintains a connection between the universal mission to the Gentiles and the cosmic order. On the basis of this quotation, Lambrecht believes that OT influence on 2 Cor 5:17 is likely. See Lambrecht 1994b:380. Cf. Beale 1989:562.

course of his argument.[56] The convergence of restoration with the new creation motif in Isaiah, as argued above, speaks against the notion that Paul uses Isaianic phraseology without regard to its theological context.[57] With the repetition of ἰδοὺ νῦν, Paul's explanation in 6:2b indicates that he insists that the prophecy of Isaiah has been fulfilled in his own time: ἰδοὺ νῦν καιρὸς εὐπρόσδεκτος, ἰδοὺ νῦν ἡμέρα σωτηρίας.

Isaiah 49 is obviously important for Paul. He not only quotes it here in 2 Cor 6:2 but likely alludes to it in his description of his calling in Gal 1:15-6 (cf. Isa 49:1, 6; Acts 13:47).[58] It is widely recognized that Paul likely saw his ministry as an embodiment of the servant traditions of Isaiah.[59] Nevertheless, not all scholars accept that 6:2 should be taken as a reference to Paul's own ministry.[60] Harris allows that there are interesting correspondences between the ministry of Paul and the discussion of the Servant in Isa 49.[61] But there are far more extensive connections than Harris recognizes.[62] A clue to the Isaianic connection may occur in Paul's self-designation as δοῦλος (Rom 1:1; Gal 1:10; Phil 1:1).[63] This connection would make all the more poignant Paul's role as light-bearer to the blind (2 Cor 4:4-6) since this was a crucial role of Isaiah's Servant (Isa 49:6).[64]

Σου and σοι have been understood in two very different ways in 2 Cor 6:2. One is that Paul applies this text to his own apostolic ministry.[65] In

---

[56] This point becomes even stronger if Webb's assertion that the fragment (2 Cor 6:14-7:1) with its catena of OT quotes is conceptually parallel to the broader context of 2 Cor 2:14-7:4 based on his research in new covenant and exilic return traditions. For a summary of his hypothesis, see Webb 1993:176-8. Contra the attempt of Schröter 1993:195 to explain the reference to the "favourable time" from the perspective of contemporary philosophy.

[57] This position is espoused, for example, in the work of Lambrecht 1999:108; Lambrecht 1989:377-91.

[58] Lindars 1961:223-4.

[59] Webb 1993:128-31; cf. Hooker 1959:114-23. See the excursus on the nature of the prophetic vocabulary in Isa 49:1-6 in Sandnes 1991:62-5.

[60] For support of this, see Beale, Hafemann, Webb and Wilk. Contra, see Thrall, Harris, Lambrecht.

[61] Namely, they are called to their ministries from birth (Isa 49:1, 5; Gal 1:15; cf. Jer 1:5), they have a joint mission to Israel and the Gentiles (Isa 49:5-6; Gal 1:16) and they both experience feelings of futility (Isa 49:4; 2 Cor 6:1). Harris 2005:460-1.

[62] It is interesting that in Luke's account of Paul's ministry in Acts 13:47 Luke has Paul using Isa 49:6 in direct reference to his own ministry: "For so the Lord has commanded us, saying, 'I have set you to be a light for the Gentiles, so that you may bring salvation to the ends of the earth.'" Cf. Acts 26:16-18. Cf. Beale 1989:563-4.

[63] Cf. Gal 1:15; Isa 49:3, 5. See Stanley 1954:415-18.

[64] Webb 1993:129-30. Note especially the more nuanced work of Gignilliat 2007:51-4. See the work of Sandnes which argues particularly that the language of 2 Cor 4:6 reflects Paul's self-understanding in relation to OT prophets. Sandnes 1991:131-45.

[65] As argued, for example, in Beale 1989:561-6.

this case, τὴν χάριν τοῦ θεοῦ would refer to Paul's apostolic ministry and the quotation would identify Paul with the servant of Isa 49. The quotation would serve as divine approval of the ministry of Paul and indicate to the Corinthians that the promises of salvation given in Isaiah have been fulfilled in the ministry of Christ of which Paul's own ministry is an extension. The other explanation is that 2 Cor 6:2 applies Isa 49:8 to the Corinthians.[66] In this case, Paul would be placing the Corinthians in the role of the exiled and estranged Israel for whom the servant of Isa 49 was the representative figure. Paul would be making an appeal for the Corinthians to allow the Gospel which had been proclaimed to them to bear fruit in their lives by being reconciled to God by means of being reconciled to his own ministry.

The recent work of M. Gignilliat, however, provides a more nuanced understanding of how we should take Paul's use of the Servant passages of Isaiah.[67] According to Gignilliat, Paul is placing himself in the line of prophetic tradition though he does not claim the identity of Isaiah's servant – a role, Gignilliat argues, which Paul reserves for Jesus.[68] He rightly asserts that Paul's purpose is not to make a particular identification with these pronouns but rather to emphasize that the work of Christ has brought about an eschatological fulfilment to the Isaianic prophecies.[69] This is clear in Paul's own commentary on the Isaianic text in 2 Cor 6:2b, "Behold! Now is the acceptable time. Behold! Now is the day of salvation."[70]

The Isaianic influence on 2 Cor 5:1-6:2 informs Paul's appeal to the Corinthians to behave according to the time in which they are living. His use of the Isaianic material draws the reader into the broader soteriological message of Isaiah and understanding this point is a crucial first step to understanding how Paul uses the concept of new creation in the context of his apostolic defence.[71] Paul's ministry heralds the new eschatological age and he bases his argument on the new criteria for evaluation characteristic of that age.[72]

---

[66] E.g. Lambrecht 1989:381.
[67] Gignilliat 2007:57-60.
[68] Gignilliat 2007:59.
[69] Gignilliat makes a case that Paul actually identifies himself with the servants of the Servant – a group largely overlooked in previous studies of Isaiah and Paul. See Gignilliat 2007:108-42.
[70] Hahn 1973:249-52.
[71] Gignilliat 2007:60-107.
[72] Cf. Wagner 2002:318.

B. New Creation Epistemology as Apostolic Defence

It is quite significant that Paul uses the idea of new creation in 2 Cor 5:17 to deal with problems he was facing with the church in Corinth. The identity of Paul's opponents there has been the subject of rigorous discussion since the time of Baur.[73] Though the image of the opponents is less than clear, we get a fair insight into their complaint. They were most likely concerned with the nature of apostleship as Paul's appearance did not match the powerful and authoritative image which they felt should be characteristic of an apostle.[74] The Corinthians had misunderstood Paul (1:14) because they misunderstood the nature of the ministry he had received from Christ whose ministry was characterised by weakness and suffering ultimately demonstrated at his crucifixion.[75] Paul defends his apostleship from this position. The theological arguments which unfold in this letter (at least in 2:14-7:4) undergird this apologetic thrust.[76]

In this section, I hope to make a case that Paul bases his apostolic defence on an eschatological inversion which effects an epistemological change. As argued previously, Paul's eschatological perspective is crucial to understanding his concept of new creation and his argument in 2 Cor 2-5. This eschatological perspective would have been informed by the Jewish apocalyptic eschatology of Second Temple Judaism and may provide one of the interpretive lenses through which Paul understood the Christ event.[77]

The contrast between Paul's eschatology and the eschatology found in the Jewish apocalyptic works is seen quite clearly in Paul's understanding of the new creation.[78] The Jewish apocalyptic idea of the division of time into two successive ages of a world hostile in its manifold rebellion against God and the new age of the Spirit when God would overcome all opposi-

---

[73] Georgi traces this discussion back to Baur's re-assessment of early Christian history from the perspective of the conflict in Corinth. Georgi 1986:2. Baur's original article of 1831, "Die Christuspartei der korinthischen Gemeinde," may be found in Scholder 1963:1-164.

[74] Sumney 1990:146. Sumney 1990:13-115 gives a very helpful methodological corrective of previous efforts to ascertain the identity of Paul's opponents in 2 Corinthians. Cf. Sumney 2005:7-58.

[75] Garland 1999:32-3.

[76] Barnett 2003:326.

[77] Beker 1980:19; cf. Humphrey 2002:113. See the discussion of this point in the preceding chapter in the section, "*Paul's modification of 'Jewish Apocalyptic Eschatology.'*"

[78] Whether the phrase was used in this manner in pre-Pauline Christian traditions is beyond the scope of this thesis. See Weima 1993:101-2.

B. New Creation Epistemology as Apostolic Defence

tion to his rule was absolutely central for Paul (cf. *4 Ezra* 4:26; 7:50).[79] The Christ event, however, served as the pivotal crux of history to bring the old age to a close and to initiate the subsequent and final age of God's reign. De Boer rightly points back to Schweitzer in claiming that "Paul's apocalyptic eschatology is not reduced to his understanding of the parousia and the end but also encompasses his understanding of Christ's advent, death, and resurrection."[80]

In this manner, Paul modified the Jewish thinking in which he had been steeped. Paul placed the time of God's most radical invasion of the world in the past in the events of the life, death and resurrection of Christ.[81] Paul inverts the future-oriented hope of God's actions described with new creation language in Jewish writings into an eschatological system where the epicentre of God's cosmic earthquake was located in the past.[82]

Some recent analyses of Paul's new creation tend to reject the cosmological influence of apocalyptic literature on the grounds that this material uses the idea of renovation or re-creation of the cosmos as the solution to an external plight. Paul, it is said, is concerned not with the external problems addressed by the apocalyptic writers but rather with the internal plight of "sin and inability."[83] This assertion, however, can neither be maintained for the apocalyptic literature nor for Paul. I have already addressed this issue in relation to the apocalyptic literature, and Paul's writings, too, resist the classification. The context of 2 Cor 5:17 reveals that the new creation does help to deal with an external problem – the pressure placed on Paul by invalid evaluations of his apostleship based on epistemology which had not been transformed to that of the new age inaugurated by Christ.[84]

That Paul's eschatological perspective is absolutely crucial to his apostolic defence is seen clearly in the literary context of 2 Cor 5:17. The argument for Paul's own apostolic authority is presented throughout the first chapters of 2 Corinthians and his conception of the new creation as the eschatological turn of the ages is the organizational matrix and the linchpin of his defence.[85] This crucial point may be seen in several ways.

---

[79] This may be seen most clearly in Paul in the contrast between the present evil age with the age of salvation (Gal 1:4; 1 Cor 10:11; Rom 12:2). This comes to expression in the Adam/Christ comparison and perhaps in the Spirit/flesh antithesis. It may also be evident in the spatial dualism of Paul's view of heaven and earth and the ethical dualism of Paul's belief in the realm of powers hostile to God (2 Cor 4:4). See Aune 1993:31-2.

[80] De Boer 2000:379.

[81] Furnish 1984:333.

[82] In the Jewish writings there was a form of inaugurated eschatology but the centre of gravity lay in the future whereas the centre of gravity for Paul lay in the past.

[83] Hubbard 2002:239.

[84] Aune 2001a:238.

[85] Martyn 1997:92ff.

First, each of the three explicit references to the resurrection in 2 Corinthians is used to defend his apostolic authority. In 2 Corinthians 1:9-10 Paul is making certain that his readers understand something of the hardships he has faced as a minister of the gospel (1:8; cf. Acts 14:22). He testifies that his feeling of being like one sentenced to death was to prevent him relying on himself and to ensure that he relied upon God "who raises the dead." Thus, Paul explains his apparent weakness as reliance upon the creative resurrection power of God. This is intensified in 4:1-15 where the peculiar nature of the powerful gospel clothed in the inglorious message of weakness (i.e. the crucifixion) proclaimed by weak and imperfect vessels (who, themselves, reflect the sufferings of Christ) is intended to show that the origin of its power is not humanly generated but that it comes directly from God. Again, Paul identifies his ministry with Christ's self-sacrificial suffering as well as the resurrection to authenticate his own authority (vv. 10-14). In 5:14-15 Paul explains his motivation for ministry in terms of Christ's death and resurrection. The immediate consequence of this is that the previous principles of evaluation are excluded (v. 16). In these passages, Paul speaks about an eschatological reversal.[86] What seemed like weakness to his readers was actually an identification with Christ's suffering and death which served as a conduit of life. His apostleship depends upon this inverted scale of eschatological life-giving.[87]

The connection between the new creation and the resurrection in early Jewish thought is crucial. The prophets anticipated a resurrection which would accompany the end of the ages. Through a physical resurrection, it was believed God would make his people part of his new creation (cf. Daniel 12:1-2).[88] This was part of the broader Jewish hope for the renewal of creation as a whole (*1 En.* 45:4-5; 72:1; *4 Ezra* 6:13-16; 7:75-80; Rev 21:1-5).[89] As "firstfruits (ἀπαρχή) of those who have died" (1 Cor 15:20, 23), Christ's physical body was the first of those to be raised in the anticipated eschatological resurrection.[90] The resurrection of Christ and the subsequent resurrection of believers should be seen as a cosmological event

---

[86] For a discussion of how Paul's view of resurrection challenged the Corinthian understanding of reality, see Johnson 2003:291-309.

[87] Martyn 1997:92ff.

[88] Beale 1997:18ff.

[89] Wright 2003:128, 205. For an interesting assessment of the complex and intriguing contribution of Josephus to our understanding of the question of life after death during Second Temple Judaism, see Elledge 2006.

[90] Christ could be spoken of in the later literature as "firstborn of all creation" (Col 1:15) and "firstborn from the dead" (Col 1:18; cf. Rom 8:11, 16-17, 29). Even though Colossians is generally considered to be deutero-Pauline, at the very least it suggests that Paul's thinking was compatible with the construct I am suggesting. For a broader discussion on Paul's cosmic Christology, see Van Kooten 2003:9-58.

because it represents the first stage of fulfilment of prophetic promises concerning the eschatological new creation.[91]

Levenson argues that the concept of resurrection was crucial to early Judaism.[92] Through the later lenses of the rabbis, he asserts that "resurrection finds its place within a larger vision not of the continuation of the world but of its redemption."[93] The important point to acknowledge here is that the idea of resurrection is associated with the redemption of the world and not just the individual. It functions as a kind of polemic based "on the long-standing conviction that God would yet again prove faithful to his promises of life for his people and that he had the stupendous might it would take to do so."[94]

Wright, too, sees the association of the concept of resurrection with the wider creation in the Hebrew Scriptures. He understands resurrection "not just as an image for the restoration of nation and land but as a literal prediction of one element in that restoration; not simply metaphor, but also metonymy."[95] Extremely significant for my argument is the idea that resurrection in the Second Temple period was seen both as restoration of Israel as well as "the newly embodied life of all YHWH's people." This event was seen as ending "the present age" and inaugurating the "age to come."[96]

Secondly, in 2 Cor 3:1-18, the letter of recommendation that Paul receives for his apostolic authority is not written with human implements. Rather, it is written with the Spirit of the living God (3:3). Later in this chapter, Paul speaks from the perspective of being a minister of a new covenant[97] made competent, again, not with human implements but "by the Spirit" (3:6).[98] Paul's thinking about the Spirit makes clear that he is writing from an eschatological perspective.[99] The Spirit as ἀρραβών looks

---

[91] It is certainly true that the general resurrection would have been considered a future event in Paul (1 Cor 15:52; Rom 6:5). However, there are also passages which suggest that the resurrection is, in some way, active in the present as well (2 Cor 4:11; Rom 6:11; cf. Eph 2:5; Col 2:13).

[92] Levenson 2006:x, 23-34. Levenson argues first from the perspective of contemporary Judaism and bases his arguments on the idea that the physical resurrection was already present in the Torah and did not simply arise as the result of apocalyptic expectation during the Second Temple Period.

[93] Levenson 2006:x.

[94] Levenson 2006:xiii.

[95] Wright 2003:128.

[96] Wright 2003:205.

[97] The Qumran community thought of itself as embodying the new covenant (1QpHab 2:3; CD 6:19; 8:21; 19:33-34; 20:12). This may have implications for Paul's understanding of his communities. Cf. Fitzmyer 2000:104-5.

[98] Barnett 1997:41-4.

[99] The new age was thought to be the age of the Spirit (cf. Joel 2:28; Acts 2:17). Dunn argues that Second Temple Judaism may be characterised by a sense that the Spirit was

both back towards the promises of God as fulfilled in Christ (1:20) and forward to what is to come in the future of God's salvific activity in the world (1:22; 5:5). The presence of the Spirit was the infusion of the future into the present and the first instalment of what God was doing to bring about the final age.[100] This is especially striking given the Spirit's role in the resurrection of Christ (the beginning of the new creation) and those who identify with him (cf. Rom 1:4; 8:11; 1 Cor 15:45; 2 Cor 3:18). Paul's motivation for doing what he has been called and commissioned to do is based on this eschatological hope (4:1; 4:16; 5:6).[101] Paul's ministry, approved by the Spirit, was characterised by the new age and was representative of the order of that new age being infused into the present. Thus, for Paul, the new creation is the foundation of and paradigm for his ministry.[102]

Finally, Paul uses temporally important terminology to locate himself on God's calendar of the ages in 5:15-16. The phrases μηκέτι, ἀπὸ τοῦ νῦν and νῦν οὐκέτι are theologically important phrases signalling that Paul, in concert with the thrust of his defence previously highlighted, punctuates his life in reference to the Christ event as the turning point of the ages. Bultmann held ἀπὸ τοῦ νῦν to be eschatological terminology and not a reference to the moment of conversion.[103] This position is echoed in Martyn who sees this as a reference to the "turn of the ages in the death/resurrection of Jesus."[104] The strength of this interpretation is that it makes the important connection between v. 16 and vv. 14-15 and maintains the importance of the centrality of the Christ event for Paul. Bultmann expressed this succinctly: "Ever since the event of verse 14 the world is new (v. 17; 6:2), the old has passed away – in the objective sense, of course, and not for me as one converted, however surely it is realized for me through my conversion."[105]

---

not fully active in Israel. There was an expectation that the age to come would be marked by a new outpouring of the Spirit to include even the Gentiles (Dunn 1998:416-19). Davies 1980:215-16 speaks of the Judaism of this period as having largely consigned the working of the Spirit to a previous time. He believes that "the Rabbinic Judaism of the first century would have regarded the Messianic Age or the Age to Come as the Era of the Spirit."

[100] This stands contra Kwon 2004:131-2 who rejects the "down payment" idea partially on the grounds that the resurrection has not yet occurred. However, the power of the resurrection had been applied to Paul's life (2 Cor 4:10; 5:5).

[101] Martyn 1997:92ff.
[102] Kertelge 1997:139-44.
[103] Bultmann 1963:17.
[104] Martyn 1997:94.
[105] Bultmann 1985:154.

Martyn argues that this language indicates Paul has in mind an event of cosmic proportions.[106] However, he goes too far with the conclusion that this must not refer to a private experience of the apostle Paul himself or his immediate audience. This underplays the importance of the individual and the actual context of the passage. First, the expressions ἀπὸ τοῦ νῦν and νῦν οὐκέτι refer to the verbs οἶδα and γινώσκω. These verbs are used in reference to human perception of reality. The phrase ἀπὸ τοῦ νῦν likely refers to the time when Paul formed the conviction mentioned in v. 14. Then, the very fact that Paul's opponents appear to be regarding him κατὰ σάρκα indicates that something had happened to him which had not happened to them.[107] Though Christ certainly inaugurated a new standard of measurement, this standard was only employed by those who were "in Him." The εἴ τις of v. 17 together with an apparent allusion to Paul's personal experience in v. 16b suggest that Paul's own conversion experience may have served as a model of the general Christian experience.[108]

The clear anthropological application of 2 Cor 5:16-17 does not preclude the broader soteriology important for Paul's understanding of new creation. Collange offers the helpful suggestion that ἀπὸ τοῦ νῦν is neither simply a reference to eschatology nor to conversion itself. It is both at the same time and should not be applied to Paul alone but also to believers from the time of their baptism. It refers to the "présent inauguré à la croix."[109] Hubbard recognizes the strength of Collange's position in refusing "to separate sharply Paul's eschatological 'now' (cf. Rom 3:21; 16:26) from his soteriological 'now' (Rom 5:9, 11; 7:6; 8:1; Gal 2:20), especially in the light of the way they are interwoven in 6:2."[110] Yet he believes that a focus on soteriology in 5:16 necessitates a stringently anthropological understanding of the phrase. However, this would seem to represent an inadequate understanding of Pauline soteriology as a whole. It implies a division between Paul's soteriology and the eschatological Christ event. As Stuhlmacher points out, Paul's soteriology has to do with a history of election which cannot be separated from a "cosmological-eschatological horizon."[111] Specifically, Stuhlmacher argues that the individual conversion should be thought of as the "individual application of the change of time brought about by Christ."[112]

---

[106] Martyn 1997:94-6.
[107] Hubbard strongly argues for the anthropological focus of this passage in Hubbard 2002:173-4.
[108] Hubbard 2002:174.
[109] Collange 1972:258.
[110] Hubbard 2002:174.
[111] Stuhlmacher 1967:4.
[112] Stuhlmacher 1967:5-6. Interestingly, Stuhlmacher points out how *Jos. Asen.*, rather than representing an individualization of the concept of new creation, demonstrates

Paul's understanding of conversion involved a union with Christ, which Paul frequently referenced with his ἐν Χριστῷ language.[113] This union draws the believer into a completely new mode of existence. It necessitates applying the Christ event to one's own life thereby exchanging distorted ways of perception for altogether new ones – perception through the atmosphere of a new creation.[114] Allowing for Paul's emphasis on the individual aspect of conversion in no way diminishes the communal and cosmic implications in his soteriology. As S. Chester argues in his work on Paul's understanding of conversion, "Paul...closely connects the individual with the communal and cosmic levels of his thought, in order to better express his all-encompassing gospel."[115] One's response to this gospel required change on an individual and social level and provided the basis for an alternative perspective on reality.

This change in perspective is the interpretive paradigm to which he appeals in 5:16 as a part of his apostolic defence. Though this verse has been variously interpreted as a digression or even as a gnostic gloss, it is actually a significant indication of Paul's transformed epistemology as well as an important connecting point for the subsequent verse which more explicitly speaks of new creation.[116] How the two κατὰ σάρκα phrases are construed is a critical interpretational issue here. If the phrases are interpreted adjectivally, modifying οὐδένα and Χριστόν, then we end up with some very opaque propositions. Paul would be saying that he did not know any people who were in a human body even though he did at one point know the human Jesus whom he knows no longer in this manner. This seems to distort Paul's argument beyond recognition. It is far more likely that Paul intended an adverbial use of the phrases, as most commentators now accept. It is significant that whenever Paul uses the phrase κατὰ σάρκα with reference to a proper noun it occurs after the noun and not before as here. It is used both before and after the verb when it functions adverbially.[117]

This supports the argument that Paul seems to be advancing in favour of his apostolic authority. Despite predominant interpretations in the past, Paul is not really making a Christological point here. What he is asserting is that there are different systems of measurement. According to the meas-

---

the link between the cosmic-eschatology of Isaiah with conversion. Cf. Kim 1984:15-6. Also, see Hengel 2003:229-44.

[113] For a study of the impact Paul's Damascus Road experience had on his life and ministry, see Kim 1984:110-12. For a way forward in the debate over whether the Damascus Road experience was a conversion or a call, see Chester 2003:157f.

[114] Stuhlmacher 1967:1-35.
[115] Chester 2003:318.
[116] Furnish 1984:332.
[117] Garland 1999:282.

ure of his opponents, his authority does not hold up. But they are evaluating him κατὰ σάρκα just as he had once evaluated the life, death and resurrection of Jesus.[118] However, that cataclysmic event marked the beginning of an entirely new mode of knowledge. The common sense rulings of the old age are foolishness in the new creation.[119] Paul "coins an epistemological locution – to know by the norm of the flesh – by which he refers to the passé, old-age manner of acquiring knowledge."[120]

The epistemological transformation spoken of by Paul would have been incredibly resonant in the Corinthian community which was inundated with Roman imperial ideology.[121] The Augustan transformation of the world amounted to a reinterpretation of reality around the person of the emperor and the city of Rome.[122] As a model Roman colony, Corinth embraced wholesale the new reality.[123] Similar to the surrounding culture, Paul sought to describe a reinterpretation of reality even if the community he envisaged stood in stark contrast to the social world created by the power of Rome.[124]

While the Pauline juxtaposition of σάρξ versus πνεῦμα is typically brought into the interpretation of this passage, Martyn proposes that the opposite to knowing κατὰ σάρκα is knowing κατὰ σταυρόν.[125] According to Martyn, Paul avoids the contrast with κατὰ πνεῦμα because this would reflect the overly confident teaching of the opponents.[126] Paul resists the pitfall of substituting extreme pessimism about the current situation with an overly optimistic view of the presence of the anticipated new age.[127]

---

[118] "Flesh" is an important concept in Paul and can be used in a number of different ways. R. Jewett's study of Paul's anthropological terms astutely points out how this term is associated with the old age (cf. Gal 4:21-31). He acknowledges that Paul uses κατὰ σάρκα in 2 Cor 5:16 to level the charge that those who are falsely evaluating his ministry are doing so according to the characteristics of the old age in conflict with those of the new age of the new creation. See Jewett 1971:453-6.

[119] Suffering could not be viewed positively in the old world. It is only acceptable because of the promise of resurrection.

[120] Martyn 1997:95-7. Martyn argues that the Corinthians would have had no problems understanding Paul on this matter on the basis of similar ideas found in Philo where the Platonic idea of true knowledge being hindered by the flesh is present (cf. *Agriculture* 97; *Migration* 14; *Unchangeable* 143; *Giants* 53).

[121] See Chapter 4.

[122] For an argument that the Augustan revolution was predicated upon an epistemological metamorphosis, see Wallace-Hadrill 2005:55-84.

[123] For example, see Walbank 1996:201-13.

[124] Horsley 2005:371-95. Cf. Meeks 1983:164-92; Chow 1992:188-90.

[125] Gloer 1996:108, 398 suggests that κατὰ πνεῦμα could be connected to κατὰ σταυρόν in Paul.

[126] Martyn 1997:101-06.

[127] Boomershine 1989:148.

Though the expression κατὰ σταυρόν is not actually used by Paul, it seems to encapsulate the meaning of his argument. Earlier, Paul had argued that it was the love of Christ which controlled or compelled him (5:14). The love of Christ is to be understood here in the context of the very next verse where the self-sacrificial action of his death and resurrection for the benefit of others is set forth. It was that event which turned the ages, which was presented to Paul by the resurrected Lord Himself on the Damascus road, which, in turn, revolutionized Paul's own understanding of the world and the times in which he lived, and which provided the paradigm for his own apostolic ministry. He understood that the message of the cross was "a stumbling block to Jews and foolishness to Gentiles" (1 Cor 1:23) but, for him, it was nothing less than the event of God's invasion into the world to display the power of his salvation (1 Cor 1:18, 24; cf. Rom 1:16). As the "cross-event" was what Paul perceived to have inaugurated the new creation, it would be more accurate in regard to 2 Cor 5:17 to describe Paul's contrast as being between evaluation κατὰ σάρκα and evaluation κατὰ καινὴν κτίσιν. The connection which Paul makes between the new creation and the Christ event has not been sufficiently treated despite its determinative role in this passage. We now turn our attention to a closer examination of that relationship.

C. The Christ Event and the New Creation

ὥστε εἴ τις ἐν Χριστῷ, καινὴ κτίσις
τὰ ἀρχαῖα παρῆλθεν, ἰδοὺ γέγονεν καινά[128]

Therefore if anyone [is] in Christ, [he is a] new creation.
The old things have passed away; behold, new things have come.

With the introductory ὥστε, we might expect verse 17 to be the logical conclusion of the immediately preceding verse. However, the content is more specific in verse 16 and it would seem more natural for the new epistemology expounded in the previous section to be the result of the more general statement of new creation in v. 17. Thus, it is more likely that vv.

---

[128] The text as it stands in the NA27 has the strongest support and should be allowed to stand. Several important manuscripts, however, include τὰ πάντα either before or after καινά. Metzger explains that if the second option were original, its exclusion could be a case of a scribe's eye passing over the τὰ πάντα because the next verse begins with τὰ δὲ πάντα. But if this were the case, we might expect there to be some evidence of an omitted δέ in v. 18. Nonetheless, given the age and character of the witnesses in support of the text and inadequate explanations of how τὰ πάντα could have been omitted, it is likely that the alternative witnesses record a scribal insertion. See Metzger 1994:511.

16-17 are parallel statements working out the implications of vv. 14-15.[129] If that is the case, being ἐν Χριστῷ (v. 17) entails participation in the representative death and resurrection of Christ mentioned in vv. 14-15. The significance of this connection has been largely underplayed by commentators on these verses. This close association with the Christ event helps to substantiate my argument that the apostle Paul's conception of new creation is an expression of his eschatologically infused soteriology which has implications for the individual, the community and the cosmos. Furnish suggests that 5:17 makes for a cosmic and eschatological interpretation of v. 14.[130] But it will be argued here that vv. 14-15 help us understand in what way v. 17 is cosmic and eschatological.

Thrall recognizes the inadequate attempts to see this passage strictly cosmologically but admits that there is something more than an individual anthropological emphasis here: "Since it is precisely through death and resurrection that this new creation is inaugurated, it is something more than the new beginning made by a proselyte to Judaism, or by an entrant to the Qumran community, or by all Jews on the Day of Atonement. It is a genuine anticipation of the eschatological transformation."[131] Thrall seems to be wrestling with the same issue as Hubbard. 2 Corinthians 5:17 resists an overly cosmological interpretation but her keen exegetical senses alert her to the fact that the verse must not be limited simply to individual experience. This becomes clear when the connection with the preceding verses is taken into account.

In 2 Cor 5:14 Paul's insistence upon the love of Christ being the motivating factor of his ministry is highly significant.[132] Contrary to the self-serving motivation of the orators, it is the self-sacrificial love of Christ (cf. Rom 5:5-6) which sustains Paul's ministry.[133] The basis of this compulsion is his conviction that Christ's death and resurrection served a representative function for the entire human race (πᾶς occurs 3 times in 5:14-15) and that those who appropriate the effects of this event are exhorted to leave behind the self-serving way of life characteristic of the previous age for the resurrection-quality life of Christ (5:15).[134] This provides a clue that Paul's

---

[129] Thrall 1994:424.
[130] Furnish 1984:329.
[131] Thrall 1994:428.
[132] With the vast majority of scholars I take τοῦ Χριστοῦ as a subjective genitive. See Harris 2005:418.
[133] The discussion regarding the origin of the ὑπέρ-tradition in Paul's thinking is diverse. For a fuller treatment of the issue, see Gloer 1996:13-32.
[134] Philo saw a similar idea of representation in his comments on Gen 7:1 where Noah is told "Go into the ark, you and all your household, for I have seen that you alone are righteous before me in this generation." Philo interprets this as an example of the principle that many may be saved through the acts of one righteous person, δι' ἕνα ἄνδρα δίκαιον καὶ ὅσιον πολλοὶ ἄνθρωποι σώζονται (QG 2.11).

understanding of new creation is not limited to an individual experience. His conviction that one has died for all should alert us to the fact that Paul is interested in the supra-individual effects of the Christ event as well as the change it brings to the individual's life.

The real *crux interpretum* comes in 14c, ἄρα οἱ πάντες ἀπέθανον. This conclusion is just the opposite of what we might expect. If one dies for all, no one else would need to die. The aorist tense of both occurrences of ἀποθνῄσκω suggests that the "all" died at the time of Christ's death.[135] Thrall's solution to this exegetical difficulty is better than most alternatives. She concludes that Paul's understanding of the individual's participation in the sin of Adam may have required a participation in the event which brought that power to an end.[136] Thrall, however, remains ambivalent as to how "realistically" Paul understood this. An examination of Paul's use of Adam-Christ typology in this context may offer some clarity. This comparison is spelt out more fully elsewhere (Rom 5:15-21; 1 Cor 15:21-22, 45-50) and it operates just beneath the surface of this text.[137]

The effect of the Adam-Christ comparison underscores that the death and resurrection of Christ has "more than individual significance."[138] Paul's use of death in Rom 5 and 1 Cor 15 should be understood in the context of his "Christological apocalyptic eschatology."[139] In the type of eschatology represented in this literature there is a strong dualism of ages where the old age is controlled by inimical powers of sin and death and the new age is characterised by righteousness and life.[140] It was the "old age" that produced the improper judgement κατὰ σάρκα of 5:16 and in which realm "the god of this world (ὁ θεὸς τοῦ αἰῶνος τούτου)" (4:4) operated. Paul knew that "the ends of the ages had come" (1 Cor 10:11). It was

---

[135] Despite attempts to relate the three occurrences of πάντες to believers, it is better taken as universal in scope. See Harris 2005:421-2.

[136] Thrall 1994:411.

[137] There are substantial differences in the way this theme is expressed. In Romans 5:12-21, "the many" died through the sin of "the one man" and the gift of grace through the one man Jesus Christ abounds to "the many". In 1 Cor 15:22, "in Adam all die" and "in Christ all will be made alive."

[138] Dunn 1988:290.

[139] De Boer 1988:181. We should beware of the term "apocalyptic" since it can be so slippery as not to mean anything at all. The warnings of Matlock are merited in that de Boer's use of the term doesn't best serve his agenda. What he is really trying to do is to "undertake an exegetical study of Paul's 'already/not yet' tension in the tradition of Käsemann and Beker, to which tradition he makes a valuable contribution." Thus, I prefer the term "eschatological" to "apocalyptic." See Matlock 1996:314-15.

[140] Although Paul has affinities with the more "forensic" stream of Jewish apocalypticism, in this instance it is the "cosmological" stream which better explains his thinking. See De Boer's discussion of the two "tracks" of Jewish apocalypticism in De Boer 1989:172-85.

C. The Christ Event and the New Creation

the death and resurrection of Christ that marked the end of the old age and the beginning of the new. Yet the facts that the physical universe remained unchanged and that judgement κατὰ σάρκα was still possible indicate that Paul's eschatology was processual. The end had arrived but had not yet come in full. For Paul the death and resurrection of Christ had begun God's end-time new creation.

This eschatological influence may be seen in Paul's understanding of Adam and Christ as representative heads of the ages. The means of transfer from one realm of influence to another is the death of Christ. The old world has been judged. Its constituency is subject to death but those who are "in Christ" enter a new sphere of existence.[141] Christ's death and resurrection function as a bridge between the old and the new age.[142] This may be seen from a closer examination of the Adam-Christ comparison in 1 Cor 15 and Rom 5.

Paul first develops the Adam-Christ comparison in 1 Cor 15:22,

ὥσπερ γὰρ ἐν τῷ Ἀδὰμ πάντες ἀποθνῄσκουσιν,
οὕτως καὶ ἐν τῷ Χριστῷ πάντες ζῳοποιηθήσονται.

The point of this comparison is to explain further the relationship between the resurrection of Christ and the general resurrection (1 Cor 15:20). Paul has been arguing against objections to the idea of resurrection from the dead (1 Cor 15:1-2, 3-8, 12) on the grounds that if there is no resurrection then the faith he proclaims is futile (κενός, μάταιος) since that would mean that not even Christ was raised (vv. 12-19). In truth, Paul asserts, Christ is the ἀπαρχή of the general resurrection (vv. 20, 23; cf. Rom 8:23).

Twice in this context, Christ is specifically referred to as the ἀπαρχή (1 Cor 15:20, 23). The concept of the firstfruits is probably based on the OT offering of the first portion of the crop as an offering of thanks to God for his provision. It signified the provision of the remainder of the harvest and the acknowledgement that all which was to follow was the Lord's. Applied to the resurrection of Christ, this indicates Paul's understanding of the connection between Christ's resurrection and the eschatological resurrection of believers.[143] Consequently, the resurrection of Christ was a "cosmic world-event" which marked the turn of the ages because it was part of the final restoration of creation expected in the last days.[144]

Paul's argument is based on the assertion that resurrection comes through a man because that is the way in which death came into the world

---

[141] De Boer 1988:185.
[142] Hooker 1994:42.
[143] Cf. De Boer 1988:109.
[144] Schweitzer 1956:23. This is in line with the view espoused in some apocalyptic literature which understood resurrection language in reference to future hopes of cosmic restoration. Cf. Beker 1980:101, 152-3.

(1 Cor 15:21).[145] In continuity with the first century Jewish understanding of the unity of humanity in Adam, Paul saw Adam as representative of the entire human race.[146] In similar fashion, Christ is representative of a new humanity (cf. Eph 2:15). The fall of Adam had cosmological significance in Second Temple Judaism (cf. *4 Ezra* 8:11) and it was believed that the new/Messianic age would need to reverse these consequences.[147]

This becomes even clearer when Paul's discussion in 1 Cor 15 explains the nature of the resurrection body (vv. 35-50). He employs in this explanation the Adam-Christ typology once again. This time, the comparison is made even more explicit. Christ is called ὁ ἔσχατος Ἀδάμ. Quoting Gen 2:7 to speak of the original creation, Paul makes two important additions to the text:

Gen 2:7b LXX =	ἐγένετο ὁ	ἄνθρωπος	εἰς ψυχὴν ζῶσαν
1 Cor 15:45a =	ἐγένετο ὁ πρῶτος	ἄνθρωπος Ἀδάμ	εἰς ψυχὴν ζῶσαν

The insertion of πρῶτος and Ἀδάμ serve to heighten the contrast between Adam and Christ, ὁ ἔσχατος Ἀδάμ. The point being made is that humanity bears the image of Adam in sharing with him a mortal existence dependent upon the evanescent body fashioned from the "dust of the earth" (Gen 2:7; cf. 1 Cor 15:47-9).[148] Paul uses the Adam-Christ comparison in his explanation of how believers share in the resurrection body of Christ. Rather than the fragile and weak nature of the body which all humanity shares with Adam, the resurrected Christ offers an incorruptible and immortal body. Adam was merely a "living being (ψυχή)," a term used generically to designate living things. Christ is referred to as a "life-giving spirit (πνεῦμα ζῳοποιοῦν)" by virtue of his resurrection (cf. 2 Cor 3:6).[149] Humanity presently bears the image of this "man of dust (τὴν εἰκόνα τοῦ χοϊκοῦ)" but will also bear the image of the "man of heaven (τὴν εἰκόνα τοῦ ἐπουρανίου)" (1 Cor 15:49).

Paul picks up again the language of the εἰκών in 2 Cor 4:4-6. Here, God's calling light out of darkness in the context of discussion about the

---

[145] Davies 1980:49 suggests this is an example of the principle of *Endzeit-Urzeit* correspondence in Paul (cf. 2 Cor 5:17).

[146] This is particularly important with regard to the discussion of Gal 6:15 where the new creation in Christ supersedes the divisions of the former creation in Adam. Cf. Horrell 2000.

[147] Cf. Davies 1980:39.

[148] For an explanation of χοϊκός as a Pauline neologism, see *TDNT* 9:472-79. The concentrated use of this term in this passage (4 times in 3 verses) highlights the strong contrast between the nature of Adamic existence and that of life in Christ, the man of heaven.

[149] See the recent work of Yates 2007.

image of God cannot help but recall the creation account of Gen 1. In the Gen text God made Adam κατ' εἰκόνα θεοῦ, in 2 Cor 4:4 Christ is referred to as the image of God. Christ is thus placed in correspondence to the representative man of the first creation. This is not meant to suggest that Paul viewed Adam as the prototypical/ideal man in the Philonic/Platonic sense. In fact, the use of the Adam-Christ comparison in 1 Cor 15 and Rom 5 shows that Adam is used as the representative figure of creation under the ill-effects of sin and decay. Paul juxtaposes Adam and the era represented by him with Christ and the new era he brings into being and he applies the creation language to conversion.[150]

The significance of this for Paul's conception of new creation is that Paul was thinking in eschatological terms when he thought about conversion. The creation imagery of chapter 4 emphasizes that Christ becomes the starting point of the new creation for which Paul is arguing in 2 Corinthians just as Adam had been the starting point of the original creation. Paul has in mind the idea of transformation from likeness to "the image (τὴν εἰκόνα) of the man of dust (τοῦ χοϊκοῦ)" (1 Cor 15:49) into the glorious image of the risen Lord "from one degree of glory to another (ἀπὸ δόξης εἰς δόξαν)" (2 Cor 3:18).[151] This transformation is evidence that the new creation had been inaugurated in the Christ event and that it was advancing through the life and ministry of Paul and his eschatological communities.[152]

Paul uses the Adam-Christ comparison in Rom 5:12-21 with a different emphasis. Whereas he had used the comparison in 1 Cor 15 to advance his argument about the resurrection, in Rom 5 the topic is justification. However, Rom 5 is still instructive for our purposes because of Paul's further use of the Adam-Christ comparison. Without pausing to deal with the many issues raised by Rom 5:12-21, we can focus on one point for the purposes of this argument: Paul views Christ as the counterpart to Adam. The point is that "everything which happened to man in Adam is paralleled, or rather reversed, by what has happened to man in Christ."[153] For him, history could be divided into two acts – each one characterised by a representative figure.[154]

---

[150] The language of 2 Cor 4:4-6 probably represents a reflection upon Paul's experience of the risen Christ on the Damascus Road and does not necessarily entail an actual description of what Paul saw. Contra Kim 1984:110ff. See Dunn 1987:251-66.

[151] See Scholla 1997:33-54.

[152] Hafemann 1996:301.

[153] Hooker 1990:28, 31. But M. Hooker argues that the parallels are not precise because Paul is actually making another contrast in this passage: "the transgression of Adam and *God's* act of reconciliation in Christ" (Rom 5:6-11). The focus on God's action in reconciliation is confirmed in 2 Cor 5:18-21.

[154] Dunn 1988:288.

All of humanity is naturally identified with Adam. Identification with Christ comes to those who receive the free gift of righteousness and is signified through the act of baptism (Rom 5:15-19; 6:3-11).[155] Immediately following an extended treatment of the effects of the one man, Adam, versus the effects of the one man, Christ, Paul attempts to deal with the question: "Are we to continue in sin that grace may abound (Rom 6:1)?" The answer to this comes through an identification of the believer with the death of Christ: "Do you not know that all of us who have been baptized into Christ Jesus were baptized into his death (6:3; cf. 2 Cor 5:14-15)?"[156] The idea of dying with Christ comes to fuller expression in the astonishing proposition of Rom 6:6: ὁ παλαιὸς ἡμῶν ἄνθρωπος συνεσταυρώθη, ἵνα καταργηθῇ τὸ σῶμα τῆς ἁμαρτίας, τοῦ μηκέτι δουλεύειν ἡμᾶς τῇ ἁμαρτίᾳ.[157]

Paul's use of the phrase ὁ παλαιὸς ἡμῶν ἄνθρωπος is intriguing as an extension of the Adam-Christ comparison from the preceding verses. This is not a reference to a *part* of Paul but to his former identity and association with the Adamic age.[158] D. Moo understands this as denoting "the solidarity of people with the 'heads' of the two contrasting ages of salvation history."[159] This collective emphasis is suggested by the presence of the ἡμῶν.[160] The purpose of the co-crucifixion with Christ of "our old man"[161] is revealed in the very next clause, ἵνα καταργηθῇ τὸ σῶμα τῆς

---

[155] In fact, it may have been through an early association with Christian baptismal rites that the idea of new creation was "de-cosmologised." Thanks to Professor William Horbury for this helpful suggestion.

[156] It should not be overlooked that there is also an identification with Christ's resurrection. This takes on an ethical quality, "Therefore we have been buried with him by baptism into death, so that, just as Christ was raised from the dead by the glory of the Father, so we too might walk in newness of life" (6:4). But this also points to a resurrection existence which transcends moral dimensions (6:5, 8) and has both future (6:8) as well as present (6:11) applications.

[157] For treatment of the background of the Pauline "with Christ" language, see Wedderburn 1987:342-59.

[158] Moo 1996:374-5. This explains how the concept is used corporately in Col 3:10-11 and Eph 2:15. For a defence of the connection of Rom 5:12-21 with Rom 6, see Tannehill 1967:26-29. Cf. Hooker 1990:23.

[159] Moo 1996:374. Moo believes this explains the apparent discrepancy between the idea that believers have become the new man already (cf. Col 3:9-11) and the command elsewhere to "put on the new man" (Eph 4:22-24). "At the heart of the contrast between "old man" and "new man" is the eschatological tension between the inauguration of the new age in the life of the believer – he or she belongs to the 'new creation' (2 Cor 5:17) – and the culmination of that new age in 'glorification with Christ' (8:17)" (Moo 1996: 375).

[160] Tannehill 1967:24-5.

[161] NRSV = "our old self."

ἁμαρτίας.¹⁶² Although Paul does use σῶμα in reference to the physical body, he also uses the term in reference to the person as a whole (e.g. Rom 6:12-13; 12:1; Phil 1:20; cf. Eph 5:28).¹⁶³ This understanding of σῶμα adds weight to Jewett's translation of τὸ σῶμα τῆς ἁμαρτίας as "its body of sin" where the τὸ receives a mildly possessive sense.¹⁶⁴ The sinful body is the individual manifestation of "our old man (ὁ παλαιὸς ἡμῶν ἄνθρωπος)." By participation in the crucifixion of Christ, humanity's solidarity with and domination by Adamic existence comes to an end.

The relationship between these Adam-Christ comparisons and 2 Cor 5:14 becomes clearer in the dying with Christ language used in v. 15. Paul expresses this theme by using the dative in combination with the verb ζάω to speak of transfer from one life to another.¹⁶⁵ The transfer expressed with this construction is clearly present in 2 Cor 5:15, καὶ ὑπὲρ πάντων ἀπέθανεν ἵνα οἱ ζῶντες μηκέτι **ἑαυτοῖς** ζῶσιν ἀλλὰ τῷ ὑπὲρ αὐτῶν **ἀποθανόντι καὶ ἐγερθέντι**. This observation alongside the presence of the εἷς-πᾶς motif affirms the presence of the Adam-Christ comparison in this passage.¹⁶⁶ This is crucial for understanding what Paul means by new creation in 5:17.¹⁶⁷ To be ἐν Χριστῷ Ἰησοῦ (Rom 6:11; cf. 2 Cor 5:17) means to have transferred from the life of the old age to the life of the new through participation in Christ's own death and resurrection. Christ's death is the representative death of the old age and his resurrection marks the beginning of the new age.¹⁶⁸

This brings me to a point of significant disagreement with the most recent study of new creation in Paul's letters. M. Hubbard recognizes the importance of the ἐν Χριστῷ in 5:17 but he misunderstands how this language functions in the context. He rightly points out that Paul's ἐν Χριστῷ is soteriological and that the τις requires an anthropological em-

---

¹⁶² The adjective παλαιός occurs in similar context in 2 Cor 3:14 where Paul uses it to describe the covenant which preceded Christ (cf. 1 Cor 5:7-8). The same verb used in 6:6 (καταργέω) is also used there to indicate that the old covenant has been made ineffective. Whereas in 2 Cor 3:13 this verb is used in reference to the glory of Moses' face, it is used here in reference to "the body of sin (τὸ σῶμα τῆς ἁμαρτίας)." See the detailed discussion of Paul's use of καταργέω in Hafemann 1995:301-9.

¹⁶³ Moo 1996:375. Moo points out Bultmann's understanding of σῶμα in this way and the subsequent corrective offered by Gundry against such an "aspectival" understanding; but he overrules the objections on the basis of frequent use of the term in the context of holistic language in Paul. Cf. Dunn 1988:319-20.

¹⁶⁴ Jewett 2007:404.

¹⁶⁵ Tannehill cites Rom 6:10-11; Gal 2:19; 5:25; cf. Rom 6:2; 7:4; Gal 6:14. Tannehill 1967:66.

¹⁶⁶ Harris 2005:420.

¹⁶⁷ Lambrecht 1994b:376.

¹⁶⁸ This is expressed clearest in 1 Cor 15:21 where the Adam-Christ comparison is used in the context of Paul's discussion of the resurrection.

phasis. However, as I have attempted to argue, the nature of the ἐν Χριστῷ language is difficult to subsume completely into the category of conversion of the individual as Hubbard's argument seems to do. Though ἐν Χριστῷ may be shorthand for being a Christian in some passages (e.g. 12:2), it misses the larger theological point being made with regard to the Adam-Christ analogy to restrict this phrase simply to that meaning.

The idea of mysticism has been used to describe Paul's participatory imagery as a way of recognizing that this type of language in Paul applied to the death and resurrection of Christ cannot be considered a mere description of baptism or of ethical or social change.[169] Rather, Paul's language points to *participation* of believers in the "cosmic movement of God centred on Christ and effected through his Spirit."[170] This participation is crucial to Paul's apologetic. Paul's own sufferings reflected those of Christ's. If the Corinthians reject Paul's ministry, they are actually rejecting the Christological path to restoration of Adam's glory.[171]

The theme of restoration is advanced in Paul's discussion of reconciliation in 2 Cor 5:18-6:2. Hubbard argues that this simply strengthens an anthropological interpretation of new creation; but this text has clear links to the Jewish idea of restoration. Hubbard correctly identifies this as having impact upon the individual. But restoration (and more generally, redemption) from the Jewish perspective was primarily seen as something that would happen to Israel corporately, not simply to individuals.[172] At the very least, this should speak for an ecclesiological interpretation of new creation in 5:17. If the above connection with Isaiah can be sustained, it should also be noted that this restoration was thought of ultimately to bring changes to the created order, itself.[173] Further, the timing of the restoration was to be eschatological. In other words, restoration was characteristic of how God would act in the new age. This creates a strong link between new creation and the Jewish perception of the ages. The connection is important

---

[169] Schweitzer's term can be misleading and is probably better understood as "participation." Cf. Tuckett 2001:60-2.

[170] Dunn 1998:404. Cf. Collins 1996:235-8.

[171] The Jewish expectation that the glory of Adam would be restored in the age to come was confirmed for Paul in Christ, the righteous sufferer. Pate 1991:137-40. On the restoration of the glory of Adam in early Judaism, note the helpful insights in Swarup 2006:123-5.

[172] See the discussion of the "Israel of God" in the previous chapter. If we are correct to see Isaianic influence here, cosmological and anthropological restoration must be interrelated. On this point, see Hooker 1990:3.

[173] Chester makes the argument that resurrection in the OT prior to Daniel was likely a metaphorical way of expressing hope for restoration. Chester 2001:47-77.

for understanding all that Paul had in mind when he used the phrase καινὴ κτίσις.[174]

The close link between Paul's use of new creation and the Christ event supports the idea that 2 Cor 5:17 refers to something more than an individual's conversion. The Christ event has efficacy prior to an individual experience.[175] The tenses of verse 14 indicate that "all" died at the time of Christ's death. Paul did not speak here of becoming convinced that Christ had died "for me" (cf. Gal 2:20) but "for all." Though Paul could certainly envisage limitations to the scope of Christ's death (Rom 5:17; 2 Cor 5:15), there is a sense in which the death of Christ has universal implications.[176] The "all died" should be understood in the light of the passing away of the old age. Paul uses this language to elucidate the cosmic implications of the death of Christ. As C. K. Barrett articulated this balance in 1962, there are "two needful elements in redemption – the cosmic act of deliverance, and the inner anthropological rectification of man's existence in the sight of God."[177] Christ's love, conceptualized in his death, is not merely a private, personal motivation for Paul and a select group who believe. It has universal and cosmic implications.[178]

As Paul's Adam-Christ comparison makes clear, all humanity is associated with the old age by virtue of its connection with Adam and his sin. Christ is the eschatological Adam which both ends the old form of existence and begins a new creation existence.[179] Those who are associated with Adam are those living in the old age under the hegemony of the power of sin and death. Christ's representative death for that age/sphere of existence marks the beginning of its destruction. Quite significant for our understanding of the new creation is the idea prevalent in later apocalyptic literature which uses this kind of temporal dualism to express the tension between the present state of the world and the final state when God acts to restore creation to its original splendour.[180]

Having examined the crucial connection between the Christ event and new creation in Paul's thinking, we now focus our attention further on 2 Cor 5:17. The well-balanced parallelism of this verse contributes to deciphering its meaning.

---

[174] Hubbard's argument misunderstands this connection.

[175] Cf. Denney 1951:82-5.

[176] See Moule's essay on the scope of Christ's death in Moule 1977:107-126. For a more recent discussion, see Wedderburn 2003:267-83.

[177] Barrett 1962:117. Note his discussion on the new creation in the individual, the church and the world in Barrett 1962:103-19.

[178] Pickett 1997:142-50.

[179] Beker refers to this as "a resurrection mode of existence." Beker 1980:100-1.

[180] Aune 2001b:177.

2 Cor 5:17a	ὥστε εἴ τις ἐν Χριστῷ	καινὴ κτίσις
2 Cor 5:17b	τὰ ἀρχαῖα παρῆλθεν	ἰδοὺ γέγονεν καινά

What is meant in the first clause is elaborated in the second. The "in Christ" language of 5:17a reminds the reader of the participatory motif and, consequently, the Adam-Christ comparison which had been operative in vv. 14-15. Thus the passing away of the "old things" invokes the death of "all" articulated in those verses as well as Paul's personal experience of that cosmically efficacious event. Given the strong connection with the Christ event in vv. 14-15 as well as the death-life imagery at work in those verses, the "new things" which have come bring to mind those who now live the resurrection life of Christ (v. 15). Though the actual physical resurrection of believers was yet to come, the resurrection of Christ began to fulfil promises of restoration expected to occur at the end of time. This in no way diminishes the individual implications of this text but neither should its individual application obscure its relationship to Paul's broader soteriology.[181]

Of course, the tenses of v. 17b prohibit us from understanding Paul's new creation primarily in terms of the physical universe. Since Paul viewed the "old"[182] as having passed away and the new as a present reality, the expression καινὴ κτίσις is not simply a reference to a re-creation or renovation of the world. But if we take Paul's inaugurated eschatological perspective seriously, as well as the link with the Christ event in vv. 14-15, there may be an additional way to speak of the physical new creation as having begun – in the resurrection body of Jesus. This would certainly not strain the evidence of passages like 1 Cor 15:20, 23 where Christ's resurrection is referred to as the "firstfruits" of the general resurrection believed to occur at the end of time (cf. Col 1:15-18; Rom 8:11, 16-17, 29). This is also compatible with the apocalyptic understanding of resurrection in the context of the re-creation of the cosmos.[183] Furthermore, if it is true that Christ's physical resurrection represented the beginning of the new crea-

---

[181] Contra Hubbard 2002:181-2.

[182] This is the only occurrence of the term ἀρχαῖος in Paul's writings. He more usually employs παλαιός (Rom 6:6; 1 Cor 5:7-8; 2 Cor 3:14). Use of this terminology in contrast with καινός supports the argument that Paul's language may reflect the influence of Isa 43:18-19 as argued above. This supports my contention that this passage is imbued with rich soteriological themes which should not be limited to the anthropological elements of Paul's thought.

[183] E.g. *1 En.* 51:1-5. I have made a fuller case for this connection in my chapter on new creation in intertestamental literature. For an argument against this cosmological understanding of vv. 14-15, see Findeis 1983.

tion, it is conceivable that the destruction of his physical body on the cross represented the beginning of the destruction of the cosmos along with the powers associated with it.[184]

A final exegetical insight deserves consideration: Paul's use of the conditional sentence. Alongside the use of τις, the conditional sentence has been said to rule out a cosmological understanding of new creation in 2 Cor 5:17.[185] Harris correctly recognizes that "the renewal of the individual in conversion prefigures the renewal of the cosmos at the end" but he believes the focus in 5:17a is "anthropological and personal" rather than "cosmological and eschatological."[186] However, the conditional sentence need not be taken in a way that reduces Paul's cosmological and eschatological focus. In the context of Paul's broader argument the conditional sentence "functions as a tool of persuasion."[187] The protasis is assumed both by Paul and by his audience and he thus urges them to live out the implications of that truth – that they are part of God's eschatological plan of redemption and that the former way of living characteristic of the old world is no longer valid or appropriate. Their judgment of his apostolic ministry revealed that they were very much still operating as participants in the old age.

D. CONCLUSIONS

Paul's writing is certainly influenced by many sources (Jewish and Greco-Roman) but it is commonly recognized that the prophecies of Isaiah are of particular importance for him. The convergence of a number of Isaianic motifs in 2 Cor 5 supports the assertion that the prophecies of Isaiah significantly influenced Paul's thinking in his understanding of new creation. As previously argued in chapter 2, the soteriology of the Isaianic material consistently maintains a connection between the individual, the nation of Israel and the world in which they lived. It is concerned with the redemption of God's people as part of his creation as a whole. Although Paul does not trade heavily in the kind of literal cosmic destruction language which appears in Isaiah and which is typical of later apocalyptic writings, the soteriological breadth of the Isaianic prophecies is important for his think-

---

[184] This may help to explain the statement of v. 14 that Christ's death implied the death of "all."

[185] Harris 2005:432.

[186] Thrall 1994:461. This leads to the conclusion that the proper background for understanding Paul's new creation is the "rabbinic description of the sinner who repents or the Gentile who converts." See Harris 2005:432-3.

[187] Wallace 1996:694.

ing.¹⁸⁸ This is clear in the way that Paul understands the work of Christ to have brought about an eschatological fulfilment of the Isaianic prophecies.

If Isaianic influence stands behind 2 Cor 5:17, Paul could well be taking up the idea that all previous acts of deliverance and works of God are completely outdone by his latest and most significant revelation in the person and work of Christ. His most powerful act of deliverance (in the Christ event) was not an isolated individual death. Christ died ὑπὲρ πάντων with the result that οἱ πάντες ἀπέθανον. What it means that "all died" cannot simply be limited to individual experience. The πάντες should be understood universally.¹⁸⁹ Paul's use of the Adam-Christ comparison in this context suggests that what passed away for Paul in 2 Cor 5:17 is not just his old thought processes and his former attitudes, though these were certainly included. Rather, the "old age" of which those things are characteristic has been dealt its death blow in the death of Christ. The individual convert, then, is a microcosm of the ultimate act of redemption which God plans for the entire cosmos.¹⁹⁰ For Paul, human nature itself reflects the larger eschatological tension.¹⁹¹ In conversion, a person moves not only from one opinion to another but from one social sphere to another. The person also moves into a new way of perceiving reality – an epistemological revolution.

At the beginning of this chapter I suggested that the particular social setting of the Corinthian church would make the epistemological revolution described in 2 Cor 5:16 especially relevant to our discussion. The Augustan transformation of the world could be conceived of in terms of a metamorphosis of Roman knowledge.¹⁹² The transformation was based upon a form of eschatology in which the emperor and the empire were seen as the apex of human history. If Paul's apostolic defence to the Corinthians was based on a new epistemology brought about by the eschatological action of God in Christ, the stage is set for a high degree of cultural resonance when Paul uses the concept of new creation in the very next verse. The imperial ideology used cosmological imagery to describe the *Pax Romana*. Imperial exploits were said to bring peace and order to the cosmos. This ideology pervaded the empire, East and West, and provides an interesting acoustic in which Paul's understanding of new creation could have reverberated.

---

¹⁸⁸ For a recent study of cosmic destruction language in the new testament, see Adams 2007.

¹⁸⁹ See the argument in Harris 2005:419-24.

¹⁹⁰ Aune 1993:32-3.

¹⁹¹ Note the different uses of παλιγγενεσία in Mt 19:28 and Tit 3:5. This term is applied both to the overlapping concepts of new age and new birth.

¹⁹² See Wallace-Hadrill 2005:55-84.

D. CONCLUSIONS

If the Corinthian colonists embraced the imperial self-understanding – and we have clear evidence to confirm they did – Paul's use of the concept of new creation could easily have taken on associations far broader than an individual's conversion. It could have suggested a completely new social order and even implied the kind of all-encompassing metamorphosis characteristic of Roman imperial ideology. This observation supports the central claim of this thesis that Paul's understanding of new creation is an expression of his eschatologically infused soteriology. The following chapter casts the exegetical net a little wider and explores how Paul uses the concept of new creation where the phrase καινὴ κτίσις does not occur.

Chapter 7

Paul's Conception of New Creation in Romans 8:18-25

This chapter attempts to show how Paul uses the concept of new creation in his letter to the churches in Rome. Although the phrase καινὴ κτίσις does not occur in Romans, the concept is clearly operative in the way that Paul builds his argument in chapters 1-8. Significantly, apart from Gal 6:15 and 2 Cor 5:17, κτίσις *only* occurs in Paul's undisputed letters in Romans 1 and 8.[1] This provides some terminological control over the inclusion of Rom 8 into the discussion of καινὴ κτίσις in Gal 6 and 2 Cor 5. In addition to the lexical convergence, the implied renewal of creation in 8:18-25 makes these verses an important text for understanding Paul's conception of new creation.[2] Under the generally accepted view that Romans provides us with a kind of theological *summa*, we should not be surprised to find the concept of creation at play if, indeed, it plays the kind of role in Paul's soteriological plan argued in this thesis.[3]

The argument proceeds with a discussion of how κτίσις is used in Romans 8 in reference to non-human creation followed by an examination of the role creation plays for Paul in the plan of chapters 1-8 as a whole. It is argued here that Paul employs creation imagery in chapter 1 of his letter to the Romans and that he advances his argument toward the redemption of that creation in chapter 8. Romans 8, in particular, provides evidence that Paul's soteriology inextricably links the salvation of people with the salvation of the world.[4] According to Paul, the fates of both were entwined with the sin of Adam and are inseparable until God's purposes in redemption are complete. After an examination of the function of creation in Romans,

---

[1] See Col 1:15, 23; Cf. 1 Tim 4:4.

[2] Vögtle understands the individual as new creation as a proleptic indicator of the coming new creation of the whole world. He sees Rom 8:19ff as irrefutable evidence for the connection between the anthropological and cosmological new creation. See Vögtle 1970a:174-6, 183-208. For an argument that the renewal of Rom 8 is strictly anthropological, see, e.g., Gager 1970; Lampe 1964.

[3] This is neither to suggest that the social situation in Rome was unimportant nor that Romans is impersonal. However, it is generally agreed that the form of the letter suggests more than a personal communication. In a manner unique among the contemporary evidence, Paul combines the letter form with that of a treatise. See Dunn 1988:lix-lx.

[4] Cf. Bolt 1995:34-51; Stuhlmacher 1994:133-5.

an attempt is made to show how this is significant for understanding Paul's use of καινὴ κτίσις.

A. Paul's Use of κτίςις in Romans[5]

Paul uses the term κτίσις seven times in his letter to the Romans, all concentrated in chapters 1 and 8.[6] The two most common uses of the term are represented in chapter 1 and its usage there is fairly clear. In Rom 1:20 κτίσις denotes the act of creating and refers to the time when God created the world (κόσμος).[7] Rom 1:25 denotes the result of the creative act and is translated by the majority of scholars as "creature."[8] The meaning of the four occurrences of κτίσις in Rom 8:19-22 has been strongly contested but is taken as a reference to non-human creation by the majority of scholars.[9] The final occurrence of κτίσις in Romans (8:39) is preceded by τις implying a created thing rather than all of creation and should be understood similarly to 1:25.

The trajectory of creation between chapters 1 and 8 reveals a great deal about Paul's overall argument. In chapter 1, the creation is presented positively as the revelation of God to the Gentiles. Paul makes clear in 1:19-20 that God's "eternal power and divinity" were revealed through the created order but humanity proved unable to comprehend this revelation because their unrighteousness suppressed the truth (τῶν τὴν ἀλήθειαν ἐν ἀδικίᾳ

---

[5] On the general theme of creation in Paul, see Baumbach 1979:196-205.

[6] See the examination of the expressions and themes relating to creation in Rom 1-8 which suggest a connection between Romans 1 and 8 in Kraftchick 1987:82-5. Cf. Walter 1989:218-26. Theobald discusses the theocentric nature of protology and eschatology in the context of Rom 1 and 8 in Theobald 2000:138-42.

[7] The preposition ἀπό takes on a temporal sense as in Rom 15:23; 2 Cor 9:2; Col 1:6, 9. Cf. BDAG, pp. 572-3; Fitzmyer 1993:280.

[8] This is contra BDAG which translates κτίσις as "creation." See, e.g., LaGrange 1950; Cranfield 1975; Dunn 1988; Fitzmyer 1993; Moo 1996; Byrne 1996; Schreiner 1998; Lohse 2003; Jewett 2007. Michel 1978 is somewhat ambivalent but probably listed among these.

[9] There have been attempts to take κτίσις in Rom 8 as referring either exclusively to unbelievers or to unbelievers in conjunction with non-human creation. Gager, for example, takes this as anthropological partially on the basis of the idea that καινὴ κτίσις refers to the converted individual. This not only seriously overrides the lexical data of the immediate context, it also makes the *a priori* assumption of an anthropologically restricted referent in Gal 6:15 and 2 Cor 5:17. See Gager 1970:328-9.

E. Adams points out the recent consensus which has emerged among scholars to interpret κτίσις in Rom 8:19-22 as a reference to the non-human creation. See Adams 2000:175-8; Cranfield 1974:225. But note the objection of Eastman who includes unbelieving humanity with the created order in Eastman 2002:273-6.

κατεχόντων, v. 18). The result was the darkening of human reason and an idolatrous relationship with creation (1:21-2; cf. Wisdom 13:1-3). The failure to honour and give thanks to God led to their thinking becoming "futile" (ματαιόω).[10] This is the only appearance of the verb ματαιόω in Romans but the nominal form appears in 8:20 where Paul argues that creation itself was subjected to futility (ματαιότης).[11] This very likely reflects the Jewish understanding of God's curse pronounced on the ground in Gen 3:17-19.[12]

Adam's sin is considered to have brought effects upon the created order – including humanity (cf. *4 Ezra* 7:11, 118). Consequently, the creation which was once the revelation of God's invisible qualities has been rendered unable to fulfil the purpose for which it was intended: displaying his glory. By the time Paul reaches Romans 8, he has already made clear that the problem with creation is tied to its inhabitants.[13] How he does this may be seen through the course of the argument and especially in his use of κόσμος in Rom 3-5 and the Adam-Christ comparison in chapter 5. We now turn to a brief examination of these issues.

B. Paul's Use of κόσμος in Rom 3-5[14]

Romans 3-5 makes the general case that all humanity alike, both Jew and Gentile, stand under sin and the righteousness of God is available to them through faith in Christ.[15] Given the strongly anthropological focus of Rom 3:4-5 and the continuation of the theme of God's judgment of people in v. 6, we should understand κόσμος in 3:6 as a reference to humanity in general.[16] The use of the term in Paul's explanation of how God maintains

---

[10] S. Moyise sees a connection between Rom 1:21 and 8:20 and a possible reliance upon the text of Ecclesiastes but he recognizes that Ecclesiastes itself may reflect the earlier tradition of the curse in Gen 3. See Moyise 2000:19-25.

[11] See Moo 2008:74-89.

[12] Barrett argues on the basis of the application of this term to idols in the LXX that it should be understood in Paul similarly to enslavement under τὰ στοιχεῖα τοῦ κόσμου (Gal 4:3, 9). See Barrett 1957:166; Lietzmann 1933:85. For other suggestions, see Cranfield 1975:413-4. For an argument that Gen 3 stands behind Paul's use of this term, see Scroggs 1966:75-112 Vollenweider views Rom 8:18ff as a reinterpretation of the *Urgeschichte*. See Vollenweider 1989:388.

[13] Cf. Theobald 2005:438-41.

[14] For a more detailed discussion, see Adams 2000:164-74. Adams, however, focuses his discussion on the different epistolary uses of κόσμος.

[15] For fuller discussion of how the genitives should be understood in the expressions διὰ πίστεως Ἰησοῦ (Rom 3:22) and ἐκ πίστεως Ἰησοῦ (Rom 3:26), see Taylor 2004.

[16] BDAG, pp. 561-3

covenant faithfulness to Jews is important, for his claims regarding Gentiles in the previous chapter could have raised serious questions in the minds of Jewish hearers (Rom 2:14-5, 26-9).[17] When κόσμος appears again in 3:19 it is used similarly to 3:6 and comes at the end of a catena of scriptural citations proving that Jews, like Gentiles (1:18-32), are "under sin" (3:9). Romans 3:19 stands in the concluding section of Paul's opening argument where he has explained that both Jew and Gentile are objects of God's wrath.[18] Along these lines, the references to "every mouth" being closed and "the whole world" held accountable deftly serve to emphasize that the Jewish people stand in the same condition before God as the rest of humanity. This is further confirmed in the very next verse (v. 20) where Paul uses the phrase πᾶσα σάρξ to reject the idea that one could be justified by works of the law.[19]

Paul uses πᾶσα σάρξ in Rom 3:20 in a similar context to that of Gal 2:16 (cf. 1 Cor 1:29). Especially in the context of his attempt to show Jews and Gentiles to be objects of God's wrath, Paul's modification of the text of Ps 142:2 (LXX) from πᾶς ζῶν is quite significant.[20] In addition to a startling challenge to the idea that the elect might be granted a reprieve at the judgment,[21] Paul's use of the phrase πᾶσα σάρξ (particularly with the further addition of ἔργων νόμου to the text of Ps 142:2) indicates that Paul specifically intended to deal with the impression that circumcision achieved a righteous status before God (cf. Rom 2:25-9). Jewett recognizes that the similarities between Paul's use of the phrase and its occurrence in *1 En.* 81:5 places Paul within a tradition which strongly emphasized general human sinfulness.[22] If this is the case, and if Paul's argument in Romans 1-8 moves from creation to new creation as this discussion suggests, it is quite salient that the phrase πᾶσα σάρξ appears in Gen 6:12 at the climax of the portrayal of humanity's sin which ultimately led to the judgment of the flood (Gen 6:17).[23]

---

[17] See Wischmeyer 1996:352-75.

[18] Dunn 1988:vii-viii.

[19] The debate regarding Paul's view of the law is beyond the scope of this argument. For a sustained critique of the New Perspective on Paul in the context of Romans, see Gathercole 2002.

[20] Most commentators acknowledge the influence of Ps 142:2 LXX on Rom 3:20. See Jewett 2007:265-7.

[21] Cf. *1 En.* 1:7-9. Note especially the cosmic destruction language of v. 7 which reflects a broader Jewish tradition of destruction and renewal of the earth.

[22] However, this stands against the stream of *1 Enoch* as a whole where the righteous come away from the judgment with a rebuke while the wicked are destroyed (cf. *1 En.* 1:7-9). Qumran has a similar view of human depravity. Cf. 1QH 16:11; 1QS 11; CD I, cited in Jewett 1971:97.

[23] Christoffersson argues for the flood tradition as background to Rom 8:18-27 in Christoffersson 1990. If the argument is accepted that the prophecies of Isaiah stand be-

Contributing to the universalizing thrust of Rom 1-8, Paul uses κόσμος in 4:13 as a way of expanding the Abrahamic land promises where the texts in Genesis have the term γῆ (Gen 12:7; 15:7, 18).[24] According to Paul, God's promise to Abraham is not restricted to the land of Canaan.[25] The geographically restricted promise to the physical descendents of Abraham is broadened to include the world. Romans 4:13 is part of a trajectory in Romans which climaxes in the vision for a redeemed world in Rom 8:18-25.

Perhaps the most significant evidence which reveals the movement of Rom 1-8 from creation to new creation is the Adam-Christ comparison in chapter 5. We have already dealt with this comparison earlier in our discussion of 2 Cor 5:14 and the discussion need not be repeated here. However, a few observations are in order about the ways Rom 5 anticipates the themes of chapter 8. Nils Dahl has argued that all the major themes of chapter 8 are anticipated in Rom 5:1-11.[26] Whether or not this can be substantiated, it is certainly the case that there is significant overlap. The trajectory of these chapters and the overall thrust of Paul's argument suggest that the parallels are more than just coincidental. In Rom 5:2 Paul boasts "in hope of the glory of God." Both passages emphasize endurance in the context of present suffering in hope of future glory and both acknowledge the enabling role of the Spirit in the process of redemption.[27] Not least, the Adam-Christ comparison in chapter 5 should be seen as the way in which Paul expects believers to "boast in hope of the glory of God" (v. 2).

Through further use of the term κόσμος in Rom 5:12-13, Paul indicates how the sin of Adam in Gen 3 influences his perception of the world.[28] The point Paul makes in 5:12-21 is that "Christ's redeeming work has undone the fateful effects of Adam's rebellious act and has provided a comprehen-

---

hind Paul's thinking about new creation, the use of πᾶσα σάρξ in Isaiah becomes exceedingly relevant. It occurs in 40:5-6 to announce universal salvation and again in Isaiah 66 in the context of the announcement of the new creation (Isa 65:17; 66:22). YHWH promises to gather the nations who will see his glory and even include some of them into the priestly order (Isa 66:18, 21). In the promised new creation "all flesh" (not just Israel) worships YHWH in Jerusalem (Isa 66:23).

[24] This is a common theme in Jewish literature as argued by Adams and is commonly recognized by scholars. See Adams 2000:167-71.

[25] Hester 1968:77 rightly concludes that "the possibility of this inheritance comes in Christ. Abraham's seed can inherit the world because they are in Christ who is Lord of the world."

[26] Dahl 1977:89, 88-90.

[27] Hope appears in Rom 8:20, 24 (4 times), 25. The theme of glory appears in Rom 8:18, 21, 30.

[28] The term κόσμος here probably means "humanity." See Adams 2000:173.

sive solution to the universal plight [of sin]."[29] Despite the absence of a specific reference to Adam in Rom 8, Paul plays on this imagery in his exposition of the renewal of creation where believers are said to be "predestined to be conformed to the image of his son," a likely reflection on Jewish traditions about the creation of mankind in the image of God.[30] This background is made clearer in a closer investigation of the text of Rom 8:18-25.

C. Eschatological Glory and the Restoration of Creation in Romans 8:18-25

Rom 8:18-30 is bracketed with the concept of glory and it is conveyed within the eschatological framework familiar in Paul. The "coming glory to be revealed" in 8:18 has an excitedly expectant air and points to the future. However, Paul places the verb δοξάζω in 8:30 in the aorist. The apparent tension may be solved if we understand Rom 8:30 in its immediate context of God's calling, foreknowledge and predestination (vv. 28-30).[31] Both ἐδικαίωσεν and ἐδόξασεν in Rom 8:30 portray the "eschatological completion of God's work on behalf of believers that began before history, and the aorist signifies the certainty that what God has begun he will finish."[32]

Paul uses the idea of glory in this passage to offer hope to the Roman believers in the midst of present suffering.[33] A series of movements from suffering to glory makes clear the importance of this motif in this section of Romans.[34] Suffering with Christ leads to being glorified with him (8:17). The present sufferings are not worthy to be compared with the hope of future glory (8:18). Creation itself undergoes suffering in its subjection to futility and eager longing for redemption, and Paul writes to the Romans that creation will be set free into the "freedom of the glory of the children of God" (Rom 8:21). Creation suffers the pains of childbirth (8:22) and groans with believers for the redemption of the body. Even the Spirit

---

[29] Adams 2000:171-2.

[30] Cf. Gen 1:27.

[31] For a list of possible options, see Jewett 2007:530.

[32] Schreiner 1998:454. The Christ event is the beginning of the fulfilment of God's salvific work.

[33] Jewett compellingly situates Paul's recognition of present suffering in the social setting of first century Rome where the utopian ideology of empire is shattered by the actual experience of the Roman underclass. Jewett 2007:46-62, 508-11. Cf. Jewett 2004:25-46. For further discussion on the importance of this ideology for understanding Paul, see Chapter 4 above.

[34] Balz 1971:33-5.

groans in anticipation of redemption (vv. 26-7). Paul concludes the section with the assurance that despite the tribulations of the present, "all things work together for good to those who love God" (8:28) on the basis of the eschatological work of redemption set in motion by him (vv. 29-30).

Paul's understanding of glory is significantly illuminated when it is considered in the light of Paul's Adam-Christ comparison.[35] Jewish tradition maintained that humanity was created to reflect the glory of God. Adam's sin forfeited the glory which he enjoyed and introduced sin and death into the world (Rom 3:23; 5:12-13).[36] Thus, Dunn's observation is correct that, "For Paul the whole of history reduces to the destinies of two men – Adam and Christ.... Only [Christ] has inherited the glory of God."[37] Those who participate with him in his sufferings have the promise of inheriting glory with him (Rom 8:17). Just as Adam was the progenitor of the original creation, Christ is the progenitor of the new creation. In the conclusion of Paul's argument in 8:28-30, his soteriology is rendered in terms of Adam Christology. Christ has fulfilled God's original purpose in creation to have humanity reflect his glory. As Adam was the image bearer in the original creation, Christ is the image bearer of the new creation and believers are to be formed according to his image (Rom 8:29).[38]

D. The Effects of Human Sin on Creation

I have argued up to this point that there is a movement in Romans from creation to new creation. With that in mind, two further points need to be elaborated for the purposes of this thesis: 1) Creation itself is affected by human sin; 2) Creation is redeemed when humanity is redeemed. If these two propositions may be shown to be true, the case for a connection between Paul's thinking about creation and his soteriology will be difficult to deny.

---

[35] Cf. Hafemann 1991:31-49.

[36] See Dunn 1988:178. For a thorough study of the theme of Adam's glory, see Fletcher-Louis 2002. The Greek text of the 2nd-3rd century Christian apocalyptic work *3 Bar.* preserves a tradition of the loss of Adam's glory in the garden, "Just as Adam through this tree was condemned and was stripped of the glory of God, thus men now who insatiably drink the wine deriving from it transgress worse than Adam, and become distant from the glory of God, and will secure for themselves eternal fire" (*3 Bar.* 4:16).

[37] Dunn 1988:464.

[38] Adams 2002:29. This article gives a careful and nuanced discussion of how we might understand the way "narrative" functions in Paul's writing.

D. The Effects of Human Sin on Creation

First, it is clear from Paul's argument in Romans 8:18-30 that he believed creation to have been affected by human sin.[39] The γάρ which connects verse 19 with verse 18 suggests a causal connnection.[40] Present sufferings are not worth comparing with future glory (v. 18) *because* these sufferings are a function of creation which has been subjected to futility (vv. 19-20) and which will ultimately be redeemed (v. 21).[41] We have already seen how the term ματαιότης connects Paul's thinking about creation in Rom 8 with chapter 1 and the subsequent discussion has added weight to the already commonly acknowledged influence of Gen 3 on Paul's thinking. A closer examination of who has done the subjecting will strengthen the force of that proposition.

There are a number of options for the subject of the verb ὑποτάσσω in Rom 8:20. Hahne presents five alternatives: God, Christ, Satan, humanity and, the most commonly held opinion, Adam.[42] The most telling argument is the use of the active participle in 8:20b, ἀλλὰ διὰ τὸν ὑποτάξαντα, ἐφ' ἐλπίδι. In the other four undisputed Pauline occurrences of this verb in the active voice, the subject is God or Christ. This argues against Satan, humanity and Adam as alternatives.[43] Of the two remaining alternatives, Christ is the subject in Phil 3:21 and in the first of the two usages in 1 Cor 15:27. However, to take Christ as the subject in Rom 8:20 would seriously compromise the sense of the message since the Christ event is actually the means of redemption.[44]

---

[39] Chrysostom's *Homilies on Romans* 14 records a similar view: "Creation became corruptible...because of you, O man! For because you have a body which has become mortal and subject to suffering, the earth too has received a curse and has brought forth thorns and thistles." See Bray 1999:224.

[40] Moo 1996:513.

[41] Meyer recognizes that vv. 18-31 serve as the basis of the hope of glorification with Christ in v. 17. Meyer 1879:68.

[42] Hahne 2006:187-8.

[43] Furthermore, it would be difficult to explain how any of these might have subjected creation "in hope."

[44] Hahne has the right idea when he claims that "the cross...is the solution for the situation described in Rom 8:20." Hahne 2006:188. However, this language is less than appropriate in the context of Romans. In fact, Paul does not employ the term σταυρός in Romans. Neither does he refer to the crucifixion apart from Rom 6:6, and there the reference is indirect. The subject of the passive verb συνεσταυρώθη is "our old man," and there is no specific connection in this verse to Jesus.

Paul is certainly not shy about the death and resurrection of Jesus in his letter to the Romans (cf. 1:4; 4:24; 5:6, 8, 10; chapter 6.). The absence of references to the cross or crucifixion can probably be explained by the fact that this letter was written to the capital city of the empire and it would be imprudent for the believing communities there to associate their Lord with that form of Roman execution especially practised upon insurgents for crimes against the state. The letter is none the less subversive to the imperial ideology but the way in which Paul challenges this attests that he is not interested in establishing a

God is the subject in the very similar construction in 1 Cor 15:27-28 and should be taken as the subject here. Notably, Paul is careful to say that Christ's subjection of "all things under his feet" does not include God, "the one who subjected all things to him."[45] Furthermore, the idea that creation is subjected οὐχ ἑκοῦσα (Rom 8:20) indicates that creation is a victim rather than a culprit in the offending action. This comports well with the Jewish Scriptural tradition that the creation was under Adam's care (Gen 1:28; Ps 8:7) and naturally suffers the consequences when he sins (cf. *4 Ezra* 7:1).[46] The subjection ἐφ' ἐλπίδι makes perfect sense in the light of Gen 3:16-19 where God pronounces a curse immediately following a promise of hope (Gen 3:15).

The ground for the hope of creation which has been subjected to futility is that it will be set free from its "slavery to corruption (δουλείας τῆς φθορᾶς)" (Rom 8:21). The term φθορά may have an ethical connotation in Paul as it seems to have in Gal 6:8 but the Pauline usage of the term generally includes the idea of physical decay.[47] In the light of Paul's earlier association of death's entrance into the world with Adam (Rom 5:12) and his discussion in Rom 8 of creation being subjected to futility, it would be difficult to deny the importance of Gen 3 as background for the argument. Without attempting to solve the question of how the writer of Genesis viewed the fall to have affected the natural world,[48] it seems clear that Paul interpreted it in this way and this point is supported in Judaism contemporary with Paul as well as a wide consensus of scholarship.[49]

Another observation from Rom 8 can be taken to support the contention that the creation is affected by human sin. In Rom 8:22, Paul makes the claim that "the whole creation groans together (συστενάζει) and suffers birth pangs together (συνωδίνει)."[50] The significance of the participatory

---

politically revolutionary movement. See my chapter on the Roman imperial ideology above and note the sustained attention to this issue throughout Jewett 2007. For an example of those who interpret this letter as a "political declaration of war," see Taubes 1993:27.

[45] Virtually the same participial phrase is repeated in 1 Cor 15:27 and v. 28.

[46] Adams 2002:28-9. Cf. Bindemann 1983.

[47] Note especially the use of the term in 1 Cor 15:42, 50 in the context of Paul's discussion of the resurrection body. The correspondence of this idea with Paul's earlier discussion of resurrection in Rom 8:11 will be discussed in the following section.

[48] That is, whether it was the actual creation or only Adam's labours that were frustrated because of sin. For a discussion of the issue in apocalyptic literature, see Gowan 1985:83-103.

[49] Braaten challenges this consensus by pointing out that the prophetic imagery of a mourning earth is a more suitable background for Rom 8. See Braaten 2006:133-7.

[50] Tsumura argues that the curse of pain in childbearing in Gen 3:16a should be considered part of the background material for Rom 8:22. Tsumura 1994:620-1. Following Lange, Tsumura holds that the metaphor of birth pangs is particularly apropos for Paul

D. The Effects of Human Sin on Creation

verbs is disputed. A minority of scholars suggest that these verbs indicate solidarity in the groaning of creation and humanity (v. 23).[51] However, the majority favour the understanding that these verbs refer to an experience common to every part of creation.[52] The latter would make better sense of Paul's expression πᾶσα ἡ κτίσις as well as the οὐ μόνον δέ in the following verse which seems to represent a change of focus from the creation in v. 22 to believers in v. 23. However, both positions support the thrust of what is being argued here – that there is a close link between creation and humanity.[53]

The recent work of L. J. Braaten makes the case that the groaning of the earth language is deeply rooted in the prophetic tradition of Israel.[54] The passages in the LXX which contain the theme of the earth's mourning employ the verb πενθέω but two (Isa 24:7; Jer 4:31) out of the nine relevant passages also contain cognates of συστενάζω which is used by Paul in Rom 8:22 (cf. vv. 23, 26).[55] These two passages contain interesting paral-

---

"not only because it announces a new birth and new form of the earth, but because it reflects in travailing Eve the fate of the travailing earth, and vice versa." Lange 1869:273. This interpretation, however, may run aground on the text of Genesis which directs this particular curse to the woman and not the earth. For a thorough discussion of the use of child-bearing language in Paul, see Gaventa 1981:189-201.

Some scholars have attempted to understand the language in the context of Jewish traditions about birth pangs of the messiah (cf. Dan 7:21-7; *2 Bar.* 25:2-3; 1 QH 3:7ff.). E.g. Byrne 1996:261; Käsemann 1980:236; Cranfield 1975:416. Despite some similarities, passages which refer to the birth pangs of the messiah are significantly different from Paul's use of the groaning earth imagery in Rom 8. See the arguments against taking this material as background to Paul's thought in Rom 8 in Hahne 2006:204-5. For further discussion of the birth pangs, see Gempf 1994:119-35.

[51] E.g. Tholuck 1844; Calvin 1993:306; Fitzmyer 1993:509; Jewett 2007:517.

[52] Cf. Cranfield 1975:416-7; Michel 1978:268-9; Dunn 1988:489; Grässer 1990:93-117; Byrne 1996:261; Moo 1996:518; Schreiner 1998:437; Lohse 2003:247;.

[53] The solidarity between humanity and creation is supported in various ways in the Jewish literature. In the OT, there is strong support for the land's being blessed or cursed according to the obedience of God's people. The connection is also recognized in apocalyptic literature on the basis of mankind's creation from the dust of the earth and mankind's place of authority over the earth. See Hahne 2006:214-15.

[54] E.g. Isa 24:1-20; Jer 4:9-12, 23-8; Hosea 4:3; Joel 1-2. Braaten maintains that Joel "offers the most comprehensive picture of the mourning creation in the scriptures" and gives us "the clearest picture of what Paul meant when he declared that 'all creation has been groaning together.'" See Braaten 2006:141-5, 149-52. For a discussion of the connection between the themes of creation and salvation in the prophets, see Fretheim 2005:181-98.

[55] Πενθέω appears twice in the Pauline letters in the context of mourning over sin (1 Cor 5:2; 2 Cor 12:21). As for the question of why Paul used συστενάζω rather than πενθέω in Rom 8:22, Braaten suggests that συστενάζω and its cognates have sufficient semantic range to "connect the earth mourning motif with the experience of the believer

lels with Paul's thinking in Romans. Jer 4:27-8 (LXX) records YHWH's devastating judgment upon the land which compels the earth itself to mourn (πενθείτω ἡ γῆ).[56] In Isa 24:4-7 (LXX) the earth (γῆ) is said to mourn (πενθέω) as a direct result of human sin, "the earth is lawless on account of its inhabitants (Isa 24:5)...." The resulting curse affects both the natural world as well as humanity,[57]

διὰ τοῦτο ἀρὰ ἔδεται τὴν γῆν ὅτι ἡμάρτοσαν οἱ κατοικοῦντες αὐτήν...πενθήσει οἶνος πενθήσει ἄμπελος στενάξουσιν πάντες οἱ εὐφραινόμενοι τὴν ψυχήν (Isa 24:6a, 7)

Therefore a curse will devour the earth because those inhabiting it have sinned...the wine will mourn, the vine will mourn, all the merry-hearted will groan.

Many of the themes which Paul addresses in Rom 8 may be found in Isa 24-7 and this provides a good test case to support Braaten's thesis that Paul's conception of the groaning earth in Rom 8 is influenced by similar prophetic traditions.[58] Paul's use of the imagery of earth's groaning encapsulates a central thread of the mourning earth motif whereby the creation itself suffers as a direct result of human sin. [59]

---

and the groaning of the Spirit." He also suggests the term may resonate with a possible use of exodus imagery in Rom 8. Braaten 2006:152-3. Cf. Keesmaat 1999:102-110.

[56] Those represented by the "Daughter of Zion" join in the lament and the sound of their groaning (στεναγμός) is compared to that of a woman giving labour to her first child (ὡς ὠδινούσης...ὡς πρωτοτοκούσης). Note Paul's association of groaning and birth pangs in Rom 8:22.

[57] Hahne erroneously argues that the verb στενάζω is used in Isa 24:7 in reference "to the groaning of the natural order due to the devastation of sin." However, the subject of the verb στενάζω in Isa 24:7 is οἱ εὐφραινόμενοι and this is confirmed by the fact that the verb is in the third person plural. Hahne 2006:201.

[58] The verbal similarities between Rom 8 and Isa 24-7 include the use of: φθορά/φθείρω (Isa 24:3; Rom 8:21); δόξα (Isa 24:14-5; Rom 8:18, 21); ἐλπίς (Isa 24:16; Rom 8:20, 24); θλῖψις (Isa 26:16; Rom 8:35); and, ὠδίνω/ὠδίν/συνωδίνω (Isa 26:17; Rom 8:22). In addition to these links, the conceptual overlap between these passages is striking. For further discussion, see Moo 2008:74-89. This becomes especially poignant since the movement from creation's mourning to its redemption spoken of in new creation terms spans the Isaianic material culminating in Isa 65-66. On this point, see my argument above in Chapter 2, "New Creation in the Old Testament."

[59] Braaten 2006:152-3. Braaten argues that the mourning of the earth in the prophetic tradition is the result of ongoing human sin and not the curse pronounced against sin in Gen 3:17.

E. Creation and Redemption

In addition to making the case that Paul understood sin to have effects on creation itself, it can also be surmised from Rom 8 that Paul understood the redemption of creation to coincide with the redemption of humanity.[60] This case has been argued thoroughly in the work of J. Gibbs who insists that "the descriptions of God's redemptive purpose at work in creation are not mere reflections of the inner working of redemption in the 'heirs,' but are rather descriptions of a reality alongside the reality of the Christian's freedom, even in suffering, for glory."[61] In other words, redemption and creation are *coordinate* concepts in Paul.[62] The critical exegetical issue is the meaning of κτίσις in Rom 8:19-23 and we have already argued (along with a consensus of scholars) for the understanding of the term as a reference to sub-human creation.[63] A closer look at the redemption of creation in Rom 8 and how it is related to the redemption of humanity will support these claims.

The OT prophetic tradition is replete with references to images of eschatological restoration which include people as well as the cosmos (Isa 11:6-9; 43:19-21; 55:12-13; Eze 34:25-31; Hos 2:18; Zech 8:12) and the motif is also represented well in later Jewish apocalyptic tradition (*1 En.* 45:4-5; 51:4-5; *4 Ezra* 8:51-54; *2 Bar.* 29:1-8; *Sib. Or.* 3:777-95).[64] The eschatological thrust of Rom 8:18-30 is undeniable.[65] Paul offers his readers comfort in the face of present struggles on the basis of a promise of future glory. The difficulty of the present (τοῦ νῦν καιροῦ), far from calling the future glory into question, serves only to point out that the first move-

---

[60] Cf. Stuhlmacher 1967:1-35; Lindeskog 1952:260.

[61] Gibbs maintains that the link between creation and redemption should be seen in Paul's cosmic Christology based on the lordship of Christ over the world and Paul's encounter with him on the road to Damascus. Gibbs 1971:34, 35-47:134-8. Cf. Gibbs 1975:13-29. This stands in direct contradiction to a number of scholars who understand Rom 8:18-30 from an anthropological-soteriological perspective. That approach has been advanced by: Lampe 1964:449-62; Vögtle 1970b:351-66; Gager 1970:327-30; Baumgarten 1975:170-4.

[62] Bolt 1995:35-6. Bolt has a thorough discussion of the problems inherent in a strictly anthropological-soteriological interpretation of Rom 8:18-27 in Bolt 1995:34-51.

[63] However, a view such as Eastman's which includes unbelieving humanity (even unbelieving Israel) in the referent of κτίσις would not contradict the point of this argument, for she acknowledges that "the fate of Israel and the fate of all creation hang together." Eastman 2002:276. Hahne gives a helpful *Forschungsbericht* in Hahne 2006:177-81.

[64] Byrne 1996:256. Cf. Thielman 1993:169-95.

[65] Gager acknowledges that in Rom 8:18ff., "the final event of the end-time is in the indispensable key to Paul's view of the present as a time of hope and suffering." See Gager 1970:336.

ment of redemption has ended with an unresolved chord.⁶⁶ The structure of the passage confirms its eschatological nature and advances through a progression from suffering to glory which picks up themes appearing in 5:1-11.⁶⁷ This eschatological thrust holds together the redemption of humanity and the natural world.⁶⁸

In Rom 8:19 creation is depicted as longing expectantly for the "revelation (ἀποκάλυψις) of the sons of God."⁶⁹ In the immediate context of suffering and glory, this probably should be understood in terms of revealing the true status of believers.⁷⁰ Despite all appearances to the contrary, Paul is fully aware that God is at work in and behind the suffering faced by believers to achieve an "eternal weight of glory" and their current situation should only be understood in that context (Rom 8:17-18, 28-30; 2 Cor 4:17). The reason creation "eagerly awaits" this ἀποκάλυψις is given in the following verses (20-22). If the argument above is correct, creation was subjected to futility as a result of human sin but Paul maintains the hope that it "will be set free *from* slavery to decay *into* the freedom of the glory of the children of God."⁷¹ That is, the freedom envisaged to apply to the children of God will also apply to creation. As if to underscore the cosmic scope of his argument, Paul makes the subject of the passive verb (ἐλευθερωθήσεται) clear; the focus of the liberation in Rom 8:21 is "creation itself (αὐτὴ ἡ κτίσις).⁷²

---

⁶⁶ Balz 1971:33.

⁶⁷ The connection with chapter 5 is elaborated in Jewett 2007:506. Moo points out that the common understanding of a threefold division arranged around the groaning of creation, believers and the Spirit (cf. Balz 1971:36-123) is not obvious in the text. His explanation divides the passage according to grammatical markers in v. 26 and v. 28. Moo 1996:510.

⁶⁸ As Vollenweider argues, the eschatological thrust of this passage is not simply to point through the difficulties of the present to a better future based on an apocalyptic understanding of the discontinuity between a hopeless present and glorious future. Rather, Paul's eschatology is based on the *continuity* of the present and the future which has already been revealed to believers. See Vollenweider 1989:385-8.

⁶⁹ Christoffersson argues that the "sons of God" are angels. See Christoffersson 1990:120-4.

⁷⁰ So the majority of commentators, e.g., Moo 1996:55.

⁷¹ The textual variant is interesting in this case because the option presented in NA27 with strong external support is διοτι (Jewett 2007:504 prefers διοτι). This would make the causal connection more clear but the ὅτι could also be translated causally. Because the ὅτι is the more vague reading and has stronger external support, it is more likely. Metzger explains the διοτι by dittography from ελπιδιοτι to ελπιδιδιοτι. Metzger 1994:456.

⁷² Irenaeus writes, "God is rich in all things, and everything is his. It is therefore fitting that the creation itself, having been restored to its primeval condition, should with-

E. Creation and Redemption

The freedom that Paul has in mind in Rom 8:21 should be understood in the context of the slavery mentioned in the immediately preceding phrase.[73] If, as we have argued, the "slavery to corruption" has in mind the entropic principle to which creation was subjected as a result of sin and which ultimately leads to death, liberation from that enslavement promises a reversal of the principle of decay and futility. For Paul, the ultimate act of reversal and restoration of creation to its proper order occurs in the resurrection of believers (Rom 8:11, 23). This is inextricably linked to his understanding of the restoration of creation.[74]

Creation groans and travails alongside believers who groan in anticipation of "adoption as sons, the redemption of [the] body" (v. 23).[75] The question of why Paul speaks of the adoption in future terms here is puzzling in the light of his emphasis on the past and present realities in Rom 8:14-17. This is probably best explained in terms of the repetition of ἀπεκδέχομαι (vv. 19, 23).[76] Although believers are called sons of God if they are led by his Spirit and are said to have received the spirit of adoption (vv. 14-15), their present circumstances argue against this reality. This tension puts believers in a position of groaning alongside creation in expectation of the fulfillment of the redemption which was already begun in them.[77]

As we have already seen in our examination of Galatians and 2 Corinthians, the importance of the resurrection cannot be overstated. It is precisely in that concept that Paul's connection between redemption and creation becomes clearest. For him, the resurrection is not redemption *from* the body as we would expect in the context of Greek philosophy.[78] Nor is it simply an individual's experience of transformation intended to create new

---

out restraint be under the dominion of the righteous" (*Against Heresies* 5.32.1). See Bray 1999:222.

[73] Cf. Keesmaat 1999:102-10.

[74] See the discussion in Chapters 5 and 6 of the resurrection of Christ as the beginning of the end-time resurrection of believers as well as the discussion of how Judaism contemporary with Paul could view the resurrection of the body as a means of restoring creation. Cf. Michaels 1999:111-12.

[75] For discussion of Paul's use of υἱοθεσία, see Scott 1992.

[76] Jewett 2007:519.

[77] Byrne 1996:263.

[78] Despite Lietzmann's assertion that Paul views resurrection here as redemption *from* the σῶμα (whether the body is equated with σάρξ or the σάρξ-*Substanz*), the genitive in the phrase τὴν ἀπολύτρωσιν τοῦ σώματος ἡμῶν is more likely objective than ablative. Paul understands resurrection to be a redemption *of* the body – a microscopic renewal of the cosmos itself. Cf. Lietzmann 1933:85.

social structures more responsible toward the created order.[79] Rather, Paul sees the redemption *of* the body as fundamental to the renewal of creation as a whole. Far from an anthropological restriction of redemption, this is an acknowledgement that the redemption of humanity is bound up in the redemption of creation.

If Paul's letters to the Corinthians and Galatians could be said to be theology on the battle field because of the conflicts and controversies which occasioned his writing, his letter to the Romans may be considered somewhat less defensive. Removed from the vicissitudes of the Corinthian and Galatian communities, Paul could be more reflective and systematic in his letter to the Romans.[80] This, however, is not to suggest that the letter is simply a theological essay. Recent scholarship has suggested that both the epistolary form of the letter as well as its occasional nature should be taken into consideration.[81] Nonetheless, the relatively late date of Paul's composition of this letter (ca. A.D. 55-7) places it towards the end of his apostolic career and many of the themes from his earlier letters are repeated in it.[82] Though this stage of Paul's literary career reflects development and greater theological maturity than the earlier writings, it is clear that his thinking, addressed to different communities, has operated along a coherent trajectory.[83]

In this light, the remarks of Jewett in relation to Rom 8:23 are significant, for he acknowledges the crucial connection between Paul's thinking about new creation in his earlier letters and that which appears in Rom 8: "The 'new creation' of 2 Cor 5:17 and Gal 6:15 is clearly in view here.... Paul's purpose is to encourage the Roman believers to begin enacting their sonship and daughtership right now, in refusing to conform to the fallen age, and resolutely acting rightly toward the groaning creation, of which their bodies are a part."[84] This connection may be further confirmed through a comparison of Paul's thought in Rom 8 with Gal 6 and 2 Cor 5. We now turn to a brief examination of correspondence between Paul's earlier letters and his thinking in Romans.

---

[79] Note the parallels in Qumran where the community plays a role in world transformation. See my argument in Part 3 of Chapter 3 in the section, *"New Creation in the DSS."*

[80] See Myers 1992:819.

[81] Scholarship is divided on what this nature is; deciding the issue is beyond the scope of this thesis. For further discussion of relevant issues, see Wedderburn 1988; Myers 1992:820-1. See the recent discussion in Das 2007.

[82] Wilckens 1978:47.

[83] Beker 1980:11-19.

[84] Jewett 2007:519.

E. Creation and Redemption

The similarities between Romans and Galatians are widely noted and need not be elaborated here.[85] It will be worthwhile, however, to take a closer look at 2 Cor 5 since that text is less often related to Rom 8. The essence of Paul's argument in 2 Cor 4:16-5:10 is that his present sufferings mark his apostolic identification with Christ whose own suffering led to resurrection and to the resurrection of those "in him." This same movement from suffering to glory (2 Cor 4:17) may be observed in Romans 8:17 where Paul embarks on a discussion of future glory in the context of creation (cf. 2 Cor 5:17).[86] In a tantalizing footnote in M. Harris's commentary on 2 Cor, he remarks that the closest "parallel to 2 Cor 4:16-5:10 as a whole is Rom 8:18-25."[87] But Harris's claim that 2 Cor 5 and Rom 8 are parallel needs to be substantiated.[88] There are at least three ways in which these texts converge.

First, there is a movement from suffering to glory in both passages. In 2 Cor, Paul is pointing out that his sufferings, which call into question his apostolic ministry in the minds of some, are actually the means by which Paul (like Jesus) attains glory (2 Cor 4:14, 17). Despite present groaning and the vicissitudes of mortality, Paul declares faith in an eternal perspective which provides the true lenses through which his situation should be interpreted (2 Cor 5:6-10). Romans 8:17b picks up explicitly the theme of identification with Christ in the move from suffering to glory, εἴπερ συμπάσχομεν ἵνα καὶ συνδοξασθῶμεν (cf. v. 18). As in 2 Cor 5, Rom 8 makes an appeal to future glory in order to relativize the current sufferings (v. 18).[89] Secondly, both texts deal with bodily resurrection and view the Spirit as an important precursor to the fulfilment of this eschatological promise (Rom 8:23; 2 Cor 5:5; cf. 2 Cor 1:22).[90] Thirdly, both texts refer to the present situation as a time of groaning (στενάζω). Whereas this is restricted to the individual in 2 Cor 5:2, 4, Rom 8:22 applies this to the creation itself, ἡ κτίσις συστενάζει.

Should we surmise that Paul limits his comments to the individual in 2 Cor 5 and includes the broader creation only in Rom 8? While it is true that 2 Cor 5 has an individual application, it should not be understood

---

[85] Longenecker 2002:58-84. Cf. Schnelle 2005:270; Borse 1972:120-43.
[86] Wright 2003:365-6.
[87] Harris 2005:409.
[88] Lindars acknowledges that Rom 8 works out the thought of 2 Cor 5:5. Lindars 1961:57.
[89] Compare Rom 8:24-25 with 2 Cor 4:18.
[90] An exploration of the Spirit's role in creation would prove fruitful at this point but is beyond the limitations of this thesis.

individualistically.⁹¹ 2 Cor 5 should be seen not as setting out a different idea but as a specific application of Paul's broader soteriology. Paul makes this abundantly clear in Rom 8 where he specifically links the groaning of creation and the groaning of believers who await the redemption of the body (vv. 22-3). It is not strange to see this combination of creation and redemption. Judaism frequently combined these ideas.⁹²

One final question may be addressed here. If Paul's understanding of new creation is similar in Gal, 2 Cor and Rom, why does he not employ the term καινὴ κτίσις in Rom 8 which is clearly cosmic in its scope? I have already argued that this term would have resonated strongly with the imperial ideology contemporary with Paul. If that is the case, the use of the phrase καινὴ κτίσις may have raised imperial suspicions about the nature of the believing communities in Rome.

As E. Adams has shown, Paul's cosmological terminology is used differently from its use in 1 Corinthians, for example, where Paul is attempting to distinguish believing groups from external society. In Romans, Paul's cosmological language serves to avoid social conflict and inculcate a degree of "social harmony with the larger society and good citizenship."⁹³ Though Paul may have maintained a polemical edge, he was careful not to use the kind of incendiary language which could have sent the wrong signal to a dominant society intolerant of sedition (e.g. cross, crucifixion).⁹⁴ The term "new creation" could have been understood in this way and Paul may have avoided its use in his letter to the Romans because of the negative repercussions it would incite from the authorities.

---

⁹¹ Hubbard 2002:183 warns against an individualistic understanding of new creation in Paul but his strict anthropocentricism misses the broader soteriology at work in Paul's letters.

⁹² This goes against the assertion that 2 Cor 5 is about realized eschatology and Rom 8 is about future expectation. Hubbard is really arguing this point about 2 Cor 5:17. But this removes that section from the broader context where Paul is, in fact, not presenting us with a particularly realized eschatology. The groaning of vv. 2, 4 make this clear. What he does do is to make the case that, despite present trouble, the future places everything in its proper perspective. It would be a mistake to speak of 2 Cor 5 as dealing solely with the present. It brings past, present and future together in the work of Christ and its effects. Furthermore, this eschatological perspective is present in Rom 8 as well. Even though Paul is addressing the groaning of believers who await redemption along with creation, he is able to say, "In this hope we *were saved* (ἐσώθημεν)" (Rom 8:24).

⁹³ Adams 2000:240.

⁹⁴ See the footnote above on "cross" and "crucifixion" in Romans.

F. CONCLUSIONS

Beginning with an analysis of Paul's uses of κτίσις and κόσμος, this chapter has sought to show how the argument in Rom 1-8 begins in Rom 1 with a focus on creation and advances a soteriological program which is expressed in new creation imagery in Rom 8. This resonates with OT prophetic traditions which envisage eschatological restoration of people and the world in which they live. The eschatological matrix which has been so influential in our discussions of other Pauline letters is certainly at play in Romans as well, and Paul uses it as a foundation for much of the hope he offers in Rom 8.

In the course of our discussion, it has become clear that Paul's references to creation in Rom 8 include the subhuman created order and that Paul believes creation itself to have been affected by human sin. Particularly the language of the groaning creation shows that Paul is operating in the stream of prophetic tradition in which sin causes the earth to mourn. The groaning of creation is set alongside the groaning of believers who hope for fulfilment of redemption which has begun in them. The redemption for which they hope is connected to the redemption for which personified creation longs. It is ultimately in resurrection that believers receive the completion of their salvation. This should be seen in the light of Jewish traditions which viewed resurrection as part of YHWH's eschatological renewal of the earth. Thus, creation is affected by human sin and it is redeemed when humanity is redeemed.

Romans 8 makes abundantly clear that Paul's cosmology and anthropology are inextricably linked. If Paul's understanding of creation and redemption are as closely related as this chapter argues, it is difficult to imagine how Paul could have used the term καινὴ κτίσις without reflection upon the relationship, even if the immediate reference of the term is anthropological. Although it is much clearer in Romans, this thesis has argued that the connection is present in Galatians and 2 Corinthians as well.

This chapter has not attempted to resolve the question of whether Paul looked forward to a complete destruction of the present cosmos followed by a totally new creation or only a restoration of the present world.[95] Both views were prevalent in Judaism contemporary with Paul as well as in early Christianity.[96] What is taken up here is that Paul's thinking, particularly his eschatology, reflects the influence of apocalyptic traditions traced back to the expression of new creation in the prophecies of Isaiah. Rather than any particular view of the fate of the cosmos, it is the connection be-

---

[95] See Adams 2007.

[96] Cf. Hahne 2006:226-8. However, Rom 8 seems to suggest that Paul did not expect a complete physical destruction of the present world followed by a new *creatio ex nihilo*.

tween creation and humanity which ties Paul to this tradition. Though Paul does not engage in detailed cosmological speculation, his understanding of new creation is no less cosmological since his perception of the nature of all reality has been altered by the Christ event. This point has been made clear in discussions of Galatians 6 and 2 Cor 5 and is strongly supported by the connection of creation and redemption in Rom 8.

The assumption that if Paul had been influenced by apocalyptic traditions, he would have provided a more vivid portrayal of the final state of creation has led to considerable confusion in attempts to understand Paul's conception of new creation. Because Paul does not employ the kind of cosmic destruction language present in Jewish and Christian apocalyptic works, it is argued, he is not concerned with cosmological issues but with anthropological-soteriology when he speaks of new creation. This chapter is intended to show how misguided is that assumption on the grounds that Paul's soteriology included both humanity and creation and these cannot be understood as mutually exclusive categories in his thinking.

Finally, the question of how Roman hearers might have processed Paul's expression of new creation in Rom 8 promises further insight into how we should interpret this important concept. As this thesis has argued, Paul's concept of new creation could have strongly conflicted with the transformation of the world envisaged in the imperial ideology.[97]

Whereas the birth of Caesar had promised transformation of the world for imperial Rome, the death and resurrection of Christ had done so for Paul.[98] In Gal, 2 Cor and Rom, Paul's new creation is expressed in the context of the Christ event. Christ's resurrection and the consequent life given to believers are testimony and preliminary fulfilment of hopes for the renewal of creation itself.[99] If, as I have argued, Paul's readers/hearers had been exposed to the concept of world-renewal as a result of the emperor's exploits, it could have profoundly influenced how they heard Paul's use of new creation language in the context of the Christ event.

With eschatological language in striking parallel to Paul's writing, the imperial propaganda of Rome was claiming that a new age had been inaugurated in which creation itself was more productive because of the *Pax Romana*. The new and purportedly eternal world created by the imperial ideology would have embraced a radically different eschatology from that

---

[97] R. Jewett, in particular, has taken pains to recognize this conflict in the context of Paul's letter to the Romans.

[98] The senate voted to declare the apotheosis of the emperor, but Jesus was "declared to be Son of God with power according to the spirit of holiness by resurrection from the dead" (Rom 1:4). Cf. Wright 2002a:173-93.

[99] The theme comes to clearest expression in Rom 8 but it is clearly linked with the resurrection of Christ in 1 Cor 15.

of the apostle Paul. If Paul felt pressure from the ubiquitous imperial ideology which presented the emperor as the saviour of the world[100] in its own cosmological and eschatological terms, it is hard to imagine a better method of dealing with that issue than with the creation/new creation themes available from the prophetic and apocalyptic traditions of Judaism.

---

[100] See Harrison 2002:87.

Conclusion

Chapter 8

Conclusion

This thesis has sought to explore the concept of new creation in the letters of Paul in a way that maintains the inherent balance between the anthropological and cosmological elements in his theology. The most recent flurry of interest in this subject has been sparked off by the work of M. Hubbard. He accurately acknowledges that the history of research on Paul's understanding of new creation may generally be arranged according to whether this phrase should be seen from an anthropological (individual or communal) or a cosmological perspective.[1] Since the increased interest in the influence of Jewish apocalyptic literature on Paul, scholarship has listed heavily towards a cosmological interpretation of Paul's new creation and this tendency is represented well in the work of U. Mell and J. L. Martyn. As the apocalyptic approach to Paul has somewhat fallen out of vogue, Hubbard's attempt to reclaim pride of place for an anthropological understanding of Paul's new creation has been well received.

This thesis has argued that a stark distinction between *anthropo-* and *cosmo-* soteriology is an inappropriate delineation of the apostle's thinking. Paul's thought should not be confined to sharply defined categories that Paul himself did not impose on the texts. That is not to say that Paul did not think of cosmological and anthropological characteristics, but it is hard to imagine Paul dividing these into isolated categories. In essence, Paul's conception of the new creation has both anthropological as well as cosmological dimensions. Consequently, I have attempted to show how Paul's καινὴ κτίσις serves as theological shorthand for a soteriology based on the efficacy of the Christ event which has anthropological as well as cosmological implications.

A. Summary

Part I of the argument focused on Paul's historical and social contexts beginning with the most explicit articulation of the concept of new creation in the Old Testament in the book of Isaiah. Modern scholarly approaches

---

[1] Hubbard 2002:1-5.

to the book of Isaiah rightly investigate its origins and attempt to understand how it may have reached its present canonical form. However, Paul would most likely have viewed the book as a literary unity. This point presents a serious problem for any argument which suggests that Paul's focus was more influenced by the anthropological soteriology in "Deutero-" Isaiah than the broader cosmological soteriology in "Trito-" Isaiah since these ideas are woven together throughout the Isaianic material.[2] Even in that OT prophetic literature used to support an anthropological understanding of new creation in Paul (e.g. Jer 31; Eze 34-6), cosmological themes are part of the prophetic message. The OT prophets, particularly Isaiah, maintained a strong connection between human sin and the state of the nation. In Isaiah even the natural world is affected by the spiritual condition of the people of God.

The apocalyptic writers further developed the Isaianic conception of new creation and put the concept to use in the context of their own struggles to preserve the identity of their communities. It would misrepresent the evidence to suggest that these writers were entirely concerned with an *external* dilemma. The problems they faced included the encroachment of Hellenistic society on the way of life they valued. However, similarly to the OT prophets, they drew a connection between the natural order and the spiritual state of the people of God. Sin led to a disruption in the natural order which was exacerbated by Satan and the Gentiles. This became clear in our focus on the theme of new creation in *Jubilees*.

It is notoriously difficult to pinpoint the actual social setting of Jewish apocalyptic literature and determining such a background for *Jubilees* is no exception. However, it is clear that the book attempts to preserve Jewish identity against the threat of assimilation to Hellenistic society. The oppressive foreign influence present for the writer of *Jubilees* is the physical manifestation of the spiritual bondage/exile in which the people of God find themselves. This spiritual problem has led to a breakdown in the proper functioning of the universe. The Law is tied to cosmic order and disobedience to it (or improper observation of it) threatens the operation of the cosmos itself. The concept of new creation is used in this book to set right what has gone wrong in the world. It has anthropological and cosmological implications and is an expression of God's eschatological program of restoration.

After a detailed analysis of new creation in *Jubilees*, we turned our attention to how this idea functioned in the DSS. Some important observations came to light as a result of that discussion. First, the DSS represent renewal as something that God would do *through* the community and *within* the temporal world. The moral and social stability of their commu-

---

[2] Cf. Hubbard 2002:17-25.

nity would result in a stable and more productive physical world. The Qumran documents suggest that these communities anticipated the future action of God who had chosen them to carry out his plans and they spoke of this future hope in terms of a renewed creation. Of course, this eschatological perspective was modified by Paul whose bifocal eschatology anticipated the future but also included the Christ event as the fulfilment of prophetic hopes for salvation. Secondly, the renewed world was to be a place where all opposition to God's rule through his people would be eradicated. The DSS communities envisaged themselves in opposition to the Jerusalem establishment but they came to view Rome as their primary enemy. This is consistent with the antagonism toward foreign oppression present in the apocalyptic and prophetic literature.

Use of the concept of new creation in pre-Pauline Jewish traditions as a way of dealing with the encroachment of foreign cultures upon Jewish identity alerts us to the cultural context in which Paul uses the concept. This becomes particularly poignant when we note the resonance which the concept would have had in the Pauline communities of Galatia, Corinth and Rome. The social world of the first century was inundated with the ideology propagated by the Roman Empire. This ideology was eschatological in the sense that it presented the Roman era as the pinnacle of human history. With eschatological language in striking parallel to Paul's writing, the ideology of the empire claimed that a new age had been inaugurated in which creation itself was more productive because of the *Pax Romana*. The new and purportedly eternal world created by the imperial ideology would have embraced a radically different eschatology from that of the apostle Paul who insisted that Rome's golden age was actually an age of evil (Gal 1:4).

The imperial message was ubiquitous in the first century and took on a cosmological flavour communicated in terms of a renewal of creation. At the same time that Paul was announcing the gospel of Jesus Christ, the Roman Empire advocated its own "gospel" message focused on the city of Rome and the person of the emperor. If at the beginning of the letter to the Galatians, the recipients heard a reference to the imperial gospel in Paul's use of εὐαγγέλιον,[3] it could be that the "new creation" at the end further set Paul's message in contrast to that of Rome.

The content of the imperial gospels was that an emperor had been born who would establish a new world order of peace and prosperity. Those emperors were lauded as sons of god and some of them were apotheosised by senatorial decree upon their death. The content of Paul's gospel, on the other hand, was "received ... through a revelation (ἀποκαλύψεως) of Jesus Christ" (Gal 1:12). This revelation consisted of God's eschatological ac-

---

[3] This has been argued convincingly in Stanton 2004:39-40.

tion of the cross. The crucifixion and resurrection of Christ had transformed time and inaugurated the new age expected at the end of history. This established a new order which transformed the way people were evaluated and created an entirely new society defined not by the morality of imperial legislation but by the law of Christ (cf. Gal 6:2). The new order this gospel proclaimed was spoken of as καινὴ κτίσις. The distinctions of the old age were irrelevant. All that mattered was the eschatological order established by the death and resurrection of Jesus (cf. 2 Cor 5:16).

Like the imperial gospel, Paul's gospel dealt with a turning of the ages. But the new age for Paul was not a cyclical event that could be repeated. It was something that had taken place once and for all in God's invasion of the world through the cross of Christ. The eschatology of Rome had to be re-articulated when a new emperor rose to power. Paul could imagine no further improvement upon Christ's work on the cross. Paul's gospel offered a peace and established a new world order. However, the peace Paul declared was based on something radically different from the imperial propaganda. For him, the new creation was based on the death and resurrection of Jesus. This eschatological event brought a peace so pervasive that even the deepest divisions of humanity were brought into unity. In a society deeply concerned with status and distinctions, Paul wrote about a new order in which the old distinctions were no longer important. All that mattered was what Jesus had done. One's identity in the Pauline communities did not depend upon the distinctions recognized within the old order but upon identifying with Christ – first in his death but also in his new creation. This was a cosmological and social concept very different from imperial Roman propaganda.

Rome's colonies advanced its ideology in the provinces and throughout the known world. Paul, too, was establishing an outpost for another kind of kingdom – one with an altogether different ethic based on a surprising eschatological soteriology.

The Roman propaganda machine created nothing less than a completely transformed social world where relationships between individuals and between subject and ruler reflected the imperial ideology. Proclamations of the emperor's role as saviour of the world, Lord of the cosmos and guarantor of peace, concord and prosperity could hardly have avoided contradiction with Paul's proclamation of Christ.

Thus, it is suggested here that Paul's understanding of new creation sprang from Jewish soil already concerned with the establishment of God's people in the face of foreign opposition. The ideology of the Roman Empire would have made the use of this tradition an obvious choice and exceedingly germane to the world in which he ministered. This insight provides evidence which supports the idea that Paul was, in fact, influenced by Jewish prophetic and apocalyptic traditions which maintained a connec-

A. Summary

tion between cosmological and anthropological realities in their understanding of what was involved in God's new creation.[4] The cosmological overtones of these streams of thought were not superfluous mythology but, rather, critical elements of his thinking. The ways in which cosmological language was used to express social change in the ancient world would be a fascinating area for further study – particularly since the cosmos and the state were connected.[5]

The approach taken to the background material in this thesis acknowledges Paul's missionary thrust. Paul's theological matrix was formed from his Jewish roots but his message was articulated in Greco-Roman culture. Such an understanding of the way that Paul employed Israel's scripture advances our insight into how Paul used the OT in his writing.[6] It also helps to explain how the various backgrounds for Paul's letters are not mutually exclusive.

As much as the background information informs us of Paul's thinking, it should not be allowed to upstage the evidence we have in Paul's letters themselves. For that reason, Part II of this thesis attempts detailed exegetical work in the three Pauline passages deemed most important for understanding his thinking regarding new creation. If the central claim of this thesis stands, it must stand on the exegesis of the actual letters of Paul.

In a chapter on Paul's conception of new creation in Galatians, I took the position that καινὴ κτίσις should be understood as an eschatologically charged expression which appears in the letter closing and is used to encapsulate the major ideas which Paul articulated throughout the letter. In an important series of contrasts, Paul sets καινὴ κτίσις over against his crucifixion to the world and the crucifixion of the world (κόσμος) itself (Gal 6:14).

The only other occurrence of the term κόσμος in Galatians is in 4:3 where Paul refers to the στοιχεῖα τοῦ κόσμου. The connection Paul makes between the Law and the cosmos provides strong support to the notion that Paul is making use of themes which we have shown to be present in apocalyptic literature. The contrast between κόσμος and καινὴ κτίσις would certainly have contributed to thinking along these lines. Given that κόσμος was viewed as the sum of all existence in the Greco-Roman world and the individual was considered to be a microcosm of the cosmos itself, it is highly likely that Paul's reference to καινὴ κτίσις in this context

---

[4] The later application of the idea of new creation to the individual convert in texts such as *Joseph and Aseneth* should not control our approach to Paul's understanding of new creation since Paul, I have argued, is influenced by traditions which combine cosmological and anthropological interests.

[5] Cf. Adams 2000:3-36.

[6] This is taken up more fully in Wagner 2002. Cf. Moyise 2000; Aageson 2006:152-81.

would have been understood to incorporate something more than an individual conversion experience. Exactly how this is the case becomes clearer when we see how Paul's καινὴ κτίσις in Gal 6:15 is an eschatologically charged expression.

If my argument that the opening and the closing of this letter are organically related may be sustained, the new creation in 6:15 should be seen in the light of the reference to the resurrection in 1:1 and acts as a way of speaking about the new age envisaged to occur at the end of time. This kind of eschatology sets Paul's thinking apart from his Jewish roots and the Greco-Roman world in which he operated. Paul modified the Jewish thinking which projected the watershed of God's action for his people into the future. Rather than a simple focus on the future, Paul understood God's end-time actions to have already begun in the Christ event. This eschatological position is at work throughout Paul's argument and comes to fullest expression in his use of καινὴ κτίσις in 6:15. Christ's death and resurrection certainly had an effect on Paul's own life but it also destroyed the old world order of which the Law itself was a part and at the same time inaugurated a new age. The key is the role played by the Christ event in Paul's thinking. Identification with Christ and consequent freedom from the demands of Torah lie at the heart of the soteriological engine of this letter. In addition to a modification of Jewish traditions, the eschatological thrust of the letter would have directly challenged the contemporary Roman ideology.

As the Roman ideology was proclaimed throughout Asia Minor, it is not altogether unlikely that Paul's proclamation of the new creation would have alerted the sensibilities of those familiar with the imperial message. Paul's letter to the Galatians relates a gospel categorically different from that of the emperors of Rome. Like the imperial gospel, Paul's gospel dealt with a turning of the ages. But the new age for Paul was not a cyclical event that could be repeated. It was something that had taken place once and for all in God's invasion of the world through the cross of Christ. The eschatology of Rome had to be re-articulated when a new emperor rose to power. Paul could imagine no further improvement upon Christ's work on the cross.

Like Rome's imperial message, Paul's gospel offered a peace and established a new world order. However, the peace Paul declared was based on something radically different from the imperial propaganda. For him, the new creation was based on the death and resurrection of Jesus. This eschatological event brought a peace so pervasive that even the deepest divisions of humanity were brought into unity. In a society deeply concerned with status and distinctions, Paul wrote about a new order in which the old distinctions were no longer important. All that mattered was what Jesus had done. One's identity in the Pauline churches did not depend upon the distinctions recognized within the old order but upon identifying with Christ – first in his death but also in his new creation. This was a cosmological and social concept very different from imperial Roman ideology.

The next chapter deals with the use of καινὴ κτίσις in 2 Cor 5:17 and begins with an acknowledgment that this phrase occurs in the context of strong Isaianic reverberations. Although this association is commonly acknowledged, its significance for our understanding of 2 Cor 5:17 has not been fully addressed. Even though 5:17 reflects Isaianic language, the nature of the Isaianic influence on Paul's thinking is hotly debated. I have attempted to show that the consistent application of the Isaianic material in the immediate literary context of this verse makes a strong case that Isaianic concepts (and not just language) were influential for Paul's understanding of new creation in 2 Cor 5:17.

Four major themes in the literary context of this verse reflect Isaianic influence. First, 2 Cor 5:4 is probably an echo of Isa 25:8. The quotation of Isa 25:8 when Paul dealt with a similar theme in 1 Cor 15:54 supports this claim.[7] The idea of resurrection may be used differently in these two passages but the application of Isa 25:8 is consistent. Secondly, Paul's ministry of reconciliation spoken of in 2 Cor 5:18-21 is likely to have been influenced by the restoration prophecies of Isaiah. The Isaianic material often communicates the concept of reconciliation with cosmological language. Given the combination of restoration and new creation themes in Isaiah – especially in Isa 43:18-19 which is likely reflected in 2 Cor 5:17 – it is highly probable that Paul's expression of new creation immediately followed by a discussion of reconciliation is influenced by this tradition.

Thirdly, the only direct quotation of OT tradition in the immediate context of 2 Cor 5:17 is the use of Isa 49:8 in 2 Cor 6:2. This confirms that Paul is drawing out how the work of Christ has brought about an eschatological fulfilment to the Isaianic prophecies. Finally, the presence of these themes in conjunction with the use of Isaianic language in 2 Cor 5:17 presents a strong cumulative case that Paul understands the new creation in Christ as a fulfilment of Isaianic prophecies which maintain a strong link between the salvation of people and world. Further exploration on how Paul's use of καινὴ κτίσις in Gal 6:15 may appear in the context of Isaianic themes would support this argument and could help offer further insight into the way that Paul applies OT traditions to his own message.

Similarly to the Galatian situation, Paul's apostolic authority was being questioned in Corinth and the concept of new creation is used in the context of defending his position. The basis of Paul's defence is the eschatological inversion where the epicentre of God's cosmic "earthquake" was located in the death and resurrection of Christ. This eschatological inver-

---

[7] Also, note the significant reflection of Isa 24-7 in Rom 8 discussed in Chapter 7.

sion evokes an epistemological change in which the previous criteria for evaluating strengths and weakness are no longer valid. The epistemological transformation spoken of by Paul would have been incredibly resonant in the Corinthian community which was inundated with Roman imperial ideology. Paul's reinterpretation of reality envisaged a community which stood in stark contrast to the social world created by the power of Rome.

Like the Roman ideology which constructed reality around the person of the emperor and the city of Rome, Paul's epistemological transformation was predicated upon the supreme figure of the new order and understanding this connection is absolutely crucial for understanding Paul's use of καινὴ κτίσις in 2 Cor 5:17. Being ἐν Χριστῷ entails participation in the representative death and resurrection of Christ mentioned in 5:14-15. The close association with the Christ event indicates that Paul's thinking is not limited to an individual conversion experience. Through an application of the familiar Adam-Christ comparison in 2 Cor 5:14, Paul makes the case that the Christ event has inaugurated a new age. All humanity is associated with the old age by virtue of its connection with Adam and his sin. Christ is the eschatological Adam which both ends the old form of existence and begins the new creation. The association of new creation with the Christ event confirms the supra-individual effects of Paul's conception of new creation and the cultural climate of the city of Corinth provides evidence of how resonant such a connection would have been in the first century.

Although the phrase καινὴ κτίσις does not appear in the NT outside Gal and 2 Cor, a chapter on Paul's use of the theme of new creation in Rom 8 offers strong support for the central contention of my argument – Paul's understanding of new creation involved both cosmological and anthropological elements. In Paul's undisputed letters, the term κτίσις only occurs in Gal 6:15, 2 Cor 5:17, Rom 1 and Rom 8, and this underscores the importance of incorporating the evidence from Paul's letter to the Romans in this discussion.[8] Paul's argument in Romans 1-8 utilizes the imagery of creation. Presented in a positive light in 1:20, the creation in Rom 8 is shown to be subjected to futility because of human sin.

A deft comparison between Adam and Christ in Rom 5 shows that Paul viewed both Adam's sin as well as Christ's work to have universal effects. The soteriology of Rom 8 is rendered in terms of Adam Christology. Christ has fulfilled God's original purpose in creation to have humanity reflect his glory. Paul's movement from creation to new creation in Rom 1-8 takes the position that creation itself is affected by human sin and Rom 8 makes clear that, for Paul, the redemption of humanity was part of the redemption of creation. The redemptive connection between humanity and creation be-

---

[8] The only other use of the term is in Col 1:15, 23 and the importance of these verses will be addressed anon.

comes clearest in Paul's use of the resurrection. Paul sees the redemption of the body as fundamental to the renewal of creation as a whole. Readers or hearers of Paul's letter in the city of Rome would have heard Paul's proclamation of creation's need for liberation in a world supposed to have been restored to liberty and moral rectitude by the Roman emperor.[9] Rather than the idyllic visions of Virgil, Paul understood creation to be groaning in longing for God's final and ultimate act of redemption of his people and his world.[10]

This thesis has attended to the various ways in which Paul employs the concept of new creation in various communities and has maintained that his understanding of the idea is consistent throughout his writings. A number of similarities in the different contexts support this claim. Both occurrences of καινὴ κτίσις appear in the context of an "appearance versus reality motif;" both hold καινὴ κτίσις in antithesis to σάρξ and thereby embody a strongly pneumatological thrust; both appear in similarly terse syntax; both are expanded beyond an individual experience.[11]

In addition to these similarities, both occurrences of καινὴ κτίσις in Paul's letters appear in the context of a defence of his apostolic authority. His understanding of new creation is strongly soteriological and necessarily includes conversion but his appeal is not simply to the conversion experience of individuals. The eschatological situation brought about by the death and resurrection of Christ is what alters reality in Paul's thinking and this suggests that his understanding of new creation should be interpreted through broad soteriological lenses. The two occurrences of καινὴ κτίσις as well as the use of the concept in Romans 8 are intricately related to the Christ event. This association is indispensable for understanding Paul's thinking since he views the resurrection of Christ to be the beginning of the eschatological restoration envisaged in the OT.

For Paul, the new creation is an eschatologically charged concept. He has modified the eschatological perspectives of Jewish traditions and he writes in the atmosphere of a society influenced by the eschatological claims of Roman imperial ideology. This eschatological thrust is common to each of the three new creation passages examined in this thesis.

---

[9] *Res Gestae Divi Augusti 1.1*.

[10] In the ancient world, there was an inextricable link between the cosmos and the state. As early as Hesiod, the earth was said to groan as an effect of the war between Olympians and Typhoeus (*Theogony* 840-50). Further study on the ancient understanding of the groaning of creation could prove helpful, especially given the fact that the Roman Empire contemporary with Paul articulated the imperial propaganda in cosmological terms. See, e.g., Virgil, *Eclogue*, Book IV; Paterculus II,89. Cf. Jones 1977:47.

[11] Hubbard's study recognizes these convergences but does not observe the further similarities noted below. See Hubbard 2002:231-2.

The question remains why Paul did not make more explicit the cosmological elements of his thinking. With the evidence available to us we can only surmise that Paul's pastoral concerns in various communities must have outweighed the importance of theological speculation on these issues. The incomplete epistolary evidence from Paul prohibits us from a complete picture of his view of the final state of God's new creation in terms of how it might look and in what sense it would be new. Did Paul believe in the destruction of the physical universe and a completely new creation, or did he think more along the lines of a renovation/renewal of the present world? In truth, both lines of thought are represented in Jewish literature which might have influenced Paul (sometimes even in the same work). Paul's own writings tend towards the idea of renovation/renewal but it is difficult to make a conclusive decision given the limitations of the evidence.

B. Implications and Considerations for Further Study

Paul's application of Jewish traditions in the cultural milieu of the Greco-Roman world in which he operated may be understood in terms of his missionary thrust. Informed by the eschatological promises of the prophetic literature and influenced by the intertwined cosmological and anthropological soteriology represented there, Paul's ministry was carried out in a society in which at least one of the pervasive world-views – that of the imperial ideology – was articulated in eschatological, cosmological and even soteriological terms. I have argued that Paul's understanding of new creation is eschatologically infused and contains both cosmological and anthropological elements, and this proposition is supported by both Jewish and Greco-Roman background material as well as detailed analysis of the Pauline literature itself. In the course of the summarizing conclusions discussed above I addressed a number of issues for additional consideration. A number of other thought-provoking questions have been raised by this study and these provide intriguing and worthwhile avenues for further lines of enquiry.

First, there has been a tendency in Pauline studies, represented, for example, in the work of J. L. Martyn, to downplay salvation historical observations in Paul in favour of Paul's alleged use of apocalyptic categories. As I have already indicated, the apocalyptic approach to Paul no longer enjoys the wide support it once did and neither does interest in Paul's connection to salvation historical concerns. This thesis suggests that these different approaches to understanding Paul's thought may be more compatible than has been assumed. Throughout my argument I have acknowledged that Paul's writings reflect apocalyptic influence and, at the same time, show interest in affirming OT promises of salvation. I have also suggested ways in which the apocalyptic influence may be seen to be compatible with these OT expectations. If this is correct it would offer fresh insight into how Paul could well have sustained salvation historical concerns even if he adopted apocalyptic categories of thought.

Secondly, the growing interest in the political background to Paul would be greatly enhanced by the recognition that an incorporation of the political elements of Paul's thought should not be understood outside the context of his Jewish tradition. Paul was not simply an anti-imperial liberation theologian. He does, however, challenge the contemporary world views which contradict his message and the imperial "gospel" is not excluded from that challenge. While interest in the political implications of Paul's writing has been enlightening, it cannot be the singular interpretive key to his thought. This thesis could serve as an example for how we might maintain an interest both in the Jewish thought world which undoubtedly influenced Paul and the Greco-Roman world in which he articulated his message.

Thirdly, since identification with Christ is such an important theme for Paul (especially in the context of both passages which include καινή κτίσις), it would be helpful to come to a fuller understanding of what it meant to identify oneself with Roman society. With concepts such as Augustus's role as "father of the country," to what extent was Roman society viewed as a family? If he represented the corporate personality of the empire, how closely were individuals actually related to the emperor himself? In his letter of consolation to Polybius, Seneca writes concerning Caesar (Claudius), "So long as he is alive, your dear ones are alive – you have lost nothing. Your eyes ought to be not only dry, but even happy; in him you have all things, he takes the place of all (*in hoc tibi omnia sunt, hic pro omnibus est*)."[12]

For Seneca, the wellbeing of the emperor ensured not only the wellbeing of the empire in general but relativized particular events within it. The emperor stood as representative and source of all things and one's complete sphere of existence could be spoken of as "in him." The emperor's personality represented the corporate personality of the empire.[13] Although every constituent of the Roman Empire may not have resonated with this identification, this is how the emperor himself wanted to be perceived. It was the message that the elite of Rome perpetuated and, as such, it represents the ideology they attempted to communicate. How this idea is impor-

---

[12] Seneca, *To Polybius, On Consolation* 7.4. The importance of the figure of the emperor is also attested, for example, in the work of Suetonius in *Augustus* 98.2. Cf. Acts 17:28.

[13] Brent 1999:66.

tant for Paul's use of "in Christ" language, identification with Christ and the Church as body with Christ as its head deserves further consideration and may advance our understanding of Paul's participatory language.

Finally, it was unfortunately beyond the limitations of this thesis to include a study of the use of the theme of new creation in the letters of disputed Pauline authorship. Two letters in particular make significant use of the theme even though the phrase καινὴ κτίσις does not appear: Ephesians and Colossians. In the letter to the Ephesians, the verb κτίζω is used four times. God, the creator of all things (Eph 3:9), creates a new man (καινὸν ἄνθρωπον) in his own likeness (Eph 4:24). Putting off the old man and putting on the new is part of Paul's conversion imagery but it is interesting that in Eph 2:15 the creation of the new man refers not to an individual convert but to the unified body of Christ, which is to include Jew and Gentile (cf. Gal 6:15-16). At the very least, this indicates that for the writer of Ephesians the concept of new creation was part of a broad soteriology. The concern of this letter with the heavenly/spiritual dimension, its interest in the ages as well as the connection between the resurrection of Christ and believers (Eph 2:6) would be worth exploring in the context of new creation themes in this letter. How this relates to Paul's understanding of new creation in Gal, 2 Cor and Rom would be a worthwhile expansion of this research.

The concept of the new man is also used in Col 3:10 followed by a similar appeal to unity in the body of Christ in 3:11 (cf. Gal 3:28). In its closing assertion that "Christ is all and in all ([τὰ] πάντα καὶ ἐν πᾶσιν Χριστός)," Col 3:11 represents the cosmic Christology so important to the writer of Colossians.[14] If there is any doubt about the scope of the reconciliation discussed by Paul in 2 Cor 5:18-21, the writer of Colossians makes clear its cosmic scale. Christ, in whom the fullness of God dwelt, was the agent through whom God "reconciled to himself all things (τὰ πάντα), whether on earth or in heaven, making peace through the blood of his cross" (Col 1:20). This reconciliation language occurs in the context of strong emphasis on the cosmic role of Christ who is twice called πρωτότοκος (Col 1:15, 18; cf. Rom 8:29). He is both firstborn over all creation (Col 1:15) and firstborn ἐκ τῶν νεκρῶν (Col 1:18).[15] Such rich cosmic Christology, whether from Paul himself or his earliest interpreters, was not considered inconsistent with the undisputed letters since we have no evidence of objections to the acceptance of Colossians by the early church. Further study on how this relates to Paul's undisputed letters would be a helpful starting point for an examination of how the theme of

---

[14] Cf. Col 1:15-16

[15] Might the latter phrase signal Paul's understanding of the Christ event to have inaugurated the new creation expected to occur in the eschaton?

new creation is used in the New Testament as a whole and may even contribute to the debate over the authenticity of this letter.

This thesis attempts to take seriously the historical and social settings of the Pauline letters and at the same time to give adequate attention to those Jewish sources which would have influenced Paul's thinking. I have suggested how Paul was influenced by Jewish traditions and why these traditions might have appealed to him in the cultural settings in which he ministered. In particular, I have sought to understand how the Roman imperial ideology might have created an atmosphere in which Paul's understanding of new creation would have been especially resonant. This suggests that Paul's concept of new creation was a way of encapsulating a broad eschatologically infused soteriology, and examination of the most relevant Pauline texts supports this claim. This work is intended as an important nuance to our understanding of Paul's new creation and offers a number of implications and suggestions for further research. It is hoped that the thesis here advocated will help to advance our understanding of Paul's conception of new creation and will suggest a helpful model for interpreting Paul's writing within its missionary context.

Bibliography

Aageson, James W. "Written Also for Our Sake: Paul's Use of Scripture in the Four Major Epistles, with a Study of 1 Corinthians 10." In *Hearing the Old Testament in the New Testament*, ed. Stanley E. Porter, 152-81. Grand Rapids: Eerdmans, 2006.

Adams, Edward. *Constructing the World*, Studies of the New Testament and Its World, ed. John Barclay, Joel Marcus and John Riches. Edinburgh: T&T Clark, 2000.

—. "Paul's Story of God and Creation." In *Narrative Dynamics in Paul: A Critical Assessment*, ed. Bruce W. Longenecker, 19-43. London: Westminster John Knox Press, 2002.

—. *The Stars Will Fall from Heaven: Cosmic Catastrophe in the New Testament and Its World*. New York: T&T Clark, 2007.

Anderson, Bernhard W. *From Creation to New Creation*, Overtures to Biblical Theology, ed. Walter Brueggemann, et. al. Minneapolis: Fortress Press, 1994.

Ando, Clifford. *Imperial Ideology and Provincial Loyalty in the Roman Empire*. Vol. VI. VII vols., Classics and Contemporary Thought, ed. Thomas Habinek. London: University of California Press, 2000.

Arnold, Clinton E. "Returning to the Domain of the Powers: Stoicheia as Evil Spirits in Galatians 4:3, 9." *Novum Testamentum* 38, no. 1 (1996): 55-76.

Aune, David E. "Apocalypticism." In *Dictionary of Paul and His Letters*, ed. Gerald F. Hawthorne and Ralph P. Martin, 25-35. Downers Grove: InterVarsity Press, 1993.

—. "Anthropological Duality in the Eschatology of 2 Cor 4:16-5:10." In *Paul Beyond the Judaism/Hellenism Divide*, ed. Troels Engberg-Pederson, 215-39. London: Westminster John Knox Press, 2001a.

—. "From the Idealized Past to the Imaginary Future: Eschatolgical Restoration in Jewish Apocalyptic Literature." In *Restoration: Old Testament, Jewish, and Christian Perspectives*, ed. James M. Scott, 72, 147-77. Boston: Brill, 2001b.

Aymer, A.J.D. "Paul's Understanding of KAINH KTISIS: Continuity and Discontinuity in Pauline Eschatology." Drew University, 1983.

Baer, David A. *When We All Go Home: Translation and Theology in LXX Isaiah 56-66*. Vol. 318, JSOTSS, ed. David J.A. Clines and Philip R. Davies. Sheffield: Sheffield Academic Press, 2001.

Balz, Horst. *Heilsvertrauen und Welterfahrung: Strukturen des paulinischen Eschatologie nach Römer 8,18-39*. Münich: Kaiser, 1971.

Barclay, John. *Obeying the Truth: Paul's Ethics in Galatians*. Vancouver: Regent College Publishing, 1988.

Barnett, Paul. *The Second Epistle to the Corinthians*, NICNT, ed. Gordon D. Fee. Grand Rapids: William B. Eerdmans, 1997.

—. "Paul, Apologist to the Corinthians." In *Paul and the Corinthians: Studies on a Community in Conflict. Essays in Honour of Margaret Thrall*, ed. Trevor J. Burke and J. Keith Elliott, 109, 313-26. Leiden: Brill, 2003.

Barrett, C.K. *A Commentary on the Epistle to the Romans*, Black's New Testament Commentaries. London: A&C Black, 1957.

—. *From First Adam to Last: A Study in Pauline Theology*. London: Adam & Charles Black, 1962.
Baumbach, G. "Die Schöpfung in der Theologie des Paulus." *Kairos* 21-22 (1979-80): 196-205.
Baumgarten, Jörg. *Paulus und die Apokalyptik*. Neukirchen-Vluyn: Neukirchner, 1975.
Beale, G.K. "The Old Testament Background of Reconciliation in 2 Corinthians 5-7 and its Bearing on the Literary Problem of 2 Corinthians 6:14-7:1." *New Testament Studies* 35 (1989): 550-581.
—. "The Eschatological Conception of New Testament Theology." In *'The Reader Must Understand': Eschatology in Bible and Theology*, ed. K.E. Brower and M.W. Elliot, 11-52. Leicester: Apollos, 1997.
—. "Peace and Mercy Upon the Israel of God: The Old Testament Background of Galatians 6:16b." *Biblica* 80 (1999): 204-223.
—. "The Old Testament Background of Paul's Reference to 'the Fruit of the Spirit' in Galatians 5:22." *BBR* 15, no. 1 (2005): 1-38.
Beker, J. *Paul the Apostle: the Triumph of God in Life and Thought*. Philadelphia: Fortress Press, 1980.
Berges, Ulrich. "Der neue Himmel und die neue Erde im Jesjabuch: Eine Auslegung zu Jesaja 65:17 und 66:22." In *The New Things: Eschatology in Old Testament Prophecy*, ed. F. Postma, K. Spronk and E. Talstra, 9-15. Maastricht: Shaker Publishing, 2002.
Bergey, Ronald. "The Song of Moses (Deuteronomy 32:1-43) and Isaianic Prophecies: A Case of Early Intertextuality?" *JSOT* 28, no. 1 (2003): 33-54.
Betz, H.D. "The Literary Composition and Function of Paul's Letter to the Galatians." *NTS* 21, no. 3 (1975): 353-79.
—. *Galatians: A Commentary on Paul's Letter to the Churches in Galatia*, Hermeneia, ed. Helmut Koester. Philadelphia: Fortress Press, 1979.
Beuken, Willem A. M. "Isaiah Chapters LXV-LXVI: Trito-Isaiah and the Closure of the Book of Isaiah." In *Congress Volume: Leuven 1989*, ed. J.A. Emerton, 43, 204-21. Leiden: Brill, 1991.
—. "The Literary Emergence of Zion as a City in the first Opening of the Book of Isaiah (1:1-2, 5)." In *Gott und Mensch im Dialog: Festschrift für Otto Kaiser zum 80. Geburtstag*, ed. Markus Witte, 345/I, 457-470. Berlin: Walter de Gruyter, 2004.
Beyer, H.W. "ΚΑΝΩΝ." In *TDNT*, ed. G. Kittel, 3, 596-602. Grand Rapids: Eerdmans, 1965.
Bickerman, Elias J. *The God of the Maccabees: Studies on the Meaning and Origin of the Maccabean Revolt*. Translated by Horst R. Moehring. Vol. 32, Studies in Judaism in Late Antiquity, ed. Jacob Neusner. Leiden: Brill, 1979.
Bindemann, W. *Die Hoffnung der Schöpfung: Röm 8:17-27 und die Frage einer Theologie der Befreiung von Mensch und Natur*. Neukirchen: Neukirchner, 1983.
Blenkinsopp, Joseph. *Isaiah 40-55: A New Translation with Introduction and Commentary*. Vol. 19A, The Anchor Bible, ed. William Foxwell Albright and David Noel Freedman. New York: Doubleday, 2002.
—. *Isaiah 56-66: A New Translation with Introduction and Commentary*. Vol. 19B, The Anchor Bible, ed. William Foxwell Albright and David Noel Freedman. New York: Doubleday, 2003.
Blinzer, J. "Lexikalisches zu dem Terminus ΤΑ ΣΤΟΙΧΕΙΑ ΤΟΥ ΚΟΣΜΟΥ bei Paulus." In *Studiorum Paulinorum Congressus Internationalis Catholicus 1961*, 2, 429-43. Rome: Pontifical Biblical Institute, 1963.
Boismard, Marie-Emile. *Our Victory Over Death: Resurrection?* Collegeville, MN: Liturgical Press, 1999.

Bolt, John. "The Relation between Creation and Redemption in Romans 8:18-27." *CTJ* 30 (1995): 34-51.
Bookidis, Nancy. "Religion in Corinth: 146 B.C.E. to 100 C.E." In *Urban Religion in Roman Corinth: Interdisciplinary Approaches*, ed. Daniel N. Schowalter and Steven J. Friesen, 53, 140-64. Cambridge, MA: Harvard University Press, 2005.
Boomershine, Thomas E. "Epistemology at the Turn of the Ages in Paul, Jesus, and Mark: Rhetoric and Dialectic in Apocalyptic and the New Testament: Essays in Honor of J. Louis Martyn." In *Apocalyptic and the New Testament*, ed. J. Marcus and M.L. Soards, 24, 147-67. Sheffield: JSOT Press, 1989.
Borse, Udo. *Der Standort des Galaterbriefes*. Köln: Peter Hanstein Verlag, 1972.
Bovon, François. "Une formule prépaulinienne dans l'Épitre aux Galates (Ga 1, 4-5)." In *Paganisme, Judaïsme, Christianisme: influences et affrontements dans le monde antique: mélanges offerts a Marcel Simon*, ed. F.F. Bruce and et. al., 91-107. Paris: Editions E. de Boccard, 1978.
Bowman, Alan K., Edward Champlin, and Andrew Lintott, eds. *The Cambridge Ancient History*. Vol. X. Cambridge: Cambridge University Press, 1996.
Braaten, Laurie J. "All Creation Groans: Romans 8:22 in Light of the Biblical Sources." *Horizons in Biblical Theology* 28, no. 2 (2006): 131-60.
Branigan, Keith. "Images – Or Mirages – of Empire? An Archaeological Approach to the Problem." In *Images of Empire*, ed. Loveday Alexander, 122, 316. Sheffield: JSOT Press, 1991.
Braund, David C. *Augustus to Nero: A Sourcebook on Roman History (31 B.C. - A.D. 68)*. London: Croom Helm, 1985.
Bray, Gerald, ed. *1 & 2 Corinthians*. Vol. VII, Ancient Christian Commentary on Scripture. Downers Grove, IL: IVP, 1999a.
—, ed. *Romans*. Vol. VI, Ancient Christian Commentary on Scripture. Downers Grove, IL: IVP, 1999b.
Brent, Allen. *The Imperial Cult and the Development of Church Order: Concepts and Images of Authority in Paganism and Early Christianity before the Age of Cyprian*. Vol. 45, Supplements to Vigiliae Christianae, ed. J. Den Boeft. Leiden: Brill, 1999.
Brinsmead, Bernard Hungerford. *Galatians – Dialogical Response to Opponents*, SBL Diss, ed. W. Baird. Chico, CA: Scholars Press, 1982.
Bruce, F.F. *The Epistle of Paul to the Galatians*, The New International Greek Testament Commentary, ed. I. Howard Marshall and W. Ward Gasque. Exeter: Paternoster Press, 1982.
Brueggemann, Walter. *Isaiah 1-39*, Westminster Bible Companion, ed. Patrick D. & David L. Bartlett Miller. Louisville: Westminster John Knox Press, 1998.
Brunt, P. A. *Roman Imperial Themes*. Oxford: Clarendon Press, 1990.
Bultmann, R. *Exegetische Probleme des zweiten Korintherbriefes*. Darmstadt: Wissenschaftliche Buchgesellschaft, 1963.
—. *The Second Letter to the Corinthians*. Translated by Roy A. Harrisville. Minneapolis: Augsburg Publishing House, 1985.
Burton, Ernest De Witt. *The Epistle to the Galatians*. Edinburgh: T&T Clark, 1921.
Byrne, Brendan. *Romans*. Collegeville, MN: Liturgical Press, 1996.
Calvin, John. *Commentary on Romans 1-16*. Translated by John Owen. Vol. 19, Calvin's Commentaries. Grand Rapids, Michigan: Baker Book House, 1993.
Cancik, Hubert. "The End of the World, of HIstory, and of the Individual in Greek and Roman Antiquity." In *The Encyclopedia of Apocalypticism. Vol 1: The Origins of Apocalypticism in Judaism*, ed. John J. Collins, 1, 84-125. London: Continuum, 2000.

Carter, Warren. *Matthew and Empire: Initial Explorations*. Harrisburg: Trinity Press International, 2001.
Castriota, David. *The Ara Pacis Augustus and the Imagery of Abundance in Later Greek and Early Roman Imperial Art*. Princeton: Princeton University Press, 1995.
Charlesworth, M.P. "Gaius and Claudius." In *The Cambridge Ancient History*, ed. S.A. Cook, F.E. Adcock and M.P. Charlesworth, 10, 653-701. Cambridge: CUP, 1966.
Chester, Andrew. "Jewish Messianic Expectation and Mediatorial Figures and Pauline Christology." In *Paulus und das antike Judentum*, ed. M. Hengel and U. Heckel, 17-89. Tübingen: Mohr, 1991.
—. "Resurrection and Transformation." In *Auferstehung – Resurrection*, ed. Friedrich Avemarie and Hermann Lichtenberger, 135, 47-77. Tübingen: Mohr Siebeck, 2001.
Chester, Stephen J. *Conversion at Corinth: Perspectives on Conversion in Paul's Theology and the Corinthian Church*, Studies of the NT and Its World, ed. John Barclay, Joel Marcus and John Riches. London: T&T Clark, 2003.
Childs, Brevard S. *Introduction to the Old Testament as Scripture*. London: SCM, 1979.
—. *Isaiah*, The Old Testament Library, ed. James Luther Mays, Carol A. Newsom and David L. Petersen. Louisville: Westminster John Knox Press, 2001.
Chisholm, Kitty, and John Ferguson, eds. *Rome: The Augustan Age*. Oxford: Oxford University Press, 1981.
Chow, John K. *Patronage and Power: a Study of Social Networks in Corinth*. Vol. 75. Sheffield: JSOT Press, 1992.
Christoffersson, Olle. *The Earnest Expectation of the Creature: The Flood-tradition as Matrix of Romans 8:18-27*, Coniectanea Biblica, 23; New Testament Series. Stockholm: Almqvist & Wiksell International, 1990.
Ciampa, Roy E. *The Presence and Function of Scripture in Galatians 1 and 2*. Vol. 102. 449 vols., WUNT. Tübingen: Mohr Siebeck, 1998.
Clements, R.E. "Zion as Symbol and political Reality: A Central Isaianic Quest." In *Studies in the Book of Isaiah*, ed. Jacques Van Ruiten and M. Vervenne, 132, 3-17. Leuven: University Press, 1997.
Clifford, Richard J. *Creation Accounts in the Ancient Near East and in the Bible*. Vol. 26, The Catholic Biblical Quarterly Monograph Series, ed. S.S. Barré, Michael L. Washington: Catholic Biblical Association of America, 1994.
Collange, J.-F. *Enigmes de la Deuxieme Epitre de Paul aux Corinthiens: Etude Exegetique de 2 Cor. 2:14-7:4*, SNTSM, ed. Matthew Black. Cambridge: CUP, 1972.
Collins, Adela Yarbro. "Introduction: Early Christian Apocalypticism." *Semeia* 36 (1986): 1-11.
—. *Cosmology and Eschatology in Jewish and Christian Apocalypticism*. Vol. 50, Supplements to the Journal for the Study of Judaism, ed. John J. Collins. Leiden: E.J. Brill, 1996.
—. "The Worship of Jesus and the Imperial Cult." In *The Jewish Roots of Christological Monotheism: Papers from the St. Andrews Conference on the Historical Origins of the Worship of Jesus*, ed. C.C. Newman, J.R. Davila and G.S. Lewis, 63, 234-57. Leiden: Brill, 1999.
Collins, John J. "Cosmos and Salvation: Jewish Wisdom and Apocalyptic in the Hellenistic Age." *History of Religions* 17, no. 2 (1977): 121-42.
—. "Apocalyptic Literature." In *Early Judaism and its Modern Interpreters*, ed. R.A. Kraft and George W.E. Nickelsburg, 345-70. Chico, CA: Scholars Press, 1986.
—. *The Apocalyptic Imagination: An Introduction to Jewish Apocalyptic Literature*. 2nd ed. Grand Rapids: William B. Eerdmans Publishing Company, 1998.
—. "Eschatology." In *Encyclopedia of the Dead Sea Scrolls*, ed. Lawrence H. Schiffman and James C. VanderKam, 1, 256-61. Oxford: OUP, 2000.

Cousar, Charles B. *A Theology of the Cross: The Death of Jesus in the Pauline Letters*. Minneapolis: Fortress Press, 1990.
Cramer, Frederick H. *Astrology in Roman Law and Politics*. Philadelphia: The American Philosophical Society, 1954.
Cranfield, C.E.B. "Some Observations on Romans 8:19-21." In *Reconciliation and Hope: New Testament Essays on Atonement and Eschatology*, ed. Robert Banks, 224-30. Exeter: Paternoster Press, 1974.
—. *The Epistle to the Romans*. Vol. 1. 2 vols., ICC. Edinburgh: T&T Clark, 1975.
Crossan, John D., and Jonathan L. Reed. *In Search of Paul: How Jesus's Apostle Opposed Rome's Empire with God's Kingdom*. San Francisco, CA: HarperSanFrancisco, 2004.
Dahl, N.A. "Christ, Creation and the Church." In *The Background of the New Testament and its Eschatology*, ed. W.D. Davies and D. Daube, 422-43. Cambridge: CUP, 1956.
—. *Studies in Paul: Theology for the Early Christain Mission*. Minneapolis: Augsburg Publishing House, 1977.
Daise, M.A. "Biblical Creation Motifs in the Qumran Hodayot." In *The DSS Fifty Years after their Discovery: Proceedings of the Jerusalem Congress, July 20-25, 1997*, ed. L.H. Schiffman, E. Tov and James C. VanderKam, 293-305. Jerusalem: Old City Press, 2000.
Das, A. Andrew. *Solving the Romans Debate*. Minneapolis: Fortress Press, 2007.
Davenport, Gene L. *The Eschatology of the Book of Jubilees*. Leiden: E.J. Brill, 1971.
Davies, Philip R. "The Social World of Apocalyptic Writings." In *The World of Ancient Israel: Sociological, Anthropological and Political Perspectives*, ed. R.E. Clements, 251-71. Cambridge: Cambridge University Press, 1989.
Davies, W.D. *Paul and Rabbinic Judaism: Some Rabbinic Elements in Pauline Theology*. 4th ed. Philadelphia: Fortress Press, 1980.
—. "Paul and the New Exodus." In *The Quest for Context and Meaning: Studies in Biblical Intertextuality in Honor of James A. Sanders*, ed. Craig A. Evans and Talmon Shemaryahu, 442-63. New York: Brill, 1997.
—. "Paul from the Jewish Point of View." In *The Cambridge History of Judaism: The Early Roman Period*, ed. William Horbury, W.D. Davies and John Sturdy, 3, 678-730. Cambridge: Cambridge University Press, 1999.
De Boer, M.C. *The Defeat of Death: Apocalyptic Eschatology in 1 Corinthians 15 and Romans 5*. Vol. 22, JSNTSS, ed. David Hill. Sheffield: JSOT Press, 1988.
—. "Paul and Jewish Apocalyptic Eschatology." In *Apocalyptic and the New Testament: Essays in Honor of J. Louis Martyn*, ed. J. Marcus and M.L. Soards, 169-90. Sheffield: Academic Press, 1989.
—. "Paul and Apocalyptic Eschatology." In *The Encyclopedia of Apocalypticism: The Origins of Apocalypticism in Judaism and Christianity*, ed. John J. Collins, 1, 345-383. London: Continuum, 2000.
—. "The Meaning of the Phrase ΤΑ ΣΤΟΙΧΕΙΑ ΤΟΥ ΚΟΣΜΟΥ in Galatians." *NTS* 53 (2007): 204-24.
Delling, D. "ΣΤΟΙΧΕΩ, ΣΥΣΤΟΙΧΕΩ, ΣΤΟΙΧΕΙΟΝ." In *TDNT*, ed. G. Friedrich, 7, 666-87. Grand Rapids: Eerdmans, 1971.
Denney, James. *The Death of Christ*. London: Tyndale Press, 1951.
Derrett, J.D.M. "New Creation: Qumran, Paul, the Church and Jesus." *Revue de Qumran* 13 (1988): 597-608.
Dim, Emmanuel Uchenna. *The Eschatological Implications of Isa 65 and 66 as the Conclusion of the Book of Isaiah*, Bible in History, ed. Joseph Alobaidi. Bern: Peter Lang, 2005.
Dodd, C.H. *According to the Scriptures*. London: Nisbet, 1952.

Doering, Lutz. "The Concept of the Sabbath in the Book of Jubilees." In *Studies in the Book of Jubilees*, ed. Matthias Albani, Jörg Frey and Armin Lange, 65, 179-205. Tübingen: Mohr Siebeck, 1997.

Downing, F. G. "Cosmic Eschatology in the First Century: 'Pagan', Jewish and Christian." *L'Antiquité Classique* 64 (1995): 99-109.

Doyle, Brian. *The Apocalypse of Isaiah Metaphorically Speaking: A Study of the Use, Function and Significance of Metaphors in Isaiah 24-27*. Vol. 151, Bibliotheca Ephemeridum Theologicarum Lovaniensium. Leuven: Leuven University Press, 2000.

Du Toit, Andrie. "Vilification as a Pragmatic Device in Early Christian Epistolography." *Bib* 75 (1994): 403-12.

Duff, N.J. "The Significance of Pauline Apocalyptic for Theological Ethics." In *Apocalyptic and New Testament*, ed. J. Marcus and M.L. Soards, 279-96. Sheffield: Sheffield Press, 1989.

Duhaime, Jean. *The War Texts: 1QM and Related Manuscripts*. London: T&T Clark, 2004.

Dumbrell, William J. "Some Observations on the Political Origins of Israel's Eschatology." *The Reformed Theological Review* 36, no. 2 (1977): 33-41.

Dunn, James D. G. "'A Light to the Gentiles': the Significance of the Damascus Road Christophany for Paul." In *The Glory of Christ in the New Testament: Studies in Christology*, ed. D. Hurst and N. T. Wright, 251-66. Oxford: Clarendon Press, 1987.

—. *Romans 1-8*. Vol. 38A, WBC, ed. Ralph P. Martin. Dallas: Word Books, 1988.

—. *The Epistle to the Galatians*, Black's NT Commentary, ed. Henry Chadwick. Peabody: Hendrickson, 1993.

—. *Paul and the Mosaic Law: The Third Durham-Tübingen Research Symposium on Earliest Christianity and Judaism*, WUNT. Tübingen: Mohr, 1996.

—. *The Theology of Paul the Apostle*. Grand Rapids: William B. Eerdmans, 1998.

Eastman, Susan. "Whose Apocalypse? The Identity of the Sons of God in Romans 8:19." *JBL* 121, no. 2 (2002): 263-77.

Eckstein, Hans-Joachim. "Auferstehung und gegenwärtiges Leben nach Röm 6,1-11: Präsentische Eschatologie bei Paulus?" *Theologische Beiträge* 28 (1997): 8-23.

Edwards, Mark, ed. *Galatians, Ephesians, Philippians*. Vol. VIII, Ancient Christian Commentary on Scripture. Downers Grove, IL: IVP, 1999.

Ego, Beate. *Im Himmel wie auf Erden: Studien zum Verhältnis von himmlischer und irdischer Welt im rabbinischen Judentum*. Vol. 34, WUNT. Tübingen: J.C.B. Mohr, 1989.

—. "Heilige Zeit – heiliger Raum – heiliger Mensch: Beobachtung zur Struktur der Gesetzesbegründung in der Schöpfungs- und Paradiesgeschichte des Jubiläenbuchs." In *Studies in the Book of Jubilees*, ed. Matthias Albani, Jörg Frey and Armin Lange, 65, 207-19. Tübingen: Mohr Siebeck, 1997.

Ehrenberg, Victor, and A. H. M. Jones. *Documents Illustrating the Reigns of Augustus and Tiberius*. 2nd ed. Oxford: Clarendon Press, 1976.

Elledge, C.D. *Life after Death in Early Judaism: The Evidence of Josephus*. Vol. 208, WUNT. Tübingen: Mohr Siebeck, 2006.

Elliott, Neil. *Liberating Paul: The Justice of God and the Politics of the Apostle*. Maryknoll, NY: Orbis Books, 1994.

Endres, John C. *Biblical Interpretation in the Book of Jubilees*. Vol. 18, The Catholic Biblical Quarterly Monograph Series, ed. Robert J. Karris. Washington, D.C.: The Catholic Biblical Association of America, 1987.

Engels, Donald. *Roman Corinth: an Alternative Model for the Classical City*. Chicago: The University of Chicago, 1990.

Esler, Philip F. "Rome in Apocalyptic and Rabbinic Literature." In *The Gospel of Matthew in its Roman Imperial Context*, ed. John Riches and David C. Sim, 9-33. London: T&T Clark, 2005.
Favro, Diane. *The Urban Image of Augustan Rome*. Cambridge: Cambridge University Press, 1996.
Fee, Gordon D. *The First Epistle to the Corinthians*. Grand Rapids: Eerdmans, 1987.
—. *God's Empowering Presence*. Peabody: Hendrickson, 1994.
—. *Pauline Christology: an exegetical theological study*. Peabody: Hendrickson, 2007.
Findeis, H.-J. *Versöhnung-Apostolat-Kirche: eine exegetisch-theologische und rezeptionsgeschichtliche Studie zu den Versöhnungsaussagen des Neuen Testaments (2 Kor, Röm, Kol, Eph)*. Vol. 40, Forschung zur Bibel. Würzburg: Echter Verlag, 1983.
Fishwick, Duncan. *The Imperial Cult in the Latin West: Studies in the Ruler Cult of the Western Provinces of the Roman Empire; Volume I,1*. Vol. 108. 2nd ed., Études Préliminaires aux Religions Orientales dans l'Empire Romain, ed. M. J. Vermaseren. Leiden: E. J. Brill, 1993.
—. *The Imperial Cult in the Latin West: Studies in the Ruler Cult of the Western Provinces of the Roman Empire; Volume III: Provincial Cult; Part 3: The Provincial Centre*. Vol. 147, Religions in the Graeco-Roman World, ed. H.S. Versnel, D. Frankfurter and J. Hahn. Leiden: E. J. Brill, 2004.
Fitzmyer, J.A. *Romans*. Vol. 33, The Anchor Bible. New York: Doubleday, 1993.
—. "Paul and the Dead Sea Scrolls." In *The Dead Sea Scrolls After Fifty Years: A Comprehensive Assessment*, ed. P.W. Flint and James C. VanderKam, 2, 599-621. Leiden: Brill, 1999.
—. *The Dead Sea Scrolls and Christian Origins*. Grand Rapids: Eerdmans, 2000.
Fletcher-Louis, Crispin. *All the Glory of Adam: Liturgical Anthropology in the Dead Sea Scrolls*. Vol. 42, Studies on the Texts of the Desert of Judah. Leiden: Brill, 2002.
Forbes, Chris. "Paul's Principalities and Powers: Demythologizing Apocalyptic?" *JSNT* 82 (2001): 61-88.
French, D. *Roman Roads and Milestones of Asia Minor*. Oxford: B.A.R., 1981.
Fretheim, Terence E. *God and the World in the Old Testament: A Relational Theology of Creation*. Nashville: Abingdon Press, 2005.
Frey, Jörg. "Zum Weltbild im Jubiläenbuch." In *Studies in the Book of Jubilees*, ed. Matthias Albani, Jörg Frey and Armin Lange, 65, 261-92. Tübingen: Mohr Siebeck, 1997.
Friesen, Steven J. *Imperial Cults and the Apocalypse of John: Reading Revelation in the Ruins*. Oxford: Oxford University Press, 2001.
—. "Satan's Throne, Imperial Cults and the Social Settings of Revelation." *JSNT* 27, no. 3 (2005): 351-73.
Fritz, Volkmar. *The City in Ancient Israel*. Sheffield: Sheffield Academic Press, 1995.
Furnish, V.P. *II Corinthians*. Vol. 32A, The Anchor Bible, ed. William Foxwell Albright and David Noel Freedman. Garden City, NY: Doubleday & Co., 1984.
Gager, John G. "Functional Diversity in Paul's Use of End-Time Language." *JBL* 89 (1970): 325-37.
Galinsky, Karl. *Augustan Culture*. Princeton: Princeton University Press, 1996.
Garland, D. *2 Corinthians*. Vol. 29, The New American Commentary, ed. E. Ray Clendenen. Nashville: Broadman & Holman, 1999.
—. *1 Corinthians*, Baker Exegetical Commentary on the New Testament, ed. R.W. Yarbrough and R.H. Stein. Grand Rapids: Eerdmans, 2003.
Gathercole, Simon J. *Where is Boasting? Early Jewish Soteriology and Paul's Response in Romans 1-5*. Grand Rapids: William B. Eerdmans, 2002.

Gaventa, Beverly R. "The Maternity of Paul: An Exegetical Study of Gal 4:19." In *The Conversation Continues: Studies in Paul and John in Honor of J. Louis Martyn*, ed. Robert T. Fortna and Beverly R. Gaventa, 189-201. Nashville: Abingdon, 1981.

—. "Galatians 1 and 2: Autobiography as Paradigm." *Novum Testamentum* XXVIII, no. 4 (1986): 309-326.

—. "The Singularity of the Gospel: A Reading of Galatians." In *Pauline Theology*, ed. Jouette Bassler, David M. Hay and E. Elizabeth Johnson, 1, 147-59. Minneapolis: Fortress Press, 1991.

Gempf, C.H. "The Imagery of Birth Pangs in the New Testament." *Tyndale Bulletin* 45, no. 1 (1994): 119-35.

Georgi, Dieter. *The Opponents of Paul in Second Corinthians*. Philadelphia: Fortress Press, 1986.

—. *Theocracy in Paul's Praxis and Theology*. Translated by David E. Green. Minneapolis: Fortress Press, 1991.

—. "Who is the True Prophet?" In *Paul and Empire: Religion and Power in Roman Imperial Society*, ed. Richard A. Horsley, 36-46. Harrisburg, Pennsylvania: Trinity Press International, 1997.

Gibbs, John G. *Creation and Redemption: A Study in Pauline Theology*. Vol. 26, Supplements to Novum Testamentum, ed. W.C. van Unnik. Bilthoven. Leiden: Brill, 1971.

—. "Cosmic Scope of Redemption According to Paul." *Biblica* 56, no. 1 (1975): 13-29.

Gignilliat, Mark. *Paul and Isaiah's Servants: Paul's Theological Reading of Isaiah 40-66 in 2 Corinthians 5:14-6:10*. Vol. 330, Library of New Testament Studies. London: T&T Clark, 2007.

Gill, David W.J. "The Roman Empire as a Context for the New Testament." In *Handbook to Exegesis of the New Testament*, ed. Stanley E. Porter, 25, 389-406. Leiden: Brill, 1997.

Gillman, J. "A Thematic Comparison: 1 Cor 15:50-57 and 2 Cor 1:1-5." *JBL* 107 (1988): 439-54.

Glasson, T. Francis. "2 Corinthians 5:1-10 versus Platonism." *SJT* 43, no. 2 (1990): 145-55.

Gloer, W. Hulitt. *An Exegetical and Theological Study of Paul's Understanding of New Creation and Reconciliation in 2 Cor. 5:14-21*. Vol. 42, Mellen Biblical Press Series. Lewiston: Mellen Biblical Press, 1996.

Gordon, Richard. "The Veil of Power." In *Paul and Empire: Religion and Power in Roman Imperial Power*, ed. Richard A. Horsley, 126-137. Harrisburg, Pennsylvania: Trinity Press International, 1997.

Gordon, Robert P. *Holy Land, Holy City: Sacred Geography and the Interpretation of the Bible*, Didsbury Lectures, 2001. Waynesboro, GA: Paternoster Press, 2004.

Gordon, T.D. "A Note on ΠΑΙΔΑΓΩΓΟΣ in Galatians 3:24-25." *NTS* 35, no. 1 (1989): 150-4.

Gowan, Donald E. "The Fall and Redemption of the Material World in Apocalyptic Literature." *Horizons in Biblical Theology* 7, no. 2 (1985): 83-103.

—. *Eschatology in the Old Testament*. 2nd ed. Edinburgh: T&T Clark, 2000.

Grabbe, Lester L., and Robert D. Haak, eds. *Knowing the End from the Beginning: The Prophetic, the Apocalyptic and their Relationships*. Vol. 46. London: T&T Clark International, 2003.

Gradel, Ittai. *Emperor Worship and Roman Religion*, Oxford Classical Monographs. Oxford: Clarendon Press, 2002.

Grässer, Erich. "Das Seufzen der Kreatur (Röm 8,19-22). Auf der Suche nach einer 'biblischen Tierschutzethik'." *Jahrbuch für Biblische Theologie* 5 (1990): 93-117.

Griffin, Miriam. "Urbs Roma, Plebs and Princeps." In *Images of Empire*, ed. Loveday Alexander, 122, 19-46. Sheffield: JSOT Press, 1991.

Grimal, Pierre. *Roman Cities*. Translated by G. Michael Woloch. Madison, Wisconsin: The University of Wisconsin Press, 1983.

Hafemann, Scott J. "The Glory and Veil of Moses in 2 Cor 3:7-14: An Example of Paul's Contextual Exegesis of the OT – A Proposal." *Horizons in Biblical Theology* 14, no. 1 (1991): 31-49.

—. *Paul, Moses and the History of Israel: The Letter/Spirit Contrast and the Argument from Scripture in 2 Corinthians 3*. Vol. 81, WUNT, ed. Martin Hengel and Otfried Hofius. Tübingen: J.C.B. Mohr, 1995.

—. "Paul's Argument from the Old Testament and Christology in 2 Cor 1-9: The Salvation-History/Restoration Structure of Paul's Apologetic." In *The Corinthian Correspondence*, ed. R. Bieringer, 125, 277-303. Leuven: Leuven University Press, 1996.

—. "The Spirit of the New Covenant, the Law, and the Temple of God's Presence: Five Theses on Qumran Self-Understanding and teh Contours of Paul's Thought." In *Evangelium Schriftauslegung Kirche: Festschrift für Peter Stuhlmacher zum 65. Geburtstag*, ed. Jostein Adna, Scott J. Hafemann and Otfried Hofius, 172-89. Göttingen: Vandenhoeck & Ruprecht, 1997.

Hahn, Ferdinand. "'Siehe, jetzt ist der Tag des Heils': Neuschöpfung und Versöhnung nach 2. Korinther 5,14-6,2." (1973).

Hahne, Harry A. *The Corruption and Redemption of Creation: Nature in Romans 8:19-22 and Jewish Apocalpytic Literature*. Vol. 336, LNTS, ed. Mark Goodacre. London: T&T Clark, 2006.

Hall III, John F. "The Saeculum Novum of Augustus and its Etruscan Antecedents." In *Principat*, ed. Hildegard Temporini and Wolfgang Hasse, II.16.3, 2564-2589. Berlin: Walter De Gruyter, 1986.

Hall, Robert G. *Revealed Histories: Techniques for Ancient Jewish and Christian Historiography*. Vol. 6, Journal for the Study of the Pseudepigrapha Supplement Series, ed. James H. Charlesworth. Sheffield: JSOT Presss, 1991.

Halpern-Amaru, Betsy. "The First Woman, Wives, and Mothers in Jubilees." *Journal of Biblical Literature* 113 (1994): 609-626.

Hamilton, Neill Q. *The Holy Spirit and Eschatology in Paul*. Vol. 6, SJT Occasional Papers. London: Oliver and Boyd, 1957.

Hanson, Paul D. *The Dawn of Apocalyptic: The Historical and Sociological Roots of Jewish Apocalyptic Eschtology*. Revised ed. Philadelphia: Fortress Press, 1979.

—. *Isaiah 40-66*, Interpretation, ed. James Luther Mays. Louisville: John Knox Press, 1995.

Hardie, Philip R. *Virgil's Aeneid: Cosmos and Imperium*. Oxford: Clarendon Press, 1986.

Hardin, Justin. *Galatians and the Imperial Cult: A Critical Analysis of the First-Century Social Context of Paul's Letter*, WUNT. Tübingen: Mohr Siebeck, 2008.

Harnack, Adolf von. "Die Terminologie der Wiedergeburt und verwandter Erlebnisse in der ältesten Kirche." *Texte und Untersuchungen zur Geschichte der altchristlichen Literatur* 42.3 (1918): 97-143.

Harrington, Daniel J., S.J. "'Holy War' Texts Among the Qumran Scrolls." In *Studies in the Hebrew Bible, Qumran, and the Septuagint Presented to Eugene Ulrich*, ed. P.W. Flint, E. Tov and James C. VanderKam, 175-83. Leiden: Brill, 2006.

Harris, Murray J. *The Second Epistle to the Corinthians: A Commentary on the Greek Text*, The New International Greek Testament Commentary, ed. I. Howard Marshall and Donald A. Hagner. Grand Rapids: William B. Eerdmans, 2005.

Harrison, J.R. "Paul, Eschatology and the Augustan Age of Grace." *Tyndale Bulletin* 50, no. 1 (1999): 79-91.

—. "Paul and the Imperial Gospel at Thessaloniki." *JSNT* 25, no. 1 (2002): 71-96.
Harrisville, Roy A. "The Concept of Newness in the New Testament." *Journal of Biblical Literature* 74, no. 2 (1955): 69-79.
Hays, Richard B. *Echoes of Scripture in the Letters of Paul*. New Haven: Yale University Press, 1989.
—. *The Moral Vision of the New Testament: A Contemporary Introduction to New Testament Ethics*. San Francisco: Harper Collins, 1996.
—. *The Conversion of the Imagination: Paul as Interpreter of Israel's Scripture*. Grand Rapids: Eerdmans, 2005.
Hellerman, Joseph. "Purity and Nationalism in Second Temple Literature: *1-2 Maccabees* and *Jubilees*." *JETS* 46, no. 3 (2003): 401-21.
Hempel, Charlotte. "The Place of the Book of Jubilees at Qumran and Beyond." In *The Dead Sea Scrolls in their Historical Context*, ed. Timothy Lim, 187-96. Edinburgh: T&T Clark, 2000.
Hendrix, Holland Lee. "Archaeology and Eschatology." In *The Future of Early Christianity*, ed. Birger A. Pearson, 107-118. Minneapolis: Fortress Press, 1991.
Hengel, M. *Crucifixion in the Ancient World and the Folly of the Message of the Cross*. Translated by John Bowden. London: SCM Press, 1977.
—. "'Salvation History': The Truth of Scripture and Modern Theology." In *Reading Texts, Seeking Wisdom: Scripture and Theology*, ed. David F. Ford and G.N. Stanton, 229-44. Grand Rapids: Eerdmans, 2003.
Hengel, Martin. *Judentum und Hellenismus: Studien zu ihrer Begegnung unter besonderer Berücksichtigung Palästinas bis zur Mitte des 2. Jh.s v. Chr. 2. Auflage*. Vol. 10, WUNT, ed. Joachim Jeremias and D. Otto Michel. Tübingen: J.C.B. Mohr, 1973.
—. *Judaism and Hellenism : Studies In Their Encounter In Palestine During the Early Hellenistic Period*. Translated by John Bowden. Vol. 1. 2 vols. London: SCM Press, 1974.
—. "Messianische Hoffnung und politischer "Radikalismus" in der "jüdisch-hellenistischen Diaspora"." In *Apocalypticism in the Mediterannean World and the Near East: Proceedings of the International Colloquium on Apocalypticism. Uppsala, August 12-17, 1979*, ed. D. Hellholm, 655-86. Tübingen: J.C.B. Mohr, 1989.
—. "Qumran and Hellenism." In *Religion in the Dead Sea Scrolls*, ed. J. J. Collins and R. A. Kugler, 46-56. Grand Rapids: Wm. B. Eerdmans, 2000.
—. "Judaism and Hellenism Revisited." In *Hellenism in the Land of Israel*, ed. John J. Collins and Gregory E. Sterling, 13, 343. Notre Dame: University of Notre Dame Press, 2001.
Hester, James D. *Paul's Concept of Inheritance: A Contribution to the Understanding of Heilsgeschichte*. Vol. 14, SJT Occasional Papers. Edinburgh: Oliver and Boyd, 1968.
Hickling, C.J.A. "Paul's Use of Exodus in the Corinthian Correspondence." In *The Corinthian Correspondence*, ed. R. Bieringer, 125, 367-76. Leuven: Leuven University Press, 1996.
Hoegen-Rohls, Christina. "Wie klingt es, wenn Paulus von Neuer Schöpfung spricht? Stilanalytische Beobachtungen zu 2 Kor 5,17 und Gal 6,15." In *"...was ihr auf dem Weg verhandelt habt": Beitrage zur Exegese und Theologie des Neuen Testaments; Festschrift für Ferdinand Hahn zum 75. Geburtstag*, ed. Peter Müller, Christine Gerber and Thomas Knöppler, 143-53. Neukirchen-Vluyn: Neukirchener, 2001.

Hofius, Otfried. "Erwägungen zur Gestalt und Herkunft des paulinischen Versöhnungsgedankens." *Zeitschrift für Theologie und Kirche* 77, no. 2 (1980): 186-99.
—. "Das vierte Gottesknechtslied in den Briefen des Neuen Testamentes." *NTS* 39 (1993): 414-37.
Holm-Nielsen, Svend. *Hodayot: Psalms from Qumran.* Vol. 2, Acta Theologica Danica, ed. T. Christensen, E. Neielsen, J Munck and R. Prenter. Denmark: Universitetsforlagfet I Aarhus, 1960.
Hooker, Morna. *Jesus and the Servant: the Influence of the Servant Concept of Deutero-Isaiah in the New Testament.* London: SPCK, 1959.
—. *From Adam to Christ: Essays on Paul.* Cambridge: CUP, 1990.
—. *Not Ashamed of the Gospel: New Testament Interpretations of the Death of Christ.* Carlisle: Paternoster, 1994.
—. "Did the Use of Isaiah 53 to Interpret His Mission Begin with Jesus?" In *Jesus and the Suffering Servant: Isaiah 53 and Christian Origins*, ed. Jr. Bellinger, William H. and William R. Famer, 88-103. Harrisburg, PA: Trinity Press International, 1998.
—. "Raised for our Acquital (Rom 4:25)." In *Resurrection in the New Testament: Festschrift for J. Lambrecht*, ed. R. Bieringer, V. Koperski and B. Lataire, 165, 323-41. Leuven: Leuven University Press, 2002.
Hoover, Joel Herbert. "The Concept of New Creation in the Letters of Paul." University of Iowa, 1979.
Horbury, William. *Messianism among Jews and Christians: Twelve Biblical and Historical Studies.* London: T&T Clark, 2003.
Horrell, David G. "'No Longer Jew or Greek' Paul's Corporate Christology and the Construction of Christian Community." In *Christology, Controversy and Community: New Testament Essays in Honour of David R. Catchpole*, ed. David G. Horrell and Christopher M. Tuckett, 99, 321-44. Leiden: Brill, 2000.
—. "Introduction." *JSNT* 27, no. 3 (2005): 251-55.
Horsley, Richard A. *Jesus and the Spiral of Violence: Popular Jewish Resistance in Roman Palestine.* San Francisco: Harper & Row, 1987.
—. "Paul's Assembly in Corinth: An Alternative Society." In *Urban Religion in Roman Corinth*, ed. Daniel N. Schowalter and Steven J. Friesen, 53, 371-95. Cambridge: Harvard University Press, 2005.
—, ed. *Paul and Empire: Religion and Power in Roman Imperial Society.* Harrisburg, PA: Trinity Press International, 1997.
Houtman, Cornelis. *Der Himmel im Alten Testament: Israels Weltbild und Weltanschauung.* Vol. 30, Oudtestamentische Studiën, ed. A.S. van der Woude. Leiden: Brill, 1993.
Howard-Brook, Wes, and Anthony Gwyther. *Unveiling Empire : Reading Revelation Then and Now*, The Bible and Liberation, ed. Norman K. Gottwald and Richard A. Horsley. Maryknoll, N.Y.: Orbis Books, 1999.
Hubbard, Moyer. *New Creation in Paul's Letters and Thought.* Vol. 119, Society for New Testament Studies Monograph Series, ed. Richard Bauckham. Cambridge: Cambridge Universtity Press, 2002.
Hübner, Hans. *Law in Paul's Thought.* Translated by James C.G. Creig, Studies of the New Testament and its World, ed. John Riches. Edinburgh: T&T Clark, 1984.
Hughes, J.A. *Scriptural Allusions and Exegesis in the Hodayot.* Vol. 59, Studies on the Texts of the Desert of Judah, ed. F.G. Martínez. Leiden: Brill, 2006.
Humphrey, Edith M. "Ambivalent Apocalypse: Apocalyptic Rhetoric and Intertextuality in 2 Corinthians." In *The Intertexture of Apocalyptic Discourse in the New Testament*, ed. Duane F. Watson, 14, 113-35. Atlanta: Society of Biblical Literature, 2002.

Instinsky, Hans Ulrich. "Kaiser und Ewigkeit." *Hermes* 77 (1942): 313-355.
Iwry, Samuel. "A New Designation for the Luminaries in Ben Sira and in the Manual of Discipline (1QS)." *Bulletin of the American Schools of Oriental Research*, no. 200 (1970): 41-7.
Jewett, Robert. *Paul's Anthropological Terms: A Study of Their Use in Conflict Settings.* Vol. X, Arbeiten zur Geschichte des Antiken Judentums und des Urchristentums, ed. D. Otto Michel and M. Hengel. Leiden: Brill, 1971.
—. "The Corruption and Redemption of Creation." In *Paul and the Roman Imperial Order*, ed. Richard A. Horsley, 25-46. London: Continuum, 2004.
—. *Romans: A Commentary*, Hermeneia, ed. Helmut Koester. Minneapolis: Fortress Press, 2007.
Johnson, Andrew. "Turning the World Upside Down in 1 Corinthians 15: Apocalyptic Epistemology, the Resurrected Body and the New Creation." *EQ* 75:4 (2003): 291-309.
Jones, A. H. M. *Augustus*. London: Chatto & Windus, 1977.
Kahn, C. H. *Anaximander and the Origins of Greek Cosmology*. New York: Columbia University Press, 1960.
Käsemann, E. "Some Thoughts on the Theme 'The Doctrine of Reconciliation in the New Testament'." In *The Future of Our Religious Past*, 49-64. New York: Harper & Row, 1971.
—. *Commentary on Romans*. Translated by Geoffrey W. Bromiley. Grand Rapids: Eerdmans, 1980.
Kee, Howard Clark. "Pauline Eschatology: Relationships with Apocalyptic and Stoic Thought." In *Glaube und Eschatologie*, ed. Erich and Otto Merk Grässer, 135-158. Tübingen: J.C.B. Mohr, 1985.
Keesmaat, Sylvia C. "Paul and His Story: Exodus and Tradition in Galatians." In *Early Christian Interpretation of the Scriptures of Israel: Investigations and Proposals*, 148, 300-33. Sheffield: Sheffield Academic Press, 1997.
—. *Paul and his Story: (Re)Interpreting the Exodus Tradition*. Vol. 181, Journal for the Study of the New Testament Suppllement Series, ed. Stanley E. Porter. Sheffield: Sheffield Academic Press, 1999.
Kegley, Charles W., ed. *The Theology of Rudolf Bultmann*. London: SCM Press, 1966.
Keown, Gerald L., Pamela J. Scalise, and Thomas G. Smothers. *Jeremiah 26-52*. Vol. 27, Word Biblical Commentary, ed. David A. Hubbard and Glenn W. Barker. Dallas: Word Books, 1995.
Kern, P.H. *Rhetoric and Galatians. Assessing an Approach to Paul's Epistle*. Vol. 101, SNTSMS. Cambridge: CUP, 1998.
Kertelge, Karl. "'Neue Schöpfung': Grund und Massstab apostolischen Handelns (2 Kor 5,17)." In *Eschatologie und Schöpfung : Festschrift für Erich Grässer zum siebzigsten Geburtstag*, ed. Martin Evang, Helmut Merklein and Michael Wolter, 89, 139-44. Berlin: De Gruyter, 1997.
Kiesow, Klaus. *Exodustexte im Jesajabuch*. Vol. 24, Orbis Biblicus et Orientalis. Göttingen: Vandenhoeck & Ruprecht, 1979.
Kim, Seyoon. *The Origin of Paul's Gospel*. 2 ed., WUNT. Tübingen: Mohr, 1984.
Kirschläger, Walter. "Zu Herkunft und Aussage von Gal 1,4." In *L'Apôtre Paul: Personnalité, Style et Conception du Ministère*, ed. A. Vanhoye and et. al., 73, 332-39. Leuven: Leuven University Press, 1986.
Klaiber, Walter. *Rechtfertigung und Gemeinde: eine Untersuchung zum paulinischen Kirchenverständnis*. Vol. 127, FRLANT. Göttingen: Vandenhoeck & Ruprecht, 1982.
Klijn, A.F. "The Sources and the Redaction of the Syriac Apocalypse of Baruch." *JSJ* 1 (1970): 65-76.

Knibb, Michael A. *Jubilees and the Origins of the Qumran Community*. London: King's College, 1989.
—. "Eschatology and Messianism in the Dead Sea Scrolls." In *The Dead Sea Scrolls after Fifty Years: A Comprehensive Assessment*, ed. P.W. Flint and James C. VanderKam, 2. Leiden: Brill, 1999.
Knohl, Israel. *The Messiah before Jesus: The Suffering Servant of the Dead Sea Scrolls*. Translated by David Maisel. Berkeley: University of California Press, 2000.
Kraftchick, S. "Paul's Use of Creation Themes: A Test of Romans 1-8." *Ex Auditu* 3 (1987): 72-97.
Kraus, H.-J. *Das Evangelium des unbekannten Propheten. Jesaja 40-66*, Kleine biblische Bibliothek. Neukirchen-Vluyn: Neukirchen Verlag, 1990.
Kraus, W. *Das Volk Gottes: Zur Grundlegung der Ekklesiologie bei Paulus*. Tübingen: Mohr, 1996.
Kreitzer, Larry J. *Striking New Images: Roman Imperial Coinage and the New Testament World*. Vol. 134, Journal for the Study of the New Testament Supplement Series, ed. Stanley E. Porter. Sheffield: Sheffield Academic Press, Ltd., 1996.
Kubusch, K. *Aurea Saecula, Mythos und Geschichte: Untersuchung eines Motivs in der Antiken Literature bis Ovid*. Vol. 28, Studien zur klassischen Philologie. Frankfurt am Main: Lang, 1986.
Kuhn, Heinz-Wolfgang. *Enderwartung und Gegenwärtiges Heil*. Göttingen: Vandenhoeck & Ruprecht, 1966.
Kwon, Yon-Gyong. *Eschatology in Galatians*. Vol. 183, WUNT, ed. Jörg Frey. Tübingen: Mohr Siebeck, 2004.
LaGrange, Marie-Joseph. *Saint Paul: Épitre aus Romains*, Études bibliques. Paris: Gabalda, 1950.
Lambrecht, J. "The Favorable Time: a Study of 2 Cor 6,2a in its Context." In *Vom Urchristentum zu Jesus : für Joachim Gnilka*, ed. Hubert Frankemölle and Karl Kertelge, 377-91. Freiburg: Herder, 1989.
—. "The Eschtological Outlook in 2 Corinthians 4:7-15." In *Studies on 2 Corinthians*, ed. R. Bieringer and J. Lambrecht, 112, 335-49. Leuven: Leuven University Press, 1994a.
—. "'Reconcile Yourselves...' A Reading of 2 Corinthians 5,11-21." In *Studies in 2 Corinthians*, ed. R. Bieringer and J. Lambrecht, 112, 363-412. Leuven: Leuven University Press, 1994b.
—. "The Universalistic Will of God: the True Gospel in Galatians." In *Pauline Studies*, ed. J. Lambrecht, 115, 299-306. Leuven: University Press, 1994c.
—. *Second Corinthians*. Vol. 8, Sacra Pagina, ed. Daniel J. Harrington, S.J. Collegeville, MN: The Liturgical Press, 1999.
Lampe, G.W.H. "The New Testament Doctrine of ΚΤΙΣΙΣ." *SJT* 17 (1964): 449-62.
Lanci, John R. *A New Temple for Corinth: Rhetorical and Archaeological Approaches to Pauline Imagery*. Vol. 1, Studies in Biblical Literature, ed. H. Gossai. New York: Peter Lang, 1997.
Lange, Armin. "Divinatorische Träume und Apokalyptic im Jubiläenbuch." In *Studies in the Book of Jubilees*, ed. Matthias Albani, Jörg Frey and Armin Lange, 65, 25-38. Tübingen: Mohr Siebeck, 1997.
Lange, J.P. *The Epistle of Paul to the Romans*. Translated by J.F. Hurst. Edinburgh: T&T Clark, 1869.
Lee, Stephen. *Creation and Redemption in Isaiah 40-55*, Jian Dao Dissertation Series 2: Bible and Literature 2, ed. Philip P. Chia and Yeo Khiok-khng, 1995.
Levenson, Jon D. *Resurrection and the Restoration of Israel: the Ultimate Victory of the God of Life*. New Haven: Yale University Press, 2006.

Lichtenberger, Hermann. "Auferstehung in den Qumranfunden." In *Auferstehung – Resurrection: The Fourth Durham-Tübingen Research Symposium: Resurrection, Transfiguration and Exaltation in Old Testament, Ancient Judaism and Early Christianity*, ed. Friedrich Avemarie and Hermann Lichtenberger, 135, 79-91. Tübingen: Mohr Siebeck, 2001.
Lietzmann, Hans. *An die Römer*. 4th ed., Handbuch zum Neuen Testament. Tübingen: Mohr, 1933.
Lightfoot, J.B. *Saint Paul's Epistle to the Galatians*. London: Macmillan and Co., 1896.
Lim, Timothy. "Kittim." In *Encyclopedia of the Dead Sea Scrolls*, ed. L.H. Schiffman and James C. VanderKam, 1, 469-71. Oxford: OUP, 2000.
Lind, Millard C. "Political Implications of Isaiah 6." In *Writing and Reading the Scroll of Isaiah: Studies of an Interpretive Tradition*, ed. Craig C. Broyles and Craig A. Evans, 1, 317-38. Leiden: Brill, 1997.
Lindars, Barnabas. *New Testament Apologetic: The Doctrinal Significance of the Old Testament Quotations*. London: SCM Press, 1961.
Lindeskog, Gösta. *Studien zum neutestamentlichen Schöpfungsgedanken*. Uppsala: Lundequistska Bokhandeln, 1952.
Lohse, Eduard. *Der Brief an die Römer*. Göttingen: Vandenhoeck & Ruprecht, 2003.
Longenecker, Bruce W. *The Triumph of Abraham's God: The Transformation of Identity in Galatians*. Nashville: Abingdon Press, 1998.
—. "Sharing in Their Spiritual Blessings? The Stories of Israel in Galatians and Romans." In *Narrative Dynamics in Paul: A Critical Assessment*, ed. Bruce W. Longenecker, 58-84. London: Westminster John Knox Press, 2002.
Longenecker, R.N. *Galatians*. Vol. 41, WBC, ed. David A. Hubbard and Glenn W. Barker. Dallas: Word Books, 1990.
Mansoor, Menahem. *The Thanksgiving Hymns: Translated and Annotated with an Introduction*. Vol. 3, Studies on the Texts of the Desert of Judah, ed. Van der Ploeg. Leiden: Brill, 1961.
Martin, Ralph P. *2 Corinthians*. Vol. 40, WBC, ed. Ralph P. Martin. Waco: Word Books, 1986.
Martínez, F.G. *The DSS Translated: the Qumran texts in English*. Leiden: Brill, 1996.
Martyn, J. Louis. "Apocalyptic Antinomies." In *Theological Issues in the Letters of Paul*, ed. John Barclay, J. Marcus and John Riches, 111-123. Edinburgh: T&T Clark, 1997a.
—. "Christ and the Elements of the Cosmos." In *Theological Issues in the Letters of Paul*, ed. John Barclay, J. Marcus and John Riches, 125-40. Edinburgh: T&T Clark, 1997b.
—. *Galatians: A New Translation with Introduction and Commentary*. Vol. 33A, The Anchor Bible, ed. William Foxwell Albright and David Noel Freedman. London: Doubleday, 1997c.
—. *Theological Issues in the Letters of Paul*, Studies of the New Testament and Its World, ed. John Barclay, Joel Marcus & John Riches. Edinburgh: T&T Clark, Ltd., 1997d.
Matera, F.J. "The Culmination of Paul's Argument to the Galatians: Gal 5,1-6,17." *JSNT* 32 (1988): 79-91.
—. "Apostolic Suffering and Resurrection Faith: Distinguishing Between Appearance and Reality (2 Cor 4:7-5:10)." In *Resurrection in the New Testament: Festschrift for J. Lambrecht*, ed. R. Bieringer, V. Koperski and B. Lataire, 165. Leuven: Leuven University Press, 2002.

Matlock, R. Barry. *Unveiling the Apocalyptic Paul: Paul's Interpreters and the Rhetoric of Criticism*. Vol. 127, JSNTSS, ed. Stanley E. Porter. Sheffield: Sheffield Academic Press, 1996.
McDonough, Sean M. "Of Beasts and Bees: the View of the Natural World in Virgil's *Georgics* and John's Apocalypse." *NTS* 46 (2000): 227-44.
McLaren, James S. "Jews and the Imperial Cult: From Augustus to Domitian." *JSNT* 27, no. 3 (2005): 257-78.
Meeks, Wayne A. *The First Urban Christians: The Social World of the Apostle Paul*. New Haven: Yale University Press, 1983.
Meggitt, Justin. "Taking the Emperor's Clothes Seriously: The New Testament and the Roman Emperor." In *The Quest for Wisdom: Essays in Honour of Philip Budd*, ed. Christine E. Joynes, 143-169. Cambridge: Orchard Academic, 2002.
Mell, Ulrich. *Neue Schöpfung: Eine traditionsgeschichtliche und exegetische Studie zu einem soteriologischen Grundsatz paulinisher Theologie*. Berlin: Walter de Gruyter, 1989.
Merklein, Helmut. "Im Spannungsfeld von Protologie und Eschatologie: zur kurzen Geschichte der aktiven Beteiligung von Frauen in paulinishen Gemeinden." In *Eschatologie und Schöpfung : Festschrift für Erich Grässer zum siebzigsten Geburtstag*, ed. Martin Evang, Helmut Merklein and Michael Wolter, 89, 231-59. Berlin: De Gruyter, 1997.
Metzger, Bruce M. *A Textual Commentary on the Greek New Testament*. 2nd ed. Stuttgart: Biblia-Druck, 1994.
Meyer, H.A.W. *Critical and Exegetical Handbook to the Epistle to the Romans*. Vol. 2. 2nd ed. Edinburgh: T&T Clark, 1879.
—. *Galatians*. Edinburgh: T&T Clark, 1884.
Michaels, J. Ramsey. "The Redemption of our Body: the Riddle of Romans 8:19-22." In *Romans and the People of God: Essays in Honor of Gordon D. Fee on the Occasion of His 65th Birthday*, ed. Sven K. Soderlund and N.T. Wright, 92-114. Grand Rapids: Eerdmans, 1999.
Michel, O. *Der Brief an die Römer*. Göttingen: Vandendoeck & Ruprecht, 1978.
Milgrom, Jacob. *Leviticus 23-27: A New Translation with Introduction and Commentary*. Vol. 3B, The Anchor Bible, ed. William Foxwell Albright and David Noel Freedman. New York: Doubleday, 2001.
Minear, Paul S. "The Cosmology of the Apocalypse." In *Current Issues in New Testament Interpretation: Essays in Honour of Otto A. Piper*, ed. William Klassen and Graydon F. Snyder, 23-37. London: SCM Press, 1962.
—. "The Crucified World: The Enigma of Galatians 6,14." In *Theologica Crucis – Signum Crucis*, ed. Carl Andresen and Günter Klein, 395-407. Tübingen: J.C.B. Mohr, 1979.
Mitchell, Stephen. *Anatolia: Land, men and Gods in Asia Minor*. Vol. I. Oxford: Clarendon Press, 1993.
Moo, Douglas J. *The Epistle to the Romans*, NICNT, ed. Gordon D. Fee. Grand Rapids: WmBEerdmans, 1996.
Moore, G.F. *Judaism in the First Centuries of the Christian Era: The Age of the Tannaim*. Vol. 1. 3 vols. Cambridge: Harvard University Press, 1927.
Morales, Rodrigo José. "The Spirit and the Restoration of Israel: New Exodus and New Creation Motifs in Galatians." Duke, 2007.
Motyer, J.A. *The Prophecy of Isaiah*. Leicester: IVP, 1993.
Moule, C.F.D. *The Origin of Christology*. Cambridge: CUP, 1977.
Moulton, J.H., and George Milligan. *The Vocabulary of the Greek Testament: Illustrated from the Papyri and Other Non-Literary sources*. London: Hodder and Stoughton, 1930.

Moyise, Steve. "Intertextuality and the Study of the Old Testament in the New Testament." In *The Old Testament in the New Testament: Essays in Honour of J.L. North*, ed. Stanley E. Porter, 189, 14-41. Sheffield: Sheffield Academic Press, 2000.
Mußner, Franz. *Der Galaterbrief.* Freiburg: Herder, 1974.
Myers, Charles D. "Epistle to the Romans." In *ABD*, ed. David Noel Freedman, 5, 816-30. New Yord: Doubleday, 1992.
Nickelsburg, George W.E. *Resurrection, Immortality, and Eternal Life in Intertestamental Judaism.* Vol. 26, Harvard Theological Studies. Cambridge, MA: HUP, 1972.
——. "Social Aspects of Palestinian Jewish Apocalypticism." In *Apocalypticism in the Mediterannean World and the Near East: Proceedings of the International Colloquium on Apocalypticism. Uppsala, August 12-17, 1979*, ed. D. Hellholm, 641-54. Tübingen: J.C.B. Mohr, 1989.
Nock, A.D. "Religious Developments from the Close of the Repbulic to the Death of Nero." In *The Cambridge Ancient History*, ed. S.A. Cook, F.E. Adcock and M.P. Charlesworth, 10, 465-511. Cambridge: CUP, 1966.
North, C.R. "The 'Former Things' and the 'New Things' in Deutero-Isaiah." In *Studies in Old Testament Prophecy*, ed. H.H. Rowley, 111-26. Edinburgh: T&T Clark, 1950.
Oakes, Peter. *Philippians: From People to Letter.* Vol. 110, Society for New Testament Studies Monograph Series, ed. Richard Bauckham. Cambridge: Cambridge University Press, 2001.
——. "Re-mapping the Universe: Paul and the Emperor in 1 Thessalonians and Philippians." *JSNT* 27, no. 3 (2005): 301-22.
O'Brien, Peter T. *Introductory Thanksgivings in the Letters of Paul.* Vol. 49, Supplements to Novum Testamentum. Leiden: Brill, 1977.
Oropeza, B.J. "Echoes of Isaiah in the Rhetoric of Paul: New Exodus, Wisdom, and the Humility of the Cross in Utopian-Apoclayptic Expectation." In *The Intertexture of Apocalyptic Discourse in the New Testament*, ed. Duane F. Watson, 14, 87-112. Atlanta: Society of Biblical Literature, 2002.
Oswalt, John N. *The Book of Isaiah: Chapters 1-39*, The New International Commentary on the Old Testament, ed. R. K. Harrison. Grand Rapids: Wm. B. Eerdmans, 1986.
——. "Righteousness in Isaiah: Chapters 55-66." In *Writing and Reading the Scroll of Isaiah: Studies of an Interpretive Tradition*, ed. Craig C. Broyles and Craig A. Evans, 1, 177-91. Leiden: Brill, 1997.
——. *The Book of Isaiah: Chapters 40-66*, The New International Commentary on the Old Testament, ed. R. K. Harrison and R. L. Hubbard. Grand Rapids: Wm. B. Eerdmans, 1998.
Panagopoulos, Johannes. "Schöpfung und Neuschöpfung in der Theologie der griechischen Kirchenväter." *Jahrbuch für Biblische Theologie* 5 (1990): 153-71.
Pate, C. Marvin. *Adam Christology and the Exegetical & Theological Substructure of 2 Corinthians 4:7-5:21.* Lanham: University Press of America, 1991.
Pearson, Michael Parker, and Colin Richards. *Architecture and Order: Approaches to Social Space.* London: Routledge, 1994.
Philip, Finny. *The Origins of Pauline Pneumatology: The Eschatological Bestowal of the Spirit upon Gentiles in Judaism and in the Early Development of Paul's Theology.* Vol. 194, WUNT. Tübingen: Mohr, 2005.
Photopoulos, John. *Food Offered to Idols in Roman Corinth: a Social Rhetorical Reconsideration of 1 Corinthians 8:1-11:1.* Tübingen: Mohr Siebeck, 2003.
Pickett, Raymond. *The Cross in Corinth: The Social Significance of the Death of Jesus.* Vol. 143, JSNTSS, ed. Stanley E. Porter. Sheffield: Sheffield Academic Press, 1997.

Porter, Stanley E. *Katallasso in Ancient Greek Literature with Reference to the Pauline Writings.* Vol. 5, Estudios De Filologia Neotestamentaria. Cordoba: Ediciones el Almendro, 1994.

—. "Reconciliation and 2 Cor 5,18-21." In *The Corinthian Correspondence*, ed. R. Bieringer, 125, 693-705. Leuven: Leuven University Press, 1996.

—, ed. *Paul & His Opponents.* Vol. 2, Pauline Studies. Leiden: Brill, 2005.

Price, S. R. F. *Rituals and Power: The Roman Imperial Cult in Asia Minor.* Cambridge: Cambridge University Press, 1984.

Puech, E. *La croyance des Esséniens en la vie future: immortalité, résurrection, vie éternelle? Histoire d'une croyance dans le Judaïsme ancien.* 2 vols. Paris: Cerf, 1993.

Räisänen, Heikki. *Paul and the Law.* Vol. 29. 2nd ed., WUNT. Tübingen: Mohr, 1987.

Ramsey, John T., and A. Lewis Licht. *The Comet of 44 B.C. and Caesar's Funeral Games.* Vol. 39, American Classical Studies, ed. David L. Blank. Atlanta: Scholars Press, 1997.

Ravid, Liora. "Purity and Impurity in the Book of Jubilees." *Journal for the Study of the Pseudepigrapha* 13, no. 1 (2002): 61-86.

Rehak, Paul. *Imperium and Cosmos.* Madison: University of Wisconsin Press, 2006.

Rendtorff, Rolf. "Zur Komposition des Buches Jesaja." *Vetus Testamentum* 34, no. 3 (1984): 295-320.

Reynolds, Joyce M. "Ruler-cult at Aphrodisian in the Late Republic and Under the Julio-Claudian Emperors." In *Subject & Ruler: The Cult of the Ruling Power in Classical Antiquity*, ed. Alastair Small, 17, 41-50. Ann Arobor, MI: Thomson-Shore, 1996.

Richardson, Peter. *City and Sanctuary: Religion and Architecture in the Roman Near East.* London: SCM Press, 2002.

Riches, John. "Why Write a Reception-Historical Commentary?" *JSNT* 29, no. 3 (2007): 323-32.

—. *Galatians Through the Centuries*, Blackwell Bible Commentaries. Oxford: Blackwell, 2008.

Ringgren, Helmer. *The Faith of Qumran: Theology of the Dead Sea Scrolls.* Translated by E.T. Sander. New York: Crossroad, 1995.

Roetzel, Calvin J. *The World that Shaped the New Testament.* 2nd ed. Louisville: Westminster John Knox Press, 2002.

Rosner, Brian S. *Paul, Scripture and Ethics: A Study of 1 Corinthians 5-7.* Vol. 22, Arbeiten zur Geschichte des antiken Judentums und des Urchristentums. Leiden: Brill, 1994.

—. "'With What Kind of Body Do They Come?' (1 Corinthians 15:35b): Paul's Conception of Resurrection Bodies." In *The New Testament in Its First Century Setting*, ed. P.J. Williams, Andrew D. Clarke, Peter M. Head and David Instone-Brewer, 190-205. Cambridge: WmBEerdmans, 2004.

Rowe, Cavin. "Luke-Acts and the Imperial Cult: A Way Through the Conundrum?" *JSNT* 27, no. 3 (2005): 279-300.

Rowland, Christopher. *The Open Heaven: A Study of Apocalyptic in Judaism and Early Christianity.* New York: Crossroad, 1982.

—. "Apocalypse, Prophecy and the New Testament." In *Knowing the End from the Beginning: The Prophetic, the Apocalyptic and their Relationships*, ed. Lester L. Grabbe and Robert D. Haak, 46, 148-66. London: T & T Clark, 2003.

Rusam, D. "Neue Belege zu dem ΣΤΟΙΧΕΙΑ ΤΟΥ ΚΟΣΜΟΥ (Gal 4,3.9; Kol 2,8.20)." *ZNW* 83 (1992): 119-25.

Russell, D.S. *The Method and Message of Jewish Apocalyptic, 200 BC-AC 100*, Old Testament Library. London: SCM Press, 1964.

Russell, David M. *Divine Disclosure: An Introduction to Jewish Apocalyptic*. Minneapolis: Fortress Press, 1992.
—. *The "New Heavens and New Earth": Hope for the Creation in Jewish Apocalyptic and the New Testament*. Vol. 1, Studies in Biblical Apocalyptic Literature. Philadelphia: Visionary Press, 1996.
Ryberg, Inez Scott. "Vergil's Golden Age." *Transactions and Proceedings of the American Philological Association* 89 (1958): 112-131.
Sals, Ulrike. *Die Biographie der "Hure Babylon": Studien zur Intertextualität der Babylon-Texte in der Bibel*. Vol. 6, Forschungen zum Alten Testament, 2. Reihe, ed. Bernd Janowski, Mark S. Smith and Hermann Spieckermann. Tübingen: Mohr Siebeck, 2004.
Sanders, E.P. *Paul, the Law, and the Jewish People*. Philadelphia: Fortress Press, 1983.
—. *Judaism: Practise and Belief 63 BCE-66CE*. London: SCM Press, 1992.
Sandmel, S. "Parallelomania." *JBL* 81 (1962): 1-13.
Sandnes, Karl Olav. *Paul – One of the Prophets? A Contribution to the Apostle's Self-Understanding*. Vol. 43, WUNT, ed. M. Hengel and Otfried Hofius. Tübingen: J.C.B. Mohr, 1991.
Sappington, Thomas J. "The Factor of Function in Defining Jewish Apocalyptic Literature." *JSP* 12 (1994): 83-123.
Sasse, H. "ΑΙΩΝ." *TDNT* 1 (1964): 197-209.
Sawyer, Deborah F. "Gender-Play and Sacred Text: A Scene from Jeremiah." *JSOT* 83 (1999): 99-111.
Schiffman, L.H. *The Eschatological Community of the DSS*. Vol. 38, SBLMS. Atlanta: Scholars Press, 1989.
Schiffman, Lawrence H. "The Concept of Restoration in the Dead Sea Scrolls." In *Restoration: Old Testament, Jewish, and Christian Perspectives*, ed. James M. Scott, 72, 203-21. Boston: Brill, 2001.
Schlier, Heinrich. *Der Brief an die Galater*. Göttingen: Vandendoeck & Ruprecht, 1962.
Schneider, Gerhard. "Die Idee der Neuschöpfung beim Apostel Paulus und ihr religionsgeschichtlicher Hintergrund." *TThZ* 68 (1959): 257-70.
Schnelle, Udo. *Apostle Paul: His Life and Theology*. Translated by M. Eugene Boring. Grand Rapids, MI: Baker, 2005.
Schnider, F., and W. Stenger. *Studien zum Neutestamentlichen Briefformular*. Leiden: Brill, 1987.
Scholder, Klaus, ed. *Ausgewählte Werke in Einzelausgaben*. Vol. 1. Stuttgart-Bad Cannstatt: Frommann, 1963.
Scholla, Robert W. "Into the Image of God: Pauline Eschatology and the Transformation of Believers." *Gregorianum* 78, no. 1 (1997): 33-54.
Schrage, Wolfgang. "Schöpfung und Neuschöpfung in Kontinuität und Diskontinuität bei Paulus." *Evangelische Theologie* 65, no. 4 (2005): 245-59.
Schreiner, Thomas R. *Romans*, Baker Exegetical Commentary on the New Testament, ed. Moisés Silva. Grand Rapids: Eerdmans, 1998.
Schröter, J. *Der versöhnte Versöhner. Paulus als unentbehrlicher Mittler im Heilsvorgang zwischen Gott und Gemeinde nach 2Kor 2,14-7,4*. Vol. 10, TANZ. Tübingen: Francke, 1993.
Schwantes, Heinz. *Schöpfung der Endzeit: Ein Beitrag zum Verständnis der Auferweckung bei Paulus*. Stuttgart: Calwer, 1962.
Schweitzer, Albert. *Geschichte der Paulinischen Forschung von der Reformation bis auf die Gegenwart*. Tübingen: Mohr, 1911.

—. *The Mysticism of Paul the Apostle.* Translated by William Montgomery. 2nd ed. London: Adam & Charles Black, 1956.
Schweizer, E. "Zum religionsgeschichtlichen Hintergrund der 'Sendungsformel' Gal 4,4f., Rm 8,3f., Joh 3,16f., 1 Joh 4,9." *ZNW* 57 (1966): 199-210.
—. "Slaves of the Elements and Worshipers of Angels: Gal 4:3, 9; Col 2:8, 18, 20." *JBL* 107 (1988): 455-68.
Scott, James M. *Adoption as Sons of God: An Exegetical Investigation into the Background of ΥΙΟΘΕΣΙΑ in the Pauline Corpus.* Vol. 48, WUNT. Tübingen: Mohr Siebeck, 1992.
—. "Restoration of Israel." In *Dictionary of Paul and His Letters*, ed. Gerald F. Hawthorne and Ralph P. Martin, 796-805. Downers Grove, IL: InterVarsity Press, 1996.
—. "Exile and the Self-Understanding of Diaspora Jews in the Greco-Roman Period." In *Exile: Old Testament, Jewish, and Christian Conceptions*, ed. James M. Scott, 56, 173-218. Leiden: Brill, 1997.
—. *On Earth as in Heaven: The Restoration of Sacred Time and Sacred Space in the Book of Jubilees.* Vol. 91, Supplement to the Journal for the Study of Judaism, ed. John J. Collins. Leiden: Brill, 2005.
Scranton, R.L. *Monuments in the Lower Agora and North of the Archaic Temple.* Princeton, NJ: American School of Classical Studies at Athens, 1951.
Scroggs, Robin. *The Last Adam.* Oxford: Basil Blackwell, 1966.
Seeligmann, I. L. *The Septuagint Version of Isaiah and Cognate Studies.* Vol. 40, FAT. Tübingen: Mohr Siebeck, 2004.
Sehmsdorf, Von Eberhard. "Studien zur Redaktionsgeschichte von Jesaja 56-66 (I-II)." *ZATW* 84 (1972): 517-76.
Shotter, David. *Augustus Caesar.* London: Routledge, 2005.
Silva, Moisés. *Biblical Words and their Meaning: An Introduction to Lexical Semantics.* Rev. ed. Grand Rapids: Zondervan, 1994a.
—. "Eschatological Structures in Galatians." In *To Tell the Mystery: Essays in New Testament Eschatology in Honor of Robert Gundry*, ed. T.E. Schmidt and Moisés Silva, 140-62. Sheffield: JSOT Press, 1994b.
—. *Interpreting Galatians: Explorations in Exegetical Method.* 2nd ed. Grand Rapids: Baker Academic, 2001.
Sjöberg, Erik. "Wiedergeburt und Neuschöpfung in palästinischen Judentum." *Studia Theologica* 4, no. 2 (1950): 44-85.
—. "Neuschöpfung in den Toten-Meer-Rollen." *Studia Theologica* 9, no. 2 (1955): 131-36.
Smith, Michael J. "The Role of the Pedagogue in Galatians." *Bibliotheca Sacra* 163, no. 650 (2006): 197-214.
Stahl, Hans-Peter, ed. *Vergil's Aeneid: Augustan Epic and Political Context.* London: Duckworth, 1998.
Stanley, Christopher D. *Paul and the Laguage of Scripture: Citation technique in the Pauline Epistles and contemporary literature.* Vol. 69, SNTSMS, ed. G.N. Stanton. Cambridge: CUP, 1992.
—. *Arguing with Scripture: The Rhetoric of Quotations in the Letters of Paul.* London: T&T Clark, 2004.
Stanley, David M. "The Theme of the Servant of Yahweh in Primitive Christian Soteriology and its Transposition by St. Paul." *CBQ* 16, no. 4 (1954): 385-425.
Stanton, G.N. "The Law of Moses and the Law of Christ: Galatians 3:1-6:2." In *Paul and the Mosaic law*, ed. James D.G. Dunn, 89, 99-116. Tübingen: J.C.B. Mohr, 1996.
—. "Review of J.L. Martyn's Anchor Bible Commentary on Galatians." *J Theol Studies* 51 (2000): 264-70.
—. *Jesus and Gospel.* Cambridge: CUP, 2004.

Steck, O.H. "Der neue Himmel und die neue Erde. Beobachtungen zur Rezeption von Gen 1-3 in Jes 65,16b-25." In *Studies in the Book of Isaiah*, ed. Jacques van Ruiten and M. Vervenne, 132, 349-66. Leuven: University Press, 1997.
Steudel, A. "'End of Days' in the Texts from Qumran." *Revue de Qumran* 16, no. 2 (1993): 225-46.
Stockton, David L. "Augustus *Sub Specie Aeteritatis*." *Thought* 55, no. 216 (1980): 5-17.
Strauss, Mark L. *The Davidic Messiah in Luke-Acts: The Promise and its Fulfillment in Lukan Christology*. Vol. 110, JSNTS, ed. Stanley E. Porter. Sheffield: Sheffield Academic Press, 1995.
Stuhlmacher, Peter. *Gerechtigkeit Gottes bei Paulus*. Vol. 87, Forschungen zur Religion und Literatur des Alten und Neuen Testaments. Göttingen: Vandenhoeck & Ruprecht, 1965.
—. "Erwägungen zum ontologischen Charakter der ΚΑΙΝΗ ΚΤΙΣΙΣ bei Paulus." *Evangelische Theologie* 27, no. 1 (1967): 1-35.
—. *Paul's Letter to the Romans*. Translated by Scott J. Hafemann. Edinburgh: T&T Clark, 1994.
Stuhlmueller, Carol. *Creative Redemption in Deutero-Isaiah*. Vol. 43, Analecta Biblica. Rome: Biblical Institute Press, 1970.
Sumney, Jerry L. *Identifying Paul's Opponents: The Question of Method in 2 Corinthians*. Vol. 40, JSNTSS, ed. David Hill. Sheffield: JSOT Press, 1990.
—. "Studying Paul's Opponents: Advances and Challenges." In *Paul and His Opponents*, ed. Stanley E. Porter, 2, 7-58. Leiden: Brill, 2005.
Swarup, Paul. *The Self-understanding of the Dead Sea Scrolls Community: An Eternal Planting, a House of Holiness*. Vol. 59, Library of Second Temple Studies. London: T&T Clark, 2006.
Sweeney, Marvin A. *Isaiah 1-4 and the Post-Exilic Understanding of the Isaianic Tradition*. Vol. 171, BZAW. Berlin: de Gruyter, 1988.
—. *Isaiah 1-39 with an Introduction to Prophetic Literature*. Vol. 16, The Forms of the Old Testament Literature, ed. Rolf P. Knierim and Gene M. Tucker. Grand Rapids: Wm. B. Eerdmans, 1996.
—. "Prophetic Exegesis in Isaiah 65-66." In *Writing and Reading the Scroll of Isaiah: Studies of an Interpretive Tradition*, ed. Craig C. Broyles and Craig A. Evans, 1, 455-74. Leiden: Brill, 1997.
Talmon, Shemaryan. ""Exile" and "Restoration" in the Conceptual World of Ancient Judaism." In *Restoration: Old Testament, Jewish, and Christian Perspectives*, ed. James M. Scott, 72, 107-146. Boston: Brill, 2001.
Tannehill, R.C. *Dying and Rising with Christ: A Study in Pauline Theology*. Vol. 32, Beiheft zur Zeitschrift für die Neutestamentliche Wissenschaft und die Kunde der Älteren Kirche, ed. W. Eltester. Berlin: Verlag Alfred Töpelmann, 1967.
Taubes, Jacob. *Die politische Theologie des Paulus: Vorträge, gehalten an der Forschungsstätte derevangelischen Studiengemeinschaft in Heidelberg, 23.-27. Februar 1987*. München: Wilhalm Fink, 1993.
Taylor, John. "Paul's Understanding of Faith." University of Cambridge, 2004.
Taylor, Lily Ross, and S. R. F. Price. "Secular Games." In *The Oxford Classical Dictionary*, ed. Simon Hornblower and Antony Spawforth, 1378. Oxford: Oxford University Press, 1996.
Theobald, M. *Der Römerbrief*. Darmstadt: Wissenschaftliche Buchgesellschaft, 2000.
—. "'Welt' bei Paulus und Johannes." *Communio*, no. 5 (2005): 435-447.
Thielman, Frank. "The Story of Israel and the Theology of Romans 5-8." In *Society of Biblical Literature Seminar Papers*, ed. E.H. Lovering, 32, 169-195. Atlanta: SBL, 1993.

—. *Paul and the Law: A Contextual Approach.* Downers Grove, IL: IVP, 1994.
Thiselton, Anthony C. *The First Epistle to the Corinthians: A Commentary on the Greek Text*, NIGTC, ed. I. Howard Marshall and Donald A. Hagner. Cambridge: Eerdmans, 2000.
Tholuck, F.A.G. *Exposition of St. Paul's Epistle to the Romans.* Translated by Robert Menzies. 2nd ed. Philadelphia: Sorin and Ball, 1844.
Thompson, John B. *Ideology and Modern Culture: Critical Social Theory in the Era of Mass Communication.* Cambridge: Polity Press, 1990.
Thrall, Margaret E. *A Critical and Exegetical Commentary on the Second Epistle to the Corinthians.* Vol. 1. 2 vols., ICC, ed. J.A. Emerton, C.E.B. Cranfield and Graham Stanton. Edinburgh: T&T Clark, 1994.
Tolmie, D. Francois. *Persuading the Galatians: A Text-Centred Rhetorical Analysis of a Pauline Letter.* Vol. 190, WUNT, ed. Jörg Frey. Tübingen: Mohr Siebeck, 2005.
Tomson, Peter J. "Paul's Jewish Background in View of His Law Teaching in 1 Cor 7." In *Paul and the Mosaic law*, ed. James D.G. Dunn, 89, 251-70. Tübingen: J.C.B. Mohr, 1996.
Tsumura, D.T. "An OT Background to Rom 8:22." *NTS* 40 (1994): 620-21.
Tuckett, Christopher M. *Christology and the New Testament: Jesus and His Earliest Followers.* Edinburgh: Edinburgh University Press, 2001.
Van der Kooij, A. "The Cities of Isaiah 24-27 According to the Vulgate, Targum and Septuagint." In *Studies in Isaiah 24-27: The Isaiah Workshop*, ed. H.J. Bosman, Harm Van Grol and *et alii*, 43, 183-98. Leiden: Brill, 2000.
Van Kooten, George H. *Cosmic Christology in Paul and the Pauline School.* Vol. 171, WUNT, ed. Jörg Frey. Tübingen: Mohr Siebeck, 2003.
Van Oorschot, Jürgen. "Die Stadt – Lebensraum und Symbol. Israels Stadtkultur als Spiegel seiner Geschichte und Theologie." In *Gott und Mensch im Dialog: Festschrift für Otto Kaiser zum 80. Geburtstag*, ed. Markus Witte, 345/I, 155-179. Berlin: Walter de Gruyter, 2004.
Van Ruiten, Jacques. "The Garden of Eden and Jubilees 3:1-31." *Bijdragen, tijdschrift voor filososfie en theologie* 56 (1996): 305-317.
—. *Primaeval History Interpreted: The Rewriting of Genesis 1-11 in the Book of Jubilees.* Vol. 66, Supplement to the Journal for the Study of Jubilees, ed. J. J. Collins. Leiden: Brill, 2000.
—. "The Covenant of Noah in *Jubilees* 6:1-38." In *The Concept of the Covenant in the Second Temple Period*, ed. Stanley E. Porter and Jackqueline C.R. De Roo, 71, 167-90. Leiden: Brill, 2003.
VanderKam, James C. *Textual and Historical Studies in the Book of Jubilees.* Vol. 14, Harvard Semitic Monographs, ed. Frank Moore Cross. Missoula, Montana: Scholars Press, 1977.
—. "Enoch Traditions in Jubilees and Other Second-Century Sources." *Society of Biblical Literature Seminar Papers* 13, no. 1 (1978): 229-51.
—. *The Book of Jubilees.* Vol. 2. 2 vols., Corpus Scriptorum Christianorum Orientalium 510-11: Scriptores Aethiopici 87-88. Leuven: Peeters, 1989.
—. "Biblical Interpretation in 1 Enoch and Jubilees." In *The Pseudepigrapha and Early Biblical Interpretation*, ed. James H. Charlesworth and Craig A. Evans, 14, 96-125. Sheffield: JSOT Press, 1993.
—. "Exile in Jewish Apocalyptic Literature." In *Old Testament, Jewish, and Christian Conceptions*, ed. James M. Scott, 56, 89-109. Leiden: Brill, 1997a.
—. "The Origins and Purposes of the *Book of Jubilees*." In *Studies in the Book of Jubilees*, ed. Matthias Albani, Jörg Frey and Armin Lange, 65, 3-24. Tübingen: Mohr Siebeck, 1997b.

—. "Identity and History of the Community." In *The Dead Sea Scrolls after Fifty Years: A Comprehensive Assessment*, ed. P.W. Flint and James C. VanderKam, 2, 487-533. Leiden: Brill, 1999.

—. "Apocalyptic Tradition in the Dead Sea Scrolls and the Religion of Qumran." In *Religion in the Dead Sea Scrolls*, ed. J. J. Collins and R. A. Kugler, 113-134. Grand Rapids: Wm. B. Eerdmans, 2000a.

—. "Book of Jubilees." In *Encyclopedia of the Dead Sea Scrolls*, ed. L.H. Schiffman and James C. VanderKam, 1, 434-8. Oxford: OUP, 2000b.

—. *The Book of Jubilees*, Guides to the Apocrypha and Pseudepigrapha. Sheffield: Sheffield Academic Press, 2001.

Vermes, Geza. *The Complete Dead Sea Scrolls in English*. 4th ed. London: Penguin Books, 1998.

—. *Scrolls, Scriptures and Early Christianity*. Vol. 56, Library of Second Temple Studies, ed. Lester L. Grabbe and James H. Charlesworth. London: T&T Clark, 2005.

Vermeylen, Jacques. "L'Unité du Livre d'Isaïe." In *The Book of Isaiah: Les Oracles et leurs Relectures Unité et Complexité de l'Ouvrage*, ed. Jacques Vermeylen, 81. Leuven: Leuven University Press, 1989.

Virgil: The Eclogues, The Georgics. Translated by C. Day Lewis, Oxford World's Classics. Oxford: Oxford University Press, 1999.

Vögtle, Anton. *Das Neue Testament und die Zukunft des Kosmos*. Düsseldorf: Patmos, 1970a.

—. "Röm 8,19-22: eine schöpfungstheologische oder anthropologisch-soteriologische Aussage?" In *Mélanges Bibliques: en hommage au R.P. Béda Rigaux*, ed. A. Descampes and R.P.A. De Halleux, 351-66. Gembloux: Duculot, 1970b.

Vollenweider, Samuel. *Freiheit als neue Schöpfung: Eine Untersuchung zur Eleutheria bei Paulus und in seiner Umwelt*. Vol. 147, Forschungen zur Religion und Literatur des Alten und Neuen Testaments, ed. Wolfgang Schrage and Rudolf Smend. Göttingen: Vandenhoeck & Ruprecht, 1989.

Wagner, J. Ross. "The Heralds of Isaiah and the Mission of Paul: An Investigation of Paul's Use of Isaiah 51-55 in Romans." In *Jesus and the Suffering Servant: Isaiah 53 and Christian Origins*, ed. Jr. Bellinger, William H. and William R. Farmer, 193-222. Harrisburg: Trinity Press International, 1998.

—. *Heralds of the Good News: Isaiah and Paul "In Concert" in the Letter to the Romans*. Vol. CI, Supplements to Novum Testamentum. Leiden: Brill, 2002.

Walbank, Mary E. Hoskins. "Evidence for the Imperial Cult in Julio-Claudian Corinth." In *Subject and Ruler: The Cult of the Ruling Power in Classical Antiquity: papers presented at a conference held in the University of Alberta on April 13-15, 1994, to celebrate the 65th anniversary of Duncan Fishwick*, ed. Alastair Small, 17. Ann Arbor, MI: Thomson-Shore, 1996.

Wallace, Daniel B. *Greek Grammar Beyond the Basics: An Exegetical Syntax of the New Testament*. Grand Rapids: Zondervan, 1996.

Wallace-Hadrill, Andrew. "*Mutatis Formas:* The Augustan Transformation of Roman Knowledge." In *The Cambridge Companion to the Age of Augustus*, ed. Karl Galinsky, 55-84. Cambridge: CUP, 2005.

Walter, N. "Gottes Zorn und das Harren der Kreatur. Zur Korrespondenz zwischen Römer 1,18-32 und 8,19-22." In *Christus Bezeugen*, ed. Karl Kertelge, et. al., 218-26. Freiburg: Herder, 1989.

Watts, John D. W. *Isaiah 1-33*. Vol. 24, Word Biblical Commentary, ed. David A. Hubbard and Glenn W. Barker. Waco: Word Books, 1985.

—. *Isaiah 34-66*. Vol. 25, Word Biblical Commentary, ed. R.K. Harrison and David A. Hubbard. Waco: Word Books, 1987.

Watts, Rikki. *Isaiah's New Exodus and Mark*. Vol. 88, WUNT, ed. M. Hengel and Otfried Hofius. Tübingen: Mohr Siebeck, 1997.

Webb, William J. *Returning Home: New Covenant and Second Exodus as the Context for 2 Corinthians 6:14-7:1*. Vol. 85, Journal for the Study of the New Testament Supplement Series, ed. Stanley E. Porter. Sheffield: JSOT Press, 1993.

Wedderburn, A.J.M. *Baptism and Resurrection: Studies in Pauline Theology against its Greco-Roman Background*, WUNT. Tübingen: J.C.B. Mohr, 1987.

—. *Reasons for Romans*. Edinburgh: T&T Clark, 1988.

—. "2 Corinthians 5:14 – A key to Paul's Soteriology?" In *Paul and the Corinthians: Studies on a Community in Conflict. Essays in Honour of Margaret Thrall*, ed. Trevor J. Burke and J. Keith Elliott, 267-83. Leiden: Brill, 2003.

Weima, J.A.D. "Gal 6:11-18: A Hermeneutical Key to the Galatian Letter." *Calvin Theological Journal* 28 (1993): 90-107.

—. *Neglected Endings: The Significance of the Pauline Letter Closings*. Vol. 101, JSNTSS. Sheffield: JSOT Press, 1994.

—. "The Pauline Letter Closings: Analysis and Hermeneutical Significance." *BBR* 5 (1995): 177-98.

Wengst, Klaus. *Pax Romana and the Peace of Jesus Christ*. Translated by John Bowden. London: SCM Press, Ltd., 1987.

Westermann, Claus. *Isaiah 40-66: A Commentary*. Translated by David M.G. Stalker, The Old Testament Library, ed. G.E. Wright, et. al. London: SCM Press, 1969.

Wilckens, Ulrich. *Der Brief an die Römer*. Vol. 6, Evangelisch-katholischer Kommentar zum Neuen Testament. Zürich: Neukirchen-Vluyn, 1978.

Wilder, William N. *Echoes of the Exodus Narrative in the Context and Background of Galatians 5:18*. Vol. 23, Studies in Biblical Literature, ed. Hemchand Gossai. New York: Peter Lang, 2001.

Wilk, Florian. *Die Bedeutung des Jesajabuches für Paulus*. Vol. 179, Forschung zur Religion und Literatur des Alten und Neuen Testaments, ed. Wolfgang Schrage and Rudolf Smend. Göttingen: Vandenhoeck & Ruprecht, 1998.

—. "Isaiah in 1 and 2 Corinthians." In *Isaiah in the New Testament*, ed. Steve Moyise and Maarten J.J. Menken, 133-58. London: T&T Clark, 2005.

Wilson, Todd. "Wilderness Apostasy and Paul's Portrayal of the Crisis in Galatians." *NTS* 50 (2004): 550-71.

—. *The Curse of the Law and the Crisis in Galatia: Reassessing the Purpose of Galatians*, WUNT. Tübingen: Mohr Siebeck, 2007.

Winter, Bruce. "Secular and Christian Responses to Corinthian Famines." *Tyndale Bulletin* 40 (1989): 86-106.

—. *After Paul Left Corinth*. Grand Rapids: William B. Eerdmans, 2001.

—. "The Imperial Cult and Early Christians in Roman Galatia (Acts XIII 13-50 and Galatians VI 11-18)." In *Acts du Ier Congrès International sur Antioche de Piside*, ed. T. Drew-Bear, M. Taslialan and C.M. Thomas, 5, 67-75. Lyon: Université Lumiere-Lyon 2, 2002.

Wintermute, O. S. "Jubilees (Second Century B.C.): A New Translation and Introduction." In *The Old Testament Pseudepigrapha*, ed. James H. Charlesworth, 2, 35-142. New York: Doubleday, 1985.

Wischmeyer, O. "ΦΥΣΙΣ und ΚΤΙΣΙΣ bei Paulus: Die paulinische Rede von Schöpfung und Natur." *ZTK* 93 (1996): 352-75.

Wistrand, Erik. *Felicitas Imperatoria*. Vol. 48, Studia Graeca et Latina Gothoburgensia. Göteborg: Acta Universitatis Gothoburgensis, 1987.

Witulski, Thomas. *Die Adressaten des Galaterbriefes: Untersuchungen zur Gemeinde von Antiochia ad Psidiam*. Vol. 193, Forschungen zur Religion und Literatur des Alten und Neuen Testaments. Göttingen: Vandenhoeck, 2000.

—. *Kaiserkult in Kleinasien: die Entwicklung der kultisch-religiösen Kaiserverherung in der römischen Provinz Asia von Augustus bis Antonius Pius.* Vol. 63, Novum Testamentum et Orbis Antiquus. Göttingen: Vandenhoeck & Ruprecht, 2007.
Woodbridge, Paul. "Time of Receipt of the Resurrection Body – A Pauline Inconsistency?" In *Paul and the Corinthians: Studies on a Community in Conflict. Essays in Honour of Margaret Thrall*, ed. Trevor J. Burke and J. Keith Elliott, 241-58. Leiden: Brill, 2003.
Wright, N. T. *The New Testament and the People of God*. Minneapolis: Fortress Press, 1992.
—. "Paul and Caesar: A New Reading of Romans." In *A Royal Priesthood? The Use of the Bible Ethically and Politically*, ed. Craig Bartholomew, et. al., 173-193. Grand Rapids: Zondervan, 2002a.
—. "Romans." In *The New Interpreter's Bible*, ed. L.E. Keck, 10, 393-770. Nashville: Abingdon Press, 2002b.
—. *The Resurrection of the Son of God.* Vol. Three, Christian Origins and the Question of God. London: SPCK, 2003.
—. *Paul: In Fresh Perspective*. Minneapolis: Fortress Press, 2005.
Yates, John W. "'Lord and Life-Giver': the Spirit and Creation in Paul." University of Cambridge, 2007.
Zanker, Paul. *The Power of Images in the Age of Augustus*. Translated by Alan Shapiro. Ann Arbor: The University of Michigan Press, 1988.
Zeller, Dieter. "Die Menschwerdung des Sohnes Gottes im Neuen Testament und die antike Religionsgeschichte." In *Menschwerdung Gottes – Vergöttlichung von Menschen*, ed. Dieter Zeller, 141-76. Göttingen: Vandenhoeck & Ruprecht, 1988.
Ziegler, Joseph. *Untersuchungen zur Septuaginta des Buches Isaias*. Vol. 13, Alttestamentliche Abhandlungen, ed. A. Schulz. Münster: Aschendorffschen, 1934.

Index of Ancient Sources

A. Hebrew Scriptures and Septuagint

Genesis			*Proverbs*	
1	141		8:22-30	94
1:1	27, 95, 120			
1:2	26		*Isaiah*	
1:27	111, 155		1-39	18, 26
1:28	158		1:2-4	23
2:7	117, 140		1:4-9	23
3	152, 154, 157, 158		1:7	23
3:15	158		1:8	24
3:16-19	158		1:21	24
3:17	160		1:21-26	24
3:17-19	152		1:29	23
3:22	28		2:1-4	25
3:24	28		2:2	26
6:12	153		2:6-8	23
6:17	153		2:8	23
12:7	154		2:10-21	23
15:7	154		2:13	23
15:18	154		2:14	23
			2:18	23
Exodus			2:19	23
43:17	20		2:20	23
			2:22	23
Leviticus			3:12-15	24
25	45		5:1-30	24
			5:2-4	24
Deuteronomy			5:25-30	24
28:1	26		5:29	26
			5:29-30	24
Ezra			6:7	22
3:12	35		9:4	123
			10:20	23
Psalm			11:6	20, 26
8:7	158		11:6-8	54
18:9	22		11:6-9	26, 161
142:2	153		11:7	26
144:5	22		12:2	23

13-23	25	42:6	55
13:22	20	42:9	55, 121
14:2	55	42:17	23
20:5	23	43	18, 19, 120, 122
24:1	25	43:1	123
24:1-20	159	43:6	122
24:3	25, 160	43:7	122
24:4-7	160	43:15	123
24:5	160	43:16	123
24:5-6	25	43:17	123
24:7	159, 160	43:18	20, 119, 120, 121, 123, 146
24:10	26		
24:14-16	160	43:18-19	179
24:18-23	25	43:19	20, 55, 119, 120, 121, 123, 146
24:20	25		
24-27	22, 25, 119, 121, 160, 179	43:19-21	123, 161
		43:20	20, 122
25:6-8	119	43:21	121
25:7	28	44:3	99
25:8	28, 117, 118, 119, 179	44:20	22
		44:21-23	123
26:16	160	44:24-28	123
26:17	160	45:1-3	46
26:19	28	45:1-8	128
27:13	26, 117	45:9-13	123
30:1-5	23	45:18-20	123
30-66	113	48	18, 19, 21
31:1	23	48:1	21
34:1-4	25	48:3	121
34:4	25	48:3-7	121
34:6	26	48:5	21
34:7	26	48:6	21, 55, 121
34:13	20	48:7	55, 121
34-35	121	48:11	55
35:1	26	48:13	21
35:2	26	49:1	126
35:9	26	49:3	126
35:10	26	49:4	126
36-37	25	49:5	126
37:31	24	49:6	55, 126
37:32	24	49:8	120, 125, 127
40:2	24	49:8-13	123
40:5	154	50:10	23
40:6	154	51:1-3	123
40:22	22	51:6	27
40:28-31	123	51:9-11	123
40-55	18, 20, 26, 123	51:12-16	123
40-66	19	52-53	125
41:17-20	123	54:1-10	123
42:5-9	123	54:10	27, 113

55:6-13	123	*Jeremiah*	
55:12	161	1:5	126
56-66	18, 26	4:9-12	159
57:1	22	4:27	159
57:15	22	4:31	159
59:4	22	23-28	159
60:3	55	31	174
60:14	24	31:4-6	31
61:4	24	31:12	31
63:9	21	31:12-14	30
63:10	21, 23	31:13	31
63:18-19	21	31:15	31
64:1-2	22	31:16	31
64:6	21	31:22	17
64:9-12	22	31:23	30
65	18, 19, 21, 22, 27, 30, 97, 113, 120, 121	31:24	30
		31:27	31
		31:28	31
65:3	21	31:31	55
65:7	21	31:31-38	30
65:16	19, 21, 28, 29		
65:16-25	28	*Ezekiel*	
65:17	17, 18, 19, 20, 21, 22, 27, 28, 29, 30, 47, 100, 120, 121, 154	34-36	31, 174
		34:25-27	54
		34:25-31	161
		36:23	46
65:17-25	31, 124	36:25-30	31
65:18	26, 27, 28	37:28	46
65:19	26, 28		
65:20	28, 50, 124	*Daniel*	
65:20-22	124	2:32	71
65:20-25	26	7:21-27	159
65:21	28	12:1-2	130
65:21-25	50		
65:22	28	*Hosea*	
65:25	26, 28, 30	2:18	161
65-66	22, 29, 30, 31, 160	4:3	159
		13:14	117
66	18, 22, 97, 113, 120		
66:18	26, 154	*Joel*	
66:18-24	25	1-2	159
66:21	26, 154	2:28	99, 131
66:22	17, 18, 26, 27, 30, 47, 100, 154		
		Haggai	
66:23	26	2:3	35
		Zechariah	
		8:12	161

B. New Testament

Matthew		2:25-29	153
5:18	94	3:4-5	152
5:24	124	3:6	152, 153
19:28	10	3:9	85, 153
		3:19	153
Mark		3:20	153
1:15	104, 105	3:21	133
16:14	104	3:23	156
		3:26	152
Luke		4:12	92
1:20	105	4:13	154
12:58	124	4:24	157
		4:25	125
John		5	138, 139, 141, 152, 154, 180
7:8	104	5:1-11	154, 162
		5:2	154
Acts		5:5	137
2:17	99, 131	5:6	137, 157
5:34	39	5:6-11	141
7:26	124	5:8	157
13:47	126	5:9	133
14:19	86	5:10	123, 157
14:20	86	5:11	133
14:22	130	5:12	154, 158
16:19-24	86	5:12-13	156
17:28	183	5:12-21	138, 141, 142, 154
22:3	39	5:13	154
23:6	39	5:15-19	142
26:5	39	5:15-21	138
26:16-18	126	5:17	145
		5:21	85
Romans		6:1	142
1	150, 151, 167, 180	6:3	142
1-8	12, 150, 153, 154, 167, 180	6:3-11	142
		6:4	97, 104
1:1	126	6:4-11	97
1:4	97, 132, 157, 168	6:5	131
1:16	136	6:6	142, 146, 157
1:18-32	153	6:10	143
1:19-20	151	6:11	104, 131, 143
1:20	151, 180	6:12	143
1:21	152	6:13	143
1:21-22	152	7:6	133
1:25	151	7:8	85
2:14	153	7:11	85
2:15	153	7:17	85

7:20	85	13:1-7	62
8	10, 12, 116, 119, 150, 151, 152, 155, 157, 158, 159, 160, 161, 164, 165, 166, 167, 168, 180, 181	15:23	151
		16:26	133
		1 Corinthians	
8:1	33	1:7	107, 109
8:11	130, 132, 146, 163	1:8	109
8:18-25	165	1:9	93
8:14	163	1:18	86, 136
8:14-17	163	1:18-25	85
8:15	163	1:20	98, 109
8:16	130, 146	1:23	86, 136
8:17	130, 146, 155, 156, 162, 165	1:24	95, 136
		1:29	153
8:18	6, 152, 154, 155, 157, 160, 161, 162, 165	2:6	98
		2:6-8	109, 114
		2:8	90, 98
		3:18	98, 109
8:18-25	25, 91, 150, 154, 155	3:19	98
		4:9-13	86
8:18-27	153, 161	5:2	159
8:18-30	155, 157, 161	5:7	143, 146
8:18-31	157	5:8	143, 146
8:19	95, 107, 157, 162, 163	7	108, 109, 110
		7:17	108
8:19-22	151	7:17-20	109
8:19-23	161	7:19	106, 108, 110
8:20	152, 154, 157, 158, 160	7:21-24	109
		7:22	109
8:20-22	162	7:24	108
8:21	154, 155, 157, 158, 160, 162, 163	7:25-28	109
		7:26	109
8:22	155, 158, 159, 160, 165, 166	7:29	92
		7:29-31	92, 109
8:23	107, 139, 159, 163, 164, 165, 166	7:31	110
		7:32-35	109
8:24	154, 165, 166	7:34	110
8:25	107, 165	7:35	110
8:26	156, 159	7:39	92
8:27	156	8:5	90, 91
8:28	156	8:6	95
8:28-30	155, 156, 162	10:11	92, 109, 129
8:29	130, 156, 184	10:20	90, 91
8:30	154, 155, 156	10:21	90, 91
8:35	160	15	116, 117, 118, 119, 138, 139, 140, 141, 168
8:39	151		
9:6	112		
10:12	109	15:1	139
12:1	143	15:2	139
12:2	129	15:3-4	104

15:3-8	139	4:16-5:10	165
15:12	139	4:17	162, 165
15:20	130, 139, 146	4:18	165
15:21	138, 140, 143	5	12, 17, 115, 116
15:22	138, 139		117, 118, 119, 123,
15:23	130, 139, 146		147, 150, 164, 165,
15:23-8	91		166, 168
15:27	157, 158	5:1-5	116, 119
15:28	158	5:1-6:2	127
15:35-50	140	5:2	116, 165
15:45-50	138	5:4	116, 117, 165, 179
15:42	158	5:5	116, 118, 132, 165
15:45	117, 132, 140	5:6	132
15:47-49	140	5:6-10	165
15:49	109	5:10-14	130
15:50	158	5:11-21	115
15:50-57	116	5:12-19	139
15:52	117, 131	5:12-21	125
15:54	117, 179	5:14	118, 130, 132, 133,
15:55	117		136, 137, 138, 142,
15:51-5	91		143, 145, 146, 154,
			180
2 Corinthians		5:14-15	12, 180
1:5	86	5:15	118, 130, 132, 137,
1:8	118, 130		142, 143, 145, 146
1:9	118	5:15-16	132
1:9-10	130	5:16	118, 121, 130, 132,
1:14	128		133, 134, 135, 136,
1:20	132		137, 138, 148, 176
1:22	132, 165	5:17	4, 6, 8, 9, 12, 106,
2-5	128		111, 115, 116, 119,
2:14-7:4	128		120, 121, 122, 123,
3	99		125, 128, 129, 132,
3:1-18	131		133, 136, 137, 142,
3:3	131		143, 144, 145, 146,
3:6	131, 140		147, 148, 150, 151,
3:6-18	55		164, 165, 166, 179,
3:14	143, 146		180
3:18	132, 141	5:18	124
4:1	132	5:18-21	123, 125, 141, 179
4:1-15	130		184
4:4	99, 129, 138, 141	5:18-6:2	144
4:4-6	126, 140	5:19	124, 125
4:6	126	5:19-21	124, 125
4:7-14	118	5:20	119, 139
4:10	132	5:21	125
4:11	131	5:23	117, 139
4:14	118, 165	6:1	126
4:16	132	6:2	120, 125, 126, 127,
4:16-18	116, 118		132, 133, 179

6:3-14	125	3:14	99
6:4	86, 142	3:19-4:7	92
6:5	86, 142	3:23	104
6:8	142	3:23-6	107
8:1	125	3:24	106
9:2	151	3:25	104, 106
10:13	112	3:26	105
10:15	112	3:28	87, 91, 105, 109, 110, 111, 184
10:16	112		
11:23-29	86	3:29	87
12:2	144	4:1-5	106
12:21	159	4:1-7	90
		4:3	88, 90, 91, 92, 94, 95, 177
Galatians			
1:1	98, 103, 104	4:3-4	95
1:1-4	97	4:4	93, 104, 105
1:3b-4	75	4:4-5	114
1:4	59, 88, 89, 90, 91, 92, 98, 100, 114, 129, 175	4:4-6	103, 104
		4:4-7	75
		4:5	94, 95, 104
1:6	83	4:6	99
1:6-9	87, 100	4:7	95
1:10	86, 126	4:8	91
1:12	175	4:9	88, 93, 95
1:13	88, 112	4:10	59, 90
1:15	126	4:11	83
1:15-17	103	4:13	85
1:16	84, 85, 126	4:14	85
2	113	4:17	86
2:7-9	109	4:19	111
2:15	59	4:21-31	135
2:16	87, 153	4:23	85
2:18	97	4:25	92
2:19	97, 99, 105, 106, 143	4:29	85
		5:2	87
2:19-21	103	5:4	86, 107
2:20	85, 86, 88, 97, 105, 107, 133, 145	5:5	99, 103, 107
		5:6	12, 87, 88, 106, 107, 110
2:21	87, 105		
3	110	5:7	83
3:1	83, 86, 97	5:8	99
3:1-5	86	5:11	87
3:2	105	5:12	83, 85
3:2-5	99	5:13	85
3:3	85	5:16	85, 92
3:5	105	5:16-18	99
3:6-8	105	5:16-26	99
3:8	105	5:17	85
3:11-14	87	5:19	85
3:13	99	5:22	85

5:24	88, 93	*Colossians*	
5:25	92, 93, 143	1:6	151
6	94, 95, 105, 150, 164, 168	1:9	151
		1:15	130, 150, 184
6:2	107, 112, 143, 176	1:15-18	146
6:8	85, 103, 158	1:15-20	95
6:11-18	83, 84, 113	1:16	184
6:12	84, 85, 86, 87	1:16-17	95
6:13	84, 85, 86, 87, 88	1:18	130, 184
6:14	12, 86, 88, 89, 90, 91, 92, 95, 97, 98, 100, 103, 105, 106, 107, 124, 143, 177	1:20	124, 184
		1:22	124
		1:23	150, 180
		2:12	97
6:14-16	103	2:13	131
6:15	4, 6, 9,12, 83, 87, 88, 89, 91, 93, 94, 97, 100, 105, 106, 107, 108, 109, 110, 111, 112, 113, 140, 150, 151, 164, 178, 179, 180	2:20	95
		3:9-11	142
		3:10	142, 184
		3:11	142, 184
		1 Thessalonians	
		3:4	86
6:15-16	184	4:16	117
6:16	59, 92, 93, 100, 111, 112, 113, 114	*1 Timothy*	
		1:1	97
6:17	86, 98, 112	4:4	150
Ephesians			
1:10	104	*2 Timothy*	
2:5	131	1:12	86
2:6	97, 184	2:3	86
2:15	140, 184	2:9	86
3:9	184		
4:22-24	142	*Hebrews*	
4:24	184	1:2	104
5:28	143		
		1 Peter	
Philippians		3:10, 12	37
1:1	126		
1:20	143	*2 Peter*	
1:29	86	3:10-13	10, 29
3:5	39	3:13	100
3:10	86		
3:16	92	*Revelation*	
3:20	75, 107	11:15	117
3:21	157	21:1	100
		21:1-2	10
		21:1-5	130

C. Other Ancient Sources

1 Enoch
1:7-9	153
10	37
10:18-22	37
10:4	37
10:5	37
16	37
19	37
21	37
24	38
45:4	37
45:4-6	38
51:1-5	146
61:12	38
72:1	37, 39, 100
91:14-16	37
91:16	38, 100
91:17	100

1 Maccabees
1:11	41
1:14	41
1:15	41
1:21	48
1:28	47
1:39	42
1:41	40
1:48-50	41

1QH
3.19-22	55
4.15	55
5.11	56
11.10-14	55
11.1-18	52
11.19-21	56
11.21	56
14.25-9	53
16.4-27	55
16.11	153
19.10-14	52
19.13-14	56

1QM
1.1-17	57
1.5	53
15.12-16	61
15.15	104
16.11-16	61
19.2-8	57
18.1-3	57

1QpHab
2.3	131
6.3-5	57
7.13	104
9.4	57
11.13	55

1QS
4.18	104
4.23-25	55
4.23-26	57
4.25	56
5	55
5.1-6	56
8.1-11	53
11	153

2 Baruch
4:3	38
30:1	105
32:6	37, 100
44:11	100
44:12	39, 100
44:12-15	37
54:13-22	38
57:2	37

2 Enoch
8:1ff	38
66:6	98

3 Baruch
4:16	156

4 Ezra
6:13-16	37
6:24	37
6:25	37
7:1	158
7:11	152
7:30-32	37
7:75	37, 100

7:118	152		CD	
8:11	140		1	153
			6.19	131
4Q246			8.21	131
1-2	52		19.33	131
			19.34	131
4Q285			20.12	131
Frag. 1	57			
			Chrysostom	
4Q394-399	52		*Com. on 2 Cor*	
			61:475	8
4Q88				
9.1-5	55		*Com. on Gal*	
9.10	53		61:636	9
9.11	54			
			Homilies on Romans	
11Q5			14	157
26.9-15	54			
			Cicero	
11QT			*On the Nature of the Gods*	
29.9	56		2:11-14	96
Ambrosiaster			*Pro Rabirio*	
Commentaries			16	86
2 Cor 5:17	7			
Gal 6:15	7		*Decree of the League of Asia*	
				71, 78
ANS				
1941.131.1150	75		Dio Cassius	
1944.100.4821	75		59.3.7-8	74
1967.153.219	75		59.26.9	68
Athanasius			Dio Chrysostom	
Four Discourses			59.30.1	74
I.5.16	8			
II.21.70	8		*Gen. Rab.*	
II.26.65	8		1:1.2.B	95
			39:4	56
Aristides				
Eulogy of Rome			Gregory of Nyssa	
66	67		*Against Eunomius*	
			2.2.8	7
b. Men.			2.4.3	7
43b	110			
			Hesiod	
Barnabas			*Theogony*	
16:8	7		840-850	181
Basil				
Letters 8	9			

Horace
Carmen Saeculare
11.45-48   73
11.29-32   73

Irenaeus
Against Heresies
5.32.1   163

Jerome
Grace & Free Will
20   7

On the Bap. of Infants
1.44   7

Reply to Faustus
11.1; 19:10 7

Sermons
26.12   7
212.1   7

Joseph and Aseneth
             120, 133, 177

Josephus
Ant.
3:183   90
12:241   41
12:254   42
13:243   48
18:373   65

J.W.
1:34   42
1:35   42
6:316   57

Jubilees
1:1   46
1:9   41, 44
1:10   41
1:11   41, 46
1:13   44, 46
1:14   41
1:15   46
1:19-20   46
1:21   46
1:21-25   49
1:23   49
1:25   46
1:26   49
1:28   46
1:29   37, 38, 39, 47, 48, 49, 100
1:31   41
2:17-19   42
4:7-15   43
4:26   439, 48, 100
4:27   43
4:28   43
5:12   49
6:35-38   41
8:10   43
8:11   43
9:14   43
10:27-34   43
15:25   42
15:26   42
15:28   42, 43
15:29   42
15:31   44, 46
15:34   43, 44
16:27   42
19:25   47
22:16   41, 44
22:22   48
23:12   49
23:18   50
23:19-21   50
23:22   50
23:23   50
23:24   59
23:26   50
23:27-29   50
23:28   50
23:30   51
23:31   51
25:1   41
25:1-3   43
25:3   41
25:5   41
25:8-10   41
25:10   43
25:12   41
30   42
30:4   43
30:7-17   41, 43
31   42

40:9	48	2:48	94
46:2	48	2:51	94
50:5	47, 48		

L.A.E.
29:3   98
51:2   97

Letter of Paullus Fabius Maximus
            78

Ovid
Fasti
1.721-22   73

P Lond
1168   104

P Oxy
14.1641   104

P Tebt
2.374   104

Paterculus
2.89   181

Philo
Agriculture
97   135

Creation
1:143   95
1:3   94, 95

Eternity
1:109   94

Giants
1:49   112
53   135

Joseph
1:29   96

Migration
14   135

Moses
2:37   96

Planting
1:8   94

Posterity
1:28   112

Rewards
1:23   96

Unchangeable
143   135

QG
2.11   137

Plato
Timaeus
30   96
44   96
45   96

Plutarch
Romulus
12.1   65
12.2-6   65
12.6   65
12:2-6   114

Psalms of Solomon
17   44

Res Gestae Divi Augusti
1.1   181

Šabb.
33b   68

Seneca
To Polybius On Consolation
7.4   183

Suetonius
Augustus
28.3   76
98.2   66, 183

Nero   61

t. Ber.
7:18 110

Tacitus
Agricola
30 68

Tertullian
Against Marcion
4.1.6 7
4.11.9 7
5.4.3 7
5.12 119

On Modesty
6 7

Testament of Levi
18:10ff 38

Tg. Jer.
23:23 38

The Tebtunis Papyri
1:19 84

Theodoret
Gal 6:15 9

Virgil
Aeneid
1.278-9 64
6.756-789 72
6.788-94 71
11.243 72

Eclogue
4 181
4.4-10 72
4.18-25 64
4.40 64
4.41 64
4.50-52 64

Georgics 64

Vitruvius
On Architecture
1.2 76
1.3 76

Index of Modern Authors

Aageson, James W.   122, 177
Adams, Edward   VII, 65, 90, 92, 95, 96, 109, 111, 120, 148, 151, 152, 154, 155, 156, 158, 166, 167, 177
Anderson, Bernhard W.   25
Ando, Clifford   70
Arnold, Clinton E.   90
Aune, David E.   96, 129, 145, 148
Aymer, A.J.D.   5, 6
Baer, David A.   29
Balz, Horst   155, 162
Barclay, John   87
Barnett, Paul   128, 131
Barrett, C.K.   145, 152
Baumbach, G.   151
Baumgarten, Jorg   5, 161
Beale, G.K.   93, 113, 119, 123, 124, 125, 126, 130
Beker, J.   5, 58, 101, 128, 138, 139, 145, 164
Berges, Ulrich   28
Betz, H.D.   83, 84, 92, 98, 100, 104, 110, 112
Beuken, Willem A. M.   25
Beyer, H.W.   112
Bickerman, Elias J.   40, 41
Bindermann, W.   158
Blinzer, J.   90
Boismard, Marie-Emile   118
Bolt, John   150, 161
Bookidis, Nancy   69
Boomershine, Thomas E.   135
Borse, Udo   165
Bovon, Udo   98
Bowman, Alan K.   73
Braaten, Laurie J.   159, 160
Branigan, Keith   68
Braund, David C.   71, 73, 74, 75, 78
Bray, Gerald   9, 157, 163
Brent, Allen   66, 68, 183

Brinsmead, Bernard Hungerford   88
Bruce, F.F.   110
Brueggemann, Walter   19, 25, 28
Brunt, P.A.   60
Bultmann, R.   5, 89, 100, 132, 189
Burton, Ernest De Witt   99
Byrne, Brendan   151, 159, 161, 163
Calvin, John   4
Cancik, Hubert   78
Carter, Warren   60
Castriota, David   66
Charlesworth, M.P.   74
Chester, Andrew   94, 97, 144
Chester, Stephen J.   134
Childs, Brevard S.   18, 23
Chisholm, Kitty   76
Chow, John K.   135
Christoffersson, Olle   153, 162
Ciampa, Roy E.   85, 88, 103
Clements, R.E.   24, 191
Clifford, Richard J.   21, 70, 133
Collange, J.   133
Collins, Adela Yarbro.   60, 144
Collins, John J.   37, 48, 52
Cousar, Charles B.   111
Cramer, Frederick H.   72
Cranfield, C.E.B.   151, 152, 159
Crossan, John D.   63, 77
Dahl, N.A.   37, 38, 111, 154
Daise, M.A.   55
Das, A. Andrew   42, 111, 112, 164
Davenport, Gene L.   38
Davies, Philip R.   33
Davies, W.D.   87, 113, 132, 140
De Boer, M.C.   5, 37, 38, 90, 100, 101, 117, 129, 138, 139
Delling, D.   90, 93
Denney, James   145
Derrett, J.D.M.   54, 55
Dim, Emmanuel Uchenna   28

Dodd, C.H.   117
Doering, Lutz   42
Downing, F.G.   60
Doyle, Brian   26
Du Toit, Andrie   87
Duff, N.J.   111
Duhaime, Jean   53
Dunn, James D. G.   86, 88, 98, 108, 131, 132, 138, 141, 143, 144, 150, 151, 153, 156, 159
Eastman, Susan   151, 161
Eckstein, Hans-Joachim   97
Edwards, Mark   9, 192
Ego, Beate   42, 96
Ehrenberg, Victor   71, 78
Elledge, C.D.   130
Elliott, Neil   36, 60
Endres, John C.   43
Engels, Donald   69
Esler, Philip F.   57
Favro, Diane   76
Fee, Gordon D.   99
Ferguson, John   76
Findeis, H.-J.   146
Fishwick, Duncan   68, 76
Fitzmyer, J.A.   52, 131, 151, 159
Fletcher-Louis, Crispin   156
Forbes, Chris   90
French, D.   77
Fretheim, Terence E.   159
Frey, Jorg   41, 45
Friesen, Steven J.   61, 70
Fritz, Volkmar   24
Furnish, V.P.   102, 120, 124, 125, 129, 134, 137
Gager, John G.   150, 151, 161
Galinsky, Karl   77
Garland, D.   91, 92, 128, 134
Gathercole, Simon J.   VII, 153
Gaventa, Beverly R.   83, 92, 159
Gempf, C.H.   159
Georgi, Dieter   60
Gibbs, John G.   161
Gignilliat, Mark   127
Gill, David W.J.   69
Gillman, J.   117
Glasson, T. Francis   118
Gloer, W. Hulitt   135, 137
Gordon, Richard   70
Gordon, Robert P.   25

Gordon, T.D.   104
Gowan, Donald E.   27
Grabbe, Lester L.   35
Gradel, Ittai   69
Griffin, Miriam   68, 69
Grimal, Pierre   65
Gwyther, Anthony   59
Haak, Robert D.   35
Hafemann, Scott J.   58, 126, 141, 143, 156
Hahn, Ferdinand.   127
Hahne, Harry A.   37, 51, 157, 159, 160, 161, 167
Hall III, John F.   71
Hall, Robert G.   39
Halpern-Amaru, Betsy   43
Hamilton, Neill Q.   92, 99
Hanson, Paul D.   18, 23, 30, 36
Hardie, Philip R.   64, 65, 78
Hardin, Justin   86, 87
Harnack, Adolf von   4
Harrington, Daniel J.   53
Harris, Murray J.   124, 126, 137, 138, 143, 147, 148, 165
Harrison, J.R.   61, 62, 79, 169
Harrisville, Roy A.   6, 103
Hays, Richard B.   6, 11, 17, 109, 116
Hellerman, Joseph   41, 42, 43
Hempel, Charlotte   51
Hendrix, Holland Lee   76
Hengel, M   33, 34, 86, 134
Hengel, Martin   34, 35, 57
Hester, James D.   154
Hickling, C.J.A.   122
Hoegen-Rohls, Christina   12
Hofius, Otfried   125
Holm-Nielsen, Svend   55
Hooker, Morna   125, 126, 139, 141, 142, 144
Hoover, Joel Herbert   5, 6, 10
Horbury, William   24, 124
Horrell, David G.   60, 103, 111, 140
Horsley, Richard A.   35, 36, 60, 135
Houtman, Cornelis   27
Howard-Brook, Wes   59
Hubbard, Moyer   3, 4, 39, 40, 51, 88, 89, 98, 133, 137, 143, 144, 173
Hughes, J.A.   55
Humphrey, Edith M.   128
Instinsky, Hans Ulrich   73

Iwry, Samuel 47
Jewett, Robert 66, 135, 143, 151, 153, 155, 158, 159, 162, 163, 164, 168
Johnson, Andrew 130
Jones, A.H.M. 64, 71, 78, 181
Kahn, C.H. 64
Käsemann, E. 5, 100, 101, 125, 138, 159
Kee, Howard Clark 71
Keesmaat, Sylvia C. 98, 113, 160, 163
Kegley, Charles W. 89
Keown, Gerald L. 17, 31
Kern, P.H. 84
Kertelge, Karl 89
Kiesow, Klaus 20
Kim, Seyoon 134, 141
Kirschläger, Walter 98
Klaiber, Walter 5
Klijn, A.F. 37
Knibb, Michael 51, 52
Knohl, Israel 124
Kraftchick, S. 151
Kraus, H.-J. 28
Kraus, W. 5, 28
Kreitzer, Larry J. 67
Kubusch, K. 72
Kuhn, Heinz-Wolfgang 52
Kwon, Yon-Gyong 98
LaGrange, Marie-Joseph 151
Lambrecht, J. 119
Lampe, G.W.H. 150, 161
Lanci, Armin 69
Lange, J.P. 39, 158, 159
Lee, Stephen 20
Levenson, Jon D. 131
Licht, A. Lewis 64, 72
Lichtenberger, Hermann 53
Lietzmann, Hans 152, 163
Lightfoot, J.B. 84, 88
Lim, Timothy 57
Lind, Millard C. 21
Lindars, Barnabas 126, 165
Lindeskog, Gösta 161
Lohse, Eduard 151, 159
Longenecker, Bruce W. 85, 87, 92, 94, 95, 101, 165
Longenecker, R.N. 84, 104, 112

Mansoor, Menahem 54
Martin, Ralph P. 118, 125
Martínez, F.G. 52
Martyn, J. Louis 90, 91, 101, 106, 108, 132, 133, 135, 173, 182
Matera, F.J. 84, 118
Matlock, R. Barry 5, 98, 138
McDonough, Sean M. 64
McLaren, James S. 87
Meeks, Wayne A. 135
Meggitt, Justin 70
Mell, Ulrich 3, 4, 56, 173
Merklein, Helmut 110
Metzger, Bruce M. 136, 162
Meyer, H.A.W. 84, 86, 157
Michaels, J. Ramsey 63
Michel, O. 151, 159
Milgrom, Jacob 45
Milligan, George 84, 104
Minear, Paul S. 5, 89, 102, 110
Mitchell, Stephen 69, 74, 77
Moo, Douglas 142, 143, 151, 152, 157, 159, 160, 162
Moore, G.F. 94
Morales, Rodrigo 98, 99, 122
Motyer, J.A. 20, 23, 24, 26, 201
Moule, C.F.D. 145
Moulton, J.H. 84, 104
Moyise, Steve 117, 152, 177
Mußner, Franz 88, 108
Myers, Charles D. 164
Nickelsburg, George W.E. 34, 36, 53
Nock, A.D. 74
North, C.R. 19
Oakes, Peter 60, 61, 62, 70
O'Brien, Peter 96
Oropeza, B.J. 113, 117
Oswalt, John N. 22, 23, 26
Panagopoulos, Johannes 8
Patem C. Marvin 144
Pearson, Michael Parker 76
Philip, Finny 99
Photopoulos, John 69
Pickett, Raymond 145
Porter, Stanley 115, 123, 124, 125
Price, S.R.F 70, 72, 76
Puech, E. 53
Räisänen, Heikki 108
Ramsey, John T. 64, 72

Ravid, Liora 43
Reed, Jonathan L. 63, 77
Rehak, Paul 67, 78
Rendtorff, Rolf 18
Reynolds, Joyce M. 68
Richards, Colin 76
Richardson, Peter 76
Riches, John 6
Ringgren, Helmer 54, 57
Roetzel, Calvin J. 78
Rosner, Brian S. 109, 118
Rowe, Cavin 68
Rowland, Christopher 33, 83
Rusam, D. 90
Russell, D.S. 31, 37, 38
Russell, David M. 30, 31, 50
Ryberg, Inez 72
Sals, Ulrike 25
Sanders, E.P. 46, 52, 53, 108
Sandmel, S. 62
Sandnes, Karl Olav 103, 116, 126
Sappington, Thomas J. 33
Sasse, H. 98
Sawyer, Deborah F. 17
Scalise, Pamela J. 17, 31
Schiffman, L.H. 52, 53
Schlier, Heinrich 98
Schnelle, Udo 165
Schnider, F. 84
Scholder, Klaus 128
Scholla, Robert W. 141
Schrage, Wolfgang 37, 116
Schreiner, Thomas R. 151, 155, 159
Schröter, J. 126
Schwantes, Heinz 5, 98
Schweitzer, Albert 5, 100, 129
Schweizer, E. 90, 104
Scott, James M. 45, 50, 187
Scranton, R.L. 69
Scroggs, Robin 152
Seeligmann, I.L. 29
Sehmsdorf, Von Eberhard 22
Shotter, David 68
Silva, Moisés 97, 98, 103, 104
Sjöberg, Erik 5, 53
Smith, Michael J. 104
Smothers, Thomas G. 17, 31
Stahl, Hans-Peter 65
Stanley, Christopher D. 117, 119
Stanley, David M. 126

Stanton, G.N. VII, 6, 79, 93, 101, 175
Steck, O.H. 28
Stenger, W. 84
Steudel, A. 52, 53
Stockton, David L. 68
Strauss, Mark L. 18
Stuhlmacher, Peter 133
Stuhlmueller, Carol 20
Sumney, Jerry L. 83, 128
Swarup, Paul 144
Sweeney, Marvin 18, 29
Talmon, Shemaryan 35
Tannehill, R.C. 88, 142, 143
Taubes, J. 158
Taylor, John 104, 105, 107, 152
Taylor, Lily Ross 72
Theobald, M. 124, 151, 152
Thielman, Frank 108, 161
Thiselton, Anthony C. 92
Tholuck, F.A.G. 159
Thompson, John B. 61
Thrall, Margaret E. 115, 126, 137, 138, 147
Tolmie, D. Francois 86, 87
Tomson, Peter J. 108
Tsumura, D.T. 158
Tuckett, Christopher M. 144
Van der Kooij, A. 26
Van Kooten, George H. 130
Van Ruiten, Jacques 41, 42
VanderKam, James C. 38, 40, 43, 44, 46, 47, 51, 52
Vermes, Geza 57
Vermeylen, Jacques 18
Vögtle, A. 150, 161
Vollenweider, Samuel 93, 152, 162
Wagner, J. Ross 11, 127, 177
Walbank, Mary E. 69, 135
Wallace, Daniel B. 147
Wallace-Hadrill, Andrew 135, 148
Walter, N. 151
Watts, John D. 24, 29
Watts, Rikki 20
Webb, William J. 122, 126
Wedderburn, A.J.M. 142, 145, 164
Weima, J.A.D. 84, 88, 93, 101, 105, 128
Wengst, Klaus 67, 68
Westermann, Claus 27
Wilckens, Ulrich 164

Wilder, William N. 113
Wilk, Florian 18, 117, 121, 122, 123, 126
Wilson, Todd 83, 98
Winter, Bruce 84, 85, 86, 87, 109, 118
Wintermute, O.S. 39, 41
Wischmeyer, O. 153

Wistrand, Erik 64
Woodbridge, Paul 117
Wright, N.T. 52, 53, 62, 80, 97, 118, 119, 130, 131, 165, 168
Yates, John W. 99, 140
Zanker, Paul 61, 66, 67, 77
Zeller, Dieter 62
Ziegler, Joseph 29

Index of Subjects

Abraham 99
Adam 55, 138, 150, 154
Adam Christology 156
Age of Evil 90
Age of Peace 73
Ages 12, 71
Agitators 84
αἰών 98
Amanuensis 84
Ambassador 125
Anthropocentricism 120
Anthropological 3, 4, 51
– communal 4
– Individual 4
Anthropologically 4
Anti-imperial 59, 62
ἀπαρχή 117
Apocalyptic 11
Apotheosis 68
Architecture 66
ἀρραβών 116
Astronomical 72
Atonement 125
Augustus 60

Baptism 8, 142
Birth Pangs 158
Body 143

Calendar 78
Calendrical Observances 90
Caligula 60
Child-bearing 159
Christ Event 129
Christian 144
Christological 134
Christological Eschatology 92
Circumcised 84
Circumcision 41, 89
Citizenship 75

City 24, 65
Claudius 60
Co-crucifixion 97, 142
Colony 69
Colossians 184
Communal 51
Community 5, 53, 95
Concord 79
Continuity 37
Conversion 7, 11, 148
Convert 148
Corinth 62
Corporate Personality 183
Corruption 158
Cosmic 18, 25, 57
Cosmic Judgment 22, 24
Cosmic Renewal 22
Cosmological 3, 4, 18, 31, 51
Cosmological Speculation 168
Cosmos 5, 64, 89
Covenant 30
Created 151
Created Order 30
Creation 20, 24, 25, 34
Creative Act 151
Cross 87, 105
Crucifixion 88, 157
Cruciform 86
Cult 68

Damascus 61
Daughter of Zion 160
Death 95
Decay 158
Defence 62, 98
Destruction 30
Deutero-Isaiah 121
Deutero-Pauline 130

Earth 21, 23

Earthly 57
Earthquake 129
Ecclesiological 144
Elements 21, 111
Empire 75
ἐν Χριστῷ 12, 107, 137
Ephesians 184
Epistemological 128
Epistemology 114, 115
Eschatological 'Museum' 67
Eschatological Soteriology 5, 34
Eschatological Tension 102, 163
εὐαγγέλιον 175
εὐπροσωπῆσαι 85
Execution 157
Exile 34
Exodus 20
External 40, 49
Ezekiel 121

Family 183
Father 183
Felicitas 64
Firstfruits 8, 146
Flesh 84
Forensic 37
Form of the World 92
Former/New 19
Fullness of Time 94
Futility 152

Galatia 62
Garden 156
γῆ 154
Genesis 158
Gentile 48
Glory 55, 144, 154
Golden Age 79
Gospel 99
Gospels 79
Grace 142
Groaning 159
Heavenly 184
Humanity 25, 34

Identification 165
Identity 41
Idolatry 22
Imperial 59, 68

Imperial Ideology 6, 11
In Christ 184
Inaugurated Eschatology 102
Individual 4, 45,110
Insurgents 157
Internal 40
Internal Condition 21
Isaianic Motifs 147
Israel of God 112

Jeremiah 121
Judgment 11, 24, 119, 153

κανών 112
Kingdom 176
Kittim 56
κόσμος 95
κτίσις 151

Land 26, 45
Law 41, 153
Letter of Recommendation 131
Love 137
Ludi Saeculares 72

Macrocosm 96
Marriage 91
Mastema 47
Messiah 159
Messianic 64
Metaphor 27
Microcosm 90, 96
Milestone 77
Military 70
Mirror-read 98
Missionary 185
Mourning 159
Mysticism 144

National 45
Natural Order 94
Natural World 19, 64
Nature 20, 66
Nero 60
New Age 53, 54, 72, 98
New Birth 8, 159
New Covenant 17, 95
New Exodus 20, 122
New Heart 4, 31

New Life 97
New Spirit 4, 31
New World Order 26
Newness 28
νόμος 106

Opposites 87

παιδαγωγός 106
παλιγγενεσία 148
Paradise 64, 71
Paradisiacal Conditions 44
Parallelomania 62
Parousia 107, 118
Participation 144
Patristic Era 6
Pax Romana *168*
Peace 79
Peace and Security 73
Personification 117
Pharisees 39
Physical 57, 64
Physical Universe 27
Plight 34
Pluralism 40
Polemic 59, 62, 83
Polemical 166
Political 23, 34, 64
Present Age 98
Processual Eschatology 117
Promises 132
Propaganda 61, 67, 168
πρωτότοκος 184
Purity 41

Qumran 11

Reason 152
Reconciliation 123
Recreation 27, 30
Redemption 20, 88
Redemptive 161
Refurbishment 76
Regeneration 8
Religio licita 87
Religious 34
Renewal 27
Renovation 30
Representative 141
Restoration 11, 18, 22, 35, 144

Resurrection 8, 13, 53, 95, 97, 105
Revelation 162
Revolutionary 158
Roads, Roman 77
Rome 62

Salvation 12, 150
Salvation History 35
σάρξ 95
– κατὰ σάρκα 133
Satan 157
Saviour 79
Second Temple 33
Seed 99
SER Pattern 46, 49
Servant 127
Sin 31, 120, 156
Slavery 158
Social Order 11
Social Sphere 148
Social Structure 12
Social Theory 4
Social World 95
Society 166
Sociological 96
Sons of God 75, 162
Soterio-anthropology 88
Soterio-cosmology 88
Soteriological 9, 31, 61
Soteriological Equalization 111
Soteriology 4
Space 75
Spirit 8
Spiritual 57, 184
Spiritual Powers 90
σταυρόω 105
State 64, 157
στοιχεῖα τοῦ κόσμου 89, 90
στοιχέω 92
Subversive 57
Sufferings 157
Sundial 77
Supra-individual 180
Symbolic Universe 36
σῶμα 163

Temple 35
Terminological Control 150
Thanksgiving 83
Thanksgivings 96

Theological Summa   150
Time   75
Torah   95
Transformation   9, 60, 168
Travailing   159
Trito-Isaiah   121
Truth   151

Uncircumcision   89
Universe   47, 54

Walk   93
Wilderness   57
World   27, 31
World Perception   75
World-views   182

Wissenschaftliche Untersuchungen zum Neuen Testament
Alphabetical Index of the First and Second Series

Ådna, Jostein: Jesu Stellung zum Tempel. 2000. *Vol. II/119.*
Ådna, Jostein (Ed.): The Formation of the Early Church. 2005. *Vol. 183.*
− and *Kvalbein, Hans* (Ed.): The Mission of the Early Church to Jews and Gentiles. 2000. *Vol. 127.*
Aland, Barbara: Was ist Gnosis? 2009. *Vol. 239.*
Alexeev, Anatoly A., Christos Karakolis and *Ulrich Luz* (Ed.): Einheit der Kirche im Neuen Testament. Dritte europäische orthodox-westliche Exegetenkonferenz in Sankt Petersburg, 24.–31. August 2005. 2008. *Vol. 218.*
Alkier, Stefan: Wunder und Wirklichkeit in den Briefen des Apostels Paulus. 2001. *Vol. 134.*
Allen, David M.: Deuteronomy and Exhortation in Hebrews. 2008. *Vol. II/238.*
Anderson, Paul N.: The Christology of the Fourth Gospel. 1996. *Vol. II/78.*
Appold, Mark L.: The Oneness Motif in the Fourth Gospel. 1976. *Vol. II/1.*
Arnold, Clinton E.: The Colossian Syncretism. 1995. *Vol. II/77.*
Ascough, Richard S.: Paul's Macedonian Associations. 2003. *Vol. II/161.*
Asiedu-Peprah, Martin: Johannine Sabbath Conflicts As Juridical Controversy. 2001. *Vol. II/132.*
Attridge, Harold W.: see *Zangenberg, Jürgen.*
Aune, David E.: Apocalypticism, Prophecy and Magic in Early Christianity. 2006. *Vol. 199.*
Avemarie, Friedrich: Die Tauferzählungen der Apostelgeschichte. 2002. *Vol. 139.*
Avemarie, Friedrich and *Hermann Lichtenberger* (Ed.): Auferstehung – Ressurection. 2001. *Vol. 135.*
− Bund und Tora. 1996. *Vol. 92.*
Baarlink, Heinrich: Verkündigtes Heil. 2004. *Vol. 168.*
Bachmann, Michael: Sünder oder Übertreter. 1992. *Vol. 59.*
Bachmann, Michael (Ed.): Lutherische und Neue Paulusperspektive. 2005. *Vol. 182.*
Back, Frances: Verwandlung durch Offenbarung bei Paulus. 2002. *Vol. II/153.*
Backhaus, Knut: Der sprechende Gott. 2009. *Vol. 240.*

Baker, William R.: Personal Speech-Ethics in the Epistle of James. 1995. *Vol. II/68.*
Bakke, Odd Magne: 'Concord and Peace'. 2001. *Vol. II/143.*
Balch, David L.: Roman Domestic Art and Early House Churches. 2008. *Vol. 228.*
Baldwin, Matthew C.: Whose *Acts of Peter*? 2005. *Vol. II/196.*
Balla, Peter: Challenges to New Testament Theology. 1997. *Vol. II/95.*
− The Child-Parent Relationship in the New Testament and its Environment. 2003. *Vol. 155.*
Bammel, Ernst: Judaica. Vol. I 1986. *Vol. 37.*
− Vol. II 1997. *Vol. 91.*
Barrier, Jeremy W.: The Acts of Paul and Thecla. 2009. *Vol. II/270.*
Barton, Stephen C.: see *Stuckenbruck, Loren T.*
Bash, Anthony: Ambassadors for Christ. 1997. *Vol. II/92.*
Bauckham, Richard: The Jewish World around the New Testament. Collected Essays Volume I. 2008. *Vol. 233.*
Bauernfeind, Otto: Kommentar und Studien zur Apostelgeschichte. 1980. *Vol. 22.*
Baum, Armin Daniel: Pseudepigraphie und literarische Fälschung im frühen Christentum. 2001. *Vol. II/138.*
Bayer, Hans Friedrich: Jesus' Predictions of Vindication and Resurrection. 1986. *Vol. II/20.*
Becker, Eve-Marie: Das Markus-Evangelium im Rahmen antiker Historiographie. 2006. *Vol. 194.*
Becker, Eve-Marie and *Peter Pilhofer* (Ed.): Biographie und Persönlichkeit des Paulus. 2005. *Vol. 187.*
Becker, Michael: Wunder und Wundertäter im frührabbinischen Judentum. 2002. *Vol. II/144.*
Becker, Michael and *Markus Öhler* (Ed.): Apokalyptik als Herausforderung neutestamentlicher Theologie. 2006. *Vol. II/214.*
Bell, Richard H.: Deliver Us from Evil. 2007. *Vol. 216.*
− The Irrevocable Call of God. 2005. *Vol. 184.*
− No One Seeks for God. 1998. *Vol. 106.*
− Provoked to Jealousy. 1994. *Vol. II/63.*

Bennema, Cornelis: The Power of Saving Wisdom. 2002. *Vol. II/148.*
Bergman, Jan: see *Kieffer, René*
Bergmeier, Roland: Das Gesetz im Römerbrief und andere Studien zum Neuen Testament. 2000. *Vol. 121.*
Bernett, Monika: Der Kaiserkult in Judäa unter den Herodiern und Römern. 2007. *Vol. 203.*
Betz, Otto: Jesus, der Messias Israels. 1987. *Vol. 42.*
– Jesus, der Herr der Kirche. 1990. *Vol. 52.*
Beyschlag, Karlmann: Simon Magus und die christliche Gnosis. 1974. *Vol. 16.*
Bieringer, Reimund: see *Koester, Craig.*
Bittner, Wolfgang J.: Jesu Zeichen im Johannesevangelium. 1987. *Vol. II/26.*
Bjerkelund, Carl J.: Tauta Egeneto. 1987. *Vol. 40.*
Blackburn, Barry Lee: Theios Aner and the Markan Miracle Traditions. 1991. *Vol. II/40.*
Blanton IV, Thomas R.: Constructing a New Covenant. 2007. *Vol. II/233.*
Bock, Darrell L.: Blasphemy and Exaltation in Judaism and the Final Examination of Jesus. 1998. *Vol. II/106.*
– and *Robert L. Webb* (Ed.): Key Events in the Life of the Historical Jesus. 2009. *Vol. 247.*
Bockmuehl, Markus N.A.: Revelation and Mystery in Ancient Judaism and Pauline Christianity. 1990. *Vol. II/36.*
Bøe, Sverre: Gog and Magog. 2001. *Vol. II/135.*
Böhlig, Alexander: Gnosis und Synkretismus. Vol. 1 1989. *Vol. 47* – Vol. 2 1989. *Vol. 48.*
Böhm, Martina: Samarien und die Samaritai bei Lukas. 1999. *Vol. II/111.*
Böttrich, Christfried: Weltweisheit – Menschheitsethik – Urkult. 1992. *Vol. II/50.*
– and *Herzer, Jens* (Ed.): Josephus und das Neue Testament. 2007. *Vol. 209.*
Bolyki, János: Jesu Tischgemeinschaften. 1997. *Vol. II/96.*
Bosman, Philip: Conscience in Philo and Paul. 2003. *Vol. II/166.*
Bovon, François: New Testament and Christian Apocrypha. 2009. *Vol. 237.*
– Studies in Early Christianity. 2003. *Vol. 161.*
Brändl, Martin: Der Agon bei Paulus. 2006. *Vol. II/222.*
Breytenbach, Cilliers: see *Frey, Jörg.*
Brocke, Christoph vom: Thessaloniki – Stadt des Kassander und Gemeinde des Paulus. 2001. *Vol. II/125.*
Brunson, Andrew: Psalm 118 in the Gospel of John. 2003. *Vol. II/158.*
Büchli, Jörg: Der Poimandres – ein paganisiertes Evangelium. 1987. *Vol. II/27.*

Bühner, Jan A.: Der Gesandte und sein Weg im 4. Evangelium. 1977. *Vol. II/2.*
Burchard, Christoph: Untersuchungen zu Joseph und Aseneth. 1965. *Vol. 8.*
– Studien zur Theologie, Sprache und Umwelt des Neuen Testaments. Ed. by D. Sänger. 1998. *Vol. 107.*
Burnett, Richard: Karl Barth's Theological Exegesis. 2001. *Vol. II/145.*
Byron, John: Slavery Metaphors in Early Judaism and Pauline Christianity. 2003. *Vol. II/162.*
Byrskog, Samuel: Story as History – History as Story. 2000. *Vol. 123.*
Cancik, Hubert (Ed.): Markus-Philologie. 1984. *Vol. 33.*
Capes, David B.: Old Testament Yaweh Texts in Paul's Christology. 1992. *Vol. II/47.*
Caragounis, Chrys C.: The Development of Greek and the New Testament. 2004. *Vol. 167.*
– The Son of Man. 1986. *Vol. 38.*
– see *Fridrichsen, Anton.*
Carleton Paget, James: The Epistle of Barnabas. 1994. *Vol. II/64.*
Carson, D.A., O'Brien, Peter T. and *Mark Seifrid* (Ed.): Justification and Variegated Nomism.
Vol. 1: The Complexities of Second Temple Judaism. 2001. *Vol. II/140.*
Vol. 2: The Paradoxes of Paul. 2004. *Vol. II/181.*
Chae, Young Sam: Jesus as the Eschatological Davidic Shepherd. 2006. *Vol. II/216.*
Chapman, David W.: Ancient Jewish and Christian Perceptions of Crucifixion. 2008. *Vol. II/244.*
Chester, Andrew: Messiah and Exaltation. 2007. *Vol. 207.*
Chibici-Revneanu, Nicole: Die Herrlichkeit des Verherrlichten. 2007. *Vol. II/231.*
Ciampa, Roy E.: The Presence and Function of Scripture in Galatians 1 and 2. 1998. *Vol. II/102.*
Classen, Carl Joachim: Rhetorical Criticsm of the New Testament. 2000. *Vol. 128.*
Colpe, Carsten: Griechen – Byzantiner – Semiten – Muslime. 2008. *Vol. 221.*
– Iranier – Aramäer – Hebräer – Hellenen. 2003. *Vol. 154.*
Coppins, Wayne: The Interpretation of Freedom in the Letters of Paul. 2009. *Vol. II/261.*
Crump, David: Jesus the Intercessor. 1992. *Vol. II/49.*
Dahl, Nils Alstrup: Studies in Ephesians. 2000. *Vol. 131.*

Daise, Michael A.: Feasts in John. 2007. *Vol. II/229.*
Deines, Roland: Die Gerechtigkeit der Tora im Reich des Messias. 2004. *Vol. 177.*
− Jüdische Steingefäße und pharisäische Frömmigkeit. 1993. *Vol. II/52.*
− Die Pharisäer. 1997. *Vol. 101.*
Deines, Roland and *Karl-Wilhelm Niebuhr* (Ed.): Philo und das Neue Testament. 2004. *Vol. 172.*
Dennis, John A.: Jesus' Death and the Gathering of True Israel. 2006. *Vol. 217.*
Dettwiler, Andreas and *Jean Zumstein* (Ed.): Kreuzestheologie im Neuen Testament. 2002. *Vol. 151.*
Dickson, John P.: Mission-Commitment in Ancient Judaism and in the Pauline Communities. 2003. *Vol. II/159.*
Dietzfelbinger, Christian: Der Abschied des Kommenden. 1997. *Vol. 95.*
Dimitrov, Ivan Z., James D.G. Dunn, Ulrich Luz and *Karl-Wilhelm Niebuhr* (Ed.): Das Alte Testament als christliche Bibel in orthodoxer und westlicher Sicht. 2004. *Vol. 174.*
Dobbeler, Axel von: Glaube als Teilhabe. 1987. *Vol. II/22.*
Docherty, Susan E.: The Use of the Old Testament in Hebrews. 2009. *Vol. II/260.*
Downs, David J.: The Offering of the Gentiles. 2008. *Vol. II/248.*
Dryden, J. de Waal: Theology and Ethics in 1 Peter. 2006. *Vol. II/209.*
Dübbers, Michael: Christologie und Existenz im Kolosserbrief. 2005. *Vol. II/191.*
Dunn, James D.G.: The New Perspective on Paul. 2005. *Vol. 185.*
Dunn, James D.G. (Ed.): Jews and Christians. 1992. *Vol. 66.*
− Paul and the Mosaic Law. 1996. *Vol. 89.*
− see *Dimitrov, Ivan Z.*
−, *Hans Klein, Ulrich Luz,* and *Vasile Mihoc* (Ed.): Auslegung der Bibel in orthodoxer und westlicher Perspektive. 2000. *Vol. 130.*
Ebel, Eva: Die Attraktivität früher christlicher Gemeinden. 2004. *Vol. II/178.*
Ebertz, Michael N.: Das Charisma des Gekreuzigten. 1987. *Vol. 45.*
Eckstein, Hans-Joachim: Der Begriff Syneidesis bei Paulus. 1983. *Vol. II/10.*
− Verheißung und Gesetz. 1996. *Vol. 86.*
Ego, Beate: Im Himmel wie auf Erden. 1989. *Vol. II/34.*
Ego, Beate, Armin Lange and *Peter Pilhofer* (Ed.): Gemeinde ohne Tempel − Community without Temple. 1999. *Vol. 118.*

− and *Helmut Merkel* (Ed.): Religiöses Lernen in der biblischen, frühjüdischen und frühchristlichen Überlieferung. 2005. *Vol. 180.*
Eisen, Ute E.: see *Paulsen, Henning.*
Elledge, C.D.: Life after Death in Early Judaism. 2006. *Vol. II/208.*
Ellis, E. Earle: Prophecy and Hermeneutic in Early Christianity. 1978. *Vol. 18.*
− The Old Testament in Early Christianity. 1991. *Vol. 54.*
Elmer, Ian J.: Paul, Jerusalem and the Judaisers. 2009. *Vol. II/258.*
Endo, Masanobu: Creation and Christology. 2002. *Vol. 149.*
Ennulat, Andreas: Die 'Minor Agreements'. 1994. *Vol. II/62.*
Ensor, Peter W.: Jesus and His 'Works'. 1996. *Vol. II/85.*
Eskola, Timo: Messiah and the Throne. 2001. *Vol. II/142.*
− Theodicy and Predestination in Pauline Soteriology. 1998. *Vol. II/100.*
Fatehi, Mehrdad: The Spirit's Relation to the Risen Lord in Paul. 2000. *Vol. II/128.*
Feldmeier, Reinhard: Die Krisis des Gottessohnes. 1987. *Vol. II/21.*
− Die Christen als Fremde. 1992. *Vol. 64.*
Feldmeier, Reinhard and *Ulrich Heckel* (Ed.): Die Heiden. 1994. *Vol. 70.*
Fletcher-Louis, Crispin H.T.: Luke-Acts: Angels, Christology and Soteriology. 1997. *Vol. II/94.*
Förster, Niclas: Marcus Magus. 1999. *Vol. 114.*
Forbes, Christopher Brian: Prophecy and Inspired Speech in Early Christianity and its Hellenistic Environment. 1995. *Vol. II/75.*
Fornberg, Tord: see *Fridrichsen, Anton.*
Fossum, Jarl E.: The Name of God and the Angel of the Lord. 1985. *Vol. 36.*
Foster, Paul: Community, Law and Mission in Matthew's Gospel. *Vol. II/177.*
Fotopoulos, John: Food Offered to Idols in Roman Corinth. 2003. *Vol. II/151.*
Frank, Nicole: Der Kolosserbrief im Kontext des paulinischen Erbes. 2009. *Vol. II/271.*
Frenschkowski, Marco: Offenbarung und Epiphanie. Vol. 1 1995. *Vol. II/79* − Vol. 2 1997. *Vol. II/80.*
Frey, Jörg: Eugen Drewermann und die biblische Exegese. 1995. *Vol. II/71.*
− Die johanneische Eschatologie. Vol. I. 1997. *Vol. 96.* − Vol. II. 1998. *Vol. 110.* − Vol. III. 2000. *Vol. 117.*
Frey, Jörg and *Cilliers Breytenbach* (Ed.): Aufgabe und Durchführung einer Theologie des Neuen Testaments. 2007. *Vol. 205.*

- Jens Herzer, Martina Janßen and Clare K. Rothschild (Ed.): Pseudepigraphie und Verfasserfiktion in frühchristlichen Briefen. 2009. *Vol. 246.*
- Stefan Krauter and Hermann Lichtenberger (Ed.): Heil und Geschichte. 2009. *Vol. 248.*
- and Udo Schnelle (Ed.): Kontexte des Johannesevangeliums. 2004. *Vol. 175.*
- and Jens Schröter (Ed.): Deutungen des Todes Jesu im Neuen Testament. 2005. *Vol. 181.*
-, Jan G. van der Watt, and Ruben Zimmermann (Ed.): Imagery in the Gospel of John. 2006. *Vol. 200.*

Freyne, Sean: Galilee and Gospel. 2000. *Vol. 125.*

Fridrichsen, Anton: Exegetical Writings. Edited by C.C. Caragounis and T. Fornberg. 1994. *Vol. 76.*

Gadenz, Pablo T.: Called from the Jews and from the Gentiles. 2009. *Vol. II/267.*

Gäbel, Georg: Die Kulttheologie des Hebräerbriefes. 2006. *Vol. II/212.*

Gäckle, Volker: Die Starken und die Schwachen in Korinth und in Rom. 2005. *Vol. 200.*

Garlington, Don B.: 'The Obedience of Faith'. 1991. *Vol. II/38.*
- Faith, Obedience, and Perseverance. 1994. *Vol. 79.*

Garnet, Paul: Salvation and Atonement in the Qumran Scrolls. 1977. *Vol. II/3.*

Gemünden, Petra von (Ed.): see *Weissenrieder, Annette.*

Gese, Michael: Das Vermächtnis des Apostels. 1997. *Vol. II/99.*

Gheorghita, Radu: The Role of the Septuagint in Hebrews. 2003. *Vol. II/160.*

Gordley, Matthew E.: The Colossian Hymn in Context. 2007. *Vol. II/228.*

Gräbe, Petrus J.: The Power of God in Paul's Letters. 2000, ²2008. *Vol. II/123.*

Gräßer, Erich: Der Alte Bund im Neuen. 1985. *Vol. 35.*
- Forschungen zur Apostelgeschichte. 2001. *Vol. 137.*

Grappe, Christian (Ed.): Le Repas de Dieu / Das Mahl Gottes. 2004. *Vol. 169.*

Gray, Timothy C.: The Temple in the Gospel of Mark. 2008. *Vol. II/242.*

Green, Joel B.: The Death of Jesus. 1988. *Vol. II/33.*

Gregg, Brian Han: The Historical Jesus and the Final Judgment Sayings in Q. 2005. *Vol. II/207.*

Gregory, Andrew: The Reception of Luke and Acts in the Period before Irenaeus. 2003. *Vol. II/169.*

Grindheim, Sigurd: The Crux of Election. 2005. *Vol. II/202.*

Gundry, Robert H.: The Old is Better. 2005. *Vol. 178.*

Gundry Volf, Judith M.: Paul and Perseverance. 1990. *Vol. II/37.*

Häußer, Detlef: Christusbekenntnis und Jesusüberlieferung bei Paulus. 2006. *Vol. 210.*

Hafemann, Scott J.: Suffering and the Spirit. 1986. *Vol. II/19.*
- Paul, Moses, and the History of Israel. 1995. *Vol. 81.*

Hahn, Ferdinand: Studien zum Neuen Testament.
Vol. I: Grundsatzfragen, Jesusforschung, Evangelien. 2006. *Vol. 191.*
Vol. II: Bekenntnisbildung und Theologie in urchristlicher Zeit. 2006. *Vol. 192.*

Hahn, Johannes (Ed.): Zerstörungen des Jerusalemer Tempels. 2002. *Vol. 147.*

Hamid-Khani, Saeed: Relevation and Concealment of Christ. 2000. *Vol. II/120.*

Hannah, Darrel D.: Michael and Christ. 1999. *Vol. II/109.*

Hardin, Justin K.: Galatians and the Imperial Cult? 2007. *Vol. II /237.*

Harrison; James R.: Paul's Language of Grace in Its Graeco-Roman Context. 2003. *Vol. II/172.*

Hartman, Lars: Text-Centered New Testament Studies. Ed. von D. Hellholm. 1997. *Vol. 102.*

Hartog, Paul: Polycarp and the New Testament. 2001. *Vol. II/134.*

Hays, Christopher M.: Luke's Wealth Ethics. 2010. *Vol. 275.*

Heckel, Theo K.: Der Innere Mensch. 1993. *Vol. II/53.*
- Vom Evangelium des Markus zum viergestaltigen Evangelium. 1999. *Vol. 120.*

Heckel, Ulrich: Kraft in Schwachheit. 1993. *Vol. II/56.*
- Der Segen im Neuen Testament. 2002. *Vol. 150.*
- see *Feldmeier, Reinhard.*
- see *Hengel, Martin.*

Heiligenthal, Roman: Werke als Zeichen. 1983. *Vol. 9.*

Heliso, Desta: Pistis and the Righteous One. 2007. *Vol. II/235.*

Hellholm, D.: see *Hartman, Lars.*

Hemer, Colin J.: The Book of Acts in the Setting of Hellenistic History. 1989. *Vol. 49.*

Hengel, Martin: Jesus und die Evangelien. Kleine Schriften V. 2007. *Vol. 211.*
- Die johanneische Frage. 1993. *Vol. 67.*

- Judaica et Hellenistica. Kleine Schriften I. 1996. *Vol. 90.*
- Judaica, Hellenistica et Christiana. Kleine Schriften II. 1999. *Vol. 109.*
- Judentum und Hellenismus. 1969, ³1988. *Vol. 10.*
- Paulus und Jakobus. Kleine Schriften III. 2002. *Vol. 141.*
- Studien zur Christologie. Kleine Schriften IV. 2006. *Vol. 201.*
- Studien zum Urchristentum. Kleine Schriften VI. 2008. *Vol. 234.*
- and *Anna Maria Schwemer:* Paulus zwischen Damaskus und Antiochien. 1998. *Vol. 108.*
- Der messianische Anspruch Jesu und die Anfänge der Christologie. 2001. *Vol. 138.*
- Die vier Evangelien und das eine Evangelium von Jesus Christus. 2008. *Vol. 224.*

Hengel, Martin and Ulrich Heckel (Ed.): Paulus und das antike Judentum. 1991. *Vol. 58.*
- and *Hermut Löhr* (Ed.): Schriftauslegung im antiken Judentum und im Urchristentum. 1994. *Vol. 73.*
- and *Anna Maria Schwemer* (Ed.): Königsherrschaft Gottes und himmlischer Kult. 1991. *Vol. 55.*
- Die Septuaginta. 1994. *Vol. 72.*
-, *Siegfried Mittmann* and *Anna Maria Schwemer* (Ed.): La Cité de Dieu / Die Stadt Gottes. 2000. *Vol. 129.*

Hentschel, Anni: Diakonia im Neuen Testament. 2007. *Vol. 226.*
Hernández Jr., Juan: Scribal Habits and Theological Influence in the Apocalypse. 2006. *Vol. II/218.*
Herrenbrück, Fritz: Jesus und die Zöllner. 1990. *Vol. II/41.*
Herzer, Jens: Paulus oder Petrus? 1998. *Vol. 103.*
- see *Böttrich, Christfried.*
- see *Frey, Jörg.*
Hill, Charles E.: From the Lost Teaching of Polycarp. 2005. *Vol. 186.*
Hoegen-Rohls, Christina: Der nachösterliche Johannes. 1996. *Vol. II/84.*
Hoffmann, Matthias Reinhard: The Destroyer and the Lamb. 2005. *Vol. II/203.*
Hofius, Otfried: Katapausis. 1970. *Vol. 11.*
- Der Vorhang vor dem Thron Gottes. 1972. *Vol. 14.*
- Der Christushymnus Philipper 2,6–11. 1976, ²1991. *Vol. 17.*
- Paulusstudien. 1989, ²1994. *Vol. 51.*
- Neutestamentliche Studien. 2000. *Vol. 132.*
- Paulusstudien II. 2002. *Vol. 143.*
- Exegetische Studien. 2008. *Vol. 223.*
- and *Hans-Christian Kammler:* Johannesstudien. 1996. *Vol. 88.*

Holloway, Paul A.: Coping with Prejudice. 2009. *Vol. 244.*
Holmberg, Bengt (Ed.): Exploring Early Christian Identity. 2008. *Vol. 226.*
- and *Mikael Winninge* (Ed.): Identity Formation in the New Testament. 2008. *Vol. 227.*
Holtz, Traugott: Geschichte und Theologie des Urchristentums. 1991. *Vol. 57.*
Hommel, Hildebrecht: Sebasmata.
  Vol. 1 1983. *Vol. 31.*
  Vol. 2 1984. *Vol. 32.*
Horbury, William: Herodian Judaism and New Testament Study. 2006. *Vol. 193.*
Horn, Friedrich Wilhelm and Ruben Zimmermann (Ed.): Jenseits von Indikativ und Imperativ. Vol. 1. 2009. *Vol. 238.*
Horst, Pieter W. van der: Jews and Christians in Their Graeco-Roman Context. 2006. *Vol. 196.*
Hultgård, Anders and Stig Norin (Ed): Le Jour de Dieu / Der Tag Gottes. 2009. *Vol. 245.*
Hvalvik, Reidar: The Struggle for Scripture and Covenant. 1996. *Vol. II/82.*
Jackson, Ryan: New Creation in Paul's Letters. 2010. *Vol. II/272.*
Janßen, Martina: see *Frey, Jörg.*
Jauhiainen, Marko: The Use of Zechariah in Revelation. 2005. *Vol. II/199.*
Jensen, Morten H.: Herod Antipas in Galilee. 2006. *Vol. II/215.*
Johns, Loren L.: The Lamb Christology of the Apocalypse of John. 2003. *Vol. II/167.*
Jossa, Giorgio: Jews or Christians? 2006. *Vol. 202.*
Joubert, Stephan: Paul as Benefactor. 2000. *Vol. II/124.*
Judge, E. A.: The First Christians in the Roman World. 2008. *Vol. 229.*
Jungbauer, Harry: „Ehre Vater und Mutter". 2002. *Vol. II/146.*
Kähler, Christoph: Jesu Gleichnisse als Poesie und Therapie. 1995. *Vol. 78.*
Kamlah, Ehrhard: Die Form der katalogischen Paränese im Neuen Testament. 1964. *Vol. 7.*
Kammler, Hans-Christian: Christologie und Eschatologie. 2000. *Vol. 126.*
- Kreuz und Weisheit. 2003. *Vol. 159.*
- see *Hofius, Otfried.*
Karakolis, Christos: see *Alexeev, Anatoly A.*
Karrer, Martin und *Wolfgang Kraus* (Ed.): Die Septuaginta – Texte, Kontexte, Lebenswelten. 2008. *Vol. 219.*
Kelhoffer, James A.: The Diet of John the Baptist. 2005. *Vol. 176.*
- Miracle and Mission. 1999. *Vol. II/112.*

Kelley, Nicole: Knowledge and Religious Authority in the Pseudo-Clementines. 2006. *Vol. II/213.*
Kennedy, Joel: The Recapitulation of Israel. 2008. *Vol. II/257.*
Kieffer, René and *Jan Bergman* (Ed.): La Main de Dieu / Die Hand Gottes. 1997. *Vol. 94.*
Kierspel, Lars: The Jews and the World in the Fourth Gospel. 2006. *Vol. 220.*
Kim, Seyoon: The Origin of Paul's Gospel. 1981, ²1984. *Vol. II/4.*
– Paul and the New Perspective. 2002. *Vol. 140.*
– "The 'Son of Man'" as the Son of God. 1983. *Vol. 30.*
Klauck, Hans-Josef: Religion und Gesellschaft im frühen Christentum. 2003. *Vol. 152.*
Klein, Hans, Vasile Mihoc und Karl-Wilhelm Niebuhr (Ed.): Das Gebet im Neuen Testament. Vierte, europäische orthodox-westliche Exegetenkonferenz in Sambata de Sus, 4.–8. August 2007. 2009. Vol. 249.
– see Dunn, James D.G.
Kleinknecht, Karl Th.: Der leidende Gerechtfertigte. 1984, ²1988. *Vol. II/13.*
Klinghardt, Matthias: Gesetz und Volk Gottes. 1988. *Vol. II/32.*
Kloppenborg, John S.: The Tenants in the Vineyard. 2006. *Vol. 195.*
Koch, Michael: Drachenkampf und Sonnenfrau. 2004. *Vol. II/184.*
Koch, Stefan: Rechtliche Regelung von Konflikten im frühen Christentum. 2004. *Vol. II/174.*
Köhler, Wolf-Dietrich: Rezeption des Matthäusevangeliums in der Zeit vor Irenäus. 1987. *Vol. II/24.*
Köhn, Andreas: Der Neutestamentler Ernst Lohmeyer. 2004. *Vol. II/180.*
Koester, Craig and *Reimund Bieringer* (Ed.): The Resurrection of Jesus in the Gospel of John. 2008. *Vol. 222.*
Konradt, Matthias: Israel, Kirche und die Völker im Matthäusevangelium. 2007. *Vol. 215.*
Kooten, George H. van: Cosmic Christology in Paul and the Pauline School. 2003. *Vol. II/171.*
– Paul's Anthropology in Context. 2008. *Vol. 232.*
Korn, Manfred: Die Geschichte Jesu in veränderter Zeit. 1993. *Vol. II/51.*
Koskenniemi, Erkki: Apollonios von Tyana in der neutestamentlichen Exegese. 1994. *Vol. II/61.*
– The Old Testament Miracle-Workers in Early Judaism. 2005. *Vol. II/206.*

Kraus, Thomas J.: Sprache, Stil und historischer Ort des zweiten Petrusbriefes. 2001. *Vol. II/136.*
Kraus, Wolfgang: Das Volk Gottes. 1996. *Vol. 85.*
– see *Karrer, Martin.*
– see *Walter, Nikolaus.*
– and *Karl-Wilhelm Niebuhr* (Ed.): Frühjudentum und Neues Testament im Horizont Biblischer Theologie. 2003. *Vol. 162.*
Krauter, Stefan: Studien zu Röm 13,1-7. 2009. *Vol. 243.*
– see *Frey, Jörg.*
Kreplin, Matthias: Das Selbstverständnis Jesu. 2001. *Vol. II/141.*
Kuhn, Karl G.: Achtzehngebet und Vaterunser und der Reim. 1950. *Vol. 1.*
Kvalbein, Hans: see *Ådna, Jostein.*
Kwon, Yon-Gyong: Eschatology in Galatians. 2004. *Vol. II/183.*
Laansma, Jon: I Will Give You Rest. 1997. *Vol. II/98.*
Labahn, Michael: Offenbarung in Zeichen und Wort. 2000. *Vol. II/117.*
Lambers-Petry, Doris: see *Tomson, Peter J.*
Lange, Armin: see *Ego, Beate.*
Lampe, Peter: Die stadtrömischen Christen in den ersten beiden Jahrhunderten. 1987, ²1989. *Vol. II/18.*
Landmesser, Christof: Wahrheit als Grundbegriff neutestamentlicher Wissenschaft. 1999. *Vol. 113.*
– Jüngerberufung und Zuwendung zu Gott. 2000. *Vol. 133.*
Lau, Andrew: Manifest in Flesh. 1996. *Vol. II/86.*
Lawrence, Louise: An Ethnography of the Gospel of Matthew. 2003. *Vol. II/165.*
Lee, Aquila H.I.: From Messiah to Preexistent Son. 2005. *Vol. II/192.*
Lee, Pilchan: The New Jerusalem in the Book of Relevation. 2000. *Vol. II/129.*
Lee, Simon S.: Jesus' Transfiguration and the Believers' Transformation. 2009. *Vol. II/265.*
Lichtenberger, Hermann: Das Ich Adams und das Ich der Menschheit. 2004. *Vol. 164.*
– see *Avemarie, Friedrich.*
– see *Frey, Jörg.*
Lierman, John: The New Testament Moses. 2004. *Vol. II/173.*
– (Ed.): Challenging Perspectives on the Gospel of John. 2006. *Vol. II/219.*
Lieu, Samuel N.C.: Manichaeism in the Later Roman Empire and Medieval China. ²1992. *Vol. 63.*
Lindemann, Andreas: Die Evangelien und die Apostelgeschichte. 2009. *Vol. 241.*

Lindgård, Fredrik: Paul's Line of Thought in 2 Corinthians 4:16–5:10. 2004. *Vol. II/189.*
Loader, William R.G.: Jesus' Attitude Towards the Law. 1997. *Vol. II/97.*
Löhr, Gebhard: Verherrlichung Gottes durch Philosophie. 1997. *Vol. 97.*
Löhr, Hermut: Studien zum frühchristlichen und frühjüdischen Gebet. 2003. *Vol. 160.*
– see *Hengel, Martin.*
Löhr, Winrich Alfried: Basilides und seine Schule. 1995. *Vol. 83.*
Lorenzen, Stefanie: Das paulinische Eikon-Konzept. 2008. *Vol. II/250.*
Luomanen, Petri: Entering the Kingdom of Heaven. 1998. *Vol. II/101.*
Luz, Ulrich: see *Alexeev, Anatoly A.*
– see *Dunn, James D.G.*
Mackay, Ian D.: John's Raltionship with Mark. 2004. *Vol. II/182.*
Mackie, Scott D.: Eschatology and Exhortation in the Epistle to the Hebrews. 2006. *Vol. II/223.*
Magda, Ksenija: Paul's Territoriality and Mission Strategy. 2009. *Vol. II/266.*
Maier, Gerhard: Mensch und freier Wille. 1971. *Vol. 12.*
– Die Johannesoffenbarung und die Kirche. 1981. *Vol. 25.*
Markschies, Christoph: Valentinus Gnosticus? 1992. *Vol. 65.*
Marshall, Jonathan: Jesus, Patrons, and Benefactors. 2009. *Vol. II/259.*
Marshall, Peter: Enmity in Corinth: Social Conventions in Paul's Relations with the Corinthians. 1987. *Vol. II/23.*
Martin, Dale B.: see *Zangenberg, Jürgen.*
Mayer, Annemarie: Sprache der Einheit im Epheserbrief und in der Ökumene. 2002. *Vol. II/150.*
Mayordomo, Moisés: Argumentiert Paulus logisch? 2005. *Vol. 188.*
McDonough, Sean M.: YHWH at Patmos: Rev. 1:4 in its Hellenistic and Early Jewish Setting. 1999. *Vol. II/107.*
McDowell, Markus: Prayers of Jewish Women. 2006. *Vol. II/211.*
McGlynn, Moyna: Divine Judgement and Divine Benevolence in the Book of Wisdom. 2001. *Vol. II/139.*
Meade, David G.: Pseudonymity and Canon. 1986. *Vol. 39.*
Meadors, Edward P.: Jesus the Messianic Herald of Salvation. 1995. *Vol. II/72.*
Meißner, Stefan: Die Heimholung des Ketzers. 1996. *Vol. II/87.*
Mell, Ulrich: Die „anderen" Winzer. 1994. *Vol. 77.*

– see *Sänger, Dieter.*
Mengel, Berthold: Studien zum Philipperbrief. 1982. *Vol. II/8.*
Merkel, Helmut: Die Widersprüche zwischen den Evangelien. 1971. *Vol. 13.*
– see *Ego, Beate.*
Merklein, Helmut: Studien zu Jesus und Paulus. Vol. 1 1987. *Vol. 43.* – Vol. 2 1998. *Vol. 105.*
Merkt, Andreas: see *Nicklas, Tobias*
Metzdorf, Christina: Die Tempelaktion Jesu. 2003. *Vol. II/168.*
Metzler, Karin: Der griechische Begriff des Verzeihens. 1991. *Vol. II/44.*
Metzner, Rainer: Die Rezeption des Matthäusevangeliums im 1. Petrusbrief. 1995. *Vol. II/74.*
– Das Verständnis der Sünde im Johannesevangelium. 2000. *Vol. 122.*
Mihoc, Vasile: see *Dunn, James D.G.*
– see *Klein, Hans.*
Mineshige, Kiyoshi: Besitzverzicht und Almosen bei Lukas. 2003. *Vol. II/163.*
Mittmann, Siegfried: see *Hengel, Martin.*
Mittmann-Richert, Ulrike: Magnifikat und Benediktus. *1996. Vol. II/90.*
– Der Sühnetod des Gottesknechts. 2008. *Vol. 220.*
Miura, Yuzuru: David in Luke-Acts. 2007. *Vol. II/232.*
Moll, Sebastian: The Arch-Heretic Marcion. 2010. *Vol. 250.*
Mournet, Terence C.: Oral Tradition and Literary Dependency. 2005. *Vol. II/195.*
Mußner, Franz: Jesus von Nazareth im Umfeld Israels und der Urkirche. Ed. von M. Theobald. 1998. *Vol. 111.*
Mutschler, Bernhard: Das Corpus Johanneum bei Irenäus von Lyon. 2005. *Vol. 189.*
Nguyen, V. Henry T.: Christian Identity in Corinth. 2008. *Vol. II/243.*
Nicklas, Tobias, Andreas Merkt und Joseph Verheyden (Ed.): Gelitten – Gestorben – Auferstanden. 2010. *Vol. II/273.*
Niebuhr, Karl-Wilhelm: Gesetz and Paränese. 1987. *Vol. II/28.*
– Heidenapostel aus Israel. 1992. *Vol. 62.*
– see *Deines, Roland.*
– see *Dimitrov, Ivan Z.*
– see *Klein, Hans.*
– see *Kraus, Wolfgang.*
Nielsen, Anders E.: "Until it is Fullfilled". 2000. *Vol. II/126.*
Nielsen, Jesper Tang: Die kognitive Dimension des Kreuzes. 2009. *Vol. II/263.*
Nissen, Andreas: Gott und der Nächste im antiken Judentum. 1974. *Vol. 15.*

Noack, Christian: Gottesbewußtsein. 2000. *Vol. II/116.*
Noormann, Rolf: Irenäus als Paulusinterpret. 1994. *Vol. II/66.*
Norin, Stig: see *Hultgård, Anders.*
Novakovic, Lidija: Messiah, the Healer of the Sick. 2003. *Vol. II/170.*
Obermann, Andreas: Die christologische Erfüllung der Schrift im Johannesevangelium. 1996. *Vol. II/83.*
Öhler, Markus: Barnabas. 2003. *Vol. 156.*
− see *Becker, Michael.*
Okure, Teresa: The Johannine Approach to Mission. 1988. *Vol. II/31.*
Onuki, Takashi: Heil und Erlösung. 2004. *Vol. 165.*
Oropeza, B. J.: Paul and Apostasy. 2000. *Vol. II/115.*
Ostmeyer, Karl-Heinrich: Kommunikation mit Gott und Christus. 2006. *Vol. 197.*
− Taufe und Typos. 2000. *Vol. II/118.*
Paulsen, Henning: Studien zur Literatur und Geschichte des frühen Christentums. Ed. von Ute E. Eisen. 1997. *Vol. 99.*
Pao, David W.: Acts and the Isaianic New Exodus. 2000. *Vol. II/130.*
Park, Eung Chun: The Mission Discourse in Matthew's Interpretation. 1995. *Vol. II/81.*
Park, Joseph S.: Conceptions of Afterlife in Jewish Insriptions. 2000. *Vol. II/121.*
Pate, C. Marvin: The Reverse of the Curse. 2000. *Vol. II/114.*
Pearce, Sarah J.K.: The Land of the Body. 2007. *Vol. 208.*
Peres, Imre: Griechische Grabinschriften und neutestamentliche Eschatologie. 2003. *Vol. 157.*
Perry, Peter S.: The Rhetoric of Digressions. 2009. *Vol. II/268.*
Philip, Finny: The Origins of Pauline Pneumatology. 2005. *Vol. II/194.*
Philonenko, Marc (Ed.): Le Trône de Dieu. 1993. *Vol. 69.*
Pilhofer, Peter: Presbyteron Kreitton. 1990. *Vol. II/39.*
− Philippi. Vol. 1 1995. *Vol. 87.* − Vol. 2 ²2009. *Vol. 119.*
− Die frühen Christen und ihre Welt. 2002. *Vol. 145.*
− see *Becker, Eve-Marie.*
− see *Ego, Beate.*
Pitre, Brant: Jesus, the Tribulation, and the End of the Exile. 2005. *Vol. II/204.*
Plümacher, Eckhard: Geschichte und Geschichten. 2004. *Vol. 170.*
Pöhlmann, Wolfgang: Der Verlorene Sohn und das Haus. 1993. *Vol. 68.*

Pokorný, Petr and *Josef B. Souček:* Bibelauslegung als Theologie. 1997. *Vol. 100.*
− and *Jan Roskovec* (Ed.): Philosophical Hermeneutics and Biblical Exegesis. 2002. *Vol. 153.*
Popkes, Enno Edzard: Das Menschenbild des Thomasevangeliums. 2007. *Vol. 206.*
− Die Theologie der Liebe Gottes in den johanneischen Schriften. 2005. *Vol. II/197.*
Porter, Stanley E.: The Paul of Acts. 1999. *Vol. 115.*
Prieur, Alexander: Die Verkündigung der Gottesherrschaft. 1996. *Vol. II/89.*
Probst, Hermann: Paulus und der Brief. 1991. *Vol. II/45.*
Räisänen, Heikki: Paul and the Law. 1983, ²1987. *Vol. 29.*
Rehkopf, Friedrich: Die lukanische Sonderquelle. 1959. *Vol. 5.*
Rein, Matthias: Die Heilung des Blindgeborenen (Joh 9). 1995. *Vol. II/73.*
Reinmuth, Eckart: Pseudo-Philo und Lukas. 1994. *Vol. 74.*
Reiser, Marius: Bibelkritik und Auslegung der Heiligen Schrift. 2007. *Vol. 217.*
− Syntax und Stil des Markusevangeliums. 1984. *Vol. II/11.*
Reynolds, Benjamin E.: The Apocalyptic Son of Man in the Gospel of John. 2008. *Vol. II/249.*
Rhodes, James N.: The Epistle of Barnabas and the Deuteronomic Tradition. 2004. *Vol. II/188.*
Richards, E. Randolph: The Secretary in the Letters of Paul. 1991. *Vol. II/42.*
Riesner, Rainer: Jesus als Lehrer. 1981, ³1988. *Vol. II/7.*
− Die Frühzeit des Apostels Paulus. 1994. *Vol. 71.*
Rissi, Mathias: Die Theologie des Hebräerbriefs. 1987. *Vol. 41.*
Röcker, Fritz W.: Belial und Katechon. 2009. *Vol. II/262.*
Röhser, Günter: Metaphorik und Personifikation der Sünde. 1987. *Vol. II/25.*
Rose, Christian: Theologie als Erzählung im Markusevangelium. 2007. *Vol. II/236.*
− Die Wolke der Zeugen. 1994. *Vol. II/60.*
Roskovec, Jan: see *Pokorný, Petr.*
Rothschild, Clare K.: Baptist Traditions and Q. 2005. *Vol. 190.*
− Hebrews as Pseudepigraphon. 2009. *Vol. 235.*
− Luke Acts and the Rhetoric of History. 2004. *Vol. II/175.*
− see *Frey, Jörg.*
Rüegger, Hans-Ulrich: Verstehen, was Markus erzählt. 2002. *Vol. II/155.*

Rüger, Hans Peter: Die Weisheitsschrift aus der Kairoer Geniza. 1991. *Vol. 53.*
Sänger, Dieter: Antikes Judentum und die Mysterien. 1980. *Vol. II/5.*
- Die Verkündigung des Gekreuzigten und Israel. 1994. *Vol. 75.*
- see *Burchard, Christoph*
- and *Ulrich Mell* (Ed.): Paulus und Johannes. 2006. *Vol. 198.*

Salier, Willis Hedley: The Rhetorical Impact of the Semeia in the Gospel of John. 2004. *Vol. II/186.*
Salzmann, Jorg Christian: Lehren und Ermahnen. 1994. *Vol. II/59.*
Sandnes, Karl Olav: Paul – One of the Prophets? 1991. *Vol. II/43.*
Sato, Migaku: Q und Prophetie. 1988. *Vol. II/29.*
Schäfer, Ruth: Paulus bis zum Apostelkonzil. 2004. *Vol. II/179.*
Schaper, Joachim: Eschatology in the Greek Psalter. 1995. *Vol. II/76.*
Schimanowski, Gottfried: Die himmlische Liturgie in der Apokalypse des Johannes. 2002. *Vol. II/154.*
- Weisheit und Messias. 1985. *Vol. II/17.*

Schlichting, Günter: Ein jüdisches Leben Jesu. 1982. *Vol. 24.*
Schließer, Benjamin: Abraham's Faith in Romans 4. 2007. *Vol. II/224.*
Schnabel, Eckhard J.: Law and Wisdom from Ben Sira to Paul. 1985. *Vol. II/16.*
Schnelle, Udo: see *Frey, Jörg.*
Schröter, Jens: Von Jesus zum Neuen Testament. 2007. *Vol. 204.*
- see *Frey, Jörg.*

Schutter, William L.: Hermeneutic and Composition in I Peter. 1989. *Vol. II/30.*
Schwartz, Daniel R.: Studies in the Jewish Background of Christianity. 1992. *Vol. 60.*
Schwemer, Anna Maria: see *Hengel, Martin*
Scott, Ian W.: Implicit Epistemology in the Letters of Paul. 2005. *Vol. II/205.*
Scott, James M.: Adoption as Sons of God. 1992. *Vol. II/48.*
- Paul and the Nations. 1995. *Vol. 84.*

Shi, Wenhua: Paul's Message of the Cross as Body Language. 2008. *Vol. II/254.*
Shum, Shiu-Lun: Paul's Use of Isaiah in Romans. 2002. *Vol. II/156.*
Siegert, Folker: Drei hellenistisch-jüdische Predigten. Teil I 1980. *Vol. 20* – Teil II 1992. *Vol. 61.*
- Nag-Hammadi-Register. 1982. *Vol. 26.*
- Argumentation bei Paulus. 1985. *Vol. 34.*
- Philon von Alexandrien. 1988. *Vol. 46.*

Simon, Marcel: Le christianisme antique et son contexte religieux I/II. 1981. *Vol. 23.*
Smit, Peter-Ben: Fellowship and Food in the Kingdom. 2008. *Vol. II/234.*
Snodgrass, Klyne: The Parable of the Wicked Tenants. 1983. *Vol. 27.*
Söding, Thomas: Das Wort vom Kreuz. 1997. *Vol. 93.*
- see *Thüsing, Wilhelm.*

Sommer, Urs: Die Passionsgeschichte des Markusevangeliums. 1993. *Vol. II/58.*
Sorensen, Eric: Possession and Exorcism in the New Testament and Early Christianity. 2002. *Vol. II/157.*
Souček, Josef B.: see *Pokorný, Petr.*
Southall, David J.: Rediscovering Righteousness in Romans. 2008. *Vol. 240.*
Spangenberg, Volker: Herrlichkeit des Neuen Bundes. 1993. *Vol. II/55.*
Spanje, T.E. van: Inconsistency in Paul? 1999. *Vol. II/110.*
Speyer, Wolfgang: Frühes Christentum im antiken Strahlungsfeld. Vol. I: 1989. *Vol. 50.*
- Vol. II: 1999. *Vol. 116.*
- Vol. III: 2007. *Vol. 213.*

Spittler, Janet E.: Animals in the Apocryphal Acts of the Apostles. 2008. *Vol. II/247.*
Sprinkle, Preston: Law and Life. 2008. *Vol. II/241.*
Stadelmann, Helge: Ben Sira als Schriftgelehrter. 1980. *Vol. II/6.*
Stein, Hans Joachim: Frühchristliche Mahlfeiern. 2008. *Vol. II/255.*
Stenschke, Christoph W.: Luke's Portrait of Gentiles Prior to Their Coming to Faith. *Vol. II/108.*
Sterck-Degueldre, Jean-Pierre: Eine Frau namens Lydia. 2004. *Vol. II/176.*
Stettler, Christian: Der Kolosserhymnus. 2000. *Vol. II/131.*
Stettler, Hanna: Die Christologie der Pastoralbriefe. 1998. *Vol. II/105.*
Stökl Ben Ezra, Daniel: The Impact of Yom Kippur on Early Christianity. 2003. *Vol. 163.*
Strobel, August: Die Stunde der Wahrheit. 1980. *Vol. 21.*
Stroumsa, Guy G.: Barbarian Philosophy. 1999. *Vol. 112.*
Stuckenbruck, Loren T.: Angel Veneration and Christology. 1995. *Vol. II/70.*
–, *Stephen C. Barton* and *Benjamin G. Wold* (Ed.): Memory in the Bible and Antiquity. 2007. *Vol. 212.*
Stuhlmacher, Peter (Ed.): Das Evangelium und die Evangelien. 1983. *Vol. 28.*
- Biblische Theologie und Evangelium. 2002. *Vol. 146.*

Sung, Chong-Hyon: Vergebung der Sünden. 1993. *Vol. II/57.*

Svendsen, Stefan N.: Allegory Transformed. 2009. Vol. II/269.
Tajra, Harry W.: The Trial of St. Paul. 1989. Vol. II/35.
– The Martyrdom of St.Paul. 1994. Vol. II/67.
Tellbe, Mikael: Christ-Believers in Ephesus. 2009. Vol. 242.
Theißen, Gerd: Studien zur Soziologie des Urchristentums. 1979, ³1989. Vol. 19.
Theobald, Michael: Studien zum Römerbrief. 2001. Vol. 136.
Theobald, Michael: see Mußner, Franz.
Thornton, Claus-Jürgen: Der Zeuge des Zeugen. 1991. Vol. 56.
Thüsing, Wilhelm: Studien zur neutestamentlichen Theologie. Ed. von Thomas Söding. 1995. Vol. 82.
Thurén, Lauri: Derhethorizing Paul. 2000. Vol. 124.
Thyen, Hartwig: Studien zum Corpus Iohanneum. 2007. Vol. 214.
Tibbs, Clint: Religious Experience of the Pneuma. 2007. Vol. II/230.
Toit, David S. du: Theios Anthropos. 1997. Vol. II/91.
Tolmie, D. Francois: Persuading the Galatians. 2005. Vol. II/190.
Tomson, Peter J. and Doris Lambers-Petry (Ed.): The Image of the Judaeo-Christians in Ancient Jewish and Christian Literature. 2003. Vol. 158.
Toney, Carl N.: Paul's Inclusive Ethic. 2008. Vol. II/252.
Trebilco, Paul: The Early Christians in Ephesus from Paul to Ignatius. 2004. Vol. 166.
Treloar, Geoffrey R.: Lightfoot the Historian. 1998. Vol. II/103.
Tsuji, Manabu: Glaube zwischen Vollkommenheit und Verweltlichung. 1997. Vol. II/93.
Twelftree, Graham H.: Jesus the Exorcist. 1993. Vol. II/54.
Ulrichs, Karl Friedrich: Christusglaube. 2007. Vol. II/227.
Urban, Christina: Das Menschenbild nach dem Johannesevangelium. 2001. Vol. II/137.
Vahrenhorst, Martin: Kultische Sprache in den Paulusbriefen. 2008. Vol. 230.
Vegge, Ivar: 2 Corinthians – a Letter about Reconciliation. 2008. Vol. II/239.
Verheyden, Josef: see Nicklas, Tobias
Visotzky, Burton L.: Fathers of the World. 1995. Vol. 80.
Vollenweider, Samuel: Horizonte neutestamentlicher Christologie. 2002. Vol. 144.
Vos, Johan S.: Die Kunst der Argumentation bei Paulus. 2002. Vol. 149.

Waaler, Erik: The Shema and The First Commandment in First Corinthians. 2008. Vol. II/253.
Wagener, Ulrike: Die Ordnung des „Hauses Gottes". 1994. Vol. II/65.
Wahlen, Clinton: Jesus and the Impurity of Spirits in the Synoptic Gospels. 2004. Vol. II/185.
Walker, Donald D.: Paul's Offer of Leniency (2 Cor 10:1). 2002. Vol. II/152.
Walter, Nikolaus: Praeparatio Evangelica. Ed. von Wolfgang Kraus und Florian Wilk. 1997. Vol. 98.
Wander, Bernd: Gottesfürchtige und Sympathisanten. 1998. Vol. 104.
Wasserman, Emma: The Death of the Soul in Romans 7. 2008. Vol. 256.
Waters, Guy: The End of Deuteronomy in the Epistles of Paul. 2006. Vol. 221.
Watt, Jan G. van der: see Frey, Jörg
Watts, Rikki: Isaiah's New Exodus and Mark. 1997. Vol. II/88.
Webb, Robert L.: see Bock, Darrell L.
Wedderburn, A.J.M.: Baptism and Resurrection. 1987. Vol. 44.
Wegner, Uwe: Der Hauptmann von Kafarnaum. 1985. Vol. II/14.
Weiß, Hans-Friedrich: Frühes Christentum und Gnosis. 2008. Vol. 225.
Weissenrieder, Annette: Images of Illness in the Gospel of Luke. 2003. Vol. II/164.
–, Friederike Wendt and Petra von Gemünden (Ed.): Picturing the New Testament. 2005. Vol. II/193.
Welck, Christian: Erzählte ‚Zeichen'. 1994. Vol. II/69.
Wendt, Friederike (Ed.): see Weissenrieder, Annette.
Wiarda, Timothy: Peter in the Gospels. 2000. Vol. II/127.
Wifstrand, Albert: Epochs and Styles. 2005. Vol. 179.
Wilk, Florian: see Walter, Nikolaus.
Williams, Catrin H.: I am He. 2000. Vol. II/113.
Wilson, Todd A.: The Curse of the Law and the Crisis in Galatia. 2007. Vol. II/225.
Wilson, Walter T.: Love without Pretense. 1991. Vol. II/46.
Winn, Adam: The Purpose of Mark's Gospel. 2008. Vol. II/245.
Winninge, Mikael: see Holmberg, Bengt.
Wischmeyer, Oda: Von Ben Sira zu Paulus. 2004. Vol. 173.
Wisdom, Jeffrey: Blessing for the Nations and the Curse of the Law. 2001. Vol. II/133.

Witmer, Stephen E.: Divine Instruction in Early Christianity. 2008. *Vol. II/246.*
Wold, Benjamin G.: Women, Men, and Angels. 2005. *Vol. II/2001.*
Wolter, Michael: Theologie und Ethos im frühen Christentum. 2009. *Vol. 236.*
– see *Stuckenbruck, Loren T.*
Wright, Archie T.: The Origin of Evil Spirits. 2005. *Vol. II/198.*
Wucherpfennig, Ansgar: Heracleon Philologus. 2002. *Vol. 142.*
Yates, John W.: The Spirit and Creation in Paul. 2008. *Vol. II/251.*
Yeung, Maureen: Faith in Jesus and Paul. 2002. *Vol. II/147.*
Zangenberg, Jürgen, Harold W. Attridge and *Dale B. Martin* (Ed.): Religion, Ethnicity and Identity in Ancient Galilee. 2007. *Vol. 210.*

Zimmermann, Alfred E.: Die urchristlichen Lehrer. 1984, ²1988. *Vol. II/12.*
Zimmermann, Johannes: Messianische Texte aus Qumran. 1998. *Vol. II/104.*
Zimmermann, Ruben: Christologie der Bilder im Johannesevangelium. 2004. *Vol. 171.*
– Geschlechtermetaphorik und Gottesverhältnis. 2001. *Vol. II/122.*
– (Ed.): Hermeneutik der Gleichnisse Jesu. 2008. *Vol. 231.*
– see *Frey, Jörg.*
– see *Horn, Friedrich Wilhelm.*
Zugmann, Michael: „Hellenisten" in der Apostelgeschichte. 2009. *Vol. II/264.*
Zumstein, Jean: see *Dettwiler, Andreas*
Zwiep, Arie W.: Judas and the Choice of Matthias. 2004. *Vol. II/187.*

www.ingramcontent.com/pod-product-compliance
Lightning Source LLC
Chambersburg PA
CBHW051634230426
43669CB00013B/2302